The Art and Science of Persuasion

THE ART AND SCIENCE OF
Persuasion

DEIRDRE D. JOHNSTON
Carroll College

Boston, Massachusetts Burr Ridge, Illinois Dubuque, Iowa
Madison, Wisconsin New York, New York San Francisco, California St. Louis, Missouri

McGraw-Hill

A Division of The **McGraw·Hill** *Companies*

3 4 5 6 7 8 9 0 QPB/QPB 9 0 9

ISBN 0–697–12890–3

Editor *Stan Stoga*
Developmental Editor *Mary E. Rossa*
Production Editor *Peggy Selle*
Photo Editor *Karen Hostert*
Permissions Editor *Mavis M. Oeth*
Visuals/Design Developmental Consultant *Marilyn A. Phelps*
Visuals/Design Freelance Specialist *Mary L. Christianson*
Publishing Services Specialist *Sherry Padden*
Marketing Manager *Carla J. Aspelmeier*
Advertising Manager *Jodi Rymer*
Executive Vice President/General Manager *Thomas E. Doran*
Vice President/Editor in Chief *Edgar J. Laube*
Vice President/Sales and Marketing *Eric Ziegler*
Director of Production *Vickie Putman Caughron*
Director of Custom and Electronic Publishing *Chris Rogers*

Cover and title page image: © Superstock/Mark Ari

Cover and interior design by Rebecca Lemna

Copyedited by Barbara Bonnett

Library of Congress Catalog Card Number: 92–74424

http://www.mhcollege.com

To Jim

Contents

Preface

Experience and reason accord to establish that men believe themselves free only because they are conscious of their actions and not of what determines them.

Benedict de Spinoza, *Ethics*, III

The origins of human thought and action lie somewhere in the interaction of individual and society—specifically, the communication process by which the individual is influenced by societal messages, constructs social meanings, and simultaneously influences his or her social world. This interaction between individual freewill and societal influence is a central theme in *The Art and Science of Persuasion*. Integrating research from a variety of academic disciplines and a range of theoretical perspectives, *The Art and Science of Persuasion* explains the persuasion process at the individual level of analysis with examples that are relevant to the undergraduate's personal experiences. Based on this explanation of the persuasion process, the reader's knowledge of persuasion is applied to more complex functions of persuasion at the societal level. In this manner, the reader acquires a holistic perspective of persuasion that explains the process and function of persuasion in his or her personal experiences, as well as the process and function of persuasion in the society at large.

One of my objectives upon embarking on this project was to create a persuasion text that was substantive in theory, yet fun and engaging to read. The result is a book that is comprehensive in its discussion of persuasion theories and principles, yet incorporates stories, case studies, cartoons, popular culture examples, visuals, advertisements, and college student conversations, to make persuasion research applicable to the reader's experiences.

Throughout this text, I have included from political speeches, advertisements, and social movements examples of persuasion that are designed to challenge you to think critically. I could have selected issues that were less controversial, but the avoidance of controversy is not conducive to shaking us out of our complacency and challenging us to question, evaluate, argue, and formulate opinions on social issues. Those who gain the most from this book will not necessarily agree with these persuasive messages, nor will they summarily dismiss those messages that are counter to their pre-existing opinions. Those who gain the most from this book will critically analyze the persuasive intentions and strategies underlying the messages, they will explore alternative meanings of the messages, and they will argue with the analyses of the messages provided in the text.

The Art and Science of Persuasion differs from other texts in its focus on both sender and receiver in the persuasion process. In our increasingly technological, mobile, service-oriented, and communication-dependent society, people must be both competent persuaders and critical message receivers. Competent persuaders are successful in work endeavors and personal relationships as a result of their ability to take the perspective of others, to build mutual understanding, and to collaborate with others to satisfy both their own and others' task and relational goals. As the world shrinks to a global community in which the actions of one person or country impact others, it is imperative that we also learn to be critical message receivers who evaluate and challenge the persuasive messages of friends, business spokespersons, social leaders, and government officials. We live at a time when mass media technology makes possible the presentation of a single message to millions of people around the globe, a time when our potential for mass destruction through unchecked technological growth, ecological deterioration, or atomic weapons is everpresent, and consequently, a time when our success and survival are dependent upon an informed and critical populace. Considering the ubiquitous and inevitable persuasive forces in our society, this book continually reminds the reader of the role of the ethical and competent persuader, as well as the role of the critical message receiver. This focus on an active message receiver illustrates the interactional, dynamic, yet subtle emergence of **mutual influence** and **shared meaning** through persuasive interaction.

A central assumption underlying *The Art and Science of Persuasion* is that persuasion is primarily a *communication process,* and that once one understands the theoretical foundation for persuasive communication, one can apply knowledge of persuasion to numerous social phenomena. Thus, the textbook is not limited to a "mass media focus" or an "interpersonal focus," but explicates the principles of persuasion by providing examples from numerous persuasive contexts, including interpersonal persuasion (e.g., doctor-patient, professor-student, significant other, parent-child, and supervisor-employee); group persuasion (e.g., organizations, families, and student groups); public persuasion (e.g., legal trials, social movements, and religious organizations), and mass mediated persuasion (e.g., advertising, political campaigns, movies, television, and music). These examples emphasize the interdisciplinary relevance of persuasion.

The text is organized into four sections: 1) **Definitions and Issues of Persuasion;** 2) **Components of Persuasion;** 3) **The Process of Persuasion;** and 4) **The Impact of Persuasion on Society.** The definitional and ethical issues addressed in the first section establish a foundation for an in-depth analysis of the components that comprise the persuasion process, which is explored in the second section. An understanding of the components of the persuasion process should lead the reader to question how these components interact to influence message construction and interpretation, and how these components interact to produce cognitive and/or behavioral changes, a process that is addressed in the third section. The final section of the text helps the reader grasp the gestalt process of persuasion by exploring the operation and impact of persuasion at the societal level.

In keeping with the *process* theme, theories of persuasion are introduced according to their relationship to the process of persuasion, rather than by "type" of theory. This focus on process helps the readers perceive how the components of persuasion interact to produce persuasive effects. The reader is better able to comprehend the interaction of variables that comprise persuasive encounters, as well as recognize the gestalt process.

This text emphasizes and develops several areas of persuasion research that are often neglected. The discussion of **persuasion ethics** (chapter 3) is placed in the first section of the textbook, both to emphasize its importance and to encourage the reader to recognize the Aristotelean perspective that ethics and persuasion are inextricably intertwined such that we cannot discuss one without considering the other. Two chapters are devoted to **meaning and symbols.** One chapter includes a discussion of symbols as a component of persuasion (chapter 4), and the other explores how shared meaning evolves through the selection and modification of symbols (chapter 11). Chapter 11 also takes readers through the steps of a semiotic analysis to illustrate the underlying cultural meanings of symbols employed in persuasive messages. The impact of communicators' **goals and strategies** on the construction and effect of persuasive messages is addressed in chapter 5. This is a relatively new, but growing, area of research in persuasion. Another often neglected topic of persuasion is the process of **self-presentation and impression formation** (chapter 7). Self-presentation and impression formation influence the attributions communicators make about each other and consequently influence message effectiveness. Since persuasion consists of attitudinal or behavioral change, and constructing opinion questionnaires has become a favorite activity of businesses and social organizations, the **definition and measurement** of attitudes, beliefs, and behaviors is discussed in chapter 10. A final area of persuasion research that is critical to our understanding of the impact of persuasion on society is the analysis of **sociological propaganda** (chapter 14) and **persuasion campaigns and movements** (chapter 15). These chapters reflect timely issues that our society should be critically analyzing. These chapters challenge the reader to question the effects of societal persuasion on their self-identities, their goals, and their behaviors. As critical receivers, we must be aware of the ways in which persuasion defines and shapes our society and ourselves.

The Art and Science of Persuasion and the accompanying *Instructor's Resource Manual* incorporate three basic principles of learning: learning by application, learning by doing, and learning by integration with previous knowledge. The campaign analysis project described in the instructor's manual facilitates students' ability to apply persuasion theory. The project enables students to pick an on-going persuasion campaign (e.g., the Red Cross, Amnesty International, or People for the Ethical Treatment of Animals) and collect persuasive messages for analysis. The project assignments parallel the textbook readings and help students to apply specific principles and issues of persuasion discussed in the text to their chosen campaign. Students are challenged to use textbook principles to critique the effectiveness of the campaign they have studied throughout the semester.

Although this book focuses on principles of persuasion over skills, classroom exercises described in the instructor's manual provide the opportunity for students to learn by doing. Research findings seem to be best understood and remembered when the theory is actually used to construct a persuasive message or to analyze a persuasive principle. These "learning by doing" exercises include role-playing scenarios and simple social influence experiments. The Instructor's Resource Manual also includes information and exercises on persuasive speaking.

The discussion questions at the end of each chapter provide opportunities to facilitate the integration of new principles with experiential knowledge. These questions challenge the reader to relate the principles discussed in the text to familiar interpersonal situations as well as familiar social contexts, such as the analysis of the rhetoric of advertisements, political campaigns, sales presentations, and social movements. Two additional aids to facilitate the integration of knowledge are the use of boldface key concepts throughout the text and a study guide at the end of each chapter.

ACKNOWLEDGEMENTS

I am indebted to a great number of people who have influenced me and the content of this book. Conversations over dinner and at conferences, late night calls to colleagues and friends, and discussions with students have all inspired ideas and crystallized my approach to various topics.

But perhaps the greatest influence on this book, and the greatest debt I owe, is to my persuasion studies mentors: Professor Donovan Ochs and Professor Greg Shepherd. Over the years they continue to challenge, inspire, question, and cajole. They are the best of teachers, the most astute of scholars, and the most valued of friends.

It was my spouse, however, who had to live with this project day after day. It was he who never failed to answer the calls from the study to rephrase an awkward sentence, generate an example, or critique and edit a chapter. His job on the front lines was backed up by insightful reviewers: Randall Bytwerk, Calvin College; Kenneth D. Frandsen, University of New Mexico; James Heflin, Cameron University; Judy Jones, New England College; Donald Lumsden, Kean College; Darrell G. Mullins, University of Wisconsin, Whitewater; William J. Schenck-Hamlin, Kansas State University; Brant Short, Idaho State University; and John Kares Smith, State University of New York, Oswego, who provided both support and constructive criticism for which I will always be thankful. I am also grateful for the encouragement, suggestions, and necessary prodding from Stan Stoga, Mary Rossa, and many others at Brown & Benchmark, without whom this book would never have reached completion. Mary provided especially helpful suggestions on the manuscript.

My students also deserve special recognition. They not only served as guinea pigs for the rough drafts of this text, but provided many ideas and examples that I have incorporated into the book. I also wish to thank my work study helpers, Bonita Goist, Betsy Randow, and Laura Braunritter, who spent tireless hours securing permissions and searching the library stacks for articles and books. I also appreciate the hard work of yet another student, Deneen Winchester, an especially talented artist, who created a persuasion cartoon for this book.

Last, but certainly not least, I want to recognize Carroll College and the support of my colleagues. Joe Hemmer, Pete Settle, and Joe Dailey picked up the departmental overloads on more than one occasion to enable me to work on this manuscript. I also wish to thank the Carroll College Research and Educational Innovations Committee. The members of this committee recognized this project while it was still a vision and awarded a much-needed grant to hire work-study students to aid in manuscript preparation.

I

The Nature of the Beast: Definitions, Myths & Issues

1

*Defining Persuasion:
Mutual Influence,
Manipulation or Coercion?*

Julie is an attractive, happy, vivacious, intelligent woman of 24. During our interview she talked about her family, high school activities, and coming to college. Her appearance, interests, anxieties, and pastimes in no way distinguished her from the other students at the pub where we talked. Julie is very close to her family; in fact, Julie says that she had always known that if she had a problem or if anything went wrong, she could always go home; she could always rely on her family for support. It was hard to believe that Julie spent two years as a Hare Krishna.

Julie was considered part of the popular clique in high school and college. During her freshman year at a mid-sized state university she joined a sorority. Yet Julie says that she never felt as if she "fit in" with the social groups with whom she "hung out." In fact, she prided herself on being unique and original. She liked to throw people off guard, and she says that the "more (she) didn't fit in—the more (she) tried not to fit in."

It was also during her freshman year that Julie encountered the Krishnas on campus. The Krishnas were giving away food. Julie was curious about different lifestyles, religions, and foods, and ended up talking to one of these "weird, bald, orange-robed gurus" for about two hours.

During her junior year in college, Julie's fiance, and confidant of three years, committed suicide. At this time, Julie had just returned to campus after taking a year off; she had lost contact with most of her college friends during her absence. One day, a few weeks after the death of her fiance, a young woman approached Julie as she walked across campus. The woman struck up a conversation and communicated concern for Julie. This concern was all Julie needed to prompt her to disclose her grief, her apathy toward her schoolwork, and her lack of direction following the loss of her lover and best friend. Over the next few days the woman "conveniently ran into" Julie on campus, and a friendship developed. Julie found that she and her new friend had many similar interests. In fact, everything Julie mentioned, including her birthday, seemed to be shared by this new friend.

During their first week of acquaintance, Julie's friend invited her to try the vegetarian food that the Krishnas were giving away. Julie had no idea the woman was a Krishna herself. Julie went to the dinner, served in a college building, complete with Indian music, decorations, and incense. The atmosphere piqued Julie's curiosity.

Julie describes herself as "the artsy-type." She is interested in drawing, guitar, sculpting, and different musical styles. Julie's new friend suggested that they start hanging out at the Krishna house where a friend could show Julie how to play the Indian instruments that had interested Julie at the Krishna dinner. During Julie's visits to the house, her new friends would dress her up in saffron robes and beads, and they would laugh together at the effect. When Julie started playing the new instruments, her new friends were amazed at how talented she was. They asked her to record music with their group so that they could sell the tapes and records. Soon, Julie was spending almost every evening at the Krishna house. Julie largely forgot her schoolwork, and the Krishnas assumed responsibility for meeting her intellectual needs. They gave her books on philosophy and religion to read, marveled at her ability to understand these complex issues, and gently refuted her arguments and concerns.

During these months Julie never considered herself a Hare Krishna. She still had her own apartment, she never wore the Krishna clothes outside the house, she still went for an occasional beer with her college friends, and she watched television. These "sins" were at first tolerated by her Krishna friends. Over the course of several months, however, their tolerance increasingly changed from gentle concern, to disappointment, to annoyance.

About four months after her first contact with the Krishnas, Julie's Krishna friends asked her to go on a road trip to the Krishna temple and commune in West Virginia. Julie had a wonderful time in West Virginia. The people there welcomed her and her questions. The atmosphere of togetherness, caring, incense-filled rooms, the beautiful temple, the pure unmaterialistic lifestyle, the vegetarian foods, and the novel musical rhythms mesmerized Julie. She was learning something new every day. Julie enjoyed the lifestyle of discussing philosophy, cooking novel foods, playing music, and talking with newfound friends.

When Julie came back to campus, she moved into the Krishna house. The Krishnas became firmer with her—scheduling her day, instructing her behavior, and punishing her transgressions—but in many ways she had never been happier.

Julie was soon instructed in strategies to recruit new members. Julie learned how to raise up to $950 in a single afternoon selling bumper stickers and visors. The card Julie wore identified her not as a member of the Krishnas, but as a member of the State Food Co-op, and she quickly learned interpersonal sales messages to get passersby to donate money: "Hey! I'm going to have to give you a ticket! You look like you're having too much fun! (passerby stops, laughs) Well, maybe I'll let you off the hook this time. . . . How would you like one of these visors? They're just five dollars, and the money goes to feed poor families. The Midwest Food Co-op can feed a family of four for a month on your donation of five dollars!" The money, of course, went directly to the Krishna organization. Yes, Julie was now a Krishna, and she stayed with the Krishnas for over two years.

In the end, Julie reports that her parents paid de-programmers $75,000 to kidnap her, lock her in a cellar for two weeks, and break her loyalty to the Krishnas. For two weeks, one of the two de-programmers stayed with Julie every minute. They would not even let her out of their sight when she used the doorless bathroom in the cellar in which she was held captive. Julie had no idea where she was or how many days passed while she was held in the cellar.

The de-programmers tried to shock Julie into remembering the life she had left two years before. According to Julie, the de-programmers defiled tenets of the Krishna belief system in any manner possible. The Krishnas worshipped their spiritual leaders; the de-programmers defiled the pictures of the spiritual leaders. The Krishnas taught celibacy; the de-programmers advocated sexual experience. The Krishnas taught that eating meat was a sin; the de-programmers forced meat down Julie's throat. After two weeks, the de-programmers dropped Julie off at her parents' home. Her parents could not risk her making contact with the Krishnas, so they alternated taking weeks of vacation from their respective jobs, so that Julie would never be alone. Her parents disconnected the phones and placed locks on the door of Julie's room. These actions continued for three months.

Julie's experience illustrates how communication can radically change a person's beliefs, attitudes, and/or behavior. The Krishnas influenced Julie's beliefs gradually, over an extended period of time, by providing consistent, continual, and persistent messages. The Krishnas persuasive strategies were effective because they adjusted their tactics to Julie's needs. When Julie was lonely and needed a friend, the Krishnas provided friendship. When Julie conveyed that she was bored and apathetic about school, the Krishnas provided exciting and novel experiences. When Julie was confused, the Krishnas provided spiritual instruction. Once Julie was dependent upon their friendship and their social and intellectual stimulation, the Krishnas shaped her behavior by communicating intolerance for her "worldly" pastimes. To persuade her to give up television, alcohol, and outside contacts, the Krishnas presented an alternative—the peaceful utopian lifestyle in the West Virginia Commune. Once Julie gave up her apartment and outside contacts (thereby making it more difficult to return to campus life), the Krishnas became more forceful in their demands and more intolerant of any behavioral transgressions.

Although most of us have not experienced persuasion by a cult, we are subjected to hundreds of persuasive messages each day. Just as the Hare Krishnas had a subtle effect on Julie over a period of time, advertisers, parents, teachers, religious leaders, musicians, politicians, and friends similarly mold and shape our beliefs and behaviors. Just as Julie failed to realize the subtle changes in her values, we fail to recognize the effects of mass mediated messages and conversations on our own values.

The purpose of this book is twofold: 1) to teach you persuasive communication skills; and 2) to enhance your critical thinking and persuasion resistance skills. To be successful in our families, marriages, social lives, careers, community services, and civic duties, we must be skillful persuaders. Competence in persuasion means not only accomplishing our goal, but also doing so in a responsible, equitable, and positive manner. That is, it does us little good to change the behavior of an employee if that employee is going to resent us, thereby jeopardizing all future interactions. Skillful persuaders are necessary to coordinate and develop our social systems. The ability to motivate, inspire, or cajole others to behave according to our wishes is necessary for success in any aspect of life. For this reason, this textbook will focus on improving persuasive communication skills.

It is also the purpose of this textbook to help people resist persuasive influences and recognize unethical or invalid persuasive appeals. Only by understanding how persuasion occurs can a person be a critical receiver of persuasive messages. Critical message receivers are alert to the use of persuasion for unethical purposes and/or the use of unethical persuasion tactics. As persuasive strategies become increasingly sophisticated, it is imperative that we be able to identify, analyze, and resist persuasion.

Persuasion is a pervasive communication phenomena that you encounter each day. In this chapter we will discuss the important societal role persuasion plays, and we will analyze the definitional characteristics of persuasion. The final section of this chapter will present three alternative approaches to the study of persuasion: one can compare and analyze persuasive communication according to context (the situation in which persuasion occurs), function (the purpose or outcome of the persuasive encounter), or process (the components that interact to produce persuasion).

THE ROLE OF PERSUASION IN SOCIETY

Persuasion influences our lives in important ways. We encounter thousands of persuasive messages each day. Every time you send or receive a message that affects your attitudes, beliefs, or behavior, persuasion has occurred. Perhaps in a typical day, you wake up to a radio station, you listen to the television news, you put on your college T-shirt, your sports cap, and your designer label blue jeans. You ask your roommate to meet for lunch. You walk out your front door and are confronted with fast-food signs, billboards, and highway signs. You face more signs on the door of the college building where you go to your first class. There your professor professes profoundly on world events, you make a date for the weekend, and a friend talks you into skipping that afternoon class to go to the lake. Later that day, Mom calls and asks you to straighten out little brother, you cajole the cafeteria worker into giving you an extra brownie, and so on and so on. You are the receiver or sender of persuasive messages from the time you put on your labeled clothes in the morning until you turn out the lights on your roommate late at night.

Persuasion not only guides our personal behavior, but also serves to establish, modify, and maintain our entire social system. Without persuasion, we would not have education, religion, families, laws, commerce, or even a government. Indeed we would not have a society. Our educational system persuades people to learn and promotes changes in our beliefs, attitudes, and behaviors. Religious and political leaders must employ persuasion to attract followers and must convince people to accept particular belief systems, such as Catholicism, Protestantism, Judaism, Socialism, or Communism. Without persuasion, no laws or rules of conduct could be adopted, and the only means of modifying behavior would be physical force. Commerce is dependent upon establishing a fair exchange, and a fair exchange requires negotiation, a form of persuasion. Without persuasion, we would have to meet all of our survival needs (shelter, food, and clothing) individually. And without mutual agreement and cooperation, there would be no kinship systems or families.

As you can see, education, religions, kinship systems, laws, commerce, and governments are created and refined according to the persuasive skills of the society. One could organize animal species on a continuum to reflect the degree to which they live and hunt alone (except for mating purposes) or live in cooperative groups through the use of rudimentary persuasion. The development of persuasive skills is correlated with the organizational sophistication of societies. In the last few hundred years we have enhanced our persuasive skills to such a degree that we can convince people to look beyond the concrete exchange of goods (food, clothing, and tools) to the more abstract exchange of services (consultation, insurance, communication). Interestingly enough, we no longer rely on people's existing needs for the exchange of goods and services; we can *create* needs for new products through persuasive advertising. Societies vary in the degree to which they achieve organization and cooperative effort through coercion and fear at one extreme, and persuasion and free-will at the other. Organizing large groups of people by free-will, rather than by fear, requires sophisticated persuasive practices.

ANATOMY OF A DEFINITION

Persuasion is a transactional process among two or more persons whereby the management of symbolic meaning reconstructs reality, resulting in a voluntary change in beliefs, attitudes, and/or behaviors. Inherent in this definition are several principles of persuasion and communication that we will discuss in depth.

Persuasion as Process

In a **process** there is no beginning or end. Persuasion may have its roots in existing personality systems or experiences unknown to the current persuader. In *Julie's Story* the persuasion process flowed from her personality, her freshman year experience talking to the Krishnas, her emotional vulnerability at the time of her fiance's death, to her curiosity in Krishna rituals. It is impossible to identify the beginning of the process. Similarly, it is impossible to identify the end of the process; Julie's Krishna experience will influence her thoughts and actions throughout her life.

A process is also dynamic and fluid. Persuasion is not uni-directional; it is not something one person *does* to another. Rather, persuasion involves a fluid, continual shaping of meaning among two or more persons, in which the intended target of the message influences the sender of the persuasive message. In the beginning, Julie's interests in her outside friends, maintaining her own apartment, drinking an occasional beer, and watching television influenced the forcefulness with which the Krishnas pushed their philosophy—the Krishnas got the message that they should not chastise Julie for these behaviors, or they might lose her. Julie interpreted the Krishnas' behavior as acceptance of her and her behavior and the preservation of her free-will. The persons participating in the persuasion process simultaneously assume the roles of persuader and target of persuasion. By its very nature, *interaction* suggests mutual influence, and *process* suggests influence that develops over time, through contact with many people and experiences.

The Transactional Nature of Persuasion

Transaction literally means "across actions," or "to change actions." Since we have defined a process as continual and dynamic, a process is by definition transactional. The importance of the concept of transaction in our study of persuasion, however, warrants its discussion as a separate definitional corollary.

A behavior or even an exchange would not be "transactional" if it had no effect beyond the given action. The transactional nature of persuasion suggests that for every action there is a reaction, and that a given action cannot be contained, but that it reverberates in many different directions.

We often discuss communication as **inter**action, an action between two or more persons. By describing persuasion as **trans**actional we emphasize the possible long-term effects of persuasive communication. A change in one's beliefs, attitudes, and/or behavior may have far-reaching implications. Can you think of ways in which Julie's experience will influence her perceptions of events throughout her life?

According to Jean Kilbourn, the perception of seemingly innocuous advertising images has transactional influence.[1] These images not only influence our buying behavior, but also dictate our definitions of gender roles in our culture.

In Figures 1.1a and 1.1b, two advertisements communicate a message about gender expectations for women during the 1940s. The first ad suggests that women who are single, fashionable, financially secure, socially active, and busy with charitable work really need a man to make them happy. As if it isn't enough to have one's happiness dictated by another person, the second ad shows a woman cowering beneath her baby while the baby gives her a condescending lecture. The cumulative effect of ads such as these tell women that happiness lies in finding a man and serving one's children. Assuming that this type of advertising influenced women's goals and lifestyle choices in the 1940s, these consumer messages had transactional impact.

If persuasion is indeed transactional, is this influence sub-conscious? Are we really aware of the ways in which past persuasive messages influence our behavior, attitudes, and beliefs? It is reasonable to assume that we learn and store information at a conscious level. Yet we may not be fully aware of the impact of these perceptions at a later time. We may forget the source of the original message; we may even forget the message itself. The retention of an isolated impression may be the only basis for transactional influence at a later date.

The Creation of Symbols and Meaning

Communication is **symbolic** because it employs words or images to represent objects, ideas, and relationships. We learn the meaning assigned to these symbols so that we can understand one another and reference things that do not exist in our current sphere of time and space. For example, if two persons are in the same sphere of time and space, they could communicate "table" by pointing to a table placed before them. If, however, the table existed in another spacial sphere, out of their sight, they could not reference this table without a symbol (word or image) to which they both attributed similar meaning.

The meaning of a symbol is not in the symbol but in the perceptions of the receiver. Our emotional associations influence the meaning of symbols and their persuasive power. As you know, there are many symbols with similar meanings. Persuaders can choose symbols that

FIGURE 1.1 a & b   These 1940s advertisements illustrate the transactional impact of advertising in depicting gender roles and expectations.

a) Johnson & Johnson

b) Reprinted by permission of Warner-Lambert Company

either increase or decrease the audience's emotional reactions. The Krishnas, for example, used symbols such as "enlightenment," "love," and "spiritual growth," as opposed to "withdrawal," "recruitment," and "religious indoctrination." If I want to incite people's emotions regarding nuclear power stations, I might choose symbols such as "toxic waste," "cancer," "radioactive," and "poisoning the planet." If my persuasive goal involves decreasing emotional reactions to this issue, I might choose to discuss "spent fuel" and "energy efficiency." Likewise, if we want to minimize the death of Americans in a military maneuver, headlines read "36 American Soldiers Lost" (they didn't die?) or "36 Soldiers KIA" (Killed in Action). If we want to maximize public outcry against the deaths, the headlines state: "36 Youths Massacred." Thus, symbols are the vehicles by which one person communicates persuasive intent to another.

The Reconstruction of Reality

Many communication theorists believe that the world is constructed by our minds. That is, what we believe to be true—what constitutes our reality—is a product of our interpretations of our experiences and knowledge. Consequently, your "reality" may differ from mine. Taking this idea one step further, there is evidence that our patterns of interaction and the symbols we use to refer to our world **construct** (or create) our perceptions and experiences.

Theorists who focus on constructed reality argue that there are many things that we believe are real, but that have no objective reality. Consider concepts such as God, freedom, equality, ghosts, and luck. These are ideas. They are intangible. Our minds apply meaning to these concepts, and we share these meanings through communication. Our thought processes construct, and communication creates many concepts and beliefs.

The communication of symbols focuses our perceptions. Conversely, the absence of a symbol or communication may allow us to conveniently erase those aspects of the external world we choose not to dwell on. Consider the reality of a Balinese tribesperson living in an isolated area. This person's reality is constructed by what is familiar. This person's reality includes demons that have to be appeased, or else they will destroy crops, spread diseases, and cause famines.[2] Your reality, which includes hidden atoms and molecules jumping at relative rates of speed in your clothing and furniture, would seem just as absurd to the Balinese tribesperson. Moreover, if no one had introduced you to the symbol "atom" and communicated and constructed a meaning for this symbol, "atoms" would not exist in your reality.

If reality is not objective, but is constructed through communication, we can change reality. The goal of persuasion is to alter or reconstruct an individual's reality. A person's reality (what he or she believes to be true) can be altered in several ways: 1) creating a new symbol; 2) changing the meaning of an existing symbol; or 3) invalidating an existing symbol. Consider how the Krishnas used these methods to reconstruct Julie's reality as they integrated her into the Krishna organization, and again when she was deprogrammed.

Julie was taught many new symbols. For example, repeating the chant "Hare Krishna, Hare Krishna, Hare Krishna, Hare Hare//Hare Rama, Hare Rama, Rama Rama, Hare Hare" purportedly facilitates separation from the physical world, focuses all senses on Krishna, and cleanses the soul.

Symbols that already existed in Julie's reality took on new meanings. Insects were no longer pests to be squashed but spiritual beings seeking reincarnation to a higher life form (karma). Christ was no longer the messiah, but a prophet like Krishna. Food and music were no longer hobbies, but paths to spiritual fulfillment.

The Krishnas invalidated many of the symbols that were part of Julie's reality in her old life. Her family was no longer a social support net but a distracting attachment preventing her spiritual enlightenment, and perhaps even a hostile entity removing her from her happy Krishna existence. Likewise, food, shelter, comfort, and warmth were not amenities that one should seek in life but symbols of the material world that were immaterial to the true devotee of Krishna Consciousness. The Krishnas reconstructed Julie's reality by introducing new symbols, changing the meaning of symbols, and invalidating existing symbols.

Persuasion is Voluntary

The most important characteristic distinguishing persuasion from other forms of influence, such as coercion, brainwashing, and mind control, is that persuasion is voluntary. The ability to distinguish between persuasion and more coercive forms of influence is essential for the ethical practice of persuasion. Moreover, you, as a message receiver, must learn to recognize and resist tactics that impinge upon your free choice.

Persuasion, as defined earlier, is a voluntary change in *thoughts and/or behavior.* **Coercion,** in contrast, is an involuntary change in *behavior,* and **brainwashing** (mind control) is an involuntary change in *thought.* Although one could use coercion to induce changes in behavior (e.g., putting a gun at someone's head and demanding money), it is difficult if not impossible to brainwash a person—that is, to change a person's thoughts (e.g., putting a gun at someone's head and demanding that the person *think* that socialism is a good idea).

Coercion

Under what conditions, then, is coercion likely to occur? Coercion is dependent upon the receiver's perception that he or she has no choice but to comply with the aggressor. Coercion—a change in behavior—is the result of an intolerable stress from which the victim perceives no alternative but to collaborate with his or her captors. Influence by coercion involves simple learning—a victim learns that the only way to escape aversive stimuli is to perform behaviors desired by the tormentor(s). Yet what some people consider an intolerable stress, others perceive as tolerable. Even when a gun is placed at your temple, you can decide whether or not to die fighting or to succumb to the gun holder's wishes.

Brainwashing

Is it possible to change a person's *thoughts* without his or her consent? Despite what television talk shows might lead you to believe, attempts to reconstruct a person's beliefs against his or her will have met with little success. Brainwashing is analogous to the old joke: *How many psychiatrists does it take to change a light bulb? Only one, but the light bulb must want to change.* Humans have a great deal of control over their minds, as others can not observe, and thereby, control the workings of the mind. As Streiker so aptly states, "No matter how submissive an individual is to the authority of a group, human consciousness retains a mind of its own" (p. 163).[3]

To produce brainwashing, a receiver's **intra-psychic structure** must be susceptible to influence. Psychodynamic theorists would argue that the stronger a person's sense of self-identity, the less susceptible this person would be to radical belief change. Self-identity is a result of stable and secure internalized beliefs that are largely resistant to external influences and are not subject to distortions by others.

This secure self-identity is shaped in early childhood by positive "mirroring" of the child's thoughts, actions, and feelings. A secure self-identity is the result of what Satir calls a child's five freedoms: 1) the freedom to experience the present; 2) the freedom to think our own thoughts; 3) the freedom to feel our own feelings; 4) the freedom to recognize our own desires; and 5) the freedom to reach one's own potential.[4] These five freedoms all refer to independence of thought, as opposed to being told what one *should* experience, think, feel, desire, and do. The child who establishes a secure identity knows that he or she is a good and worthy person. As a result, he or she tends to disregard any brainwashing attempts to distort these healthy self perceptions.

Identifying Coercion & Brainwashing

When labeling influence strategies as persuasive or involuntary, there is a tendency to base one's decision on the outcome rather than on the process. That is, if we believe the outcome is bad (joining a cult), we label the process brainwashing or coercion, but if the outcome is acceptable (getting out of a cult), we label the process persuasion. This semantic game is fallacious. The characteristics of the **process** of influence, not the outcome, distinguish persuasion from other forms of influence.

Now that we have defined coercion and brainwashing, let's consider a few examples of radical attempts to change people's beliefs, attitudes, or behaviors. In each of the following examples, try to identify whether the case involves persuasion (voluntary changes), coercion (involuntary changes in behavior), or brainwashing (involuntary changes in beliefs).

Julie & The Krishnas. If we distinguish persuasion from other forms of influence based on the degree of free will perceived by the receiver, the Hare Krishnas used persuasion to recruit Julie. The de-programmers' techniques, however, constitute brainwashing. Julie, the ex-Krishna, argues that she changed her belief system voluntarily when she joined the Krishnas. At least in the beginning of her indoctrination, she could have left at any time. Julie claims that the Krishnas exerted no more force in her decision than do other social groups who modify people's beliefs and behaviors through positive and negative reinforcement.

Unlike some religious cults, the Krishnas did not employ physiological deprivation. They recommended moderation: don't sleep too much or too little (six hours of sleep a night was recommended), and don't eat too much (heavy meals depress the mind and body, induce sleep, and prevent spiritual consciousness). Julie says that she never went hungry and never felt fatigued from lack of sleep.

Did Julie have a choice in her deprogramming? Although Julie now acknowledges that her parents made the right decision, Julie says she was forced to change her Krishna behaviors and beliefs. The deprogrammers held her captive, physically abused her, and bombarded her with anti-Krishna propaganda—continually asking her questions, boxing her if she did not respond, and allowing her no time to formulate her own thoughts. When Julie was returned to her parents' house two weeks later, the persuasion process to re-reconstruct her reality was begun in earnest. Ministers and counselors worked with Julie to point out inconsistencies in the Krishna doctrine. They encouraged her questions, in hopes of bringing about voluntary belief change. Many theorists believe that this voluntary belief change is necessary for long term maintenance of a new belief. That is, brainwashing may have only short-term effects. Julie agrees with this theory, stating that had she been able to contact the Krishnas after her two-week deprogramming, she would have returned to the movement.

Prisoners of War. Schein's study of American prisoners of war during the Korean War also suggests that even the most systematic strategies of mind control have only limited effects.[5] The Chinese attempted to brainwash American prisoners to forsake their country. The Chinese employed isolation, threats of physical abuse, food deprivation, psychological pressure, intense indoctrination, and complete dependency upon the captors, all in a controlled environment from which the prisoners could not escape.

The Chinese believed that "doing means believing." The Americans were required to sing Communist songs, sign peace petitions, read confessions of their "capitalist crimes" over the camp's PA system, and participate in communist ideology study groups. The Chinese sought to break down the prisoners' identities and egos. In *The Mind Manipulators*, Scheflin and Opton explain how the Chinese destroyed individual identities by forcing the prisoners to wear common uniforms and hair cuts, not allowing them to maintain their military rank, not allowing the use of personal names, and tricking the prisoners into self-betrayal by getting them to report on fellow prisoners, read Chinese propaganda, and confess to war crimes.[6]

Similar techniques were used on American soldiers in Vietnam. The book and movie *The Hanoi Hilton* provides an excellent depiction of strategies of mind control and the efforts of prisoners to resist.[7] In Vietnam, prisoners in isolation communicated to others by clanging eating utensils in code. When prisoners were videotaped reading anti-American statements (which were subsequently mailed to the United States Government), many prisoners crossed their fingers—a sign unfamiliar to their North Vietnamese captors.

The Chinese, Koreans, and North Vietnamese methodically employed plans to alter the belief structures of the POWs. The POWs had no way to escape the propaganda—in fact, their physical well-being if not their lives depended upon cooperating with their captors. Yet none of the persuaders was effective in producing widespread belief change. In Schein's study of the Korean War POWs, only 10 to 15 percent of the prisoners collaborated with the Koreans. According to Schein's research, this group included the scared, the intellectually curious, the ideologically confused, and the opportunists who wanted more cigarettes and privileges. It is doubtful whether all of the collaborators actually experienced belief change. It is quite probable that many of these collaborators exhibited behaviors that would get them rewards, whether or not these behaviors were consistent with their beliefs. Up to 90 percent of the POWs resisted persuasion, and of the 10 to 15 percent who collaborated with their captors, only a small percentage of these experienced actual changes in beliefs or attitudes.

One might argue that in both Korea and Vietnam the American prisoners interacted with other Americans, and that this interaction allowed the POWs to maintain their belief structures and constructions of reality despite the onslaught of anti-American propaganda. What then, of the person subjected to brainwashing in isolation, who cannot depend upon others for a "reality check" when persuasion produces doubt or confusion in one's belief system?

Patty Hearst & the SLA. Patty Hearst, daughter of the newspaper magnate, Randolph Hearst, was kidnapped in 1974 by a group of terrorists, the Symbionese Liberation Army. Patty Hearst was tied up and locked in a small, dark closet for fifty-seven days. Hearst claims that her captors brainwashed her and forced her to participate in illegal activities such as the famous Hibernia bank robbery in which two men were shot and killed. Hearst was captured eighteen months after her abduction and subsequently sentenced to thirty-five years in prison. The court did not believe the brainwashing story. She served two years of her sentence before being granted clemency by President Carter.

Hearst claims that she was subjected to physical duress and sexual abuse. She says that she continually feared for her life and the lives of her family. She reports intense indoctrination attempts by the SLA, in which they ridiculed her, her lifestyle, and her parents, to the extent that she became confused about her personal identity and values. The SLA dressed her in combat clothes, forced her to carry arms, and took her picture with the group. She claims that they forced her to participate in the bank robbery (the subject of a series of famous Patty Hearst pictures that have been repeatedly analyzed to determine if guns were pointed at Hearst as she pointed guns at civilians). After being seen publicly with the SLA, Hearst claims that she could no longer return to her family or turn herself in to the police. She reports that at this time she made a conscious "decision" to join the SLA.[8] What do you think? Was Patty persuaded, coerced, or brain-washed?

It is important to remember that an influence strategy that constitutes coercion or brainwashing for one person may be persuasion for another. Individuals exposed to the same influence attempt may respond differently; some individuals will perceive a choice while others will not. There are some influence tactics that restrict individual choice to such a degree that they are by their very nature considered involuntary. These would include the threat to life or limb, deceit, physiological deprivation (e.g., withholding of food, water, shelter, or sleep), hypnosis, or the exploitation of mental delusions. People obviously differ in their abilities to resist influence.

Freedom of choice is not an easy condition to assess or enforce when evaluating and regulating persuasive communication. On a daily basis we encounter persuasive tactics that reduce our resistance to influence. Are these techniques coercive or persuasive? Consider, for example, advertising to children who do not yet have the cognitive capabilities to resist influence what about using hypothetical fear scenarios to influence buying behavior, or spending up to a million dollars to design a single visual and verbal advertisement to activate our ego-needs, wants, and desires? In responding to advertising, we **perceive** that we have a choice. But do we? To what extent can strategic appeals to our desires, needs, and weaknesses dictate our responses?

Rather than trying to categorize influence attempts, it is best to visualize a continuum with voluntary at one end and involuntary at the

BOX 1.1   *Voluntary-Involuntary Persuasion Continuum*

Receiver retains free choice   Receiver's choices are restricted or dictated
              voluntary ———————————————————— involuntary

Analyze the degree to which each of the following influence attempts is voluntary or involuntary.

   a) advertising products to children during cartoons

   b) inserting pro-military messages in a feature film

   c) placing pro-suicide messages in musical recordings

   d) suspending students violating the school dress code

   e) excommunicating church members who divorce

other; in this manner voluntary becomes a matter of degree. The intra-psychic stability of the receiver and the degree to which the receiver perceives a choice in collaborating determine where an influence attempt is placed on this continuum. Try to place the influence attempts listed in Box 1.1 on the voluntary-involuntary continuum. You may find that many of the activities we typically categorize as fair-persuasion may, to your surprise, fall toward the coercive end of the continuum.

Affective, Cognitive & Behavioral Change

Persuasion requires a change in the receiver. There are three types of changes involved in persuasion: affective (attitudinal), cognitive (a change in beliefs), and behavioral (the performance of some action or the abstention from action).[9] Some scholars also include a fourth type of change—behavioral intent.[10] An intention is a promise to perform a particular behavior in the future, but a behavioral change is immediate and observable. It is important to note that if a persuasive message produces no changes in attitudes, beliefs, behavioral intentions, or behavior, persuasion has not occurred.

Attitudes, beliefs, and behavioral intentions reside in our minds. Some persuasive attempts are designed to influence attitudes, some are designed to change beliefs, some focus on behavior, and some effectively alter a combination of the three. Our attitudes, beliefs, and behavioral intentions for a given issue are all interrelated. Therefore, an influence attempt that changes two or three of the mental substrates is more powerful than an attempt that changes only one of the three.

Attitudes are relatively enduring evaluative responses to an idea, object, activity, policy, or value.[11] An attitude ranges from favorable to unfavorable. A persuasive message can change the degree to which something is deemed favorable or unfavorable. A persuader does not necessarily have to change the direction of an attitude from favorable to unfavorable for persuasion to occur; a change in degree of favorableness or unfavorableness is sufficient.

Although attitudes are strictly evaluative, **beliefs** are assertions that we hold with varying degrees of certainty. A belief represents a relationship among two or more ideas (e.g., San Diego has many bookstores, or Tom is very intelligent). A belief bridges an entity or idea with characteristics that define and explain it.

Behavioral intentions and **actions** are the changes most desired by persuaders. Many times persuaders seek a short- term change in our behavior (a vote, a donation, our time, or labor) without really caring whether or not a change in beliefs and attitudes accompanies the behavior.

To summarize, changes in attitudes, beliefs, and behavioral intentions are necessary for persuasion. Persuasive communication can, therefore, take many forms: 1) a change in the degree to which something is evaluated as favorable or unfavorable; 2) the creation of a new belief; 3) the change in the strength of an existing belief; 4) the elimination of an existing belief; 5) a change in intentions to perform a behavior (i.e., the likelihood the action will be performed); 6) a change in the performance of an action; and 7) abstention from an action previously performed. The characteristics of persuasion we have discussed can be used to recognize persuasion and to differentiate persuasion from other methods of changing people's thoughts and actions.

We have discussed six characteristics of persuasion that comprise our definition of persuasion—*persuasion is a* **transactional process** *among two or more persons whereby the management of* **symbolic meaning reconstructs reality,** *resulting in a* **voluntary change** *in* **beliefs, attitudes, and/or behavior.**

To gain a better understanding of how persuasion operates, we will explore the study of persuasion by context, function, and process. These three alternative approaches reflect scholars' struggle to find an organizing framework for the study of persuasion.

PERSUASION CATEGORIZED BY CONTEXT

The most common method of defining communication contexts is by the size of the communication group: interpersonal communication, small group communication, organizational communication, public communication, and mass mediated communication. These contexts differ according to the: 1) formality of communication rules; 2) opportunities for direct feedback; 3) relationship between sender and receiver; 4) communication goals; and 5) number of people involved in the communication encounter (Table 1.1). Researchers who take this approach to the study of persuasion assume that persuasion operates in different ways depending upon the communication context. That is, communication in a small group is

TABLE 1.1   Contexts of Communication & Persuasion.

Context	Formality	Feedback	Relationship	# of People
interpersonal	low	high	personal	few
small group	low or high	moderate	defined by group	3 or more
organizational	high	moderate/low	defined by status	many
public	high	low	impersonal	many
mass media	varies	low	impersonal with attempts to personalize	many

characteristically different from persuasion in the mass media. For this reason, we will define each of these contexts and briefly describe how each context influences persuasion.

Interpersonal communication is characterized by face-to-face conversation between two or more people. When you try to influence your friends to go out on the town, or try to influence your parents to send you money, or try to influence a sibling not to date the jerk he/she is enthralled with, you are engaging in interpersonal persuasion. Two variables that will influence what persuasive strategies you use, and how you interpret the other person's persuasive tactics are: 1) the relationship you have with the other person; and 2) the opportunity for all interactants to participate actively in the persuasion process and influence each other.[12] For example, you are likely to use different persuasion strategies with your roommate than with your professor. The opportunity to engage in persuasive discourse and the rules that govern this conversation are likely to differ between the conversation with your roommate (governed by equality) and the conversation with your professor (characterized by differential power).

Small group communication is defined as face-to-face communication among three or more people who constitute a social group. A social group is characterized by shared norms and a specified purpose. You are probably a member of many social groups—your family, your church or temple, your student organizations, your suite-mates, your class project group, etc. Group persuasion typically involves reaching a group consensus or decision. Two factors that influence persuasion in small group contexts are: 1) the complexity of the task; and 2) group interaction spirals.[13]

The role of persuasion in small group communication increases as the complexity of the task increases. A simple task requires little coordination among group members. In contrast, a complex task requires members to share information, integrate the information provided by other members, generate new perspectives, and elaborate and develop each other's ideas.

An **interaction spiral** occurs when the sharing of information leads the group to create new ideas that are more than the sum of the original information. In other words, Jane's information makes Frank think of his information in a new way, which leads Stacy to create a new perspective, upon which Bob elaborates.

Organizational persuasion may be used to coordinate members of a large group, such as a corporation. Persuasion in this context often involves the communication of the organization's rules, roles, and culture to its members. Two of the most important factors affecting persuasion within the organization are: 1) the respective power of the message senders and receivers; and 2) the use of persuasion for organizational structuration.

Power differences affect persuasion because perceptions of personal power affect the selection and interpretation of messages. Subordinates can do little to change organizational power structures, and power differences within the organization may increase the likelihood that supervisors select negative persuasive tactics (e.g., threats and punishments).

Structuration theory explains how organizational climates and networks are produced and continually reproduced as interaction rules and resources change.[14] That is, communication and organizational structure are intricately tied together; each serves to produce, maintain, and reproduce the other. You may have worked for a company, for example, in which the communication climate changed upon the replacement of a supervisor within the organizational structure. Clearly, persuasion is necessary for structuration; persuasion serves to coordinate organizational members and to influence the adoption of emerging climates and communication networks.

Public communication involves communication to an audience. In public communication, audience members may influence each other. Whether it be through formal feedback to the speaker or through interpersonal communication before, during, or after the presentation, audience members have a powerful influence on the acceptance of the message. You are less likely to think a political candidate's speech is terrific if the audience you are a member of responds unfavorably to the speech. In a public communication context, the speaker must maintain identification with the audience and ensure that the audience remains empathetic.[15] Once the speaker loses identification or empathy, the audience may identify with each other and group together in opposition to the speaker.

Persuasion in the **mass media context** is characterized by communication to a large, diverse audience with no opportunity for immediate feedback. Perhaps the most important characteristic of persuasion through the mass media is that the audience, although large, is usually segmented and isolated. That is, the receivers may not have the opportunity to interact with other receivers to share and challenge responses to the message. Compared to the public communication context, the reception of mass media messages is more likely to occur in social isolation. It follows that the mass media are more likely to influence people who have few social contacts. People who have a great many social contacts may be more influenced by their friends' reactions to the media message than by the media message itself.

The second variable affecting persuasion through the mass media is the entertainment function of the media. We expect to be entertained by the media; we relax and mindlessly let media messages flow over us. We are not on guard for persuasive influences—we are focusing on being entertained. Yet, persuasive influences are embedded in our entertainment.[16] Violent dramas persuade us to be more accepting of physical violence. Popular music tells us to "waste away in Margaritaville," or more positively, to save the rain forests. Sitcoms are laden with messages about civil rights, gender and social roles, honesty, and family values. To some extent even advertisements are viewed as entertainment. The problem is that the mindless, uncritical reception of media messages as entertainment can make us more vulnerable to persuasive influences.

We have explored the characteristics that distinguish persuasion in five different communication contexts. There are clearly some differences across contexts that may influence the process and outcome of persuasion. There are also, however, limitations to the study of persuasion by context.

Persuasion research tends to get bogged down in contextual factors and loses sight of the big picture: the process of persuasion. We tend to forget that persuasion is very similar across contexts. For example, the strategies the Krishnas used to persuade Julie are the same strategies our religious leaders, political leaders, and friends use to persuade us. The strategy used initially to get Julie involved in the Krishnas was **identification.** Her recruiter established all the things she and Julie had in common during their first meetings. The Krishnas played on Julie's interest in music, her vegetarian tendencies, and her intellectual curiosity to convince Julie that they had a lot in common. Political candidates who try to identify with the populace by stressing their origins as "an honest peanut farmer" (Jimmy Carter), or "the son of Greek immigrants" (Mike Dukakis), or "a loving grandfather" (George Bush) also use identification. We even use identification strategies to get dates: "Wow! You're a Deadhead, too! I can't believe all we have in common!"

The second limitation of the study of persuasion according to communication contexts is that there are many different ways to define context. Communication contexts can be defined by the number of communicators (i.e., interpersonal, small group, etc.) or according to social situation (i.e., religious, political, health, educational, and legal contexts). In the first case, the categories are not always distinct. The process of persuasion is often quite similar in interpersonal, small group,

This direct mail greeting card employs an identification persuasion strategy by communicating an appreciation for the receiver's busy schedule and daily joys and frustrations.

and mass mediated contexts. In the second case, we cannot produce an exhaustive list of social situations in which persuasion occurs.

PERSUASION CATEGORIZED BY FUNCTION

An alternative way to organize the study of persuasion is by function—that is, the purpose behind the message. Arnold and Bowers identify ten functions of communication, and all ten of these functions are applicable to persuasion (Table 1.2).[17] The study of persuasion by function assumes that persuasion differs in meaningful ways depending on the purpose or goal of the persuasive message. Examining each of these functions in more detail, we can generate many examples of persuasion that apply to each functional category.

You engage in **self-image** persuasion when you wear your best suit for a job interview. You engage in **informational** persuasion when you suggest an alternative way for a friend to organize an English paper, and you engage in **attitude-change** persuasion when you motivate this friend

TABLE 1.2   Arnold & Bowers' (1984) 10 Functions of Communication and Their
Persuasive Applications.

1. developing and altering self-images (i.e., persuading others to see you in a favorable light)

2. communicating information (i.e., persuading others to acquire new facts, beliefs, and opinions)

3. changing attitudes and gaining compliance (persuading others to change attitudes or behaviors)

4. pleasing (i.e., persuading others that we seek to please them and want them to do things that please us)

5. interpersonal bonding (i.e., persuading others to befriend us)

6. formation of small groups (i.e., persuading members to follow our leadership)

7. organization (i.e., persuading others to work toward a common goal)

8. communication of values (i.e., persuading others to adopt our values)

9. maintenance of public values (i.e., persuading others to adopt value standards and enforce them at a societal level)

10. mobilizing action for social movements (i.e., persuading people to give money, time, votes, and/or their lives for a social cause)

to have fun with those treacherous writing assignments. Persuasion for a **pleasing** function may occur when you pick up the restaurant tab, and persuasion for a **bonding** function may occur when you ask a friend to go to a movie. **Small group organization** may be your persuasive goal as you motivate club members to follow your leadership, and **organization** may be your persuasive goal when you encourage callers for the annual alumni phonathon. Philosophical or religious discussions are likely to involve **value persuasion,** and speeches in the legislature promote the **maintenance of public values.** Finally, your speeches and posters for Amnesty International, or some other social cause, serve an **action mobilization** function.

Although the analysis of persuasive functions does provide a richer understanding of the variety of persuasive purposes and outcomes, the category system has one major limitation. Once again, the list is not finite or exhaustive. There are additional functions of persuasion, such as entertaining, stimulating humor, creating fear, inciting an argument, or simply goading a person to produce a reaction. See if you can generate additional functions of persuasion that can not be subsumed under the list of ten functions in Table 1.2. The degree to which the list is incomplete reflects the degree to which our view of persuasion is incomplete.

PERSUASION CATEGORIZED BY PROCESS

Perhaps the most comprehensive approach to the study of persuasion is to analyze the process of persuasion. The advantage of a focus on process is that it provides both an analytical and a holistic view of persuasion in action. That is, to understand process we must analyze how all the pieces of the persuasion puzzle fit together and interact. Moreover, the study of the effects of persuasion on society informs our understanding of the pieces that comprise the process.

This textbook is organized according to the process approach. By studying in great detail how the persuasion process works at the level of the individual sender and receiver, we will build a foundation of knowledge that will be used to analyze the process of persuasion in complex social functions and contexts, such as the mass media, advertising, social movements, propaganda, political campaigns, etc.

The process approach identifies the components of persuasion and seeks to describe how the components interact. Components of persuasion include symbols, the people sending and receiving persuasive messages, message content, the interactants' self-presentations, the situation or context in which persuasion occurs, the channel in which the messages are transmitted (e.g., non-verbal, verbal, via audio or videotape), and the society and culture that influence the interactants' communication expectations and rules. These are the topics that we will explore in the second section of this textbook, Components of Persuasion.

Figure 1.2 illustrates the components influencing the persuasion process. The concentric circles are analogous to the rings you see when you throw a stone into a lake. The components of persuasion are fluid; these

FIGURE 1.2 The components of the persuasion process can be represented by concentric circles. The inner circles create the outer circles which encompass them. The persuasion process is created and defined by the interaction of these nine components.

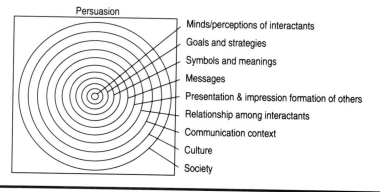

Persuasion
- Minds/perceptions of interactants
- Goals and strategies
- Symbols and meanings
- Messages
- Presentation & impression formation of others
- Relationship among interactants
- Communication context
- Culture
- Society

Model of the persuasion process. Persuasion is a cyclical process, whereby a change in attitudes, beliefs or behaviors may lead to new perceptions, new relational definitions, new goals, and new messages. This process is not limited to one message, the cycle continues to spin and evolve as new messages and meanings are negotiated. The meaning attributed to a message may cause communicators to modify their perceptions, relationship, and goals, resulting in a new persuasion cycle in which components of the process have been redefined.

FIGURE 1.3

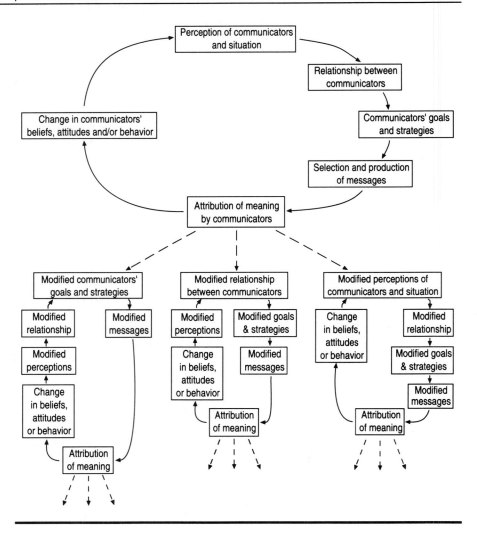

changing components shape and are shaped by the persuasion process that unfolds as two or more people interact. Each component of the persuasion process can potentially produce a wave-like effect on the other components, and as a result, the process and outcome of persuasion may change.

The study of the process of persuasion focuses on how the components of persuasion interact to bring about shared meaning among the communicators (Figure 1.3). A process approach analyzes: a) the relationship between the communicators and how the relationship affects communicators' perceptions of each other; b) how the relationship and perceptions affect communication goals and strategies; c) how all of the previously mentioned components interact in the process of message production and message interpretation; d) how the components influence individual meaning and the development of shared meaning; and finally, e) how the persuasion process leads to changes in attitudes, beliefs, and/or actions. These are the topics we will discuss in the third section of this textbook, The Process of Persuasion.

The study of the persuasion process also addresses the outcome of persuasion—the effects of persuasion on society. This topic will be addressed in the final section of the textbook, in which we discuss propaganda and the use of persuasion in campaigns and social movements.

SUMMARY

Throughout this chapter we have painted bits and pieces of a picture of persuasion, adding more detail as the chapter progresses. The discussion of the pervasive nature of persuasion established the sheer size of the canvas on which our picture of persuasion would be painted; persuasion affects all of us, everyday, in nearly everything we do.

By emphasizing the processional, transactional and symbolic nature of persuasion, and illustrating how persuasion reconstructs reality, our painting conveys the formless, magical, spiraling, changing nature of persuasion. In the course of differentiating persuasion from other forms of influence, such as coercion and brainwashing, we add strokes of humanity and respect for human dignity to our canvas.

The discussion of persuasive contexts and functions allowed us to paint the situations in which persuasion is likely to occur, and the purposes and outcomes of persuasive communication. Details were added to our portrayal of contexts and functions by filling in the components and the interactions among components. At this point the painting began to reflect the dynamic process of persuasion.

What results is a picture in our minds. An abstract picture. A colorful picture. A picture of a powerful force—but a force that is constrained and managed by the will of the communicators.

Study Guide

pervasive nature of persuasion
role of persuasion in organizing society
six definitional corollaries of persuasion
    process
    transactional
    symbols
    reconstruction of reality
        objective and constructed reality
        three methods of reconstructing reality
    voluntary
        define persuasion, coercion and brainwashing
        coercion and perceived choice
        brainwashing and intra-psychic stability
        free-choice continuum
    attitudes, beliefs, and behavior
three approaches to the study of persuasion
    persuasion contexts
        limitation of study by context
        identification as a strategy used across contexts
    persuasion functions
    persuasion components and processes

Discussion Questions

1. Think of a recent communication encounter in which you have attempted to influence a friend or family member. Describe the persuasive encounter as a process.
   a. When did the forces that led to this persuasive encounter begin?
   b. When did the effects and ramifications of this encounter end?
   c. Were you influenced in any way by the person you were trying to persuade?
   d. Did both you and the persuadee change thoughts or behaviors in an effort to establish shared meaning?

2. Do you and your friends or family share meanings for certain symbols that outsiders would not understand? Make a list of these "private" symbols, and think about how the meaning for each symbol was created.

3. Review the strategies used by the Krishnas to persuade Julie. Think about other situations in which you have experienced or observed the same influence strategies.

References

1. Kilbourn, Jean. 1987. *Still killing us softly*. Cambridge, MA: Cambridge Documentary Films, Inc. Videotape.
2. Geertz, C. 1971. "Deep play: Notes on the Balinese cockfight." In *Myth, Symbol and Culture*, C. Geertz, ed. New York: W. W. Norton.

3. Streiker, L. D. 1984. *Mind bending*. Garden City, NY: Doubleday.
4. Satir, V. 1967. *Conjoint family therapy*. Palo Alto, CA: Science & Behavior Books.

   Satir, V. 1972. *Peoplemaking*. Palo Alto, CA: Science & Behavior Books.
5. Schein, E. A. 1956. The Chinese indoctrination program of prisoners of war: A study of attempted brainwashing. *Psychiatry: Journal for the study of interpersonal processes*, 19, 149–172.
6. Scheflin, E., and J. Opton. 1978. *Mind manipulators*. New York: Paddenington Press.
7. Chetund, L. 1986. *Hanoi Hilton*. Hollywood, CA: Script City.
8. Hearst, P. C., and A. Moscow 1982. *Every secret thing*. Garden City, NY: Doubleday.
9. Katz, D., and E. Stotland. 1959. A preliminary statement to a theory of attitude structure and change. In *Psychology: A study of a science*, Vol. 3., S. Koch, ed., pp. 423–474. New York: McGraw-Hill.

   Rosenberg, M. J., and C. I. Hovland. 1960. Cognitive, affective, and behavioral components of attitudes. In *Attitude organization and change*, C. I. Hovland and M. J. Rosenberg, eds. pp. 1–14. New Haven, CT: Yale University Press, 1960.
10. Fishbein, M., and I. Ajzen. 1975. *Belief, attitude, intention and behavior: An introduction to theory and research*. Reading, MA: Addison-Wesley.
11. Keisler, C. A., B. E. Collins, and N. Miller. 1969. *Attitude change*. New York: John Wiley.
12. Cody, M., and M. L. McLaughlin. 1980. Perceptions of compliance-gaining situations: A dimensional analysis. *Communication Monographs*, 46, 132–148.
13. Bormann, E. G. 1986. Symbolic convergence theory and communication in group decision-making. In *Communication and group decision-making*, R. Hirokawa and M. S. Poole, eds. pp. 219–236. Beverly Hills, CA: Sage.

    Jarboe, S. 1988. A comparison of input-output, process-output and input-process-output models of small group problem-solving effectiveness. *Communication Monographs*, 55, 121–142.
14. Poole, M. S., and R. D. McPhee. 1983. A structuration theory of organizational climate. In *Organizational communication: An interpretive approach*, L. L. Putnam and M. Pacanowsky, eds. pp. 195–213. Beverly Hills: Sage.
15. Cronkhite, G., and J. R. Liska. 1980. The judgement of communicant acceptability. In *Persuasion: New direction in theory and research*, M. E. Roloff and G. R. Miller, eds. 101–140. Beverly Hills, CA: Sage.
16. Meyrowitz, J. 1985. No sense of place: The impact of electronic media on social behavior. New York: Oxford University Press.
17. Arnold, C. C., and J. W. Bowers. 1984. *Handbook of rhetorical and communication theory*. Boston, MA: Allyn and Bacon, Inc.

2

Six Approaches to the Study of Persuasion

"I Have a Dream speech . . ."
by
Martin Luther King

. . . This is our hope. This is the faith with which I return to the South. With this faith we will be able to hew out of the mountain of despair a stone of hope. With this faith we will be able to transform the jangling discords of our nation into a beautiful symphony of brotherhood. With this faith we will be able to work together, to pray together, to struggle together, to go to jail together, to stand up for freedom together, knowing that we will be free one day.

. . . And if America is to be a great nation this must become true. So let freedom ring from the prodigious hilltops of New Hampshire.
Let freedom ring from the mighty mountains of New York.
Let freedom ring from the heightening Alleghenies of Pennsylvania!
Let freedom ring from the snowcapped Rockies of Colorado!
Let freedom ring from the curvaceous slopes of California!
But not only that; let freedom ring from Stone Mountain of Georgia!
Let freedom ring from Lookout Mountain of Tennessee!
Let freedom ring from every hill and molehill of Mississippi. From every mountainside, let freedom ring. And when this happens—when we let freedom ring, when we let it ring from every village and every hamlet, and from every state and every city, we will be able to speed up that day when all of God's children, black men and white men, Jews and Gentiles, Protestants and Catholics, will be able to join hands and sing in the words of the old Negro spiritual "Free at last! Free at last! Thank God almighty, we are free at last!"[1]

As the conclusion of his inspirational speech demonstrates, Martin Luther King relies on rhetorical eloquence rather than physical violence to inspire change. Persuasion, throughout history, has given humans an alternative to brute force. And, just as people have pursued the study and creation of new forms of warfare, torture, or physical punishment, people have also studied strategies of persuasion. The history of persuasion gives us a sense of how our current understanding of the persuasion process has evolved, and what questions will shape persuasion research in the future.

Historical developments seldom follow a chronological timeline. Progression is cyclical, not linear. Discoveries of earlier ages are continually re-discovered and abandoned (e.g., tie-dyed fabrics were popular in the 1960s, abandoned in the 1970s and 1980s, and are fashionable once again in the 1990s). The history of persuasion research is no different. Although the classical perspective began in ancient Greece two thousand years ago, there are many scholars today who use this approach to study persuasion. Similarly, though the powerful effects perspective was most prevalent in the 1930s, there are many people who apply this approach to understanding persuasive messages in the 1990s.

In this chapter we will explore six approaches to persuasion research,: 1) the Classical Perspective, 2) the Post-Classical Perspective, 3) the Hypodermic Needle Perspective, 4) the Limited Effects Perspective, 5) the Interactional Perspective, and 6) the Cultural-Contextual Perspective. Though these perspectives are presented in a historical time frame, many of these approaches continue to be relevant to persuasion research today.

CLASSICAL PERSPECTIVE

Aristotle was the first scholar to systematically study the process of persuasion. Much of our knowledge of persuasion is based on his work. The classical era of persuasion research, roughly defined as 500 B.C. to 300 A.D., includes the work of Greek and Roman scholars, including Plato, Aristotle, Cicero, and Quintillian. These scholars studied **rhetoric**—the means of persuasion.[2]

The Greeks and Romans defined rhetoric as the art of elocution. Painting, music, and dance are all art forms used to inspire audiences. The classical scholars viewed persuasion as the *art* of inspiring others through public discourse. Students were taught to use language, gestures, and arguments poetically and emphatically.

Based on the Greeks' use of open dialogue to maintain the democratic process, the purpose of rhetoric was to promote plans of action for social causes. In Ancient Greece, it was the responsibility of a citizen to argue his own defense in a legal case and to argue his own perspective in the legislative assembly. A person's rhetorical skill was critical; one's persuasive ability was literally a matter of life, death, and protection of property. This created a role for the **sophist**—a person who traveled throughout the Greek states teaching the skills of rhetoric.[3]

Most historical accounts of persuasion theory begin with Plato. In contrast to the sophists' focus on teaching speaking skills, Plato addressed the effects of persuasion on society. It was believed that persuasive debate provided a forum through which "truth" would be revealed. It was the role of the rhetorician to inspire the citizens to support worthy and ethical causes. Plato believed that the purpose of rhetoric was to "make known the will of God." The belief that "truth" is discovered through persuasive arguments and public discourse illustrates the importance of persuasion during the classical era.

The ethics of persuasion were Plato's primary concern. In the *Phaedrus,* and in the *Gorgius,* Plato argues that persuasion promoting belief without knowledge—that is, opinion change without facts—is unethical.[4] According to Plato, the practice of arguing both sides of an issue obscures the truth. Moreover, persuasion that employs flattery, appearances, trickery, and superficial images is not based in knowledge. Plato would consider it unethical to use emotional reactions as the sole basis for persuasion. Think about advertising messages you have heard recently. Do the messages promote knowledge of the product? Or do the messages count on your mindless reaction to positive images? Plato would consider the latter unethical.

In addition to their focus on ethics, classical scholars sought to identify and label different stylistic devices (called **tropes**) used to ornament the presentation of ideas. This fueled many debates on whether persuasion should focus on style or substance.[5]

In his "I Have a Dream" speech, Martin Luther King incorporates many stylistic techniques, including repetition, antithesis, and parallel structure. **Repetition** in King's speech is illustrated by the recurring phrase "let freedom ring," in the excerpt above, and earlier in the speech in the repetition of the famous "I have a dream" phrase. **Antithesis** is the juxtaposition of opposing themes—a stylistic device by which ideas are contrasted in parallel phrases. John F. Kennedy's famous line, "Ask not what your country can do for you; ask what you can do for your country," is an example of antithesis. King also uses antithesis in the statement, "I have a dream that one day my four little children will one day live in a nation where they will not be judged by the color of their skin, but by the content of their character." **Parallel structure** is the use of phrases and sentences that incorporate the same grammatical sequence and sometimes even the same words. Repetition and antithesis both employ parallel structure, but it is also possible to have parallel structure without repetition or antithesis. King's trident plea that, "With this faith we will be able to work together, play together, to struggle together, to go to jail together, to stand up for freedom together, knowing that we will be free one day," is an example of parallel structure.

Although many classical scholars focused on style, Aristotle believed that there was more to the study of rhetoric than the classification of stylistic devices. Aristotle was one of the first scholars to focus on the pragmatics of persuasion—that is, how to construct an effective message.

Aristotle's *Rhetoric* has three books.[6] The first defines **rhetoric** and its uses in legal, ceremonial (festival and funeral oratory), and political contexts. The second book focuses on how to construct **proofs and arguments,** and the third book reiterates classical ideas of argument **style and organization.**

Aristotle's most important contributions to the study of rhetoric are addressed in his second book on intrinsic proofs. It is in this area that Aristotle made his unique contributions and changed the focus of the study of rhetoric from purely stylistic concerns. Aristotle is probably best known for his three persuasive proofs: reasoning from content or logic (**logos**), reasoning from passion and emotions (**pathos**), and reasoning from the merits and character of the speaker (**ethos**). These three persuasive proofs are similar to Cicero's (106–43 B.C.) instructions "to prove, to delight and to stir."[7]

Aristotle, who was a student of Plato, obviously had a different view of persuasion ethics. Aristotle taught his students how to appeal to the values and passions of the audience, and how to present oneself as an honest and trustworthy speaker. These strategies can lead to belief without knowledge. Unlike Plato, Aristotle did not believe that a message could be either ethical or unethical. Aristotle believed that ethics lie in people, purposes, and situations, not in arguments. According to Aristotle, rhetoric is but a tool that can be used for good or for evil, and the persuader bears the ethical responsibility for the consequences of a message. For this reason, Aristotle painstakingly outlines the characteristics of the "good man," arguing that the "good man" will use the tools of rhetoric for the common good, not for individual gain.[8]

Aristotle integrated his study of persuasive strategies with his view of ethics through the principle of moderation. The **doctrine of the mean** is a philosophy of life for Aristotle. The ethical person does all things in moderation. This doctrine is applicable to our discussion of persuasion because Aristotle proposes that truth is to be found in the *mean*. There are always two positions or sides to an issue, and extreme arguments are likely to be exaggerated rather than truthful. King demonstrates this doctrine of the mean in his call for peaceful resistance: ". . . [our fight] must not lead to a distrust of all white people, for many of our white brothers, as evidenced by their presence here today, have come to realize that their destiny is tied up with our destiny." Where it might have been easy for King to make an extreme argument using whites as a scapegoat for the injustices experienced by blacks, King opts for the ethical doctrine of the mean. For Aristotle, any appeal to a person's emotions, needs, or desires should appeal to the value of moderation. An extreme argument that is too conservative or too liberal, too exaggerated or too minimized, is unethical.

Aristotle believed that rhetoric was key to social responsibility. He believed that if people were trained in reasoning and argumentation, truth would prevail. If the side of truth failed to win in a persuasive debate, it was the fault of the speaker. Aristotle also believed that not all people had the ability to discern truth; therefore, speakers must receive training in rhetoric in order to persuade the masses to support the right causes. These speakers must also be trained, according to Aristotle, to present both sides of an argument, so that the audience can learn to analyze arguments critically and to refute the opposition.

The Romans followed in the footsteps of Plato and Aristotle. Much of their writings addressed a systematic method for teaching rhetoric (public speaking), which has become known as the five canons of persuasive discourse: 1) invention, 2) arrangement, 3) elocution, 4) memory, and 5) delivery.[9] These five tasks are basic to the creation and evaluation of persuasive speeches. Moreover, these five tasks are the basis for much of the persuasion research conducted today.

Invention involves the construction of valid, plausible, and compelling arguments. Current research in this area is concerned with the relative effectiveness of different persuasive strategies.

Arrangement simply refers to the organization of the persuasive message. Current research analyzing one- versus two-sided messages, primacy or recency effects (whether listeners remember what is said first or last), and climactic versus anti-climactic organization (whether the most important argument should be placed last or first) are all based on classical questions of arrangement. Martin Luther King's speech employed a climactic arrangement whereby the intensity and excitement of his arguments increased throughout the speech, culminating in the climactic ending, "Free at last! Free at last! Thank God Almighty, we're free at last."

Elocution includes stylistic choices in the construction of a persuasive argument. Classical rhetoricians discussed the proper use of language and word choice. Contemporary research is still pursuing this issue in studies of language intensity and stylistic devices such as repetition and poetics.

The **memory** task concerns understanding the topic and remembering the order and development of arguments. During the classical perspective persuaders spoke without notes, and one of the tools classical rhetoricians had to teach was how to memorize a speech. One of the most famous mnenomic devices involves spatial memorization in which the speaker visualizes a frequented walk and mentally places arguments along the walkway. The speaker then simply visualizes this favorite walk and mentally picks up arguments as he or she recites the speech. Since even presidents read speeches these days, contemporary scholars place little emphasis on the memory task.

The final task for the persuasive speaker is **delivery.** Classical scholars instructed students in the control of voice and body. Delivery concerns include speech rate, pitch, gestures, body movement, eye contact, and facial expressions. Contemporary scholars are still studying the effects of various delivery styles on the reception and evaluation of messages.

A sixth task, studied by Cicero, a famous Roman lawyer (106–43 B.C.) is the analysis of the situational constraints facing the speaker.[10] The study of **stasis**—the status of an issue—instructs the speaker how to analyze the situational constraints beyond his or her control, and how to use these constraints to the best advantage. The key to stasis is to refute an accusation. If, for example, you want to persuade people in Wisconsin to support the downtown district instead of shopping in climate-controlled shopping malls, an analysis of "stasis" might reveal a way to highlight the natural, exhilarating, outdoor experience—that is, to refute the fact that shopping outdoors in Wisconsin is a negative feature.

Perhaps the most significant change for the study and practice of rhetoric during Roman times was the move toward professional persuaders. Lawyers and politicians took over the persuasive responsibilities of the citizen. In contrast to Plato's and Aristotle's focus on the societal effects of persuasion, the discovery of truth, and the merits of argument, the late Roman period focused on stylistic devices, the memorization of model speeches, and the magic of language—the *how to* study of public speaking.

Although the classical approach to the study of persuasion began in ancient Greece, the classical approach is still used today. The classical approach is characterized by the analysis and evaluation of historical and contemporary public speeches, the study of Greek and Roman rhetorical theory, and an emphasis on the ethical and social implications of public persuasion. The survival of classical theories either reflects the tremendous contributions of classical rhetorical theory on our understanding of persuasion today, or conversely, reflects the lack of progress we, as contemporary scholars, have made since Greek and Roman times.

Monroe's Motivated Sequence, developed in the 1930s, is an example of a more recent application of the classical approach to teaching persuasion. Like the classical scholars, Monroe presents a prescriptive "how to" format for constructing a persuasive speech. Monroe presents five tasks that all persuasive arguments should accomplish: attention, need, satisfaction, visualization, and action.[11]

M. L. King's "I Have a Dream" speech follows these five steps in every detail. The task of **attention** is simply motivating the audience to attend to the persuasive address. King gets his audience's attention by claiming that this event "will go down in history as the greatest demonstration for freedom in the history of our nation."

Need presents a problem and establishes its relevance and importance to the audience. King next outlines the lack of freedoms and the injustices facing blacks. King's appeal to the "urgency of the moment" further punctuates the need. "This sweltering summer of the Negro's legitimate discontent will not pass until there is an invigorating autumn of freedom and equality."

The **satisfaction** stage involves a proposal that alleviates the need or problem and includes cogent arguments to support the proposal. King presents peaceful demonstration as the means to solve the problem, and continued faith as the bullice to sustain those fighting for civil rights.

The **visualization** stage allows the speaker to play with elocutionary style by using description. Through description, the speaker encourages the audience to vicariously experience what the world will be like if the proposal is implemented. King clearly illustrates visualization in six descriptive visions of the future, all beginning with the phrase, "I Have a Dream. . . ."

The **action** task is to compel the audience to change beliefs, attitudes, or behavior in favor of the proposal. King calls his followers to action by telling them to go back to their home states, to keep their faith and courage, and to continue working for peaceful change.

Monroe is just one of many contemporary scholars who rely upon the tenets of classical rhetorical theory in their work. Since the classical approach is still employed today, we should consider its merits and limitations.

The benefit of the classical approach is its focus on ethics. The classical theorists, such as Aristotle and Plato, believed that one could not teach persuasion without teaching ethics. Alternative approaches to the study of persuasion separate the study of ethics from the study of persuasive strategies. Though classical scholars evaluate a persuasive attempt in light of its ethical implications, alternative approaches evaluate persuasion according to its effectiveness. Moreover, when ethical analysis does occur in the non-classical traditions, it usually takes the form of case studies and is characterized by a reactionary "Oops! Look what happened!" The classical approach to persuasion research has a more commendable record for invoking ethical theories developed by philosophers which can be used as guidelines for ethical persuasion in many different situations. Many contemporary approaches to the study of persuasion have neglected the study of ethics.

A second benefit of the classical approach is its focus on teaching critical thinking. Aristotle and many other classical writers believed that the teaching of reasoning and argumentation was necessary for an informed society. Although we live in an information society in which hundreds of persuasive messages confront us each day, we place little attention on educating people in the art of logical reasoning, argumentation, and critical thinking. You have spent twelve to sixteen years in the

American educational system; how many classes have you taken in reasoning and argumentation? Are you prepared to discern the truth in persuasive arguments?

The primary limitation of the classical approach is that it is prescriptive—it proposes a method for persuading effectively. Our understanding of persuasion should also include explanation and prediction. Rather than trying to devise a recipe for the perfect speech, we should be working toward an explanation of how persuasion works—how people, relationships, situations, and symbols affect the persuasion process. Moreover, we need to predict under what conditions certain variables will have an effect on the persuasive outcome and what that outcome is likely to be.

The classical approach is also limited by its ability to reflect the complexity of the persuasion process. We must study the big picture, not just the speaker. Persuasion studies must take into account the receiver of the message, and the context in which the message is presented.

POST-CLASSICAL PERSPECTIVE

Compared to the impact of the classical period on contemporary persuasion scholarship, the post-classical perspective contributes very little. The study of persuasion from, roughly, 300 A.D. to the early twentieth century is characterized by a reiteration of classical works, with little original thinking or development of ideas.

Much of the research conducted during the post-classical period fell within the purview of the early Christian church.[12] Persuasion obviously played a part in the conversion of Europe to Christianity (although brute force played an equal role). In the seventeenth century, Pope Greg XV enacted a proposal to use propaganda, as an alternative to holy wars, to induce the acceptance of church doctrine.

Thomas Acquinas (St. Thomas) revived and modified the works of the classical theorists in an effort to influence church doctrine. St. Thomas struggled with the question of whether religious conviction should be the result of faith (pathos) or reason (logos). During the thirteenth century, Christian scholars tried to revive Aristotelean philosophy, and movements were afoot to make Aristotle a saint. Not surprisingly, this failed (imagine a Greek pagan a saint of the Catholic church)!

The church probably assumed they had the corner on the persuasion research market because persuasion was tied to ethics and morality, and, consequently, to religious faith and conviction. Imagine then, the impact of Machiavelli's *The Prince*.[13] This writing was a radical change from classical persuasion theory. Persuasion, according to Machiavelli's treatise, was no longer the domain of the gods, but was a means to practical political power. In contrast to the work of Aristotle and the church, *The Prince* advocates the separation of persuasion and ethics. Accordingly, the basis for ethics changed from divine will to the Lockean notion of the greatest good for the greatest number, to the contemporary cultural view of the greatest gain for the most ingenious. Machiavelli would have supported the concept of *caveat emptor*—let the buyer beware.

HYPODERMIC NEEDLE (POWERFUL EFFECTS) PERSPECTIVE

During the years preceding U.S. involvement in World War II, it was believed that persuasion was analogous to a hypodermic needle. Persuasive messages were injected into the receiver, and the passive receiver had no choice but to acquiesce. The magic bullet analogy is also used to describe these powerful effects—a magic bullet is shot into the unsuspecting audience, the bullet or idea becomes embedded in the audience member, and the audience member adopts the suggested belief, attitude, or action.

The powerful effects perspective reflects a mechanistic model of communication (Box 2.1). The source encodes a message through a channel which is decoded by a receiver. This model assumes that persuasion is something the sender *does to* the receiver, and that the receiver has little or no effect on the sender. Persuasion, according to this approach, is linear and sequential, and the message is simply transferred from sender to receiver. This model focuses on the *transmission* of a message over the construction of *meaning* by the communicators.

This model is an integration of Carroll's (1953) and Berlo's (1960) models of communication. Carroll recognized the importance of encoding (intention) and decoding (interpretation), while Berlo recognized the many source, message, and receiver variables that can impact upon the persuasion process.

BOX 2.1

COMMUNICATION PROCESS

	Source →	Encodes →	Message →	Through A Channel →	Decoded →	By Receiver
Variables	Communication skills attitudes knowledge social system culture	message construction	content code organization	see hear taste smell touch ***** mass mediated interpersonal	information processing	Communication skills attitudes knowledge social system culture

Source: Carroll, J. B. 1953. *The Study of Language.* Cambridge, MA: Harvard University Press. Berlo, D. K. 1960. *The Process of Communication.* New York: Holt, Rinehart, & Winston.

In response to the powerful effects of Nazi propaganda, the U.S. government tried its hand at persuasion.

THIS IS THE ENEMY

St. Louis Public Library, St. Louis, Mo.

During the 1930s, there were at least three events that reinforced the hypodermic needle theory of persuasion effects: 1) the perceived success of Hitler's propaganda movement; 2) the introduction of radio and mass disseminated information in society; and 3) Orson Welles' *War of the Worlds* broadcast.

Joseph Goebbels, Hitler's propaganda specialist, facilitated Hitler's rise to power during the 1930s. Goebbels produced pro-Nazi films that showed the ever-pure, blond-haired, blue-eyed youth of Germany working for the good of their country. These ideas were reinforced through four-color posters calling Germans to nationalist loyalty and focusing the German populace on a common enemy, the Jews, who were purportedly responsible for the current economic hardships. In the midst of political rallies with music, fireworks, persuasive speeches, and the chanting of slogans, Hitler rode the wave of nationalistic passion. Hitler's use of propaganda, his quick succession to power, and the zealotry of the German people frightened Americans.

About the same time, a new mass medium, radio, was sweeping the country. For the first time in history, the majority of people in a country were tied (via the airwaves) to a common source of information. Radio mesmerized people. For the first time in history a mass medium became not just a political and news mouthpiece, but a source of entertainment. In the evening the family would gather around the radio to hear entertainment and news programming. Some persuasion theorists and government officials feared that, the radio had a powerful effect on people's beliefs, attitudes, and behaviors. Some people believed that if a fascist leader could control the broadcast airwaves, he or she could control the minds of the American people.

In this environment, Orson Welles' broadcast on Halloween night, 1938, was incendiary. In addition to the powerful effects of the broadcast itself the media proclaimed the powerful persuasive effects of radio for weeks following the event. On Halloween night Orson Welles announced the beginning of the play, the *War of the Worlds*. The play began with what appeared to be news bulletins interrupting current programming: The Martians are invading the earth. . . , they are invading the United States. . . , they are invading NEW JERSEY! The news bulletins included interviews with experts (albeit fictitious experts) with impressive titles: commander of the state militia at Trenton, the vice-president of the Red Cross, and even the Secretary of the Interior! Startled descriptions by witnesses were broadcast seemingly as the events unfolded: "The darn thing's unscrewing!" "This is the most terrifying thing I have ever witnessed. . . This is the most extraordinary experience. I can't find the words. . ." The Secretary of the Interior, at a loss for constructive action, recommends that we must "place our faith in God."

An estimated six million people heard the broadcast, and an estimated one million people believed, at least for a time, that the play was real:

> "I couldn't stand it, so I turned it off. I don't remember when, but everything was coming closer. My husband wanted to put it back on, but I told him we'd better do something instead of just listen, so we started to pack."

> "I was writing a history theme. The girl from upstairs came and made me go up to her place. Everybody was so excited I felt as if I was going crazy and kept on saying, 'What can we do, what difference does it make whether we die sooner or later?' We were holding each other . . . I was afraid to die, just kept on listening."[14]

Obviously, not all listeners believed that the broadcast was real. In his analysis of the broadcast, Cantril concludes that those who were most susceptible tuned in late to the broadcast, were less educated, or did not have knowledge upon which to judge the authenticity of the Martian scenario.

A fear of nationalistic propaganda, the mesmerizing effects of radio, and people's seeming inability to distinguish fantasy from reality in media broadcasts perpetuated the hypodermic needle theory of persuasion effects. The Hypodermic Needle perspective in the 1930s was a reflection of events occurring at that time. As a result, the powerful effects approach was relatively short-lived, and a limited effects perspective replaced it. Nevertheless, we occasionally see a resurgence of the hypodermic needle perspective today. Claims that sub-audial music lyrics can turn unsuspecting youth into Satan worshippers, or that violence on television causes crime, etc., are contemporary examples of a powerful effects perspective of media influence.

LIMITED EFFECTS PERSPECTIVE

The classic studies by Lazarsfeld in the 1940s cast doubt on the powerful effects of the mass media. In one of the first quantitative studies of mass media effects, Lazarsfeld analyzed the impact of the mass media on voting behavior.[15] Lazarsfeld conducted this study in Erie, Ohio, in 1940. The panel design of the study included interviews of the same subjects during the six months prior to the election. In this manner the interviewers could monitor any changes in subjects' attitudes and beliefs.

Lazarsfeld's surprising results threw a wrench in the Hypodermic Needle perspective. Lazarsfeld found that people's families, workplace, church groups, and/or civic organizations influenced their voting behavior. People were, in fact, more influenced by the voting behavior of others than they were by the political information provided in the mass media. In contrast to the Hypodermic Needle approach, the Limited Effects perspective gives more credit to the receiver and the receiver's ability to resist persuasive influence.[16]

As a result of this study, Lazarsfeld presented the **two-step flow** of media effects: the media influence opinion leaders in a community, and the opinion leaders influence other people. That is, the mass media do not directly influence all people. This particular study of voting behavior found opinion leaders to be more involved in political issues and more attuned to mass media information. Obviously, different opinion leaders may emerge for different issues.

Lazarsfeld's discovery of the importance of the receiver in the persuasion process paralleled the research of Hovland and Janis. Hired by the War Department to study the effects of propaganda on attitude change, Hovland and Janis continued this line of research throughout the 1950s. This body of research on individual differences and conditions of persuasion has become known as the Yale School of persuasion research. The research produced by the **Yale School** provided the first systematic and

FIGURE 2.1   Model of persuasion variables researched by the Yale School

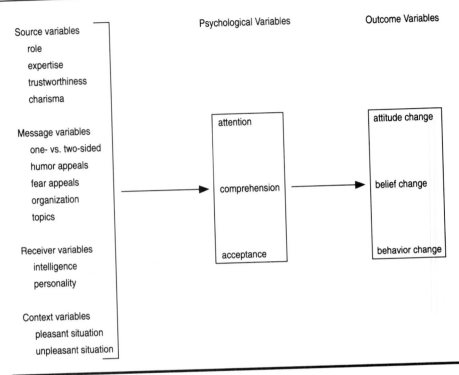

scientific study of persuasion and attitude change by experimental psychologists.[17]

An outline of the Yale School research is presented in Figure 2.1. Hovland and his colleagues systematically altered one or more variables influencing persuasion to assess the different persuasive effects rendered by different combinations of variables. Message variables included fear appeals, one- or two-sided arguments, and organization of arguments. Message source variables included the effects of credibility, self-interest, disorganization, and trustworthiness on perceptions of the source and consequent persuasive impact. Receiver variables included personality traits, involvement, and initial attitudes prior to exposure to persuasion. This approach allowed researchers to compare the impact of various message, source, and receiver variables on persuasive effects. Clearly, this perspective recognizes the complexity of the persuasion process and the numerous variables that mediate persuasion effects. Laswell's conclusion that "some messages have some effect on some people some of the

| BOX 2.2 | *Psychological Model of Communication Focusing on the Receiver* |

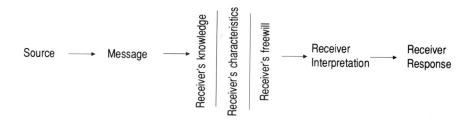

time"[18] best exemplifies this increasingly complex view of the persuasion process.

The Yale School research is revolutionary in its focus on quantitative experimental design in the study of communication, and in its focus on the individual receiver differences and their impact upon the persuasion process. Up to this time, persuasion research reflected the Aristotelean focus on source and message variables, and ignored the role of the message receiver.

A **psychological model** of communication (Box 2.2) best represents the Yale School research. The psychological model represents the increased attention to receivers' individual differences and psychological processes by the Yale School. This focus is considered an improvement over the linear mechanistic model reflecting the powerful effects perspective (Box 2.1). The receiver is a filter, and the persuasive outcome is dependent upon how this filter decodes the message and influences the meaning constructed by the receiver.

The Yale School and the limited effects perspective also have limitations. This perspective does not account for the process by which shared meaning is established between sender and receiver. Moreover, the psychological model ignores the role of the receiver in giving feedback, influencing the process of persuasion, or mutually influencing the message sender. The Yale School presents a message receiver who responds, but does not initiate influence, in the persuasive process.

INTERACTIONAL PERSPECTIVE

The Interactional Perspective is a contemporary approach to persuasion research. Although this perspective maintains a "limited-effects" view of persuasive influence, it does reflect a dramatic change from the earlier

FIGURE 2.2   Interactional model of communication.

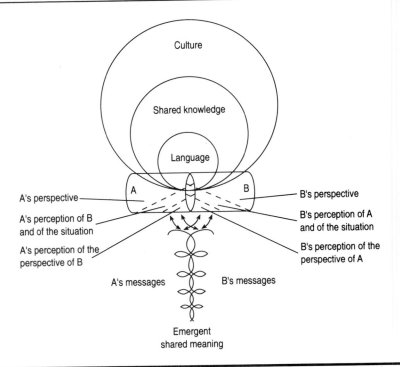

From D. L. Swanson & J. G. Delia (1972), T*he Nature of Human* Communication, p. 38. Chicago: Science Research Associates.

Yale School limited effects models. Scholars seeking to explain the interaction between communicators have promoted the interactional perspective. Rather than viewing persuasion as something one person does to another, persuasion is viewed as a process by which two or more communicators mutually influence each other and through which shared meaning evolves. Swanson and Delia's interactional model of communication is presented in Figure 2.2.

This focus broadens the study of persuasion to include interpersonal influence. Earlier limited-effects approaches to persuasion research focused on public address and the mass media and essentially ignored face-to-face persuasion in dyads or small groups.

The work of contemporary literary critic Kenneth Burke exemplifies the interactional perspective. According to Burke, persuasion is a process of **identification** or **alignment** between sender and receiver.[19] If a person causes another to identify, to some degree, with the view presented, persuasion has occurred. This identification or alignment of meaning among two or more people is the result of communication. For example, the success of Martin Luther King presumably resulted from the degree to which the people participating in the March on Washington in 1963 identified with his vision of a world in which all people could be equal and free. If people left the speech believing in a new vision of America, or believing that this vision was possible, or believing that they could help bring about this new America, identification between Martin Luther King and members of his audience occurred.

The process of identification can be explained by conceptualizing four filters through which communicators screen information: 1) **topic knowledge;** 2) **self-knowledge;** 3) **persuasion knowledge;** and 4) **cultural knowledge.** When Bob tries to persuade Sue to go out with him, Sue applies the four knowledge screens identified above. Sue activates her knowledge of dates. Her self-knowledge reminds her of the sort of people she likes to date. She also evaluates Bob's messages according to her knowledge of the "lines" males use to impress females. Sue, as an avid reader of Miss Manners, also knows the cultural expectations governing date requests. The degree to which a person is persuaded depends upon the degree to which the communicators' knowledge areas become aligned (Figure 2.3).

It is conceivable that in many persuasive situations, both interactants are simultaneously senders and receivers of persuasive messages. If you were to ask your parents for money to go to Florida for spring break, it is possible that you (the original persuader) could convince your parents to give you $800. And it is also conceivable that your parents (the original receivers) could persuade you to spend that money on a computer instead.

Mutual influence also occurs in mass mediated persuasion. In his book, *The Selling of the President,* McGinnis reports that political handlers research the idealized conception of a president and proceed to package a candidate to fulfill these expectations.[20] The audience persuades the political handlers that particular image traits are important. To the extent that we tolerate and reinforce extended attention on relatively inconsequential issues, we are responsible. As the electorate, we are both persuaders and receivers in the campaign process.

The interactional perspective on persuasion is different from the perspectives discussed earlier in its focus on the emergence of shared meaning between communicators. The interactional model portrays the dynamic, cyclical, and complex *process* of persuasion where mutual influence can occur. Whereas the classical perspective focuses on ethics and message strategies, the powerful effects perspective focuses on the message and the source, and the limited effects perspective focuses on the receiver, the interactional perspective focuses on the evolution of meaning.

Persuasion occurs when a person changes a belief, attitude or behavior in response to the direct or indirect influence of another. The most satisfactory persuasive encounters are those in which a shared meaning, which reflects the perspectives of each of the communicators, is adopted.

FIGURE 2.3

a.   Each interactant comes to a persuasive encounter with individualized knowledge and perceptions.

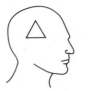

b.   Through communication knowledge is shared.

c.   Persuasion has occurred if cognitions have changed, and if cognitions are – to some degree – similar.

CULTURAL (CONTEXT-BOUND) PERSPECTIVE

Another contemporary approach to persuasion research focuses on cultural context; whereas the interactional perspective focuses on the evaluation of meaning at the individual level, the cultural perspective focuses on the situational and cultural variables that affect persuasion and meaning. Culture is a context, but we often refer to a specific persuasive situation as a context. For this reason, our discussion of this perspective will include both cultural and contextual variables. Specifically, cultural and contextual influences on the persuasion process include the socio-political philosophy of the time, the relationship of the communicators, and the situation in which the influence attempt occurs.

There are two reasons to be concerned with culture and context variables. First, to understand the meaning of a historical message, we must analyze the contextual variables influencing the audience at the time. We

Cultural knowledge is an integration of what we learn through personal experience, observation, and media exposure.

cannot impose our current perspective on the interpretation of a historical message, as the meaning would be distorted. Second, the greater the degree to which communicators perceive context variables similarly, the greater the likelihood shared meaning will evolve. For example, Martin Luther King's intentions can be interpreted only in light of the political and social climate of the Civil Rights movement in 1963. The speech has a powerful impact when we consider the intense emotional hope of the people fighting for basic civil liberties and the intense fear of the people confronting this call for social change. Moreover, the speech did not generate shared meaning for those who defined the context as a threat to the status quo, rather than as a hope for a better society.

Researchers who assume a cultural perspective believe that receivers are products of culture; cultural socialization teaches us how to think and respond. According to this perspective, the receiver of a persuasive message is likely to respond much like other individuals belonging to the same culture. Consequently, the receiver is seen as predictable and is of little interest to the culturalist. The culturalist instead focuses on the cultural climate that influences our perceptions, cognitions, and behavior.

The success of a persuasive message, according to the cultural-contextual perspective, is dependent upon its consistency with cultural beliefs and ideals. Political candidates often espouse the virtues of free speech, American ingenuity, rags-to-riches opportunism, and religious freedom. As members of American culture we have been taught that we should like these ideals and vote to preserve these ideals. As a consequence cultural beliefs can influence our interpretation and behavioral responses to a message.

According to the cultural and contextual perspective on persuasion research, the culture and the context in which a message is received influences its interpretation and effect. Cultural and contextual factors limit a message receiver's options in responding to persuasion. Consequently, we see mass trends in which many people respond similarly to a persuasive message.

SUMMARY

Our discussion of the six perspectives on persuasion reflect several historical developments. First, persuasion research is no longer limited to public speaking, as was the focus in classical studies. Second, persuasion effects are not absolutes but variables that are dependent upon a variety of factors, such as the interactional influence and development of meaning between senders and receivers. Thus, the effects of persuasion may be limited or powerful depending upon all the conditions that define the persuasive encounter. Although the six perspectives we have discussed are presented in chronological historical periods, it is important to remember that the emergence of a new perspective does not necessarily replace an old perspective. Research in persuasion today does, in fact, include studies that assume each of these perspectives.

The six perspectives presented in this chapter reflect alternative methods for studying persuasion. Each perspective is based on a set of assumptions regarding what aspect of the persuasion process is most important and what particular factor or set of factors predicts the outcome of persuasion. One could analyze or study any persuasive text, such as Martin Luther King's "I Have a Dream" speech, using any of the six perspectives. Employing the classical perspective, we might focus on the format and stylistic devices used in the speech. The use of the interactional perspective might, in contrast, focus on King's ability to establish "identification" and shared influence between speaker and audience.

It is important to keep the interactional and contextual perspectives on persuasion in mind as you read this text. As critical receivers of persuasive messages we must analyze the persuasion as a complex process involving mutual influence. Your role as a message receiver is not powerless. Similarly, an awareness of the contextual and cultural variables that might influence the interpretation of a message and its persuasive impact can help you as a receiver resist context-bound responses—that is, responses reflecting cultural and social influences rather than your thoughtful freewill.

Study Guide

classical perspective
    rhetoric
    Aristotle and ethics
    Plato and ethics
    Aristotle and three message proofs
    tropes: repetition
        antithesis
        parallel structure
    doctrine of the mean
    five canons of rhetoric
    Monroe's Motivated Sequence
    limitations of classical perspective
post-classical perspective
    persuasion and Christianity
    St. Thomas
    Machiavelli
powerful effects perspective
    three historical events
    mechanistic model
limited effects perspective
    Lazarsfeld's research
    two-step flow model of persuasive effects
    Yale School
    psychological model of persuasion
    strengths and limitations of limited-effects perspective
interactional perspective
    interpersonal influence
    interactional model
    shared meaning/mutual influence
    advantages of perspective
cultural and contextual perspective
    two reasons for studying context
    culture's influence on message reception
    creation of cultural beliefs
    role of receiver

Discussion Questions

1. In 1938, radio listeners believed that the *War of the Worlds'* broadcast was real. To what degree do you think people would be susceptible to this kind of persuasion today? To what extent do broadcast viewers or listeners believe media programs? If you believe that people are not likely to believe media broadcasts, what accounts for the change from 1938 to today?

2. Does Lazarsfeld's two-step flow of media effects reflect media influence today? Are there opinion leaders who are knowledgeable about certain topics as a result of media usage, who influence you?

3. What effects do the mass media have on you? Try to list all the ways in which mass media influence your life. Does the media have powerful, moderate, or limited effects on you?

References

1. King, Martin Luther. 1963. "I have a dream. . . ." In *Selected speeches from American history*, R. T. Oliver and E. E. White, eds. pp. 291–294. Boston, MA: Allyn and Bacon, Inc.
2. Corbett, E. P. J. 1965. Classical rhetoric for the modern student. New York: Oxford University Press.
3. Guthrie, W. K. C. 1971. *The sophists*. New York: Cambridge U. Press.
4. Plato. *Phaedrus*. Trans. L. Cooper. Ithaca, NY: Cornell University Press, 1938.
   Plato. *Gorgius*. L. Cooper, trans. Ithaca, NY: Cornell University Press, 1938.
   Brownstein, O. L. 1965. Plato's Phaedrus: Dialectic as the genuine art of speaking. *Quarterly Journal of Speech*, 51:392–398.
5. Corbett. 1965. op cit.
   Aristotle. *Rhetoric*. W. R. Roberts, trans. New York: Random House, 1954.
6. Aristotle. 1954. op cit.
   Aristotle. The basic works of Aristotle. R. McKeon, ed. NY: Random House, 1954.
7. Kennedy, G. A. 1980. *Classical rhetoric and its Christian and secular tradition from ancient to modern times*. Chapel Hill: University of North Carolina Press.
8. Aristotle. 1952. Ethics. W. D. Ross, trans. In *Great books of the western world*. R. M. Hutchins and M. J. Adler, eds. Chicago: Encyclopedia Britannica, 1952.
   Rowland, R. C., and D. F. Womack. 1985. Aristotle's view of ethical rhetoric. *Rhetoric Society Quarterly*, 15, 13–32.
9. Aristotle. Rhetoric & Poetics. W. R. Roberts, trans. New York: Random House, 1954.
10. Kennedy. 1980. op cit.
    Bitzer, L. F. 1968. The rhetorical situation. *Philosophy & Rhetoric*, 1, 1–14.
11. Monroe, A. H. 1945. *Principles and types of speech*. Glenview, IL: Scott, Foresman.
    Ehninger, D., A. H. Monroe, and B. E. Gronbeck. 1978. *Principles and types of speech communication*. Glenview, IL: Scott, Foresman.
    Kneupper, C. W. 1985. Developing rhetoric as a modern discipline: Lessons from the classical tradition. In *Oldspeak/Newspeak: Rhetorical transformations,* C. W. Kneupper, ed. pp. 108–118. Arlington, TX: Rhetoric Society of America.
12. Kennedy. 1980. op cit.
    Murphy, J. J. 1974. *Rhetoric in the Middle Ages: A history of rhetorical theory from Saint Augustine to the Renaissance*. Los Angeles: University of California Press.
13. Machiavelli, N. 1961. *The Prince*. New York: New Amsterdam Library.
14. Cantril, H. 1977. The invasion from Mars. In *The process and effects of mass communication*. W. Schramm and D. F. Roberts, eds. pp. 579–595. Urbana, IL: University of Illinois Press.
15. Lazarsfeld, P. F., B. Berelson, and H. Gaudet. 1944. *The People's Choice*. New York: Columbia University Press.

16. Smith, B. L., H. D. Lasswell, and R. D. Casey. 1946. *Propaganda, communication, and public opinion.* Princeton, NJ: Princeton University Press.

17. Hovland, C., A. Lumsdaine, and F. Sheffield. 1949. *Experiments on mass communication.* Princeton, NJ: Princeton University Press.

    Hovland, C. I., I. L. Janis, and H. H. Kelley. 1953. *Communication and persuasion.* New Haven, CT: Yale University Press.

    Delia, J. G. 1987. Communication research: A history. In *Handbook of communication science.* C. R. Berger and S. H. Chaffee, eds. pp. 20–98. Beverly Hills, CA: Sage.

18. Gordon, G. 1971. Persuasion: The theory and practice of manipulative communication. New York: Hastings House.

19. Burke, K. 1970. *A grammar of motives.* Berkeley: University of California Press.

20. McGinnis, W. J. 1968. The selling of the president. New York: Trident.

3

The Ethics of Persuasion

According to a recent report in the Utne Reader, a foreign news editor states that African famine predictions aren't real news; only when the famine translates into dead Africans is the story worthy of media coverage.[1] The article goes on to describe the famine facing Ethiopia, Somalia, Sudan, Angola and Mozambique—and the expected deaths of twenty million people. The Utne contends that Western media have not given much attention to this story. As a result, Western aid to the famine struck countries has dwindled.

We often forget the influence of communication and the fact that what we say, and even what we don't say, can affect other people. It is obvious that the influence of the mass media is far-reaching—as we have seen, the stories selected or not selected for the nightly news can affect the lives and deaths of people across the world. Bearing this in mind, we should not overlook the consequences of communication in our small sphere of influence. The evaluation of the intentions of messages, and their consequences on others, is the crux of persuasion ethics.

Ethical principles guide the evaluation of persuasion as right or wrong, fair or unfair, and moral or immoral. **Ethical principles** are standards or rules used to evaluate an action—in this case communicative behavior. Our principles are derived from moral reasoning. Three things govern the application of an ethical principle to the evaluation of a persuasive attempt: our **perspective** in viewing a situation; the **values** we believe are relevant to the situation; and our **loyalties** to the people involved in the situation.[2] As a result, people may agree on the merit of a given ethical principle, but people often differ in their perceptions of which ethical principles are applicable to a given situation. For example, you might agree that deception and lying are unethical, yet there are probably many situations in which you would tell a lie: a man with a

| BOX 3.1 | *Ten Ethical Issues for Evaluating Persuasion* |

1) **Self-interest versus mutuality**: Is it ethical for a persuader to accomplish his or her own goals with little regard for the needs of others? Does the persuader have any responsibility to others, or are others responsible for satisfying their own goals?

2) **Individual dignity and justice**: If compliance to a persuasive message causes another person embarrassment or loss of dignity, is this ethical?

3) **Accurate information**: Is it the ethical responsibility of the persuader to ensure that receivers have accurate information on all sides of an issue? Is the persuader responsible for things said, as well as things hidden or omitted? Under what conditions is deception ethical?

4) **Information evaluation**: Is it ethical to bolster the impact of a persuasive message by preventing people from communicating with each other or by hindering thoughtful analysis of the message?

5) **Consequences of the message**: Is the persuader responsible for the receivers' responses to the message? Is the persuader only responsible for the reactions the message is intended to provoke?

6) **Receiver responsibility**: Does the receiver have any ethical responsibility in a persuasive encounter? If so, what? Is the receiver responsible for being duped by a skillful persuader?

7) **Relative truth**: Is it unethical for a persuader to proclaim that his or her position reflects *truth* and that alternative positions on the issue are inherently *false*? Can we ever know the *truth*?

8) **Situational ethics**: Are ethical principles absolutes that should be adhered to in all situations? Is there an ethical standard that clearly differentiates between *right* and *wrong* and can be applied to all situations?

9) **Relative power and increased responsibility**: Should people in positions of power or influence be held more accountable for their persuasive messages?

10) **Freedom of speech**: Does freedom of speech make all persuasion ethical? Is there a difference between your *right* to say something and your ethical responsibility for the message?

gun wants to know if your roommate is home; your roommate wants to know if his non-returnable new suit looks good; or you report on a job application that you have never stolen anything, yet you habitually use office pens, paper, and envelopes for personal use. The application of a widely held ethical principle to a specific situation is clearly controversial.

In this chapter, we will take a pragmatic approach to persuasion ethics. Rather than analyzing the ethical theories of various philosophers over the centuries, we will focus our discussion on what questions you should ask in evaluating the ethics of a persuasive message. We will use ten ethical issues to guide our discussion (Box 3.1).

If a message has the power to change people's beliefs, attitudes, or behavior, this message constitutes persuasion, and its ethical burden is great. Though our society clings to the principle of *freedom of speech*, it continues to grapple with the effects of communication. Who is responsible for these effects—to what degree is the communicator responsible, and to what degree is the receiver responsible? What constitutes unethical communication? Think about the ten questions that we have raised in Box 3.1. Write down your answer to these questions before reading this chapter. As you progress through the chapter, compare the ethical standards you apply to persuasion to the principles proposed by ethical theorists. Argue with the book! Try to generate arguments that defend your perspective.

SELF-INTEREST VERSUS MUTUALITY

Gerry's parents are divorced, and he faces a difficult decision. His father wants him to go to Idaho and work in the family business for the summer. His mother assumes that he will be coming home to Illinois. His father is paying for his college education, and Gerry feels some obligation to live with his father and help him with the business. On the other hand, Gerry fears that his father's request is motivated, at least in part, by vengeance against his mother. His parents have a long history of fighting over custody, over child support, and even over Gerry's affections. When Gerry tried to explain his concerns to his father, he couldn't get a word in edgewise. Gerry's father told him: "You're expected for the summer. . ."; "You shouldn't be a 'mama's boy' and run home to your mother"; ". . . if you want to go back to the university next fall you need to work for me. . ."; and ". . . your stepmother and I will feel very hurt if you decide to stay with your mother."

Gerry's father is trying to persuade him. Is this interpersonal influence attempt unethical? What makes the father's messages fair or unfair? To answer these questions we will address the ethical criterion of self-interest.[3] Is persuasion unethical when the persuader seeks his or her own goals with little regard for the needs of others? Must persuasion reflect *mutuality*—the pursuit of mutually fulfilling goals—to be ethical?

According to the **dialogue perspective,** an ethical interpersonal conversation will have as its goal the spiritual fulfillment of each participant. Messages are chosen for their ability to help the other person realize his or her potential. Try to think of a conversation in which you felt fully understood, you communicated at an intensely personal and fulfilling level, and you felt a real connection to the other person. A conversation that enlivens you and makes you feel good about yourself and the other person probably constitutes a dialogue.

A dialogue does not involve the manipulation of another person, tactics to bolster one's own ego, or the exchange of abstract and indirect witticisms (which so frequently plague our interpersonal encounters). A dialogue is clear, direct, and honest.

Martin Buber proposes two divergent attitudes that a person may hold toward others: an "I-Thou" attitude, or an "I-It" attitude.[4] According to the dialogue perspective on interpersonal ethics, an ethical conversation is governed by an **"I-Thou" attitude.** An unethical conversation is characterized by an **"I-It" attitude** and results in a monologue. The difference between an "I-Thou" attitude and an "I-It" attitude is respect. A person with an "I-Thou" attitude respects the individuality of others, but a person with an "I-It" attitude views people as objects—entities that can serve his or her selfish needs.

A **dialogue** employing an "I-Thou" attitude is characterized by honesty and directness, rather than false presentations and pretenses. A dialogue seeks to include and confirm others; this inclusion involves taking the perspective of the other person in a disagreement and confirming the self-identity of the other person as a valuable and worthy human. The uniqueness of the other person is celebrated by an attentive focus on the other person, as opposed to being distracted, rushed, or otherwise uninvolved in the conversation. In a dialogue each person is encouraged to communicate—people are not interrupted, yelled at, judged, made fun of, or otherwise overpowered and discouraged from fully voicing their opinions. Equality and mutual respect replace power, domination, and subordination.[5]

A **monologue** is the opposite of a dialogue; it is characterized by an "I-It" attitude and is considered unethical. You can probably remember conversations you've had with bores who talk only about themselves, who turn every topic into a self-aggrandizing sermon, and who use you as an "It"—you are valuable only in your capacity to listen and to bolster their ego. In this situation, you are not an active participant in this conversation; you are the victim of a monologue. In a monologue the individual value of a person is not recognized. The communication is impersonal, self-centered, and manipulative. Ego strategies and pretenses designed to display power, importance, and status are apparent. The communication often resembles the display acts of roosters who circle each other with full plumage in an effort to establish pecking order. Monologues are often employed to influence another person—the victim, treated as an "It," is subjected to power plays, threats, empty promises, deception, and the self-assertions of the persuader.

Is persuading another person, the act of changing the person's beliefs, attitudes, or behavior, inherently unethical according to the dialogue perspective? According to this perspective, a persuasive dialogue would be ethical if it promotes shared understanding and freedom to choose one's own beliefs, attitudes, and behaviors. If a persuader assumes an "I-Thou" attitude, the persuader respects the message receiver and will seek the message receiver's input and mutual influence. Persuasive monologues, on the other hand, would be considered unethical as a result of the lack of regard for the other person. Monologues can lead to manipulation, deception, ego-displays, and impersonal persuasive strategies.

Think about the conversation between Gerry and his father. According to the dialogue perspective, how would you evaluate the ethics of this conversation? It appears that Gerry's father is looking out for his own self-interest and is not considering what is best for Gerry or Gerry's mother. Moreover, the persuasive strategies used by Gerry's father reflect an I-It perspective.

Persuasion strategies that facilitate mutual influence are clearly more ethical than those motivated by self-interest. Efforts to maintain mutuality in persuasive discourse are related to the second criteria for evaluating the ethics of persuasion: Does the persuasive strategy maintain individuals' dignity and facilitate justice for all participants?

DIGNITY AND JUSTICE

It had been a difficult year under the new department supervisor, but the research group looked forward to the upcoming Christmas party. The long standing tradition was to write an embarrassing and amusing poem about each member of the research group, and three of the managers would set the poem to music, dress up as elves at the party, and sing the humorous songs. People's strained relationship with the new supervisor made this year's party unusually tense, but the elves managed to raise everyone's spirits with their annual performance. The supervisor thought this performance was so delightful that she informed the managers that they would perform their songs at the next board meeting—to demonstrate "the team spirit and fun-loving nature of the research group." The managers were mortified—singing for the board dressed as elves was certainly inappropriate, and the use of their personalized songs to promote the supervisor's standing with the board was not their intention. Yet the managers felt pressured to comply with the supervisor in order to keep their jobs.

Was the persuasion employed by the supervisor ethical? Was the dignity of the elves violated?

Karl Wallace provides a **political perspective** for assessing individual rights in a social collective.[6] Any group, whether it be a corporation, a committee, or a government, should exercise policies that reflect: 1) the dignity of the individual; 2) fair and equal opportunity for advancement; 3) respect for the principles of freedom, justice, and responsibility; and 4) the ability of all individuals to understand, and, at some level, participate

BOX 3.2

The Political Perspective of Persuasion Ethics

Evaluate each of the following persuasion strategies according to the political perspective of preserving individual dignity and justice. Consider each of the four issues associated with the rights of the individual (e.g., dignity, opportunity, justice, and participation). Are there situations that warrant the violation of any of these four issues? If so, what conditions are necessary to warrant a violation of the political perspective?

1) *Individual Dignity*: Is individual dignity threatened when the legal system persuades people to obey drunk driving laws by printing the names of offenders in the newspaper?

2) *Equal Opportunity*: Is there a fair and equal opportunity for advancement when students are persuaded to attend a college despite high school records that suggest that it is unlikely they will succeed?

3) *Justice and Free Choice*: Are freedom, justice, and responsibility jeopardized when special interest groups attempt to persuade a politician who is under re-election pressure?

4) *Participation*: Is participatory decision making violated when a parent uses the threat of "grounding" to persuade a teen?

in the policy making process. To persuade people to behave in a manner that threatens individual dignity is unethical. Moreover, to restrict people's free will in selecting their actions is unethical.

According to these criteria, the actions of the supervisor in the preceding example are clearly wrong. The individual dignity of the managers was threatened, the managers felt that their career advancement was dependent upon their agreement to sing for the board, the managers felt coerced, and they had no input in the supervisor's decision.

Try to evaluate the ethics of each of the examples in Box 3.2, according to the political perspective. According to the criterion of individual dignity and justice, persuaders should seek input from all participants, recognize others' free will to make their own decisions, present fair and equal opportunities, and promote actions that maintain personal dignity.

One potential threat to personal dignity in a persuasive encounter occurs when the persuader does not provide complete and accurate information. The receiver may be played for a fool—and there is little dignity or justice in being deceived. This leads us to the discussion of a third criterion for evaluating the ethics of a persuasive message: access to complete and truthful information.

ACCESS TO ACCURATE INFORMATION

Oliver Stone produced a movie, *JFK*, presenting a conspiracy theory of the assassination of President John F. Kennedy. According to the movie, JFK was killed not by lone assassin Harvey Oswald, but by several gunmen representing a top-level conspiracy of CIA agents, the Mafia, and Cuban nationalists. Although the movie was based on assorted facts uncovered by various writers who have researched the Kennedy assassination, Oliver Stone was criticized for presenting a false representation of American history. Government officials and journalists censured Stone for rewriting history. They argued that the movie was deceptive. Stone argued that the movie was an account of the assassination based on facts that were elaborated with fiction.

The movie *JFK* was persuasive in challenging many viewers' beliefs and attitudes regarding government involvement in the Kennedy assassination. Did Stone use literary license to lead viewers to believe theories of the assassination that have questionable support? Probably. Does the mixing of fact and fiction with the purpose of persuading constitute deception? Probably. Is this use of deception unethical if Stone's purpose is to challenge Americans to question the Oswald theory? Is this deception unethical if Stone's purpose is merely to entertain Americans with a good mystery?

The controversy surrounding this movie leads us to question: Is deception always unethical? It is likely that you agree that Stone's movie employs the integration of fact and fiction to persuade viewers to question the government's role in the JFK assassination. But you may conclude that the juxtaposition of fact and speculation is warranted in a motion picture.

Some scholars contend that lying and deception are always wrong.[7] They argue that deception involves disrespect for the receiver and restricts the receiver's free choice.

Deception, according to some ethical scholars, also includes withholding information and the omission of relevant facts.[8] Is a politician unethical if he or she does not disclose intentions to raise taxes? What about you? Are you being unethical if you do not disclose, to your significant other, information about past relationships?

Think about situations in which you have used deception to persuade. Have you ever enhanced a friend's self-esteem by lying about the taste of a new outfit, or even about the friend's ability to succeed (aceing a class, getting a date, or winning an athletic competition)? Is this type of deceptive persuasion ethical? If the Nazis had come to your door during WWII and asked if you were harboring Jews in your attic, would this situation warrant the use of persuasion to deceive?

Is it possible that deception is ethical under certain circumstances? Let's consider an example. News reporters use deception to persuade. Yet these reporters often claim that deception is used to obtain information for the good of the public. Is this use of deception justified?

Threats to truthful news reporting include deceptive newsgathering techniques, photo and videotape retouching, and requests by the police or military to release untruthful stories for the public good. Simply telling the truth is not as easy as it first appears!

Newspaper reporters frequently go undercover to persuade sources to divulge information. The sources for this story obviously do not know that they are speaking to a reporter. Moreover, reporters frequently entrap unsuspecting people by setting up a situation in which the person is likely to act illegally. For example, the television news program 20/20 recently sent an undercover black reporter to try to rent an apartment. The landlords were videotaped telling the black reporter that the apartment was already rented and videotaped telling a white reporter that the apartment was available. Another recent case involved reporters infiltrating abortion clinics that were run by anti-abortion activists. The reporters, ostensibly seeking abortion counseling, were barraged with anti-abortion films and lectures. Should reporters lie to sources to uncover a story? Should reporters be able to report statements made by people who did not know that they were talking to a reporter?

New technology has also made it easier to alter photos and videotapes. Reporters may receive photos or videotapes that do not represent the truth. Moreover, a reporter could conceivably alter a photo or video to bias a story. In their book, *Media Ethics,* Clifford Christians, et al. report the case of a newspaper photo of a Pulitzer Prize winner in which a Coke can sitting on a table in the foreground of the photo was electronically removed.[9] Though this editing had no significant impact on the public's perception of the story, it had a tremendous impact on the news industry. Is it ethical for news reporters to alter reality?

A final ethical consideration for news reporters is compliance with officials who wish to alter a news story for persuasive purposes. In crime and hostage situations in which it is suspected that the criminals are attuned to news reports, journalists have been asked to alter their story to help police apprehend the criminals. This may take the form of withholding the report of evidence in police possession, releasing that the police have evidence that they don't have, or releasing that the police are willing to make a deal with the criminal. In any of these occurrences, the full and true disclosure of information is forsaken.

Christians, et al. also report a hostage case in which negotiators were trying to bargain with the kidnapper with promises of immunity.[10] Reporters learned from the Justice Department that immunity could not be granted. Should the reporters truthfully report this information and risk that the kidnapper, hearing this, would kill the hostage?

In the Gulf War coverage, news reporters were given false information in a press conference. The military wanted the news reporters to release false locations of ground troops in an effort to deceive the Iraqian military. The press unwittingly released this information, only to find out later that they had been duped, and that they had in turn, duped the world. Should the press trust military sources when they have been lied to in the past? Is the military justified in lying to the press? How can the press maintain their role as watchdog of the government if the government can justify lying to the press, and we the public cannot tell when the press is reporting accurate or erroneous information?

Clearly, the obvious principle that deceptive persuasion is unethical is too simplistic. A **humanist perspective** is more realistic. According to this perspective, the use of deception should be weighed by: 1) respect for all individuals affected by the message;[11] 2) the greatest benefit for the greatest number of people;[12] 3) loving kindness for others;[13] and 4) avoidance of harm.[14] The decision to deceive should be evaluated according to these four criteria. Persuaders must compare the consequences of full and honest disclosure of information with the consequences of deception. The decision to use deception should, according to these criteria, be based on the humanitarian protection of others, not on the self-interests of the persuader.

One of the risks of deceptive communication is the inability to process information that may be pertinent to the formation of attitudes, beliefs, or behaviors. The use of active, purposeful deception, as well as the passive deception of withholding information, not only violates access to truthful information, but also restricts the evaluation of information.

OPPORTUNITY TO EVALUATE INFORMATION

The Challenger space shuttle exploded January 28, 1986, just 73 seconds after take-off. The government commission established to determine the cause of the accident found that the O-ring responsible for the explosion had been labeled as a potential cause of "loss of life or vehicle" since December of 1982. Erosion of the O-ring in a July 1985 shuttle flight revealed malfunctioning of the joint, yet the launch constraint (established by the problematic O-ring) was waived for the next seven shuttle flights. Moreover, the manufacturer of the solid rocket booster, Morton Thiokol, recommended against launch on January 27. The management of Morton Thiokol later reversed this decision, against the recommendation of its own engineers, as a result of NASA's pressure to launch. The commission concluded that the Challenger disaster was as much a result of faulty decision-making as faulty equipment. NASA officials and Morton Thiokol engineers used persuasion to reach a consensus on the launch decision, and these persuasive messages prevented the decision-makers from accurately evaluating the available information.

The **information perspective** on persuasion ethics addresses the conditions necessary for appropriate evaluation of information. Persuasive strategies may be considered unethical if the exchange of information is intentionally encumbered. To be ethical, persuasive messages must promote: 1) information quality; 2) cognitive deliberation; 3) self- and other-awareness; and 4) social contact.

Information Quality

To facilitate communication processes, the best possible information must be made available to all participants. Ethical communication necessitates the disclosure of relevant information, the knowledge of alternatives, and the comprehension of consequences.[15] The communicators must feel free to present all relevant facts, and they must strive to separate facts from opinions. Most importantly, the participants must feel free to question all information and to elaborate and explore their doubts fully without being railroaded into a premature decision.

In their analysis of the decision making process leading to the launch of the Challenger, Gouran, Hirokawa, and Martz report several communication processes that jeopardized information quality. The authors note that the engineers' recommendations were constrained by: 1) role and power boundaries; 2) the use of language that minimized perceptions of risk; and 3) the failure of management to ask important questions and seek information relevant to the decision.[16]

Cognitive Deliberation

The persuasion process should encourage deliberate reasoning. Any message that focuses on images, emotions, needs, desires, or values, and thereby distracts the receiver from critically evaluating the argument, is considered unethical.[17] According to some scholars, it would be unethical for a charismatic leader to sway a group decision on the basis of his personality rather than on the basis of solid evidence. Moreover, it would be considered unethical for a person to sway others on the basis of an emotional or personal experience that is tangential to the issue: "I've just learned that my family has been in an accident . . . I hope you will decide to sign this contract today; I just can't handle any more stress. . . ."[18] (This message may seem absurd, but it is no more absurd than a presidential candidate trying to persuade voters by touting a war record or injury and ignoring his or her political record.)

Related to the criterion of cognitive deliberation is tolerance for dissent.[19] Persuaders must welcome constructive criticism and differences of opinion. If dissent is squashed in the communication process, full information exchange and cognitive deliberation cannot occur. In the case of the Challenger decision, Gouran et al. found a "perceived pressure to produce a desired recommendation and concurrence with it among those initially opposed to the launch."[20] This intolerance for dissent persuaded managers to endorse a faulty decision.

Self- and Other-Awareness

Self- and other-awareness also promotes the evaluation of information.[21] This means that each participant in the persuasion encounter is reflective and considers personal biases and prejudices that might influence his or her decision. Likewise, each person explores the motivations, goals, and values of others and is aware of how these individual biases might jeopardize the free and full exchange of information.

Self- and other-awareness were clearly missing in the communication of NASA officials in deciding whether to launch the Challenger space shuttle. Officials provided biased information and made biased decisions because they wanted to persuade superiors of the quality of their work and the quality of their previous decisions. At the time, no one questioned how his or her own motivations or the motivations of others might be biasing information exchange.[22]

Social Contact

The evaluation of information is also dependent upon people's freedom to discuss the ideas with others. Persuasion is ethical to the extent to which it facilitates the formation of groups and social contact. According to rhetorical scholar Karlyn Campbell, the purpose of language and communication is to promote the formation of social groups and to reduce individual isolation.[23] Ethical messages must lead people to self-realization about the choices available to them. Communication that prevents social contact prevents self-realization, group coordination, and educated choices. If the supervisors within the NASA or Morton Thiokol organizations restricted the engineers' access to decision-makers within these organizations, they jeopardized social contact and the free exchange of information.

There are many examples of persuasive attempts to restrict social contact. The history of authoritarian governments testifies to the effectiveness of restricting social contact to prevent the spread of information. Many coercive techniques, such as restricting protests, censoring publications, isolating dissenters, and controlling the release of information, are designed to prevent thoughtful evaluation and potential dissent. Likewise, you probably know of gag-orders issued by organizations to restrict members from talking with the press, or company policies that restrict the organization of workers, or efforts by parents to restrict the contact of their children with particular significant others or social groups. These are all examples of the restriction of social contact as a persuasion strategy to limit the free flow of ideas and information.

In sum, ethical persuasion facilitates the evaluation of information through the promotion of information quality, thoughtful deliberation, analysis of biases, and the sharing of ideas. Accordingly, it would be unethical to employ persuasive strategies that in any way restrict the evaluation of information. This leads us to our next ethical question: If a persuader upholds all of the criteria for information evaluation, is he or she still responsible if a receiver, incited by the persuader's message, engages in unethical behavior?

RESPONSIBILITY FOR CONSEQUENCES

Harriet Beecher Stowe's book *Uncle Tom's Cabin* helped promote the Civil War, and *Das Kapital* inspired leaders of the Russian Revolution. Why then, do we find it surprising that the graphic representation of criminal acts can persuade a person to imitate the modeled behavior?

Mark Chapman, the man who shot and killed John Lennon, was obsessed with the death themes illustrated in *The Catcher and the Rye.* John Hinckley, who shot President Reagan, was living the part of the main character in *Taxi Driver,* who wanted to kill a political candidate. Hinckley dressed in an Army fatigue jacket, drank peach brandy, took pills, and bought three guns—just as the character in the movie did. A man obsessed with the video *Faces of Death* shot and dismembered a young man who came to his door soliciting funds for an environmental group.

The effects of persuasive messages on particular members of society lead us to question: To what extent is a persuader ethically responsible for the consequences of a message? Is a persuader responsible for unintended outcomes—such as the use of a movie, book, picture, or song as the basis for a robbery, rape, or murder?

You may be arguing that *Uncle Tom's Cabin* and *Das Kapital* were intended to incite anger and response to social injustices. Thus, their authors intended to generate the responses to these books. You may further argue that the intention of violent movies and books is to entertain. Therefore, the creators of violent films and books are not responsible for the impact of their messages on criminal minds. Are persuaders, therefore, only responsible for intended reactions to a persuasive message?

Should persuaders be ethically responsible for unintended responses to their messages if there is probable cause that the message could produce a harmful response? Let's consider the song *Suicide Solution,* recorded by Ozzy Osbourne. A suicide victim was found shot to death with earphones on his head and a recording repeatedly playing *Suicide Solution.* The lyrics of the song suggest that "suicide is the only way out," and even advise the listener to "try it." The song ends with the repetition of "Shoot, shoot, shoot. . . ."[24]

Did Ozzy Osbourne clearly promote the act of suicide in this song? Yes. Did he intend to promote the act of suicide? Yes. Did he intend for a person to listen to this song and commit the act of suicide? Who knows?

Is Ozzy Osbourne responsible for intentionally promoting suicide? Does this song constitute unethical persuasion?

If we were to apply the humanist ethic to answer these questions, most movies, books, and pictures promoting violence would be considered unethical. Ethical scholar Henry W. Johnstone, Jr. eloquently describes the responsibilities of the persuader:

> . . . a humanist ethic requires that the **individual be responsive in his or her actions to the impact they might have on the humanity of those affected by the act.** It demands, finally, that one conduct oneself so as to maximize opportunities for cultivating in oneself and in others an awareness and appreciation of humanness. . . [The humanist ethic affirms] those human features that are most to be valued: our resourcefulness, our capacity for loving, our receptiveness to and inclination toward beauty, our emotional resilience and range of sensitivities, our capacities for foresight and self-control, our imagination, our curiosity, our capacity for wonder, our powers of passionate attachment, to name a few.[25]

Clearly, any message promoting murder, physical abuse, verbal abuse, sexual abuse, war, or suicide does not promote an "appreciation of humanness." According to the humanist ethic, persuasive messages could *report* conditions that violate the "appreciation for humanness," but should stop short of *promoting* and condoning beliefs, attitudes, or behaviors that violate valued human capacities for love and reason.

We have discussed whether a persuader is responsible for intended consequences of a message, and whether the persuader may even be responsible for unintended but foreseen consequences of a message. Yet is it fair to place the entire ethical burden of the persuasion process on the persuader? Do receivers of persuasive messages share the ethical responsibility for persuasive outcomes?

The responsibility of the receiver is illustrated by the song "We Didn't Know," recorded by the Chad Mitchell Trio in the 1960s. The lyrics suggest that individuals' fear and consequent inaction allowed the Holocaust, the Vietnam War, and civil rights violations to continue. The refrain articulates how we justify our inaction in times of social crisis by claiming "we didn't know" and "we didn't see a thing." According to the song, we deny our responsibility to help others by distancing ourselves from those who are suffering. We allow victims of social injustice to endure their hardships for fear of putting ourselves at risk. Moreover, we claim that we are ignorant and naive receivers of persuasion, and that we are not responsible for challenging unethical or harmful persuasive messages, claiming "you can't hold us to blame, what could we do?"

Many ethical scholars argue that the receiver *is* an active participant in the persuasion process and shares ethical responsibility for any consequences.[26] Specifically, Christopher Johnstone argues that resoluteness and openness must guide receivers.[27]

Resoluteness means that the receiver must not automatically "give in" to persuasion. The receiver should respond to persuasion by articulating clear arguments in support of his or her own position. The dedication to resoluteness suggests that the receiver does not remain a receiver, but becomes an active persuader.

Openness refers to the capacity of the receiver to be attentive to the communicator's arguments and to evaluate the merit of the arguments. Keller and Brown further Johnstone's position by stating that an ethical response should avoid the use of hostility, putting down the other person, or withdrawing from the debate.[28]

The 1960s folk song demonstrates the importance of receiver responsibility in the persuasion process. Just as the persuader has ethical obligations, so does the receiver. History attests to the social consequences of apathetic receivers.

It is more likely that truth and justice will prevail when everyone assumes responsibility for persuasive outcomes. Even so, the truth is evasive. In the next section we will question communicators' ability to find truth in persuasive discourse.

THE ETHICAL IMPLICATIONS OF RELATIVE TRUTH

> No human being is constituted to know the truth, the whole truth, and nothing but the truth; and even the best of [people] must be content with fragments, with partial glimpses, never with the full fruition.
>
> William Osler. The Student Life.[29]

An **existentialist perspective** on persuasion ethics suggests that we create our experiences (i.e., we define our existence) by thinking about our environment, placing values on our experiences, and communicating to others. According to this perspective, we create and construct our views of reality and knowledge. It follows that if human processes create reality, experience, and knowledge, there can be no absolute truth. When we profess some fact as true, we are simply arguing that, based on our faulty and limited human mental calculations, this truth is the best representation of knowledge as we know it at this particular point in time.

Existential theory leads us to conclude, according to rhetorical scholar Karlyn Campbell, that ethical persuasion embraces **revisionist thinking**.[30] According to this perspective, we can't be certain of anything. We must view all decisions as tentative and evaluate them for their merit at a particular point in time. Accordingly, persuaders should acknowledge that the truth remains unknown and unknowable. Therefore, any course of action must be flexible to revision as the truth-as-we-know-it changes. Revisionist thinking allows for greater flexibility in conflict resolution, bargaining, and decision making.

A persuader who proposes an absolute truth is clearly misleading the audience and is not encouraging debate on the issue. An ethical persuader will, therefore, acknowledge the relative nature of truth, and present his or her position as superior to alternatives, based on our best, but limited, understanding.

If we accept a revisionist perspective of truth, many argue that we should accept a revisionist perspective of ethics, also. Just as there is no absolute truth, there is no absolute ethical principle. Scholars who adopt this perspective believe that the situation determines ethics, and that one can revise ethical principles according to situational demands.

SITUATIONAL ETHICS

The Fourth of July is celebrated in a small community in eastern Iowa with an annual parade. The community's close proximity to the state university has led to some unique entries in the hometown parade. Many social activists use the parade to make political statements. In the 1980s a group of women protesting pornography entered the parade. The women marched in the parade—bare breasted—to demonstrate the shaming of the female body.

Although some people argue that marching bare-breasted in a parade was a legitimate and ethical persuasion strategy to protest the exploitation of the female body, fewer people, I would imagine, would condone males marching without pants to promote pornography. How can the same type of persuasive strategy be more acceptable in one situation than another? The female marchers would argue that they represent a disenfranchised group that the social power structure exploits. They would argue, therefore, that pushing the boundaries of public decency to get their message heard is appropriate. The same female marchers would likely argue that males marching without pants would be unethical because males do not represent a socially disenfranchised group, and that the males are promoting a cause (pornography) that exploits women and violates the humanist ethical perspective.

Social critic Saul Alinsky argues that social movements that have little legitimate power in society deserve ethical leniency in the strategies they use. The ethical principle often used to support the rhetoric of social movements is the **situational perspective.** The basic tenet of situational ethics is that there are no absolutes—the ethics of a message must be judged in light of the unique roles of the sender and receiver and the constraints of the situation.[31] According to the situational perspective, persuasive messages and strategies are neither

"Really babe, one's actions depend on the situation. True love is free of obligations, promises and commitments...you just gotta go with your feelings at the time!"

Deneen Kay Winchester

Deneen Kay Winchester.

ethical or unethical. Rather, the ethics reside in the effects of the message. Therefore, no ethical principle can be applied across different situations and outcomes.[32]

Alinsky argues that everyone views the ethics of a situation differently, depending on his or her role within the social power structure. In his *Rules of Radicals*, Alinsky cynically describes how social power influences how we evaluate the actions of social activists (Box 3.3).[33] Alinsky's argument is that if the goal (to correct social evils) is moral, and the social power structure oppresses the activists, the activists may be justified in the use of unethical strategies. Alinsky argues that social activists can be held accountable only for using the most ethical means available to them at the time.[34] Ethics are situational.

Other scholars vehemently disagree with situational ethics. They argue that any action can be rationalized by some situational constraint, and if any action can be justified according to situational ethics, then the whole concept of ethics becomes meaningless.[35] Consider your own code of ethics. Does it change according to the situation? Is deception ethical in some situations? Are threats, violence, and control ethical if there are no other means available and the cause is just?

Inherent in Alinsky's arguments for situational ethics is the assumption that people in positions of power have greater ethical responsibility. In the next section we will question whether we hold the mass media, for instance, more responsible for the ethical use of persuasion strategies than less powerful social groups or individuals.

BOX 3.3   *Situational Ethics: Alinsky's ''Rules for Radicals''*

1) ***Personal interest skews our ethical evaluations of the tactics of social organizations; morality is the privilege of those who have no personal interest in the issue.*** Thus, it is easy for people secure in the suburbs to condemn the riots of inner-city protesters. "Conscience is the virtue of observers and not of agents of action," according to the philosopher Goethe.

2) ***Less important issues provide greater opportunity for the selection of ethical tactics.*** The messages and actions of social activists become increasingly alarmist and one-sided, and even violent, at times when the urgency of the issue increases—such as the debate of the issue in Congress or the Supreme Court.

3) ***Ethical evaluations are biased by the social power of those judging the situation.*** People who have social power are likely to judge the actions of the powerless (the homeless, the poor, homosexuals, and minorities) more harshly than they would judge the same actions by members of their own social group. This is why socially disenfranchised groups in our society get much longer prison sentences than do white middle-class males. We fear people who are different from ourselves. We also fear people who challenge the power structure. A Greenpeace activist detained in Texas was held for $100,000 bail, while drug dealers and murderers in the same jurisdiction have been released on $10,000 bail.[36]

4) ***In social activism, as in war, the ends justify the means.*** Organizations fighting social evils and challenging the existing power structure have few resources and are often threatened by the police, military, FBI, or CIA. Chip Berlet in his article in the *Humanist* quotes the Senate Select Committee report on Intelligence Activities, which condemns the techniques the CIA and FBI "used in a sophisticated vigilante operation aimed at preventing the exercise of First Amendment rights of speech by civil rights, feminist, gay, health clinic, and food co-op organizations.[37] These groups were subjected to false arrests, surveillance, and intimidation; agents attempted to infiltrate and disrupt the organizations and sent threatening phone calls and letters.

5) ***The ethics of an act should be judged according to the situation at the time of action, rather than with the benefit of retrospection.*** The content of a message is constrained by the information available at the time the message is constructed. Knowledge of the consequences of a message may not be accurately predicted. Moreover, since ethical values change over time and across cultures, persuasion strategies should be evaluated according to the accepted standards of the time and place in which they are used.[38]

6) ***Questions of morality increase as the number of available options increases.*** If a group has a number of choices in the message appeals or information it presents, these choices represent moral dilemmas. If there is little choice, the moral responsibility of the speaker decreases.

7) ***The success or failure of the movement influences perceptions of morality.*** If an action is successful, it is more likely to be justified. Moreover, particular actions may be considered immoral when victory is assured, but may be considered justified if the actors are threatened with defeat. In most circumstances, Americans would condemn the actions of firing on retreating soldiers or bombing civilian areas. In the Gulf War, however, at a time when the public believed that the U.S. would sustain high casualties, the public considered any military tactic justified.

8) ***Appeals to emotions and values (liberty, God, freedom, duty, patriotism, etc.) are legitimate.*** Appeals to inspire people to action typically preclude reason. Throughout history we have inspired people to go to war with appeals to abstract values and emotional surges, rather than with calls for reason, evidence, and logic.

RELATIVE POWER AND INCREASED RESPONSIBILITY

Patricia Bowen claims that William Kennedy Smith raped her at the Palm Springs Kennedy estate. Kennedy Smith claims that the two engaged in consensual sex after meeting in a bar. Although Kennedy Smith was acquitted, the proceedings of the Kennedy Smith rape trial were presented on network television with a great deal of media hype. This case raises many questions about persuasion ethics. Did the television coverage influence the truth of the testimony? Was the controversial decision to air the trial made on the basis of social responsibility or advertising revenue? Did the coverage violate the privacy rights of the rape victim and/or of Kennedy Smith? Did the airing of the trial promote social justice? Will the televised trial discourage other women from pressing rape charges?

In our society, the mass media have tremendous persuasive power. Media messages reach millions of people, and people tend to believe what the media report. Should, therefore, the mass media be subjected to more strict ethical standards in relationship to the relative power the media has over the individual receiver? Moreover, should persuaders in general be held accountable for their messages according to the amount of power they have over the receiver?

There are many situations in which the persuader has more power than the receiver: 1) an employer persuading subordinates; 2) a professor persuading a student; 3) big business persuading politicians; 4) advertisers persuading consumers, especially children; and 5) news reporters persuading the public. Should relative power dictate ethical responsibility? To address this question, let's explore the ethical practices of the mass media.

The mass media have widespread persuasive influence in our society, and as a result carry a heavy ethical burden.[39] News reporters, advertisers, public relations practitioners, and network entertainment programmers all have professional codes of ethics. These written rules are typically vague—and they typically consider the ethics of the message content, devoid of the complexities of real people in real situations. For this reason, we will avoid professional codes, and our discussion will focus on real-life media situations. Our discussion of relative power and ethical responsibility will focus on: 1) the responsibility of the media to promote social justice; and 2) the ethical responsibility of advertisers.

Should the Mass Media Be Responsible for Social Justice?

What is the media's persuasive responsibility to change social wrongs, to represent disenfranchised groups, and to persuade the public to address social problems? The media's role as the public's watchdog to investigate wrongdoings is a difficult one. Social justice obligations are often at odds

Providing accurate information about the transmission of AIDS has been a controversial issue. In this ad, the Madison Advertising Federation demonstrates socially responsible advertising by confronting issues of sex and AIDS. Many publications are hesitant to run these ads, however, because they are afraid of public protest.

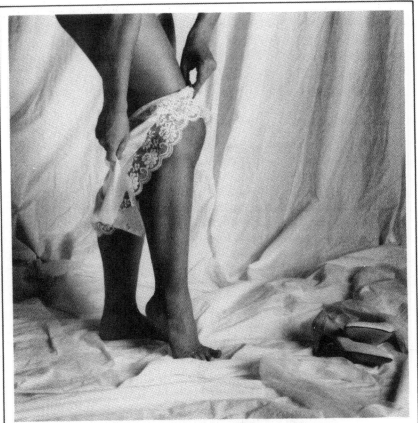

DO YOU KNOW WHO ELSE
HE'S CHARMED THE PANTS OFF OF?

You may be having sex with someone who had sex with someone who has AIDS.
To lay to rest your fear of AIDS, don't get laid by a lie. Know your partner. Demand the truth.
To know more about AIDS, call the Madison AIDS Support Network at 255-1711.

AIDS. It stops with you.

AIDS

Madison
Advertising
Federation

with big business interests and what the public wants to see. The story on the Africa famine at the beginning of this chapter is a case in point. Do the mass media have a moral obligation to seek social justice and to report stories that may not appeal to the "compassion-fatigued" public?[40]

In an article in the *Columbia Journalism Review*, Michael Moss reports that though 12.8 percent of Americans (as of 1987) are living below the poverty level, only one percent of media stories address this issue. Moreover, the stories that are run tend to play on simplistic emotional reactions to poverty, rather than to investigate the social welfare system and other causes of poverty.[41]

Is the media's role to cover the stories we want to hear, or is the media's role to seek social justice? If the media's role is to seek social justice, is it possible to maintain an unbiased perspective? Is the simplification of complex issues unethical? As the primary forum for social debate in our society, what persuasive responsibility do the mass media have to promote important social issues?

Mass media advertising plays an even more obvious persuasive role in our society. What ethical responsibilities do advertisers have to provide complete and accurate information, to avoid deceptive strategies, and to resist the temptation to persuade children who have not yet developed counter-arguing abilities?

Does the Power of Advertising Necessitate Strict Ethical Standards?

Advertising ethics are regulated by the Federal Trade Commission, advertising agencies, the advertisers, and the media. The Federal Trade Commission can require advertisers to remove "significantly" deceptive advertising, unsubstantiated comparison advertising, and unsubstantiated health claims from the media. Although we encounter hundreds of advertisements each day, the FTC rules on only a few cases a year. Advertising agencies operate under two ethical principles: autilitarian "if it works, it's good" policy, accompanies by an organizationally defined sense of moral rectitude. The client's ethics are often determined by legal liability and company image concerns—no client wants bad publicity. Whereas the FTC is most concerned with deception, the media in which the advertisements are placed are most concerned with taste. Media censors frequently refuse to run advertisements that might incite audience boycotts. Proponents of advertising argue that advertising provides a service, and that people enjoy advertising. They also argue for the libertarian marketplace of ideas which suggests that the marketplace will determine the merit of advertising claims; advertising is the quickest way to kill a bad product, and bad advertising can kill even a good product.

| BOX 3.4 | *Ethical Criticisms of Advertising* |

1) **Advertising creates needs.** Advertising persuades us to desire things we don't really need.

2) **Advertising communicates messages that influence our perceptions and behaviors.** A recent study concluded that the images presented in motorcycle advertisements—"references to power, to overtaking other motorists, to euphoria, to quest and seduction, and escape/dreams"—may promote reckless motorcycling.[42] Representatives of the Center for the Study of Commercialism in Washington, D.C., suggest that advertising influences our psychological well-being, communal values, equalitarian values, discourse, and democracy.[43] They argue that advertising promotes envy, anxiety, and insecurity; consumer values have surpassed civic values; advertising has invaded our civic organizations (schools, churches, and museums); advertising increases class differentiation; advertising promotes mindless processing of information; and that the advertising format of quick easy slogans has replaced political discourse.

3) **Advertising has become entertainment.** Advertising has been incorporated into children's cartoons—the characters and their props are now merchandise, and the cartoon story is essentially an advertisement to buy the products. Cable channels carry hour-long buying programs complete with real-life product testimonials. MTV is a continuous advertisement for recordings and celebrity concerts. The tee-shirts and hats you wear often constitute brand advertising.

4) **Advertising dictates media content.** Advertisers pull their advertising from programs or publications addressing controversial topics. This leads to very bland programming. The Lou Grant television show depicting Ed Asner as a newspaper editor had high viewership ratings, but lost advertising support as a result of controversial subject matter. This is one of the reasons the show was canceled. More recently, advertisers threatened to withdraw advertising from the television programs "Married with Children" and "thirtysomething" in response to controversial subject matter.

5) **Advertising doesn't demonstrate social responsibility.** This criticism of advertising stems from advertising's portrayal of gender roles, ethnic stereotypes, social and family relationships, and values. Many argue that the role of the mass media is to seek social justice and lead social reform. Many have also applied this role to advertising, arguing that advertising should not reflect reality, but provide models of women, minorities, and relationships to promote social change. Advocates of a social change role for advertising argue that advertising has a strong influence on people's perceptions and, consequently, perpetuates negative social stereotypes.

There are, however, many ethical criticisms of advertising. These criticisms suggest that advertising does have persuasive power to: create needs, influence behavior, persuade us under the guise of entertainment, dictate programming, and create and perpetuate social misconceptions (Box 3.4). Should advertisers, in light of their relative power over consumers, be held to more stringent ethical guidelines than other persuaders?

An ethical principle placing greater responsibility for deception and negative outcomes on people and organizations holding social power has some appeal. In addition to mass media persuasion, the principle of relative power and greater responsibility also applies to interpersonal, small group, and organizational persuasion; just as the powerful have more opportunity to persuade, they also have more opportunity to abuse their persuasive power.

It is important to remember, however, that ethical guidelines, not laws, govern the media and other power-centered people and organizations. It is therefore up to the receivers to hold people in power accountable to ethical principles. In America, freedom of speech prevents the censorship of persuasive messages, making ethical considerations in the production of persuasive messages voluntary.

THE ETHICS OF FREE SPEECH

Within the past five years, several universities have attempted to implement policies making "hate speech"—the use of speech or symbols that insult or threaten others, and that reflect discrimination on the basis of race, gender, sexual orientation, or age—punishable by expulsion. Several state supreme courts have since ruled that such a policy is an infringement of freedom of speech.

This example illustrates how judgments of a persuader's rights to produce a message are separate from judgments of the ethical responsibility of the persuader. For example, the Constitution may protect hate speech, but it may nevertheless be deemed unethical according to the principles we have discussed in this chapter.

SUMMARY: DESCRIBING THE ETHICAL PERSUASION ENCOUNTER

We have explored ten ethical criteria for evaluating persuasive messages. You might argue that these guidelines raise more questions than they answer, but the purpose of this chapter is to challenge you to evaluate critically the ethics of persuasion and develop your own position on these issues. To guide you in this process, various perspectives proposed by ethics scholars have been described: the dialogue, political, humanitarian, information, humanist, existentialist, and situational perspectives. From the discussion of these perspectives, several themes emerge that provide a picture of what might constitute an ethical persuasive interaction (Box 3.5).

Think about your own persuasive strategies. Consider how likely it is that you adhere to each of these ethical principles. Have you used ambiguous messages to hide your persuasive purpose? Have you lied or deceived a friend, lover, or relative to accomplish a persuasive

BOX 3.5   *Characteristics of Ethical Persuasion*

1) Persuaders are *clear, direct, and honest* about their intentions.

2) Communicators promote *mutual respect* and mutual satisfaction of goals, rather than self-interests.

3) Communicators use strategies that *confirm others* and preserve the dignity of others.

4) Communicators seek *input and elaboration* from each other.

5) Persuaders *avoid the use of active deception* and the withholding of relevant information, except when the truth may cause significant harm to others.

6) Communicators listen and *critically process* each others' messages.

7) Communicators welcome and explore *dissent.*

8) Communicators *analyze their own and others' biases* without defending or threatening their own or others' egos.

9) All participants in the persuasion process *share the ethical responsibility* of persuasive outcomes and respond to each other with resoluteness and openness.

10) *Communicators weigh opinions equally,* rather than on the basis of individual power or status.

11) Communicators *assess probable consequences* of their messages on others.

12) Communicators employ persuasion to *celebrate the human qualities* of diversity, personality, intelligence, passion for beliefs, humor, and reasoning.

13) Communicators encourage *social discussion and social contact.*

14) Communicators critically challenge claims of certainty and *truth.*

15) Decisions are subject to *revision* over time.

16) The *relative power* of the persuader and the receiver determines the degree of ethical responsibility.

17) Communicators maintain *free speech,* but the probability of harmful consequences guides the ethical decision to produce a persuasive message.

goal? Have you made a person feel bad (e.g., sad, hurt, or guilty) to get your way? Have you resorted to physical force when words weren't effective? Finally, how often do you try to impose your will on others with little concern for mutual accomplishment of goals? Have you withheld information, or manipulated information, to assure your persuasive success?

CONCLUSION: PERSUASION ETHICS IN THE TWENTY-FIRST CENTURY

We have explored various ethical criteria that can be used to evaluate interpersonal, small group, organizational, public, and mass mediated communication. Though each communication context represents a slightly different communication task and, consequently, a different ethical focus, there are certain ethical themes that are applicable across communication contexts. In an analysis of communication and persuasion in our increasingly complex world, Donald Cushman and Sandra King offer an ethical perspective that embraces **human diversity.** They argue that a focus on practical knowledge (e.g., understanding, respect and cooperation) should replace the focus on technical knowledge (e.g., effectiveness and goal achievement) in twentieth century communication.[44] Ethical communication, in any context, should lead to: 1) mutual self-recognition, 2) interdependence, and 3) cooperation.

Mutual self-recognition promotes the personal knowledge and fulfillment of all communication participants. Each communicator gains self- and other-insight from the interaction. Each communicator's personal dignity is respected, and each participant's attitudes, beliefs, and values are solicited.

Ethical communicators also recognize their **interdependence,** according to Cushman and King. Other people are not means to goals, but individuals who must be respected and helped. When communicators acknowledge interdependence, they embrace diversity of people, attitudes, beliefs, and values.

The final characteristic of this ethical perspective is **cooperation.** Persuasion becomes a process of identifying the interests of all people influenced by an action, working together cooperatively to solve a problem, and adapting the solution to meet the needs of all people involved.

Cushman and King argue that as we move toward a more global society in the twenty-first century, persuasion should be characterized less by the imposition of one person's will on another and more by the process of mutual interdependence and respect.

Study Guide

ethical principles
three things influencing ethical evaluations
ten issues that guide evaluation of persuasion ethics
dialogue perspective
    I-Thou attitude versus I-It attitude
    monologue versus dialogue
political perspective—four criteria
humanist perspective
    four criteria for use of deception
information perspective
    information quality
    cognitive deliberation
    self- and other-awareness
    social contact

humanist perspective and responsibility for consequences
receiver responsibility: resoluteness and openness
existentialist perspective and revisionist thinking
situational perspective
    Rules for Radicals (Alinsky)
relative power and ethical responsibility
    power of advertising
freedom of speech and ethics
characteristics of ethical persuasion
ethics in the twenty-first century
    human diversity focus
        mutual self-recognition
        interdependence
        cooperation

Discussion Questions

1. Is deception ethical? Are there situations in which you would consider a "moral lie"—that is, using deception for a good purpose? Try to write an ethical guideline regarding the appropriate and inappropriate use of deception.

2. Is there such a thing as a lie of omission? Is it unethical to withhold information? Under what circumstances would this action be unethical? Write an ethical guideline that specifies the conditions under which this omission is unethical.

3. Think of a situation in which freedom of speech is not appropriate. Are there situations in which freedom of speech has resulted in unethical persuasion?

4. Is it ethical to advertise cigarettes and alcohol? Is it ethical to target minority groups with this advertising?

5. Is it ethical to promote Satanism, suicide, and drug use in musical lyrics?

6. Is it ethical to advertise to children? the mentally ill? the mentally challenged?

7. How does the relative power of the persuader influence ethical responsibility? Is it true that as the relative power of the persuader increases, the persuader's ethical responsibility increases? Is the converse of this true? If the persuader has little social power, should the persuader be given more ethical latitude?

References

1. Washington, L. S. 1992. Africa's invisible famine. *Utne Reader,* 49, 26–27.
2. Potter, R. B. 1972. The logic of moral argument. In *Toward a discipline of social ethics.* P. Deats, ed. pp. 93–114. Boston: Boston University Press.
3. Fisher, W. 1980. Rationality and the logic of good reasons. *Philosophy and Rhetoric,* 13, 121–130.
4. Friedman, M. S. 1960. *Martin Buber: The life of dialogue.* New York: Harper Torchbook.

Pfuetze, P. E. 1961. *Self, society, existence: Human nature and dialogue in the thought of George Herbert Mead and Martin Buber.* New York: Harper Torchbook.

5. Johannesen, R. L. 1990. *Ethics in human communication,* 3rd ed. Prospect Heights, IL: Waveland Press.

6. Wallace, K. R. 1955. An ethical basis of communication. *The Speech Teacher,* 4, 1–9.
   Johannesen, R. L. 1990. *Ethics in human communication,* 3rd ed. pp. 21–39. Prospect Heights, IL: Waveland Press.

7. Fried, C. 1978. *Right and wrong.* Cambridge, MA: Harvard University Press.

8. Yoos, G. 1984. Rational appeal and the ethics of advocacy. In *Essays on classical rhetoric and modern discourse.* R. Connors, et al., eds. pp. 82–97. Carbondale, IL: Southern University Press.

9. Christians, C. G., K. B. Rotzoll, and M. Fackler. 1991. *Media ethics: Cases & moral reasoning,* 61–64. New York: Longman.

10. Ibid.

11. Kant, I. 1964. *Groundwork of the metaphysic or morals.* H. J. Paton, trans. New York: Harper Torchbooks, 62–89.

12. Mill, J. S. 1961. *Utilitarianism.* London: J. M. Dent & Sons.
    Urmson, J. O. 1953. The interpretation of the moral philosophy of J. S. Mill. *The Philosophical Quarterly,* 3, 33–39.

13. Frankena, W. 1962. *Ethics.* Englewood Cliffs, NJ: Prentice-Hall.
    Outka, G. 1972. *Agape: An ethical analysis.* New Haven, CT: Yale University Press.

14. Fletcher, J. 1964. *Situational ethics: The new morality.* Philadelphia: Westminster Press.
    Wellman, C. 1988. *Morals and ethics,* 2nd ed., p. 41. Englewood Cliffs, NJ: Prentice Hall.

15. Nielson, T. R. 1974. *Ethics of speech communication,* 2nd ed. Indianapolis: Bobbs-Merrill.

16. Gouran, D. S., R. Y. Hirokawa, and A. E. Martz. 1986. A critical analysis of factors related to decisional processes involved in the Challenger disaster. *Central States Speech Journal,* 37, 119–135.

17. Haiman, F. S. 1958. Democratic ethics in the hidden persuaders. *Quarterly Journal of Speech,* 44, 385–392.
    Johannesen, R. L. 1990. Op cit., pp. 23–24.

18. Jensen, J. V. 1981. *Argumentation: Reasoning in communication.* Belmont, CA: Wadsworth.

19. Wallace, K. R. 1955. An ethical basis of communication. *The Speech Teacher,* 4, 1–9.

20. Gouran, D. S., R. Y. Hirokawa, and A. E. Martz. 1986. *Op cit.*

21. Johnstone, C. L. 1981. Ethics, wisdom, and the mission of contemporary rhetoric: The realization of human being. *Central States Speech Journal,* 32, 177–188.

22. Gouran, D. S., R. Y. Hirokawa, and A. E. Martz. 1986. *Op cit.*

23. Campbell, K. K. 1971. The rhetorical implications of the axiology of Jean-Paul Sartre. *Western Speech Communication,* 35, 155–161.

24. Christians, C. G., K. B. Rotzoll, and M. Fackler. 1991. *Op cit.,* pp. 325–326.

25. Johnstone, C. L. 1981. Ethics, wisdom, and the mission of contemporary rhetoric: The realization of human being. *Central States Speech Journal*, 32, 177–188.

26. Diggs, B. J. 1964. Persuasion and ethics. *Quarterly Journal of Speech*, 50, 360–369.

27. Johnstone, H. W., Jr. 1981. Toward an ethics for rhetoric. *Communication*, 6, 305–314.

28. Brown, C. T., and P. W. Keller. 1979. *Monologue to dialogue: An exploration of interpersonal communication*, 2nd ed. Englewood Cliffs, NJ: Prentice-Hall.

29. Stevenson, B. 1984. *The home book of quotations*, p. 2049. New York: Greenwich House.

30. Campbell, K. K. 1971. *Op cit.*
    Sarte, J. P. Existentialism and human emotions. In *Existentialism*. V. Frechtman, trans. Secaucus, NJ: Castle.

31. Johannesen, R. L. 1990. *Op cit.*
    Rogge, E. 1959. Evaluating the ethics of a speaker in a democracy. *Quarterly Journal of Speech*, 45, 419–425.

32. Diggs, B. J. 1964. *Op cit.*

33. Alinsky, S. D. 1971. *Rules for radicals*. New York: Random House.
    Johannesen, R. L. 1990. Op cit; pp. 82–84.

34. Scott, R. L. 1976. On viewing rhetoric as epistemic: Ten years later. *Central States Speech Journal*, 27, 258–266.

35. Johannesen, R. L. 1990. Op cit., pp. 52–54.

36. Berlet, C. 1992. Activists face increased harassment. *Utne Reader*, 49, 85–88.

37. *Ibid.*

38. Schrier, W. 1930. The ethics of persuasion. *Quarterly Journal of Speech*, 16, 86.

39. Mills, R. D. 1983. Newspaper ethics: A qualitative study. *Journalism Quarterly*, 60, 589–594.

40. Christians, et al. 1991. Op cit., pp. 113–133.

41. Moss, M. 1987. The poverty story. *Columbia Journalism Review*, 25, 43–54.

42. Bachand, D. 1988. The marketing of ideas: Advertising and road safety. *International Journal of Research in Marketing*, 4, 291–309.

43. Collins, R. K. L., and M. F. Jacobson. 1992. Are we consumers or citizens? *Utne Reader*, 49, 56–57.

44. Cushman, D. P., and S. S. King, Communication, knowledge, and ethics: A twentieth century perspective. In *Human communication as a field of study*. S. S. King, ed. pp. 233–240. Albany, NY: SUNY Press.

II

Components of Persuasion

4

The Magic of Symbols

A tragic murder in Los Angeles illustrates the importance placed on symbols in our society. A young deaf woman getting out of a car was gunned down by gang members who assumed that the sign language she used to communicate represented the symbolic gestures of a rival gang. We use symbols to form impressions of other people—the tilt of a hat brim may signify allegiance to a gang, a pentadic design on jewelry may represent association with a satanic order, greek letters may reflect membership in a fraternity or a sorority. Our interpretations of symbols dictate our actions. In this manner, symbols are a powerful persuasive influence.

In this chapter we will explore what symbols are and how our symbol system is designed for persuasive purposes. This will lead us to the central issue of this chapter—a discussion of *how* symbols are used to influence others.

WHAT ARE SYMBOLS AND HOW ARE THEY USED?

We cannot underestimate the power of symbols. A symbol is something used to represent a person, place, thing, or idea. Symbols make up our communication system, which includes both verbal and non-verbal components. Symbols are analogous to cars or buses—symbols carry meaning. Symbols are necessary for thought. Without symbols, we cannot transport an idea or a concept from our environment to our brain, from one part of our brain to another, or from one person to another. To better understand symbols and how they work, we will discuss three characteristics of symbols: 1) the cognitive functions of symbols—how symbols help us think; 2) forms and types of symbols—how symbols vary; and 3) the relationship between symbols and meaning.

COGNITIVE FUNCTIONS OF SYMBOLS: HOW SYMBOLS AFFECT THOUGHT

Symbols are essential for communication. It is important to note at least four of the functions that symbols serve. First, symbols allow us to communicate about objects that are not present. Through the use of symbols we can *communicate across barriers of time and space*—I can tell you what I did *last summer* in *London*, even though it is a year later, and we are conversing in Boise, Idaho.

A second function of symbols is the opportunity to *expand knowledge and understanding*. We can create new symbols to express ideals and imaginings. Freedom, liberty, and justice have no referent—there is no object we can point to as the embodiment of freedom or liberty—but we can use the words or symbols of freedom and liberty to create certain ideals. Similarly, we have created symbols for mythical horses with single horns (unicorns), and white transparent discarnate beings (ghosts), and other entities that exist only in our imaginations.

Symbols also provide the *means for abstract thought*. Monkey, giraffe, and hippo are concrete symbols for specific types of animals. Our symbol system lets us create categories by using the single abstract term "animal" to represent innumerable species of monkeys, giraffes, hippos, lions, and bears. Abstract symbols facilitate reasoning from specific events (an argument between spouses) to general conclusions (indication of marital discord). Abstractions also allow us to make comparisons within categories and between categories (e.g., how are birds similar to and different from reptiles?). Perhaps the most important function of abstract symbols is to facilitate efficient decision making. When a large black hairy spider fell down my swimsuit in Mexico, I responded to the abstract symbol "spider," and did not bother to identify the specific type of spider before ridding myself of that long-legged, crawling creature.

In addition to allowing abstract thinking, symbols also *establish a shared social reality*. To the extent to which we have similar meaning for symbols, we can communicate ideas to one another. Members of the same culture and members of the same social group often share a view of reality based on common meanings for particular symbols. People shared a social reality of the Persian Gulf War, for example, with others who attributed the same symbol and the same meaning to the war. Liberal anti-war demonstrators used the symbol "Vietnam." Fundamental Christians invoked the symbol "Armageddon." Wall Street brokers associated the war with "recession." Each one of these groups shared an understanding with members within their group, but the war had very different meanings to people in different social groups.

Symbols serve very important communicative functions: providing a means to communicate across time and space, expanding knowledge, facilitating abstract reasoning, and establishing shared social reality. A symbol associated with Egyptian burials illustrates all four of these functions. According to tradition, when an Egyptian of high status died, his or her slaves were executed so that they could accompany the nobleperson in the afterlife. (The ancient Egyptian word for slave actually translates as "I'm doing it! I'm doing it!") Once upon a time, a very astute slave with a desire for a long life came up with an idea—why not create a symbol to represent herself in the afterlife?

The creation of this symbol demonstrates the four cognitive functions of symbols. The slave convinced people that this symbol, a small carved and painted replica of herself, could transport her services across time and space to the afterlife. This new symbol generated new theories and understanding of the afterlife and certainly facilitated abstract reasoning. The symbol itself was an abstract representation of the slave. Most importantly for the slave, society accepted this symbol, and a shared social reality regarding the meaning and power of the slave statue emerged.

The Representation of Symbols: How Symbols Vary

Symbols always stand for, or represent, an idea, person, place, or object. The thing that a symbol represents is called its **referent.** Symbols vary in the form of representation used to convey the idea, person, place, or object being symbolized. We will discuss three forms that symbols may take: verbal representations, sensory representations, or conceptual representations.

Verbal symbols are words or utterances and are the basic units of our language system. The ability to select and arrange verbal symbols to convey an experience vividly is the key to poetry, literature, and persuasive speaking.

Sensory symbols invoke our senses to produce a vicarious experience. Visual, olfactory (smell), auditory, or tactile stimuli may be used to remind us of some absent or abstract concept. If you smell chocolate chip cookies baking and remember your grandmother and your grandmother's house, the smell may symbolize or represent your memories of your grandmother. A dramatic dance may communicate a feeling of grief and symbolize the feelings experienced during bereavement. A musical march may communicate patriotism and generate strong emotions, as a symbol of the people who have died in our country's wars.

Conceptual symbols are objects used to represent abstract ideas. Conceptual symbols include flags that represent the concepts of freedom and justice, yellow ribbons that represent the concept of loyalty to overseas troops and hostages, or crosses that represent Christianity. Conceptual symbols are often combined with verbal and sensory symbols. However, the key difference is that conceptual symbols represent abstract ideals and values, and the primary purpose of the symbol is to stimulate ideas.

This advertisement for an aperitif employs conceptual symbolism to convey that the product warms you up and makes you feel whole again.

CASSANDRE, A. M. *Dubo Dubon Dubonnet.* 1932. Lithograph, printed in color, 17½ × 45½". Collection, The Museum of Modern Art, New York. Gift of Bernard Davis.

Symbols also vary in their relationship with the referent they represent. Sometimes this relationship is direct and obvious; sometimes this relationship is indirect and must be learned. It is easier to use a direct and obvious symbol for an observable object. It is more difficult to create a direct and obvious symbol for something that exists only in our minds. To define the relationship between a symbol and its referent, it is useful to characterize symbols as analogic or digital.

An **analogic symbol** resembles the idea or thing it represents. There is a logical and obvious relationship between an analogic symbol and its referent. A drawing of a bunny is an analogic symbol—the drawing looks like a bunny, and it is clear to everyone that it symbolizes a bunny. Most pictures are analogic symbols. Many nonverbal signs, such as tracking the route of a tear with your finger to symbolize crying, are analogic symbols, and the pictorial signs for handicapped, and men's and women's bathrooms are analogic symbols. People who speak a different language can usually interpret analogic symbols—the meaning of the symbol is obvious.

Analogic symbols are also used in music, art, gestures, and facial expressions to communicate evaluations (good versus bad, or happy versus sad), power (strong versus weak), and activity (fast versus slow). In contemporary political campaigns analogic symbols—such as video representations, mood music, and images of poverty and environmental damage—carry considerable persuasive weight.

Digital symbols are arbitrary. There is no obvious relationship between the symbol and its referent. Most words are digital symbols. Why does "love" symbolize the warm, fuzzy feeling we experience for certain people? Why does the written word "rabbit" or the sound I make when I

BOX 4.1   *Symbols classified by type and form*

	Analogic	Digital
Verbal	The spoken word "tick-tock"	The written word "Time"
Sensory	Painting of an old man with a beard	Hearing the music to Old Lang Syne
Conceptual	Hour glass	The ball in Times Square which drops each New Year's Eve

say "rabbit" represent the long eared animal that hops? There is no direct relationship between these symbols and their referents—the meaning of these symbols must be learned. The advantage of digital symbols is that they can be used to convey abstract concepts and associations.

What about vocalization of words such as "Boom" "Splash" and "Meow"? Are these analogic or digital symbols? Since these are symbols for sounds, and the pronunciation reproduces the sound the word represents, these words are more analogic than digital. There is a logical and obvious relationship between the symbol "Meow" and its referent, the sound a cat makes.

It is important to recognize the difference between analogic and digital symbols. The likelihood of symbol misinterpretation increases with the use of digital symbols. The meaning of digital symbols must be learned, and many digital symbols have multiple meanings.

We can distinguish different types of symbols by classifying the symbols by both form (verbal, sensory, or conceptual), and level of abstraction (analogic or digital). The matrix in Box 4.1 provides a system for distinguishing six kinds of symbols: analogic-verbal; analogic-sensory; analogic-conceptual; digital-verbal; digital-sensory; and digital-conceptual. Examples of each of the six classes of symbols are presented in the matrix cells.

Relationship Between Symbols and Meaning

A symbol may have multiple meanings, depending on the intentions of the speaker, the sentence in which the symbol is used, the emotional reactions the symbol generates in the receiver, the context in which the symbol appears, and the culture in which the symbol is understood. The relationship between a symbol and its meaning becomes quite complex when we consider the number of facts that influence how a symbol is interpreted. It is very important to remember that *meanings do not reside in a given symbol or the content of a message.* The same symbol can generate different meanings for different people—ergo, meaning resides in people, not in symbols or messages. Speakers and receivers actively construct and negotiate symbolic meaning through persuasion. In the process of assigning meaning to symbols, we rely on two guidelines—we determine whether to apply the connotative or denotative meanings for the symbols used, and we identify the speech act in which the symbol is used.

Connotative versus Denotative Meaning

My interpretation of a word may differ from the meaning you assign to the word, and the meanings we both assign may differ from the dictionary definition. If you look up the word "flag" in the dictionary, you will see the denotative, objective definition: "a rectangular piece of fabric of distinctive design used as a symbol of a nation." The **denotative meaning** of a symbol is the literal definition, while the **connotative meaning** conveys the emotional baggage that accompanies the literal definition. The connotative meanings associated with the symbol "flag" include: a reminder of the people who have given their lives to defend the country; a symbol of freedom and justice; a symbol of the hypocrisy and corruption of the government; a test of first amendment rights; hard work and progress; and the excitement of parades and ballgames.

There are many symbols (including words) that have connotative as well as denotative meanings: sex, the music "Pomp and Circumstance," pornography, death, abortion, Christmas, God, etc. It is important to remember that although people may share a common denotative meaning for a symbol, individuals may have very different connotative meanings. Persuaders can use the connotative meanings of symbols to incite receivers to action and change. Politicians often wrap themselves in the flag during campaigns to stir up connotative associations of patriotism, loyalty, and pride in America. Comedians would be hard-pressed for material if they could not count on audience's connotative meanings of sex; the denotative meaning is really not very amusing. In sum, the numerous and variant connotations that symbols can generate demonstrate that the sender and the receiver create the meaning of symbols, and that meaning does not exist within the symbol itself.

Speech Acts

Speech acts also illustrate how people influence the meaning of symbols.[1] According to Speech Act Theory, the meaning of a message can be determined only by the speaker's intent. The **speech act** used to convey a message reveals the intentions of the speaker. There are many different types of speech acts, including: questions, statements, requests, promises, commands, etc. A change in syntax (order of words) or a change in voice inflection can change a message from a request to a command, thereby changing the speech act. When you decide to produce a message, you make a decision regarding whether you will ask a question or make an assertion. The idea you intend to convey is revealed not only by your choice of words, but by your choice of speech act as well.

Persuaders can alter meaning through the selection of speech acts, and the success of persuasion is dependent upon the receiver's identifying the speech act intended by the persuader. You can use the same sentence to communicate different intentions by changing the speech act of a message. If I say, "Can you give me a refund?" as a question, it carries a different meaning from when I say the same sentence with a downward inflection, as a demand. You can also communicate the same intent using different sentences: "I'd like my money back," or "This is broken and I want to return it." It is important to note that identical messages can communicate different meanings when the speech acts differ; and different messages can communicate the same meaning when the speech act remains the same. It follows that the speech act selected by the speaker, and the identification of the speech act by the receiver determine the meaning of a message.

Persuaders may, therefore, alter the speech act used to convey a message or alter receivers' perceptions of the speech act for persuasive ends. For example, when George Bush made the statement, "Read my lips, no new taxes!" during his campaign, many people identified the speech act as a promise. Four years later, while trying to explain tax *increases* during his presidency, Bush claimed that his original statement did not constitute a *promise* but a *request* to Congress.

From our previous discussion of the characterization of symbols it is clear that our symbol system does not lead to perfect communication. Digital symbols have no logical relationship to the thing signified, connotative meanings load symbols with emotional baggage, and the meaning of symbols is dependent upon the speech act selected to convey the message.

The model of meaning in Figure 4.1 illustrates how the same symbol may conjure up very different meanings.[2] The meaning of a concept may first be distorted by the intentions of the speaker. The persuader may choose symbols that will lead the receiver to perceive a concept in an extremely favorable or unfavorable way. The second distortion occurs with the interpretation by the receiver. Past experience and learning frame the receiver's response to a symbol. Faced with triangulated meanings, persuaders may choose symbols that increase chances of establishing shared meaning with the receiver. For persuasion to be successful, the persuader must paint a symbolic picture that the receiver accepts.

Why, you might ask, is our symbol system so complex? Why is there so much inherent ambiguity in the meanings assigned to symbols? Why didn't we create a simple, direct, and precise communication system to avoid misunderstandings and conflicts? Clare Harkness answers these questions in her analysis of the origins of manipulative language. She claims that we developed a complex language system for persuasive purposes:[3]

FIGURE 4.1

The 'x' model of meaning. Meaning is the product of people, referents (the objects referred to), symbols, and individual interpretations.

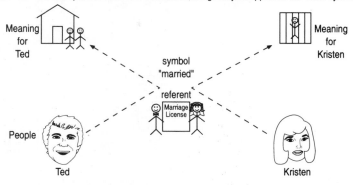

Meaning is the product of people, referents (the objects referred to), symbols and individual interpretations. This example illustrates how different meanings may be applied to the same symbol.

[R. Burling] asks what could have made our complex language, with its characteristic ambiguity, functional redundancies, and enormous vocabulary of near synonyms, selectively advantageous. He rules out the possibility that these selective advantages were obtained through use of complex language in cooperative pursuits such as group hunting or foraging. The planning and coordination required by such group tasks do not require multiple and subtle forms that language can take. Rather, for such tasks, simple, clear, and stereotyped communicative signals would best serve the hunters and foragers. He also rejects the possibility that educating young children requires sophisticated language. Teaching others requires active demonstration rather than subtle speech. Instead, he proposes that the selective advantage of complex language lies in its contribution to aspects of social influence and manipulation in the individual's search for social power and control of resources (pp. 22–23).

HOW ARE SYMBOLS USED FOR SOCIAL INFLUENCE?

How can our symbol system, with its inherent complexities, connotative meanings, and vague intentions, be designed specifically for persuasive purposes, as Harkness suggests? In this section we will explore how symbols are manipulated to create shared meanings among senders and receivers and to produce persuasive effects. In this chapter we will discuss five ways symbols are utilized by persuaders. Persuaders are like magicians—they can use symbols to make realities appear and other realities disappear. The success of their efforts lie, however, with the receivers'

Shoe by Jeff MacNelly.

Reprinted by permission: Tribune Media Services.

ability to recognize the desired symbolic meaning. Persuaders often attempt to alter symbols': 1) level of abstraction; 2) emotional associations; 3) aesthetic qualities; and 4) cognitive associations.

Altering the Level of Abstraction

As we previously discussed, symbols vary in the extent to which they are concrete (specific) or abstract (all-encompassing). Persuaders often manipulate the level of abstraction of symbols to make the symbol more desirable. Rather than responding to the specific issue, "taxes," politicians often increase the level of abstraction by talking about "revenue enhancement." The abstraction of the symbol "nuclear weapons" can similarly be increased to "national security." This process can also work in reverse. If a professor asks about your performance in a class, you may wish to avoid the issue by *decreasing* the level of abstraction and talking about a very specific case—"My dog chewed up that term paper before I could turn it in, but it won't happen again."

Changing the level of abstraction of a symbol often serves to create ambiguity. Robin Lakoff provides interesting examples of how politicians manage meaning through ambiguity.[4] As a result, receivers may construe the message in any way that appeals to their interests. If the receiver makes a negative association with an ambiguous message, the politician can always deny that this was his or her real intent.

When asked by reporters if he agreed that Martin Luther King had Communist associations, a politician recently replied, "We'll know in about thirty-five years, won't we?" referring to the fact that the FBI files on King will be declassified in thirty-five years.[5] Lakoff notes that this statement can be interpreted in many different ways. Does the politician believe that King was a Communist supporter? Is the politician hinting at information that he has and we don't? Is the politician implying he knows the answer? Or is he merely joking?

Another technique politicians use is vagueness. Rather than delivering a message that has multiple meanings, a politician may decide to produce a message that has no substantive meaning. In other words, the politician takes no clear position. Asked to report on a recent summit meeting, a politician made the following statement during a press conference:

> "And I tell you, one of the things that has been marvelous about his summit is the understanding that our values, that alliance's values—but our values are winning the battle around the world. . . . There's no longer a question of whether we've been on the right side of democracy and freedom and those things (p. 274)."[6]

If the purpose of communication is to establish a shared and understood meaning between sender and receiver, both of the politicians quoted above are trying *not* to communicate. The manipulation of the level of abstraction may allow the persuader and receiver to agree on an issue. We selectively focus on those aspects of the message with which we can identify and agree. If the rest of the message is ambiguous, we have a tendency to fill in the missing details with our own minds and conclude that the speaker is in agreement with us. We may be able to agree at an abstract level when we would disagree on a specific case, and vice-versa. Or, we may not realize that our partner in persuasion is using different levels of abstraction, and we may both perceive agreement where no agreement exists. The use of ambiguity and vagueness allows politicians, for example, to appear to be the champions of a multitude of causes reflecting the values of many different types of people. Ambiguity and vagueness hide inconsistent positions. We the public have allowed this to happen by not holding politicians accountable for the meaning, or lack of meaning, in their messages.

Altering the level of abstraction of symbols through the use of ambiguity, vagueness, or switches from specific to general cases makes it difficult for receivers to construct a clearly defined meaning or to critically analyze the message. It is hard to disagree with a message if you have no idea what meaning the speaker intends.

In this ad, the level of abstraction is manipulated by making the act of drinking a beer an intercultural experience.

Altering a Symbol's Emotional Intensity

Robin Lakoff provides a wonderful example of symbols that vary in emotional capacity. Lakoff contends that Republicans are much better than Democrats at changing the emotional intensity of political symbols.[7] Whereas the Democrats use the symbol "choice," the Republicans use the symbol "life." Whereas the Democrats discuss "competence," the Republicans describe "a kinder, gentler nation." Lakoff states:

> [Republicans] appeal to the gut, where the Democrats' . . . good words are good in the head: we have to think to realize what they mean and why they are good . . . we don't get carried away. But we want to get carried away, we want the trance induced by being part of a cheering throng. Words like 'life' have instantaneous and profound resonance. . . . In a world where more and more experiences are synthetic, plastic, manufactured, those feelings evoked in the gut are all we have that we know for sure are real. We trust (our gut emotions), and gladly give our allegiance to anyone who evokes them. (p. 261–62).

Manipulating the emotional intensity of symbols is a common persuasive strategy. If receivers already hold an attitude that is consistent with the persuader's message, high intensity symbols can incite people and move them to action. If the receivers are opposed to the persuader's position, it is wise to decrease the emotional intensity of symbols.[8] I recently advised a student working on a persuasive speech on doctors' right to provide reproductive counseling in federally subsidized Planned Parenthood clinics to avoid using the word *abortion* in her speech. Her speech responds to the congressional gag rule mandating that a physician can not discuss abortion options with patients in a federally funded clinic. The student stands a better chance of persuading her classmates if she focuses on the free speech rights of physicians to provide medical information, rather than associating her position with the emotionally charged symbol, "abortion."

Altering a Symbol's Aesthetics

Changing the form or aesthetic qualities of a symbol may increase the degree to which the symbol is visually or verbally appealing. Thus, airbrushing the face of a model who represents your product line constitutes a change in the aesthetics of a symbol. Any change that makes a symbol more attractive and desirable constitutes an aesthetic change.

A study of cigarette advertising from 1960 to 1985 illustrates how advertisers have altered the aesthetic associations of cigarettes.[9] In response to increasing health concerns, cigarette advertisers have presented cigarettes in pleasing contexts to make cigarettes more appealing. In youth magazines, advertisers increasingly present the cigarette in adventurous,

The symbolic representation of fire, heat, heroism, an oxygen mask, and a baby in distress increase the emotional intensity of this ad.

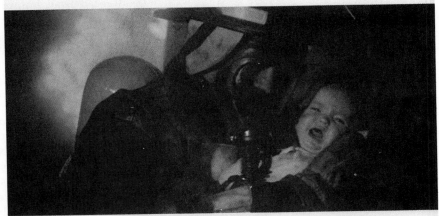

Sometimes what you wear to work makes all the difference.

At 1,500 degrees Fahrenheit, dressing for success is no cliche. It's a matter of life and death.

Which is why DuPont engineers worked to create Nomex® and Kevlar® fire resistant fibers. The remarkable performance of these fibers has made them the standard for state-of-the-art firefighting clothing all over the world.

And everyday, they not only save the lives of thousands of firefighters rushing into fires, but those they carry out as well.

At DuPont, we make the things that make a difference.

Better things for better living.

sensation-seeking, and recreational contexts. The study found that in women's magazines, cigarettes are associated with erotica. The cigarette is a sign of sex appeal, sophistication, and elegance. Although the form of the cigarette has not changed, the aesthetics surrounding the cigarette have. The attractiveness of the cigarette increases by association with aesthetically pleasing contexts.

Creating New Associations for Symbols

Perhaps the most common tactic used by persuaders is to change the meaning of a symbol—that is, modify the associations the receiver makes. Symbols generate many attributions, and the job of the persuader involves changing the favorable or unfavorable evaluation of existing associations, changing the importance of these associations, or creating new associations.

Cicero illustrates how the *evaluation* of an existing symbol can be changed for persuasive purposes. As a trial lawyer, Cicero defended many of Rome's most notorious murderers by arguing that the defendant had not committed a heinous murder, but had, in fact, performed a community service by ending the life of a particularly vile victim.

Communication researchers have recently studied the evaluation of symbols used to communicate sexual desire. Researchers have found that males involved in intimate behavior interpret a "no" response from a female as meaning "maybe," when many females intend to communicate a polite, but firm "no." Counselors working on college campuses to prevent date rape are attempting to change the meaning of these sexual desire symbols to make intentions clear. College students are being educated to say "no" only when they mean "no" and not when they intend a coy "maybe." Likewise, "no" means "no" and should be respected. College students are also learning to define sexual conversations as an information exchange rather than a persuasive encounter.

There are numerous ways in which a persuader can *create new associations* and meanings for a familiar symbol. Joseph Goebbels, Hitler's minister of propaganda, once said: "It would not be impossible to prove with sufficient repetition . . . that a square is in fact a circle. What after all are a square and a circle? They are mere words, and words can be molded until they clothe ideas in disguise."[10]

A marketing study, for example, revealed that changing a company's name without any corresponding change in management or product quality was sufficient to increase sales.[11] The researchers concluded that a new name (symbol) signified improvements in performance and production to prospective buyers.

Another study found that advertisers and marketers are very successful in giving products a symbolic meaning. "Positioning" is the process by which marketers instill a product with an image that appeals to a

In this advertisement, the National Rifle Association changes perceptions of the symbol "voting" by associating voting with power—the power to "fire" someone from a job and the "firing" power of a rifle. Voting is compared to the power of hunting through references to an "open season on politicians" and this visual of a pencil forging a bullet hole.

National Rifle Association of America

specific target. We, as consumers, take this positioning information so seriously that we use it to construct our social reality. Recall that our social reality is a culturally shared perception of the people, places, and things in our environment. An especially intriguing study provided two groups of college students with a description of a date. In one version, the male drove a Chevrolet Camaro. In the alternative version of the story, the male drove a Honda Accord. Although the description of the male and his behavior were identical in both versions of the story, students rated the Camaro driver as more sexually aggressive than the Honda Accord driver.[12] For college students in this study, "Camaro" clearly has more symbolic meaning than "a car used to get from point A to point B." In another study by the same author, subjects rated the "social worth" of other people by looking at their shopping lists.[13] These studies suggest that product symbols are so powerful that we use these symbols to form impressions of other people.

SYMBOLS AND PERSUASION

We have discussed four ways in which symbols may be manipulated for persuasive purposes. To illustrate these methods of symbol manipulation let's examine how a journalist might persuade or bias readers based on symbol manipulation. When I lived in Texas, a driver missed a curve going onto a bridge and ran his car into the river. He swam out of the river and hired a wrecking company to retrieve his sunken car. The wrecking company pulled out a car, but it wasn't his. The wrecking company continued to pull out at least six cars, with various numbers of bodies in them, that had been sitting at the bottom of the river for some time. If our journalist wants to persuade people to rally for safety measures on this particular road, the journalist could decrease the level of abstraction from a group of dead bodies to specific individuals whose lives were lost. He/she could intensify emotional reactions by using emotionally charged symbols, such as "tragedy," "disaster," "mass accidental death," and "people trapped as cars sink." The inclusion of gory pictures would certainly influence the aesthetics of the symbols, and the journalist could manipulate the meaning of the symbols by associating the deaths with negligence on the part of county highway officials. Our journalist could manipulate quite a different view of reality by increasing the level of abstraction, decreasing emotional intensity, using non-offensive pictures, and associating these symbols with driver negligence.

SUMMARY

Symbols are used to carry meaning. Even though meaning resides within the sender and the receiver and is dependent upon the symbols and speech acts they select and interpret, symbols can be altered to influence meaning. Symbols paint a picture of reality, and the objective of persuasion is to change another person's reality (i.e., their beliefs, attitudes, or behaviors). The persuader has little control over the interpretation of a message by the receiver, but the persuader can control the symbols used to construct a message and the speech act selected to present the message. In this manner, the persuader can emphasize particular connotations, intentions, aesthetic qualities, emotions, and associations.

To critically evaluate persuasive messages, the receiver should question: 1) why a symbol is presented in a particular form (i.e., verbal, visual, or conceptual); 2) how the type of symbol (i.e., analogic or digital) allows for multiple variations in meaning; 3) what connotations the symbol generates; 4) how the symbol works in conjunction with the speaker's speech act; and 5) how the speaker has altered the symbol's level of abstraction, emotional intensity, aesthetic appeal, and meaning associations.

Study Guide

symbols
     four cognitive functions of symbols
     referent
     verbal, sensory, and conceptual symbols
     analogic versus digital symbols
meaning
     meanings are in people
     connotative versus denotative meanings
     speech act theory
     model of meaning
     language complexity and persuasion
symbols and persuasion
     level of abstraction
     emotional intensity
     aesthetics
     creating associations

Discussion Questions

1. Generate examples of each of the methods persuaders use to alter symbolic meaning. Is the altering of symbolic meaning in each of these examples ethical or unethical? Why or why not?

2. What role do receiver characteristics play in the interpretation of symbolic meaning? Do you think that some people have a more difficult time recognizing persuaders' manipulation of symbols? Why or why not? How would you train receivers to recognize symbols, symbolic meaning, and manipulations of meaning?

3. What symbols generate strong connotations for you? Are you susceptible to persuasive messages that incorporate these symbols?

References

1. Searle, J. R. 1969. Speech acts: An essay in the philosophy of language. Cambridge: Cambridge University Press.
2. Ogden, C. K., and I. A. Richards. 1936. *The meaning of meaning: A study of the influence of language upon thought and the science of symbolism.* New York: Harcourt, Brace & Company.
3. Harkness, C. D. 1990. Competition for resources and the origins of manipulative language. In *Seeking compliance.* J. P. Dillard, ed. pp. 21–40. Scottsdale, AZ: Gorsuch Scarisbrick.
4. Lakoff, R. T. 1990. *Talking power: The politics of language in our lives.* New York: Basic Books.
5. *Ibid.,* p. 266.
6. *Ibid.,* p. 274.
7. Lakoff, op cit.
8. Bradac, J. J., J. W. Bowers, and J. A. Courtright. 1979. Three language variables in communication research: Intensity, immediacy, and diversity. *Human Communication Research,* 5, 257–269.
9. Altman, D. G., M. D. Slater, C. L. Albright, and N. Maccoby. 1987. How an unhealthy product is sold: Cigarette advertising in magazines, 1960–1985. *Journal of Communication,* 37, 95–106.
10. Pratkanis, A., and E. Aronson. 1991. Cited in *Age of propaganda: The everyday use and abuse of persuasion,* p. 49. New York: W. H. Freeman.
11. Horsky, D., and P. Swynggedouw. 1987. Does it pay to change your company's name? A stock market perspective. *Marketing Science,* 6, 320–335.
12. Baran, S. J. 1987. Automobile "positioning" and the construction of social reality. In *Studies in communication,* vol. 3. G. Thomas, ed. pp. 133–138. Norwood, NJ: Ablex.
13. Baran, S. J., et al. 1989. You are what you buy: Mass-mediated judgments of people's worth. *Journal of Communication,* 39, 46–54.

5

The Mind of the Source—Communication Goals and Strategies

The marketing of a new beer named "Powermaster" might have been accomplished with little attention or controversy had someone not analyzed the goals and strategies underlying the advertising message. Heilemann's goal to market a beer to urban black males led to the development of a strategy to make the target believe the beer was associated with masculinity, social and physical power, and self-determination—"power master." The analysis of Heilemann's persuasive goal and strategy led to public outcries of racism and sexism. Heilemann canceled their advertising campaign after being condemned for associating the use of a product with the empowerment of a socially disadvantaged group. The fact that the product associated "empowerment" with alcohol didn't help.

The analysis of persuasive goals and strategies can help you understand the underlying implications of persuasive messages and increase your ability to evaluate persuasive messages critically. In this chapter we will explore how communication goals and strategies are generated and selected. Specifically, we will discuss: 1) communication goals; 2) persuasive strategies; 3) the modification of goals and strategies during persuasive interactions; and 4) the consolidation of goals and strategies into persuasive plans.

COMMUNICATION GOALS

Communication goals are the objectives one hopes to achieve through communication with others. There are three factors that determine what goals will be brought to bear upon a persuasive encounter: the **personality** and **ability** of the communicator and the constraints of the **situation** or task. If you have problems with a group member working on a class project, your **personality** may dictate whether your communication goal is to make friends and resolve your differences, or to persuade the person to drop the class. Similarly, your **ability** as a communicator determines the number of goals that will be activated. You may, for example, generate task goals only—the primary goal is to coerce the person into doing more work. Or you may generate multiple goals—you want the person to do more work, but you also want him/her to like you, and you want to maintain a friendship. The **situation** or task obviously makes some goals more salient than others. In asking a person for a date you may want to communicate your attractiveness, but this goal is less likely to be activated when getting a group member to do more work.

It is important to identify and study communication goals because the goals made salient by the communicator's ability, personality, and/or situation influence the production of persuasive messages.[1] Several studies indicate that when a person is made aware of multiple communication goals, the person produces more sophisticated messages,[2] and the person engages in more strategic planning of messages during ongoing interaction.[3] In addition, goals drive message production. Goals are used to interpret feedback, and they are the basis for assessing the effectiveness of a persuasive encounter. Therefore, the recognition of other's goals and the ability to generate communication strategies to pursue one's own goals are important predictors of persuasive effectiveness.

Types of Communication Goals

Recent research has attempted to classify and categorize meaningful lists of communication goals that are relevant across situations. There are three types of communication goals that have been reported in numerous studies and numerous situations: **self-identity** goals (e.g., making a good impression); **task goals** (e.g., accomplishing the task at hand); and **relationship goals** (e.g., maintaining a favorable relationship).[4] If you decide to break up with your significant other, it is conceivable that all three types of goals may be activated. The task goal is to communicate clearly that you want to break up and date other people. A relationship goal might be to remain friends, and a self-identity goal might be to communicate sympathy and sensitivity.

An additional goal that influences communication is **arousal management.**[5] The arousal management goal may guide the selection of

---

BOX 5.1	*Goal types and goal dimensions*

Goal types: self identity goals
                        relationship goals
                        task goals
                        arousal management goals

Goal dimensions:
goal to inform ←————————————————→ goal to facilitate social interaction
self focus of goal ←————————————————→ other person is focus of goal
task accomplishment goal ←————————————————→ favorable impression goal

---

communication strategies by dictating a preferred level of arousal—that is, excitement, anxiety, or stimulation. Some people may choose aggressive and argumentative strategies because they like heightened arousal.[6] Other people may choose cooperative strategies because they prefer tranquil interactions. You probably know people who seem to thrive on strife and arguments in their interpersonal relationships. When addressing a conflict, these people may seek high arousal. Or they may even instigate conflicts to create arousal. In contrast, other people avoid both conflict and excitement in their communication encounters; they prefer low arousal.

Studies conducted by Doug McCann and Tory Higgins present the most comprehensive and theoretical classification of goals.[7] Rather than organizing goals into categories that don't reflect interrelationships among goals, McCann and Higgins advocate a dimensional classification of goals. Dimensions are lines anchored by opposite adjectives (Box 5.1). When goals are placed in categories, we don't get a picture of how goals are alike or different. **Goal dimensions** reflect the extent to which a goal has or does not have particular characteristics.

There are three dimensions for communication goals: 1) **informing versus interacting;** 2) **self versus other;** and 3) **task versus impression management.** This means that any communication goal can be described by where it falls on each of these three dimensions. This does not mean that a person cannot have more than one goal or have conflicting goals. This is quite possible. The dimensions merely suggest that any one goal can be characterized according to the degree to which it reflects one of the anchors on each dimension.

The informing versus interacting dimension differentiates goals that include getting information, expressing opinions, and checking ideas from the more social goals of entertaining, interacting socially, and having fun. The second dimension, self versus other, distinguishes those goals that are purely self-centered from those goals that involve giving assistance and maintaining a good relationship. The third dimension, task versus impression, distinguishes goals that focus on getting the job done from those goals that involve getting approval and creating a positive personal image. In sum, you should be able to describe any communication goal according to where it falls on each of the three dimensions. For example, persuading people to vote for you might be characterized by high information, high self-focus, and high impression management.

As you can tell, there are numerous types of goals that may be activated for a particular communicative encounter. The **primary goal** in a persuasive situation will usually be the task—the attitude, belief, or behavioral change you are promoting. Fotheringham describes the primary goals of persuasion as: **adoption, continuance, deterrence,** or **discontinuance.** A primary goal may be specifically defined as: 1) convincing a person to adopt a new idea or action (e.g., valuing physical fitness and health); 2) strengthening a person's commitment to a current idea or action (e.g., continue exercising at least once a week); 3) refraining from a potential idea or action (e.g., avoid eating convenient, yet unhealthy foods); and 4) discontinuing an existing idea or action (e.g., stop eating high fat desserts). **Secondary goals** include all of the additional relationship, identity, arousal, informational, and social interaction goals (e.g., you want to maintain a friendship, you want to be perceived as a health expert—not a quack, you want to motivate but not anger the receiver and you want to impart information in a fun and interesting way).[8] Both primary and secondary goals influence your choice of persuasive strategies.

PERSUASIVE STRATEGIES

It is important at this point to differentiate persuasive goals and persuasive strategies. If goals are the intended outcome driving message production, strategies are the steps taken to achieve goals. Strategies are the plans necessary to accomplish a goal: "I'm going to flatter her so she will give me a 20 percent discount"; "I'm going to be very stern and serious to convince him never to drive drunk again"; "I'm going to reward her so that she continues to pay for our dates." Flattery, severity, and rewards are all persuasive strategies—methods for accomplishing persuasive goals.

Initial research on persuasive strategies resulted in attempts to list all strategies used in persuasion. Gerald Marwell and David Schmitt's list of sixteen compliance-gaining strategies represents the first venture in this regard (Table 5.1).[9] (Throughout our discussion of persuasive strategies you may want to refer to examples of these strategies in Table 5.1). The usefulness of a list of persuasive strategies is limited for several reasons. First, it is impossible to produce an exhaustive list that accounts for every strategy available to the message producer. Furthermore, lists do not explain what strategy will be chosen. A communicator's goals, the situation at hand, the personality of the communicator, the type of relationship the

TABLE 5.1   Typology of sixteen compliance-gaining techniques.

Technique	Example
promise	If you comply, I will reward you.
threat	If you don't comply, I will punish you.
expertise (positive)	If you comply, you will be rewarded in life, in the future.
expertise (negative)	If you don't comply, you will be punished in life, in the future.
liking	I will get you into a good mood so you will comply.
pre-giving	I will reward you in advance for the behavior that I expect you to perform.
aversive stimulation	I will continue to punish you until you comply with my wishes.
debt	You owe me. I've complied with your requests in the past, so you must comply with mine now.
moral appeal	You are immoral if you don't comply.
self-feeling (positive)	You will feel better about yourself if you comply.
self-feeling (negative)	You will feel bad about yourself if you don't comply.
altercasting (positive)	A "good" person would comply.
altercasting (negative)	Only a "bad" person would not comply.
altruism	I need your compliance very badly, so do it for me.
esteem (positive)	People you value will think better of you if you comply.
esteem (negative)	People you value will think worse of you if you don't comply.

Source: Marwell & Schmitt (1967). *Sociometry*, 30. p, 357.

communicator has with the receiver, and the ability of the communicator to juggle multiple and often conflicting goals all influence strategy selection. It follows that a list is merely descriptive, not explanatory or predictive. That is, a list does not explain or predict when or why a communicator will employ a specific strategy.

The limitation of strategy lists has led researchers to place strategies on various dimensions. Similar to goal dimensions, strategy dimensions allow researchers to evaluate the extent to which a strategy reflects particular descriptive characteristics. The problem is that there is little agreement among researchers as to which dimensions are the most useful for describing persuasive strategies. Persuasive strategies have been organized on dimensions ranging from: 1) **powerful to powerless;** 2) **polite to impolite;** 3) **direct to indirect;** 4) **reward-oriented to punishment-oriented;** and 5) **modified to the listener's needs to focusing on the persuader's needs.**[10]

Perhaps the best way to make sense of research on persuasive strategies is to consider the factors that influence strategy selection. This focus allows us to draw some conclusions regarding when particular strategies are likely to be employed. We will discuss the effects of five factors on strategy selection: situations, goals, communication ability, personality characteristics and politeness.

Situational Factors and Strategy Selection

Situational factors may influence what type of message strategy a persuader employs. There are numerous factors that define the persuasive situation, including: the relationship between speaker and receiver; rhetorical conventions and situational ethics; the historical, political, and cultural conditions defining the situation; and the dominant issue plaguing the receivers.

The **relationship among communicators** may influence the selection of positive or negative persuasive strategies.[11] Persuaders are more likely to use friendly persuasion strategies, such as liking and pre-giving (see Box 5.2) in interpersonal situations, and to use more blunt and negative strategies in impersonal situations. Interpersonal situations are those in which you have an existing friendship or long-term contact with the other person, and impersonal situations are those in which you communicate to strangers. Bluntly direct requests and threatening strategies may accomplish the persuasive objectives but are unlikely to enhance the relationship with the message recipient.

Rhetorical conventions and ethics may influence the specific positive or negative strategy that will be acceptable in a given situation. **Rhetorical conventions** are those rules of communication that establish what is or is not appropriate behavior. We know that a deep burp may break the social ice at a loud, informal party, but it is unlikely to achieve the same goal at a formal dinner. Moreover, **ethical constraints** may dictate the acceptance of persuasion strategies. As discussed in chapter 3, a disenfranchised group with little social power may be more likely to employ unethical persuasion strategies than a group that has the support of the social order.

Other situational factors that communicators should consider before selecting a persuasive strategy are the **historical and political context,** the **social and cultural context,** and the **issues dominating the situation.**[12] If you seek to increase feminist activism on your college campus, you might use direct, agitational strategies to reawaken people who are aware of the historical, political, and social development of feminist issues in America. If you seek to increase feminist activism in the Caribbean, you must broach the subject much more carefully, because receivers are not likely to expect or readily accept your message. Historically and politically, women in Caribbean cultures have fewer rights than their American counterparts. The social and cultural climate is one in which a married woman is submissive to her husband. Women's issues are not widely discussed. One of the dominant issues facing women in these cultures is the double standard by which men's extra-marital affairs are culturally condoned and are expected to be tolerated. This issue might be a foundation upon which you could base your feminist arguments and persuasive strategy.

Overall, the research on persuasion suggests that situational information alone does not explain the selection of message strategies. Situational factors, such as historical, political, and cultural issues, are probably more important in the selection of persuasion strategies in formal speaking situations than in interpersonal situations. It is also possible that people differ in their reliance on situational information in selecting strategies, or perhaps the personality and skills of the persuader supersede situational influences.[13] That is, a skilled persuader will have more strategy options in any situation. Suffice it to say that situational information does influence strategy selection, but situational factors alone are not sufficient to predict what strategy a persuader will use.

Recognition of Goals and Strategy Selection

Since situational information did not clearly reveal what type of strategy a persuader would select, researchers turned to other explanations. A number of studies suggest that the salience of particular types of goals influence the characteristics of the persuasive strategy selected.

Ruthe Ann Clarke found two goals that are predictive of message selection: **self interest** in the outcome and **desire for being liked.**[14] If you desperately want tickets to a sold-out concert (activating high self-interest goals) you will chose persuasive strategies that exert pressure (e.g., reminders of debts owed and threats). If you are attempting to acquire these tickets from a friend (activating desired liking goals), the strategies you choose must appeal to the relationship (e.g., altruism, esteem, and self-feeling strategies).

A number of studies have found that persuasive strategies differ according to goal focus. Consider the situation of presenting a proposal to a business client. When the **task goal** is the central focus, people will use more logical strategies and are more likely to employ aggressive strategies. Thus, the proposal might be presented in a direct, logical, and serious manner—"use our business, here's what's in it for you." When **self-identity goals** (e.g., creating a good impression) are salient, people employ less direct strategies and try to assess the effects of the strategies prior to message production. In this case, the business proposal might be presented with high-tech graphics and in a manner that displays the presenter's wit and intelligence. Heightened awareness of **relationship goals** (e.g, maintaining a friendship) prompt the selection of positive, rather than negative, strategies and the avoidance of blunt requests.[15] In this scenario, the presenter might joke with the client, attempt to get to know the client better, and make the presentation in a less formal manner.

It has probably occurred to you that a person might recognize multiple, perhaps even conflicting, goals in a situation. Both task and relational goals are apparent in negotiating a job salary. Should you reveal the salary you want and make this request very directly, thereby facilitating the task? Or should you protect yourself from rejection (self-identity goal) by avoiding the request? Or should you protect your relationship with your boss by using hints, an approach that jeopardizes the task? When confronted with conflicting goals, a communicator's ability often determines strategy selection.

Ability and Strategy Selection

When people are presented with a list of message strategies and asked to select which strategy they would use in a given situation, their choices tend to be socially desirable.[16] That is, people pick message strategies that are nice. When people are asked to generate their own message strategies (without a list to consult), the messages they write are not nearly as nice. This suggests that people have the ability to recognize a good persuasive strategy that attends to self-identity and relationship goals, but that far fewer people have the ability to generate a message that accomplishes multiple goals.

In fact, Barbara O'Keefe proposes three ability levels that distinguish people according to their ability to address multiple and conflicting goals in a persuasive message.[17] O'Keefe argues that people differ in their ability to reason from goals, to strategies used to accomplish these goals. O'Keefe refers to people who comprise each of these three ability levels as expressives, conventionals, and rhetoricals. **Expressive communicators** are people who select one goal when confronted with multiple goals in a situation. The goal expressives usually select is the primary task goal. **Conventional communicators** separate conflicting goals. Thus, part of the conventional's message addresses the task goal, and part of the message addresses the relationship goal. The **rhetorical communicator** who is able to integrate both task and relational goals simultaneously into a single message demonstrates the greatest communication ability.

Particular types of message strategies (Box 5.2) characterize each ability level. The expressive communicator is more likely to use verbal aggression, obscenities, and explicit directives. In contrast, the conventional communicator, attempting to balance both task and relational goals, is likely to use polite strategies and indirect hedges. The rhetorical communicator attempts to use creative message strategies that redefine reality so that no conflict between task and relationship goals exists.

Ralph is confused about his relationship and wants to break up with Bitsy. As an **expressive communicator,** Ralph has the ability to select only one goal, so he selects the primary task goal—"break up with Bitsy." Ralph will focus his message on the task and will be direct: "Bitsy. I want to break up now. I have to choose a graduate school and I can't let our relationship

BOX 5.2   *Communicator Styles and Goal Management*

Goal management

Communicator style	Selection	Separation	Integration
Expressive	direct messages explicit anger task focus		
Conventional		indirect message politeness forms separate task and relationship goals	
Rhetorical			direct but inoffensive message redefine situation to avoid conflict accomplish task and relationship goals simultaneously

get in my way." This message strategy efficiently accomplishes the task but forsakes self-identity and relationship goals.

If Ralph were a conventional communicator, his message would be more polite. As a **conventional communicator** Ralph could address both task and relational goals by breaking the message into two parts: "Bitsy, I really like you, and I want us to be friends . . . even after I tell you what I have to tell you. Bitsy, I don't want to hurt you, but [switch from relationship to task] I want to break up. It's time for both of us to think about our careers." As you can see, Ralph-the-conventional-communicator essentially uses two message strategies—one that addresses the relationship goals and one that addresses the task goals.

With even greater ability, Ralph would be able to generate a **rhetorical** message strategy that integrates task and relational goals. How can Ralph redefine the situation so that there is no longer a conflict between relational and task goals? How can he produce a message that accomplishes the break-up with Bitsy but simultaneously maintains a good relationship and makes him look like a great guy? "Bitsy, I want you to be able to pick the best law school, without having to worry about my finding a graduate program in the same city. You are bright and talented and have a great career before you, and you can't make the decisions you need to make with our relationship clouding your vision. The best thing I can do for you right now is to get out of your way. Maybe after you get settled and I get settled, we can re-evaluate our relationship, but for now it will be best for both of us if we make a clean break." Though this is a less direct way to accomplish the task, Bitsy might leave with a more favorable attitude toward Ralph and their relationship than she would with either the expressive or conventional messages.

O'Keefe's research demonstrates that communication ability determines what message strategies communicators are likely to select. Some people have the ability to address multiple goals in messages; some people do not. When confronted with conflicting goals, the expressive communicator is overwhelmed and **selects** task-oriented strategies, often blundering the relationship. The conventional communicator **separates** task and relational goals by using politeness strategies and hedges, and the rhetorical communicator **integrates** task and relational goals by creating a persuasive strategy that accomplishes both. It is not enough to recognize persuasive goals—the persuader must also have the ability to translate these goals into message strategies.

Personal Characteristics and Message Strategy Selection

There are innumerable characteristics that may be related to message strategy selection in compliance-gaining situations. We will discuss three individual characteristics that have received considerable research interest: rhetorical sensitivity, locus of control, and interpersonal cognitive complexity.

Rhetorical Sensitivity

The categorization of expressive, conventional, and rhetorical communication styles reflects a progression from very self-centered strategies (expressive) to an approach that reflects the needs of others (rhetorical). In addition to communication ability, personality characteristics can also influence this difference in strategy selection. Rhetorical sensitivity, for example, is a trait that reflects people's ability to acknowledge the needs of others and to monitor their communication messages according to the responses of others.[18] People who are individualistic and self-absorbed in their communication are called **noble selves,** and people who constantly monitor and change their behavior based on the reactions of others are called **rhetorical reflectors.** In contrast, people who seek understanding and take the perspective of others are labeled **rhetorically sensitive.** The trait of rhetorical sensitivity provides a nice parallel with O'Keefe's three communication ability levels. We would expect a noble self, who does not analyze the effects of a message on the receiver prior to delivering the message, to be an expressive communicator. Rhetorical reflectors, who constantly change their self presentation to please others, are likely to be conventional communicators. And, many—although not all—people who are rhetorically sensitive and take the perspective of others can achieve the skills of the rhetorical communicator. A person's level of rhetorical sensitivity does appear to be a logical predictor of the type of persuasion strategy a person is likely to choose.

Locus of Control

Locus of control is a personality characteristic that reflects people's perceptions of the degree to which they control their lives. People with an **internal locus of control** believe that they have greater ability to change events in their lives than people with an **external locus of control,** who believe that they have little influence over life's circumstances. Locus of control influences message selection strategy because people with an internal locus of control perceive that they are more effectual in changing the attitudes, beliefs, and behaviors of others. It follows that people with an internal locus of control are more likely to analyze their persuasion goals and use these goals strategically to select message appeals.[19]

Studies have shown that people with an internal locus of control are less likely to use threats or coercion in persuasion and are more likely to use cooperative, encouraging, understanding, and assertive tactics. People with an external locus of control may have less confidence in their ability to influence others and therefore feel compelled to manipulate power, either through the use of competitive and aggressive strategies, or through flattery and subservience. Locus of control differences may explain why different bosses use different types of messages to influence subordinates; bosses with an external locus of control may feel less secure in their abilities to influence others, and may therefore employ threats and punishments; bosses with an internal locus of control may feel more confident in their abilities to persuade and, consequently, use positive and supportive strategies.[20]

In sum, how people perceive their ability to control and influence life situations predicts the likelihood of their selecting particular types of message strategies. Locus of control is a characteristic that predicts a great deal of variance in message strategy selection. People with an external locus of control seem to overestimate the need for force or coercion in effective persuasion, whereas people with an internal locus of control believe in their effectiveness to such an extent that they can use more subtle strategies.

Interpersonal Cognitive Complexity

People may be characterized as either high or low in interpersonal cognitive complexity. One's interpersonal cognitive complexity influences how one forms impressions of other people. People with a **high level of interpersonal cognitive complexity** employ a greater number of personal characteristics to evaluate others. Furthermore, people with a high level of interpersonal cognitive complexity integrate both good and bad dispositional traits in their evaluations of others. If you are cognitively complex in regard to other people, you may have twenty-five or more different personal criteria upon which you evaluate other people, such as your roommate: friendly, generous, serious, intelligent, hard working, attractive, and so on. Moreover, you may acknowledge and integrate both good and bad traits: "My roommate is a very serious thinker but has a limited sense of humor," and "My roommate is very generous with others but has no ability to manage his finances."

In contrast, people **low in interpersonal cognitive complexity** may use a small number of personal characteristics to evaluate others and may bias their evaluation as all good or all bad. I've heard some low complexity college students who use only two interpersonal dimensions to evaluate potential friends: "Is the person rich?" and "Is the person physically attractive?"

Interpersonal cognitive complexity influences the selection of message strategies in persuasion situations in several ways. A person high in interpersonal cognitive complexity has greater insight into other people's dispositions and characteristics. This helps the cognitively complex person to second-guess the listener's reaction and select message strategies that take the listener's perspective.[21] In general, people with higher levels of interpersonal cognitive complexity are more likely to address relational and task goals in selecting a message strategy, and are more likely to be effective interpersonal persuaders.[22]

Social Politeness Rules and Strategy Selection

Numerous studies of message strategies have noted that messages vary in the extent to which they are direct (less polite) or indirect (more polite). Hinting at a request may be more polite ("This hot weather sure works up a thirst!") than a direct request ("Give me a glass of soda.") Politeness is also related to *losing face*. If you use a direct message strategy, you may *lose face* or *threaten the face* of another person.

Brown and Levinson introduced the concept of **face** to communication and persuasion studies. "Face" is your social worth—that is, your perceived value in the eyes of others. If other people perceive you to be an "okay person," you have a favorable image—you have "face." On the other hand, if other people perceive you in a negative way, your *face*, or social worth, is diminished. Your *face* may be increased or decreased by the situation you are in and the people you are with. When you return to a fancy party with toilet paper stuck to your shoe, you have "lost face."

In interaction you strive to maintain your face (social worth), and you cooperatively help other people to avoid *losing face*. One way to maintain *face* in persuasive situations is to use **indirect message strategies.**[23] Indirect messages allow you to state your opinions and beliefs without threatening other people's esteem or power.

BOX 5.3   *Direct and Indirect Message Strategies*

Example message

Direct

Baldly on record:	"Can you stop smacking your gum!"
Positive politeness (no embarrassment)	"Hey! (laugh) Your mouth sounds like the 4th of July and I've gotta take this test!"
Negative politeness (no imposition)	"I'm sorry to bother you, but if it's not too much trouble could you kind of soften the gum sounds—I can't concentrate. . . ."
Off-record request	"Hummm . . . (exasperation) (move around in chair noisily) I can't concentrate!"
Avoid request	No message

Indirect

Two types of *face* come into play in persuasive situations: positive face and negative face. **Positive face** is social acceptance and approval. **Negative face** is free will and power. In communication encounters we strive to protect our own and others' positive and negative face. If "Crash" asks you to lend him your car, your negative face has been threatened—Crash has made a request that threatens your free will and power to control the use of your car. If "Crash" argues that he is a better driver than you are, he has threatened your positive face—your social acceptance.

Brown and Levinson propose that persuasive message strategies can be categorized according to the degree to which they are direct or indirect, and the degree to which the strategy is a threat to a listener's positive or negative face.[24] Any persuasive request is inherently threatening to the positive and negative face of the target. You may redress a threat to negative face by acknowledging how your request imposes on the persuasive target (e.g., "I don't want to put you on the spot, but could I borrow your class notes sometime before the test"). You may redress a threat to positive face by recognizing how important the persuasive target is to you (e.g., "You are the best notetaker in the class. Can I borrow your notes tonight?"). Box 5.3 provides examples of messages which vary in level of directness—ranging from avoiding making the request to stating the request baldly on-record.

In a persuasive situation, the directness of the message strategy and, consequently, the focus on positive or negative face depends upon several factors: 1) how **considerate** you are of the *face* of the listener; 2) the nature of your **relationship** with the person you are trying to persuade; 3) the **power or status** you have relative to the other person; 4) the **size of the request** ; and 5) the **situation**.[25]

If you have little regard for another person's *face* needs, you are more likely to use a direct message strategy. You may have a personality that places little value on considerateness, or you may perceive that accomplishing your task warrants trashing another person's "face." Traditionally, doctors have used direct message strategies to convey orders to nurses. This direct communication is clear—a less direct message might be misunderstood. Moreover, the direct message takes less time to generate and encode. The desire to validate the nurses' social worth and not to impose on the nurses' free will is considered secondary to efficiency in patient care.

Tae Seop Lim's research has demonstrated how persuasive strategies differ according to the relationship between the persuader and target.[26] Lim has found that we are most likely to use direct strategies that attack the ego and esteem (positive face) of a persuasive target when we have either an impersonal or a highly intimate relationship with the target. In other words, we are likely to be rude to people we do not know well (e.g., sales clerks and waiters), or to the people we know most intimately (e.g., parents, siblings, and lovers). It follows that we are most likely to be polite with people we have moderately intimate relationships with (e.g., acquaintances and social friends).

We are most likely to use direct requests that impose on the target (threaten negative face) if we know the target well. We somehow believe that it is our relational right to impose on significant others and family members, when we would balk at making the same request of a friend or acquaintance. We assume that our intimates have an obligation to comply with our requests. For this reason, even if an intimate rejects a request, we are likely to repeat the request directly, make counter offers, amplify our needs, and elaborate upon the intimate's obligations to us.[27]

If we have interpersonal power in a relationship, we are more likely to use direct messages. People in power are less concerned about imposing on others or validating others' social worth. In situations in which we have little power, we are likely to use indirect messages so that we do not offend or threaten the person in power.

The size of the request also determines the extent to which a message will be direct or indirect. As the size of the request increases, the imposition on the receiver increases, and we are likely to counter this imposition with an indirect message. Large requests require the persuader to flatter the receiver (build up positive face) and decrease the perceived imposition on the receiver (redress negative face).

A final consideration in determining the use of direct message strategies is the communication situation. Robin Lakoff describes three situations: distance situations, deference situations, and camaraderie situations.[28] In **distance situations,** the relationship is perceived to be equal, but is governed by formality and rules. Personal involvement is minimized in distance situations by using formal grammar and low intensity language. Indirect message strategies are most common in distance situations. Communication

Different communication strategies are employed in distance, deference, and camaraderie situations. (a) This welcoming ceremony for Americans visiting Kazahkstan suggests a distance situation governed by formal communication rules. (b) This deference situation of an American professor interacting with preschoolers in Kazahkstan, is characterized by unequal power. As is typical for a deference situation, the children's communication is restrained, respectful and polite. (c) Communication in camaraderie situations, as exemplified by this gathering of college friends, is informal, direct, personal and flexible.

a)

b)

c)

in **deference (low power) situations** is characterized by reliance on questions over statements, raised inflections, and indirect message strategies. In contrast, **camaraderie situations** are characterized by direct strategies. Camaraderie communication illustrates a "new form of politeness," according to Lakoff. This is the type of communication used with your friends; it assumes no power threat; it is open, direct, and peppered with understanding checks such as "y'know?" and "I mean. . . ."

As you can see, a person who selects a direct message strategy may be addressing task goals at the expense of relational goals. Or a person may be so concerned about being polite that the request is avoided, or relationship goals are addressed at the expense of the task. In general, the most effective message strategies fall in the middle of the direct-indirect continuum and make amends to the positive and negative face threats that making a request creates. These strategies acknowledge both the social worth of the receiver and the imposition placed on the receiver.

From our discussion we can conclude that situational variables, the persuader's recognition of goals, communication abilities, locus of control, cognitive complexity, and politeness all influence what message strategy communicators will select in a persuasive encounter.

The weight of this research leads us to conclude that no single factor is sufficient for predicting what message strategy persuaders will select. Rather, a unique combination of speaker, receiver, and situational variables determines message strategy selection. Consequently, we see both individual differences and cultural similarities in the selection of persuasive strategies. Individual differences in abilities, traits, and goals explain why different people select different strategies. Yet cultural face-saving rules predict the selection of socially appropriate message strategies.

MODIFICATION OF GOALS AND STRATEGIES IN INTERACTION

Our ability to predict and explain individuals' selection of persuasive goals and strategies becomes increasingly complicated when we consider that goals and strategies often change in the course of, and as a result of, communication with the persuasive target. To understand message production fully we must explore the goals and strategies of the speaker, the goals and strategies of the receiver, and the ways in which the interaction between speaker and receiver results in changes in communication goals and strategies.

Changing Goals and Strategies as a Result of Receiver Resistance

If a goal or strategy is meeting resistance, there are four ways a persuader may respond: 1) replace the goal or strategy with a new goal or strategy; 2) modify the original goal or strategy; 3) disengage from the interaction, and abandon pursuit of a goal; or 4) be oblivious to the resistance or the need for change, and relentlessly maintain an ineffectual goal or strategy.[29] Let's consider each of these four responses in detail.

Though it is certainly possible to **replace a goal or strategy** with a different goal or strategy during the course of a conversation, this is relatively rare. It is much more likely that the speaker will adhere to the original goal (e.g., get a date) but test alternative message strategies (e.g, promises, rewards, etc.) to reach the goal.

The persuader may **modify** an original goal or strategy during interaction to reflect the reality of the situation and the likelihood of success. For example, the persuader may expand a goal (e.g., get a date and get the person to drive) or reduce a goal (e.g., just get the person to agree to meet at the party).

The third response, **disengagement** from the interaction, may be behavioral or mental. Disengagement occurs when the speaker physically or mentally exits the conversation and abandons the influence attempt. Behavioral disengagement is readily observed—the persuader physically leaves, refuses to listen to the response of the receiver, and/or acts bored in an effort to end the interaction. Mental disengagement may not be as easy to observe, but the effect is the same—the persuader has abandoned the persuasive goal. The persuader may mentally disengage from a conversation by daydreaming or engaging in task-irrelevant thinking. If the thwarted persuader exhibits anger, disappointment, or frustration, these may be last ditch attempts to secure compliance and are therefore signs of strategy modification, not disengagement.

Perhaps the most interesting response is when the persuader appears unaware of the ineffectiveness of the strategies used and **pursues the same strategy** over and over. This response may be the result of previous successes in wearing the receiver down, lack of communication skill, or an anxiety that effectively freezes the brain's production of alternative strategies.

Changing Goals and Strategies as a Result of Persuader Abilities

There are several reasons a speaker's goals and strategies might change during interaction.[30] The speaker may become **distracted** and/or forget the intended goal—as when you call a friend and, upon hanging up, discover that you forgot to make the request or impart the information that was the initial purpose of the call. As a result of a **deficit in skill, knowledge, or motivation,** the speaker may be unable to pursue the intended goals and translate these goals into message strategies. Soap operas thrive on this scenario—lovesick characters intend to communicate their undying devotion but end up stammering, offending, and ultimately alienating their lovers. The **constraints of the situation** may also create barriers to goal pursuit. You may plan to propose to your significant other on a particular day only to discover a situation in which a rowdy group of friends has intruded on your romantic evening. A final, often overlooked, factor that may result in goal change is **anxiety.** Research has shown that

When people value goal attainment more than social appropriateness, they may resort to verbal aggression as in the case of this angry customer who could not obtain a full refund for returned concert tickets.

people who are anxious or lack confidence in goal attainment will spend less time and effort pursuing a goal, and are more likely to change or abandon their goals.[31] You may, for example, intend to tell off your boss but, as a result of anxiety, you change your communication goal upon entering the boss' office.

When Friendly Persuasion Fails

Several studies have explored what happens when a person's persuasive goals are thwarted. What determines whether a person will resort to verbal aggression or even physical abuse? There are at least three factors that help us predict the change from friendly persuasive strategies to the use of aggression: 1) the degree to which the persuader values efficiency over social appropriateness; 2) the persuader's nonverbal communication skills; and 3) the interpersonal or impersonal nature of the relationship with the persuasive target.

The meta-communication goals of efficiency (accomplish the goal as quickly and as completely as possible) and social appropriateness (maintain a favorable relationship with the persuasive target) are often at odds. When a target is resisting persuasion, and the persuader is at an impasse, the persuader may have to decide which goal is most important. If the persuader values **goal attainment** (efficiency) more than the relationship (social appropriateness), there is increased likelihood that he or she will employ verbal aggression (e.g., threats, punishments, insults, etc.).[32]

The persuader's **nonverbal communication skills** often help the persuader use more efficient and direct persuasive strategies while maintaining social appropriateness. A persuader may be able to ask direct questions or emphatically state controversial opinions if he/she accompanies the verbal messages with a smile, a laugh, or the communication of respect, understanding, or empathy. The persuader lacking the ability to encode these nonverbal messages is more likely to offend the receiver and is more likely to be perceived as aggressive.

The use of aggressive persuasive strategies is also dependent upon the **relationship between persuader and target.** A study by Mark deTurck found that if a persuader experiences resistance from an interpersonal friend, the persuader is likely to use strategies that up the ante—that is, strategies that increase rewards for the target.[33] In an interpersonal relationship, the persuader needs to cajole the receiver into compliance because the persuader values the relationship and cannot risk alienating the receiver. In contrast, when a persuader encounters resistance in interaction in a non-intimate relationship, the persuader is more likely to resort to punishment-oriented persuasive strategies. The persuader is, in effect, punishing the receiver's non-compliance.

In determining the effects of relationships on the modification of message strategies during conversation, we should not overlook the interactional nature of relationships. Regardless of the intimate or impersonal nature of the relationship, if a receiver demonstrates negative resistance (e.g., anger, belligerence, disengagement, etc.), the persuader is likely to respond in kind. Conversely, if a receiver disagrees but still listens, interacts, and communicates respect and understanding to the speaker (positive resistance), the persuader is likely to avoid aggressive or abusive strategies.

PERSUASION SCHEMAS: COMBINING GOALS AND STRATEGIES

A schema is a subset of knowledge that may be activated in a given situation to make sense of events and people's behavior.[34] A **schema** includes information regarding what type of objects, behavior, people, and messages are to be expected in a given situation or for a person assuming a particular role. Your "grandmother" schema, for example, may include images of a chubby, gray-haired woman baking goodies. Your schema may include helpful hints for communicating with your grandmother, such as talking loudly, giving a hug and a kiss in greeting, asking her about her plants and pets, and referring to current politicians as "those dirty birds."

Schemas help us to interpret messages and behavior, and schemas guide us in producing appropriate behavior and messages. You have a lecture schema and a party schema that tell you what type of behavior and events are associated with each. With the activation of your schema, you can determine, upon walking into a room, whether people are preparing for a lecture or for a party. Consider the following story:

> The procedure is actually quite simple. First you arrange things into different groups. Of course, one pile may be sufficient depending on how much there is to do. If you have to go somewhere else due to lack of facilities that is the next step . . . it is better to do a few things at once than too many . . . A mistake can be expensive as well. At first the whole procedure will seem complicated. Soon, however, it will become just another facet of life. It is difficult to foresee any end to the necessity for this task . . . but then one never can tell. After the procedure is completed one arranges the materials into different groups again. Then they can be put into their appropriate places. Eventually they will be used once more and the whole cycle will then have to be repeated. . . .[35]

This story may make little sense to you until I activate your "doing laundry" schema. Now if you reread the story, it will make sense.

Is it possible that we also have persuasion schemas that provide instructions for persuading people? Several researchers, observing similarities in people's persuasion goals and strategies, have argued that this is the case.[36] Persuasion schemas integrate situational knowledge with various goals that may be pursued in different situations, and sets of persuasive strategies that can be employed to achieve a particular goal. In other words, persuasion schemas would help us relate our knowledge of a given situation or role (e.g., go to a concert with a date) with particular persuasive goals (e.g., impress date with knowledge), and plans for translating goals into strategies and specific messages (e.g., impart anecdotes about the band members). Schemas provide a conceptual model for how situational knowledge, goals, and strategies are integrated, leading up to the generation of a persuasive message.

Researchers continue to argue whether we have one grand persuasion schema that we activate in all persuasive situations, or whether we have numerous mini-persuasion schemata that are situationally specific (e.g., a date-getting persuasion schema, a money-borrowing persuasion schema, and a job-getting persuasion schema).[37] Regardless, we can draw several conclusions regarding persuasion schemata: 1) there are individual differences in persuasion schemata; 2) there are cultural differences in persuasion schemata; 3) and there are situational differences in persuasion schemata.

Individuals differ in the number of persuasive strategies or alternative actions associated with a particular situational goal. Charles Berger argues that people differ in the complexity of their persuasive plans. More complex persuasive plans include a greater number of alternative strategies for goal attainment. We might speculate that people with more complex persuasive plans would be more effective and skilled persuaders. After all, a person with a variety of alternative actions available to pursue a persuasive goal should be able to invoke additional strategies if he/she finds a particular strategy ineffective.

Charles Berger found that this relationship between **complexity of a persuasive schema** and persuasive effectiveness is not always consistent.[38] If a person has a complex persuasive schema (including a large number of alternative actions) for a situation that is unfamiliar, the person is likely to produce a fluent persuasive message. If, on the other hand, a person has a complex schema for a familiar situation, Berger argues that the person becomes befuddled in deciding which action to pursue, and fluency in message production actually decreases. Note the obvious limitation of this study—message production fluency was the only measure of persuasive effectiveness, and there are obviously numerous variables, such as number of arguments produced and quality of arguments that also impact upon the effectiveness of a persuasive message.

Cultural differences in persuasion schema are also readily observed. In the recent Persian Gulf conflict President Bush and Iraqi leader Saddam Hussein had different goals. Bush had a typically American task-oriented goal—get Hussein out of Kuwait. Hussein had a traditionally Arabic identity-oriented goal—don't give in to a powerful Western leader. Given the variance of these goals, the only way Bush could have accomplished his task would have been to demand that Hussein stay in Kuwait; Hussein would then have had to withdraw from Kuwait to avoid giving in to a Western leader. Obviously, this example recognizes only one of many factors leading to the Gulf War and provides only a superficial analysis of cultural differences in persuasion goals. Suffice it to say that cultural differences in persuasion goals are extensive and complex, and these differences are often ignored in the analysis of conflict situations.

In addition to activating different situational goals, cultural diversity leads to the employment of different strategies, even in the pursuit of similar goals. Americans are perceived throughout the world for communication strategies that are direct, assertive, and lacking in subtlety. Americans often seek the most direct and efficient route to goal attainment, while people from other cultures, notably the Japanese, are more patient in pursuing indirect, circuitous, subtle, and ambiguous communication strategies. An American businessperson may bluster through introductions and announce intentions to enter a foreign market within a year, but the Japanese businessperson may respond with a lengthy description of the metamorphosis of the butterfly and a walk through the garden.

Persuasion schemas also vary by **situation.** Though global goals, such as making a good impression, protecting the face of the target, maintaining a relationship, and accomplishing the task may be activated in any situation, the priority of these global goals may change. To take an absurd example, the task goal of getting out of a burning house may supersede self-identity goals of not running down the block in your underwear. Yet another situational factor that influences strategy selection is the relationship between the persuader and target.

The persuasion schema is a useful concept because it helps us imagine how situational knowledge and persuasive goals and strategies interact in the generation of persuasive messages. Persuasion schemas also help us explain how persuasive goals and strategies differ among various individuals, cultures, and situations. Individuals' persuasive schemas may differ in complexity. The appropriateness of particular goals and strategies may be culturally determined. And situational factors may change the priority of persuasive goals and the perceived politeness of strategies.

SUMMARY

Communication goals and strategies are integral to our understanding of persuasion. Interpersonal influence involves the management of numerous, sometimes conflicting goals and the negotiation of goal conflicts between the persuader and the receiver. Moreover, even when sender and receiver have compatible goals, communication may break down as a result of the use of different communication strategies to accomplish the same goal.

To illustrate how communication goal differences and communication strategy differences can affect communication effectiveness, let's take a brief look at male-female interactions. A student recently observed that when she complains of school or relationship woes, a female friend will respond by empathizing and sharing similar experiences. In contrast, when she voices these same concerns, a male friend is likely to respond by offering a solution and ending the conversation. In her book, *You Just Don't Understand Me*, Deborrah Tannen explains that, as a result of cultural socialization, men and women often have different goals in advice-seeking situations.[39] Some women have a tendency to seek understanding and support, and some men have a tendency to seek quick solutions. This difference in perceived goals can lead to misunderstanding: males wonder why females don't solve their problems and move on, and females wonder why males don't commiserate with them about their problems.

Even when two or more people share the same goal, they may invoke different communication strategies to accomplish the goal. From the safety of the back seat, I quietly observed the interaction between my sister and brother-in-law when we got lost in a large city. My sister, exasperated, repeatedly suggested that we stop and ask for directions. Although we had been circling the area for over fifteen minutes, my brother-in-law, just as stubbornly, insisted that we could find our way. Though both shared a common goal—reaching their destination—they relied on different strategies to accomplish the goal (trial and error versus asking for directions).

In this chapter we have identified global persuasive goals that guide most persuasive encounters. Situational constraints, goal recognition, communication ability, and the personality of the persuader influence the selection of persuasive strategies to achieve these global goals. Adding to the complexity of our understanding of message production, we must recognize that goals and message strategies may change during the course of interaction. Persuasion is clearly bi-directional—the receiver simultaneously influences the persuader, and goals and strategies may be modified accordingly. At a conceptual level we can understand the interaction of all these factors influencing message production by imagining a schema that includes situational knowledge, persuasive goals, and persuasive strategies for achieving particular goals in a particular situation with a particular type of receiver.

Study Guide

communication goals
    three factors that influence goal selection
    four types of communication goals
    three dimensions of communication goals
    primary and secondary goals
communication strategies
    factors influencing strategy selection
        situational factors
        recognition of goals
            self-interest goals
            desired liking goals
            task, relational, and self-identity goals
        communication ability
            expressive communicators
            conventional communicators
            rhetorical communicators
            goal selection
            goal separation
            goal integration
        personal characteristics
            internal and external locus of control
            high and low interpersonal cognitive complexity
            politeness
            direct versus indirect messages
changes during interaction
    goal or strategy replacement
    goal or strategy modification
    physical or mental disengagement
    strategy repetition
    reasons for goal changes in interaction
    predictors of selection of aggressive strategies
persuasion schemas
    definition
    individual, cultural, and situational differences

Discussion Questions

1. Think about a recent communication encounter with your family. What were the apparent task, relational, self-identity, and arousal-management goals governing this conversation? Did different family members have different goals? How were these goals balanced and managed during the conversation?

2. Identify a communication goal you have had recently (e.g., to ask someone out on a date, to get a loan from your parents, to influence a social group to which you belong, etc.) Where does this goal fall on each of the three goal continuums, ranging from information-focused to social interaction, self-oriented to other-oriented, and task-focused to creating an impression?

3. Consider some of the more difficult communication situations you have experienced. What communication style best describes your behavior (i.e., expressive, conventional, or rhetorical)?

4. Brainstorm a list of situations in which you have lost positive face. What are situations in which you have lost negative face?

5. The degree to which your message strategy addresses the positive and negative face of the receiver is dependent upon your relationship, the power differential, and the size of the request. Consider situations in which you have made a request. Did you use a direct or indirect message strategy? Analyze this situation in terms of relationship, power, and size of request. Did these factors influence your strategy selection?

References

1. Wilson, S. R., and L. L. Putnam. 1990. Interaction in negotiation. In *Communication yearbook,* vol. 13. J. Anderson, ed. Beverly Hills, CA: Sage.
   Carver, C. S., and M. F. Scheier. 1990. Principles of self-regulation: Action and emotion. In *Handbook of motivation and cognition: Foundations of social behavior,* vol. 2. E. T. Higgins and R. M. Sorrentino, eds. New York: Guilford Press.
   Berger, C. R. 1988. Planning, affect and social action generation. In *Communication, social cognition, and affect.* L. Donohue, H. E. Sypher, and E. T. Higgins, eds. 93–116. Hillsdale, NJ: Lawrence Erlbaum.
2. O'Keefe, B. J., and J. C. Delia. 1982. Impression formation and message production. In *Social cognition and communication.* M. E. Roloff and C. R. Berger, eds. 33–72. Beverly Hills: Sage.
   Kline, S. L. 1984. Social cognitive determinants of face support in persuasive messages. Unpublished doctoral dissertation. Urbana, IL: University of Illinois.
3. Greene, J. O., E. Lindzey, and J. Hawn 1988. Social goals and speech fluency: Effects of number of goals on pausal phenomena. Paper presented to the annual meeting of the Speech Communication Association, New Orleans.
4. Clark, R. A., and J. C. Delia. 1979. Topoi and rhetorical competence. *Quarterly Journal of Speech,* 65, 187–206.
5. Dillard, J. P., C. Segrin, and J. M. Harden. 1989. Primary and secondary goals in the production of interpersonal influence messages. *Communication Monographs,* 56, 19–38.

6. Corsaro, W., and T. Rizzo. 1990. Disputes in the peer culture of American and Italian nursery school children. In *Conflict talk.* A. Grimshaw, ed. 21–66. Cambridge: Cambridge University Press.

7. McCann, C. D., and E. T. Higgins. 1988. Motivation and affect in interpersonal relationships: The role of personal orientations and discrepancies. In *Communication, social cognition, and affect.* L. Donohue, H. E. Sypher, and E. T. Higgins, eds. 53–79. Hillsdale, NJ: Lawrence Erlbaum.

   McCann, C. D., and E. T. Higgins. 1984. Individual differences in communication: Social cognition determinants and consequences. In *Understanding interpersonal communication: Social cognitive and strategic processes in children and adults.* H. E. Sypher and J. L. Applegate, eds. 172–210. Beverly Hills, CA: Sage.

8. Dillard, J. P., C. Segrin, and J. M. Harden. 1989. Primary and secondary goals in the production of interpersonal influence messages. *Communication Monographs,* 56, 19–38.

9. Marwell, G., and D. R. Schmitt. 1967. Dimensions of compliance-gaining behavior: An empirical analysis. *Sociometry,* 39, 350–364.

10. O'Keefe, D. J. 1990. Persuasion theory and research, 201–223. Beverly Hills, CA: Sage.

11. Hample, D., and J. M. Dallinger. 1987. Individual differences in cognitive editing standards. *Human Communication Research,* 14, 123–144.

    Miller, G., F. Boster, M. Roloff, and D. Seibold. 1977. Compliance-gaining message strategies: A typology and some findings concerning effects of situational differences. *Communication Monographs,* 44, 37–51.

12. Andrews, J. R. 1990. The practice of rhetorical criticism (pp. 16–28). New York: Longman.

13. Dillard, J. P., and M. Burgoon. 1985. Situational influences on the selection of compliance-gaining messages: Two tests of the predictive utility of the Cody-McLaughlin typology. *Communication Monographs,* 52, 289–304.

    Jackson, B., and D. Backus. 1982. Are compliance-gaining strategies dependent on situational variables? *Central States Speech Journal,* 33, 469–479.

14. Clark, R. A. 1979. The impact of self-interest and desire for liking on the selection of communicative strategies. *Communication Monographs,* 46, 257–273.

15. Hample, D., and J. M. Dallinger. 1987. Individual differences in cognitive editing standards. *Human Communication Research,* 14, 123–144.

16. Burleson, B. R., S. R. Wilson, M. S. Waltman, E. M. Goering, T. K. Ely, and B. B. Whaley. 1988. Item desirability effects in compliance-gaining research: Seven studies documenting artifacts in the strategy selection procedure. *Human Communication Research,* 14, 429–486.

17. O'Keefe, B. J. 1988. The logic of message design: Individual differences in reasoning about communication. *Communication Monographs,* 55, 80–103.

18. Hart, R. P., R. E. Carlson, and W. F. Eadie. 1980. Attitudes toward communication and the assessment of rhetorical sensitivity. *Communication Monographs,* 47, 1–22.

19. Lefcourt, H. M. 1982. Locus of control: Current trends in theory and research. 2nd ed. Hillsdale, NJ: Erlbaum.

20. Canary, D. J., M. J. Cody, and P. J. Marston. 1986. Goal types, compliance-gaining and locus of control. *Journal of Language and Social Psychology,* 5, 249–269.

21. Burleson, B. R. 1989. The constructivist approach to person-centered communication: Analysis of a research exemplar. In *Rethinking communication*. Vol. 2. Paradigm exemplars. B. Dervin, L. Grossberg, B. J. O'Keefe, and E. Wartella, eds., 29–46. Newbury Park, CA: Sage.
22. O'Keefe, B. J. 1988. *Op cit.*
23. Brown, P., and S. Levinson. 1987. *Politeness*. Cambridge, England: Cambridge University Press.
24. Craig, R. T., K. Tracy, and F. Spisak. 1986. The discourse of requests: Assessment of a politeness approach. *Human Communication Research*, 12, 437–468.
25. Brown, P., and S. Levinson. 1978. Universals in language usage: Politeness phenomena. In *Questions and politeness: Strategies in social interaction*. E. Goody, ed. 56–289. Cambridge, England: Cambridge University Press.
26. Lim, T. S. 1990. Politeness behavior in social influence situations. In *Seeking compliance: The production of interpersonal influence messages*. J. P. Dillard, ed. 75–86. Scottsdale, AZ: Gorsuch Scarisbrick.
27. Roloff, M. E., C. A. Janiszewski, M. A. McGrath, C. S. Burns, and L. A. Manrai. 1988. Acquiring resources from intimates: When obligation substitutes for persuasion. *Human Communication Research*, 14, 364–396.
28. Lakoff, R. T. 1990. *Talking power: The politics of language in our lives*. New York: Basic Books.
29. Berger, C. R. 1988. *Op cit.*
30. Carver, C. S., and M. F. Scheier. 1990. *Op cit.*
    Berger, C. R. 1988. *Op cit.*
31. Carver, C. S., and M. F. Scheier. 1990. *Op cit.*
32. O'Keefe, B. J. 1988. *Op cit.*
33. deTurck, M. A. 1985. A transactional analysis of compliance-gaining behavior: Effects of noncompliance, relational contexts, and actors' gender. *Human Communication Research*, 12, 54–78.
34. Schank, R., and R. Abelson. 1977. *Scripts, plans, goals and understanding*. Hillsdale, NJ: Erlbaum.
35. Glass, A. L., and K. J. Holyoak. 1986. *Cognition*. New York: Random House.
36. Rule, B. G., G. L. Bisanz, and M. Kohn. 1985. Anatomy of a persuasion schema: Targets, goals and strategies. *Journal of Personality and Social Psychology*, 48, 1127–1140.
37. Schank, R., and R. Abelson. 1977. *Op cit.*
    Berger, C. R., S. H. Karol, and J. M. Jordon. 1989. When a lot of knowledge is a dangerous thing: The debilitating effects of plan complexity on verbal fluency. *Human Communication Research*, 16, 91–119.
38. Berger, C. R., et al. 1989. *Ibid.*
39. Tannen, D. 1990. *You just don't understand*. New York: Ballantine.

6

The Content of the Message

What differentiates an influential persuasive message from a mediocre one? Part of what makes a persuasive message powerful is the delivery of the message. Part of what makes a message powerful is the charisma and personality of the speaker. Yet even a charismatic speaker with a refined delivery style can produce a mediocre message. There are clearly some characteristics of the message itself that enhance its effectiveness.

In this chapter we will explore the construction of a persuasive message. The persuader faces three decisions in the construction of a persuasive message: 1) What type of appeal will be used to motivate the receiver? 2) What type of reasoning will be used to support claims? and 3) How will the message be organized?

The purpose of this chapter is to make you a more effective (and ethical) persuader and to make you a more wary receiver. Knowledge regarding the construction of a persuasive message helps you to pick the best persuasive appeal for a particular persuasive task, to use ethical and effective reasoning in presenting evidence for your claims, and to organize your message to promote the greatest impact. As a receiver, you should know how persuaders use different types of appeals to motivate audiences. You should be able to identify fallacious reasoning. And you should recognize that the organization of a message can change the persuasive impact.

PERSUASIVE APPEALS

There are various ways of defining and categorizing persuasion appeals. A persuasive appeal is essentially a method of motivating the receiver. An appeal leads the receiver to evaluate a message with a particular mindset.

A discussion of persuasive appeals must necessarily begin with Aristotle. He was the first to outline the **three types of proof** that constitute the "available means of persuasion." Following our discussion of logos, pathos, and ethos, we will analyze a more recent approach that outlines **three methods of motivating** a receiver. Our discussion of persuasive appeals would not be complete without also analyzing the use of fear and humor appeals that are designed to elicit an **emotional response** from the receiver.

Logos, Pathos and Ethos

According to Aristotle there are three types of proof that a persuader may incorporate into a persuasive message: appeals to logos, pathos, and ethos.[1] An appeal to **logos** depends upon logic, (note the similarity in word form: logos = logic). A logical appeal is structured according to the rules of logic. One example of a logical structure is the "If A, Then B" format: "*If* you lie in tanning beds for prolonged periods of time, *then* you increase your chances of skin cancer." Another example of a logical appeal is: "All people are animals. All animals stink. Therefore, all people stink."

As you can see, a logical appeal is not always logical in the rational sense. A logical appeal is merely structured in a logical format. Often the mere form rather than an analysis of the *content* of a logical appeal persuades people—"Why, that politician/minister/salesman sounds logical to me, Myrtle!" The ethical persuader and the wary receiver must remember that the real *proof* of an appeal to logos lies in the content, not just the form, of the message. Unethical persuaders may purposely try to mislead receivers by presenting an illogical argument in a logical format or by presenting a lot of arguments, hoping that the receiver doesn't recognize the low quality of the arguments.

In discussing logos, Aristotle illustrates a logical pattern called a **syllogism.** A broad claim is presented, and this broad claim is then applied to a specific case. If the major premise (the broad claim) and the minor premise (the specific case) are true, then a logical conclusion follows. Syllogisms, as exemplified in the "all people stink" argument above, can take the following form: 1) If A is B; and 2) If B is C; 3) therefore, A is C. If you agree with the major premise that "all people are animals," and if you accept the minor premise that "all animals stink," you should conclude that "all people stink!" If, however, either of the major or minor premises is false, the conclusion is also false.

A similar logical pattern called **enthymenes** are often used in persuasion. An enthymene is an incomplete syllogism. An enthymene may include the premises of a logical argument and leave the receiver to draw the logical conclusion. For example, if the police announce that 90 percent of serial murderers seek young women victims, and that they have just received a letter from a person who claims to be a serial murderer living in the city, you are likely to make the conclusion that young women in this particular city are at risk.

Persuaders often use enthymenes to promote the receiver to persuade him or herself. Advertisers, for example, use enthymenes in advertising high-fiber products. Relying on the major premise that high fiber prevents cancer, advertisers market breakfast cereals as a source of fiber. We the consumers are led to conclude that a particular cereal product prevents cancer. Recognizing the absurdity of some of these advertising claims, Saturday Night Live spoofs these ads in a mock commercial promoting a new breakfast cereal called, "Colon Blast!"

An appeal to **pathos** plays upon one's passions (pathos = passion). According to Aristotle, the proof of a persuasive message may lie in the extent to which the message activates receivers' passions (Figure 6.1). Aristotle describes appeals to pathos as those that activate listeners' virtues, such as courage, wisdom, generosity, self-restraint, justice, and prudence in judgement. In modern terms, we speak more of values than virtues. A speaker could invoke pathos by appealing to our values of equality, family, religion, world peace, or environmental preservation.

An appeal to pathos is usually highly descriptive and dramatic, inciting the receiver to experience vicariously the condition described. The activation of people's passions can be transferred to the support of a specific persuasive goal. For example, I might persuade you to contribute to a fund for veterans by arguing that we should be loyal to our service people, just as they have demonstrated their loyalty to us:

> During WWII, a troop ship carrying 524 soldiers, the S.S. Dorchester, was struck by a torpedo. As the ship began to sink, the men jumped overboard, grabbing onto life jackets, floating debris, or life boats. There were too few life jackets, however, for the number of soldiers on the ship. Four Army chaplains, a Catholic priest, a Jewish Rabbi, and two protestant ministers gave their life jackets away, making a conscious decision to go down with the ship. As the soldiers floated away from the sinking ship, they watched and listened to the four men who had sacrificed their lives. The four held hands and prayed, as the flames and waves engulfed them.

Employing a testimonial, a story, or an anecdote activates the receivers' passions by allowing the receiver to experience a situation vicariously. Experience is a powerful persuader, and to the extent the audience is drawn vicariously into the experience, they suspend criticism and resistance. The Dorchester anecdote is likely to elicit a more spontaneous reaction from the audience, than is the dry presentation of arguments supporting patriotism and support for veterans.

An award-winning television ad for the Missing Children Help Center presents another emotional example of the use of pathos in persuasion. The ad begins with snapshots of a beautiful young child. The voices of the parents who are reliving the memories—the first day of school, Cindy's first puppy—are interspersed with the sound of the parents' voices, first inquisitive, then becoming increasingly hysterical, calling "Cindy? Cinnndy?? Cinnnnddddyyyy!!" The ad ends with an empty page in the photo album and the frantic cries of the parents. Each semester that I show this ad, I (and usually a few of my students) am wiping away tears by the end of the thirty-second commercial. The appeal to pathos is so powerful that viewers vicariously experience the parents' terror and grief.

Aristotle's third mode of persuasion, **ethos,** concerns the credibility of the persuader. Aristotle believed that a speaker must have three merits: good sense, good moral values, and good will. Good sense guarantees that the persuader employs sound reasoning and makes wise decisions. Good moral values ensure that the speaker employs his or her persuasive skills for only ethical purposes. And good will suggests that the persuader has the audience's interests at heart and seeks the outcome that is best for the audience. As you can see, ethos is intricately tied to ethics.

Persuaders use appeals to ethos to establish their expertise, trustworthiness, or goodwill. Though a persuader may use ethos to persuade receivers that he or she is ethical and has the receivers' best interests at heart, persuaders may use ethos to deceive. Jim Bakker's attempt to maintain his loyal television audience following his indictment is an appeal to ethos: "I went into this courtroom innocent of the charges against me, and I come out today still innocent of the charges against me."[2] In a last ditch effort Bakker changed tactics from Christian martyr to sorry sinner in his attempts to salvage his pock-marred image: "I'm deeply sorry for the people I have hurt. I have sinned. I have made mistakes. But never in my life did I intend to defraud anyone."

Appeals to ethos are also frequently used to undermine the credibility, trustworthiness, or expertise of others. The Willie Horton Ad, which ran in the 1988 presidential election, is likely to become a classic advertisement—and will be used as an example of a credibility attack for many years to come. The ad, sponsored by Republicans, featured a picture of Willie Horton, a murderer who escaped from a Massachusetts prison while participating in a prison release program. The escape occurred during the Democratic opponent's tenure as governor of Massachusetts. The ad shows Willie Horton passing through a revolving door—associating the Democratic candidate with a revolving door policy on crime. The ad clearly threatened the Democrat's credibility.

Aristotle's three modes of persuasion provide an easy categorization system for persuasive appeals. Yet there are many persuasive messages that do not fit neatly into one of Aristotle's three categories. Many messages meld emotion with logic and ethos. Consider the message, "Drinking and driving can kill a friendship!" Or consider the Partnership for a Drug-free American's ad: "This is your brain. This is your brain on drugs (frying egg in pan)." The structure of the messages are logical, but the implications are emotional.

Motivational Appeals: Sanctions, Needs, and Rationales

Schenck-Hamlin, et al. have proposed an alternative system for class-ifying persuasive appeals.[3] Schenck-Hamlin, among others, suggests that we should distinguish between appeals and the manner in which the ap-peal is presented. The same type of appeal (a fear appeal, for example) could be presented in a logical format ("Tobacco causes cancer in labora-tory animals"), an emotional format ("My 22-year-old brother is just like you. He likes music, baseball, and a good chew. Except my brother vom-its and groans in pain while we wait for him to die of cancer"), or a credibility format ("The Surgeon General of the United States has deter-mined that smoking causes cancer").

Accordingly, Schenck-Hamlin argues that there are three types of ap-peals: sanctions, needs, and rationales. Whereas Aristotle focused on how logic, emotion, and credibility may constitute the *proof* for a persuasive message, Schenck-Hamlin focuses on how sanctions, needs, and ration-ales are alternative *ways* to *motivate* receivers.

Sanctions motivate people through the use of rewards or punish-ments. Sanctions are messages that illustrate how receivers will benefit by modifying an attitude, belief, or action, or how receivers will lose by maintaining their current attitude, belief, or action. **Needs** are appeals to human motivations and values. Humans are often motivated to satisfy belonging, self-esteem, self-awareness, or self-improvement needs. Simi-larly, acceptance of a persuasive message may be associated with uphold-ing values important to the receiver, such as patriotism, hardwork, or religious doctrine. **Rationales** are appeals to evidence or support. Just as the word implies, rationales provide reasons to bolster a request. Addi-tional examples of appeals to sanctions, needs, and rationales are pre-sented in Table 6.1.

Schenck-Hamlin also argues that persuasive appeals vary according to how they are presented. Appeals may be presented in a manner that is direct or indirect, positive or negative, and dominant or equal.

The **directness** of a strategy concerns the degree to which the per-suader's intent is obvious. One could conceivably use a direct approach, "I'm going to persuade you to buy a brand new car today," or an indi-rect (tricky) approach, "I'm not really a salesperson here, but I can tell you which cars are the best value for the money." In addition to direct-ness, a persuader chooses whether to present an appeal in a **positive or negative manner**. Sanctions, for example, may be presented in a positive manner using strategies of promise and reward, rather than using the more negative strategies of threat, guilt, or warning. Persuasive appeals may also be formulated to represent varying degrees of control. **Control** refers to the extent to which the persuader is dominant, passive, or equal. When control is dominant, the receiver is restricted in his or her freedom to respond to the message and in his or her choice of action. In sum,

FIGURE 6.1   Greenpeace is known for the use of pathos in its advertising.

Farmers around the Three Mile Island and Chernobyl nuclear power plants have reported mutations, stillbirths, and sterility among their farm animals.

Unfortunately, the ill effects of nuclear power have spread to humans as well. Massachusetts residents living near the Pilgrim nuclear power plant are up to four times more likely to develop leukemia. In the Soviet Union, the death toll from Chernobyl may stretch into the hundreds of thousands, with more than a million children still awaiting medical treatment.

Yet the U.S. Council for Energy Awareness, a nuclear industry front group, wants to build hundreds of new nuclear power plants on U.S. soil. They want you to believe that there is a solution to nuclear waste.

Nothing could be further from the truth. Their "solution" to radioactive waste is to call some of it "Below Regulatory Concern" and to put it in land-fills, burn it in incinerators, recycle it into jewelry, belt buckles, and other consumer products, or just dump it down the drain.

Solar energy, wind power, and other safe sources of energy already provide us with more usable energy than nuclear power—without hundreds of billions in taxpayer dollars, without more accidents, without "routine" radiation leaks, and without the mutations.

After all, our furry friends weren't asked if they wanted nuclear power any more than you were.

For more information, contact Greenpeace Action, Suite 201-A, 1436 "U" St., NW, Washington, DC 20009.

NUCLEAR ENERGY MEANS A POISONED PLANET!
Support GREENPEACE ACTION and create a Nuclear Free Future.

Illustration by R. J. Matson for Greenpeace.

TABLE 6.1   Examples of Sanctions, Needs, and Rationales

Types of appeals	Examples
Sanctions	
fear	If you don't do this, horrible things will happen to you.
promise	If you do this, I will do something for you or give something to you.
ingratiation	I have already done nice things for you so that you will honor my request.
debt	You owe me for past favors.
allurement	Other people will reward you for this behavior.
aversive stimulation	I will continue to punish you relentlessly until you concede.
warning	Other people or events will cause you unhappiness if you don't comply.
Needs	
belonging	Other people will like you if you comply.
security	You will be safe if you comply.
esteem (positive)	Your self-worth will increase if you comply with my request.
esteem (negative)	Your self-worth will decrease if you don't comply. Other people will think less of you.
Rationales	
direct request	Please do this.
explanation	This is the logical thing to do. (Evidence provided)
hinting	I'm not going to tell you what to do.
	I'm going to give you hints until you do this of your own accord.

persuaders can present sanctions, needs, and rationales in different forms reflecting varying degrees of directness, positivism, and control (Table 6.2).

Integration of Proofs and Motivations

So how, you might ask, do Aristotle's proofs correspond to Schenck-Hamlin's motivational appeals? Logos, pathos, and ethos specify where the proof of a persuasive message resides: in the content, the emotional experience, or in the persona of the speaker. As demonstrated earlier, one could construct a sanction appeal (e.g., fear appeal to stop smoking) using a logical, emotional, or credibility proof.

Motivational appeals and proofs work in combination in persuasive appeals; different motivational appeals (sanctions, needs, or rationales) can incorporate different bases of proof (logos, pathos, or ethos) (Box 6.1). Our revised model demonstrates three types of persuasive appeals: sanctions, needs, and rationales. Persuaders may construct these appeals with any of three different types of proof: logos, pathos, or ethos. Each path of

TABLE 6.2   Persuasion Appeals that Vary in Terms of Directness, Positivism, and Control

Direct appeal:	"Vote for politicians like me who support environmental-protection legislation."
Indirect appeal:	"Today, I'm going to talk to you about a subject that I feel strongly about—environmental issues."
Positive appeal:	"We made a difference. We decreased industrial emissions in Washington County by 45 percent."
Negative appeal:	"Greenhouse gases emitted by industrialized countries increased the ozone destruction by 50 percent in just four years. You've let other issues direct your voting decisions for years—now it's time to vote for the environment."
High control:	"You are angry about environmental legislation. Vote for me and I will help you."
Low control:	"We need to join together to find solutions to our environmental problems. Organizations like yours help me by drawing my attention to important environmental legislation coming before the House. Together we can make a difference."

the model represents a different persuasive appeal available to the persuader.

It is important to note that we could present six different matrixes in Box 6.1. We could change the messages in each matrix to reflect one of six different forms: positive or negative, direct or indirect, and dominant/passive or equal.

In Box 6.1, all the messages are fear appeals. This represents a negative form of persuasive appeals. Humor, on the other hand, represents a positive form of persuasive appeals. Although it is beyond the scope of our discussion to analyze all possible combinations of proofs, motivation, and forms used to classify persuasive appeals, we will address the use of fear and humor appeals in some depth.

Fear Appeals

There are several conditions that govern the use of fear strategies for purposes of persuasion.[4] The general rule of thumb is that a moderate level of fear results in the greatest attitude or belief change. The receiver may dismiss a mild level of fear as inconsequential, and a high level of fear is too frightening for the receiver to confront, so the receiver consequently rejects it as unbelievable or unlikely. In 1983 the nuclear holocaust movie *The Day After,* in which a nuclear bomb lands on Lawrence, Kansas, aired on network television. It was a surprise to many that little attitude and belief change regarding the proliferation of nuclear weapons resulted from the movie. Research on fear appeals suggests that the fear level was so intense (millions of people instantaneously combusting on the TV screen) that people chose, for their mental health, to put the movie and its persuasive arguments out of mind.

BOX 6.1

Model of persuasive appeals incorporating Aristotle's logos, pathos, and ethos with Schenck-Hamlin's sanctions, needs, and rationales

Location of proof	Sanction	Type of appeal Need	Rationale
Logos	"Smoking causes heart disease and cancer."	"Smoking causes other people to dislike you."	"Smoking is the inhalation of carcinogins."
Pathos	"It's hard to maintain one's self-dignity lying helpless in a hospital bed with no voice box and no jaw. Don't smoke."	"Mary's doing her Christmas shopping early. She'll be dead by June. Without your life, you have nothing. Smoking throws your life away."	(direct request) "Please stop smoking, Daddy." (hint) "I want you to see me graduate, marry, and have kids, Daddy."
Ethos	"I'm Yul Brenner and I'm dying of cancer."	"I've had my larynx removed. I have to fight this cancer. So, I quit smoking. Don't wait as long as I did. Quit today."	"I'm the Surgeon General of the United States. Smoking causes cancer."

There are conditions, however, under which high levels of fear can be used.[5] One such condition is the presentation of a message by a **highly credible source.** Shortly before his death from cancer, actor and movie star Yul Brenner made a personalized television ad outlining the risks of smoking. Witnessing the debilitation of the once-powerful voice and presence of Yul Brenner made for a highly emotional and fearful ad. Yet given the credibility of Brenner and the inherent credibility of his illness, one would expect this to be a highly successful message. Receivers are less likely to dismiss a fear message as unbelievable or unlikely when it is presented by a person whom they believe is knowledgeable and trustworthy.

A higher level of fear can also be used when the message provides **reasonable solutions** to prevent the fearful consequences. These solutions should be relatively easy to adopt. Early anti-smoking campaigns showed gruesome pictures of gangrenous limbs, cancerous lips and lungs, and bald chemotherapy patients. The ads would end with the simple solution: "Quit!" These ads were not effective; for the person addicted to nicotine, "Quit!" is not an easy and reasonable solution. More effective ads provided information on steps to quitting, contacts for support groups, and anti-smoking products. A receiver asks two questions when evaluating a fear appeal: 1) How effective are the recommendations in preventing the fearful outcome? and 2) Am I capable of enacting the recommendations? In sum, the persuader can use a higher level of fear appeal when he/she provides a reasonable solution for the prevention of the fearful consequences.

Another condition influencing the reception of a fear appeal is whether or not the **risk information is specific.** The receiver is likely to process and remember more specific information. That is, concrete and explicit risks to the receiver are more likely to have an impact on the receiver's recall and consequent attitudes, beliefs, and behaviors than are vague, abstract, or uncertain risks. It follows that a higher level of fear may be used when accompanied by specific risk information.

Even with all these considerations, fear appeals are often **short-lived.** Researchers have found that the effects of fear appeals begin to dissipate within twenty-four hours, and one study reports that fear levels decreased only ten minutes after exposure to a fearful message. For this reason, it may be necessary to use a high level, rather than a moderate level of fear, assuming that a residual level of fear may be sustained to influence the receiver. Moreover, Mary Jane Smith suggests that if one desires any enduring change in beliefs or behaviors, receivers must be periodically reexposed to the fearful stimuli.[6]

Humor Appeals

Overall, in comparison tests, humor appeals are no more effective in producing attitude change than are non-humorous appeals. Advertisers even speak of the "Curse of the Clios."[7] It is a paradox in the advertising business that those ads that win awards for creativity and humor are often associated with companies, products, or advertising agencies that go out of business.

The effective use of humor in mass persuasion contexts is dependent upon several factors. First, the humor must be **relevant** to the persuasive goal; the audience must remember your product, not your joke. Second, the message has to be **funny;** the persuader runs the risk that what is funny in Chicago may not be funny in Peoria. Third, the **repetition** of humorous messages can offend your audience. And fourth, the development of a humorous idea takes **valuable air-time or copy space** that you could use to present attributes of your product or evidence for your persuasive argument.

There are fewer obstacles to the use of humor in interpersonal contexts. Effective humor can help the interpersonal persuader build **rapport** with the persuadee. People like a good sense of humor, especially when the humor is directed at a common situation or at the message source (the persuader). Humor can be effective in increasing **source attractiveness** and equalizing communicators' relationships. Humor is also effective in getting the receivers' **attention.** Research has found that when presenting a dull message, people like speakers who use humor, but

The use of humor in advertising can build receiver rapport, increase attention to the ad, and enhance perceptions of the product.

If Your Fantasies Include Large Green Lips And Well Rounded Dorsals, We've Got Your Boat.

If you're fanatical enough about bass fishing to appreciate our superior rough-water handling, innovative deck layouts, and **SKEETER** **Eat. Sleep. Fish.** one of the most performance oriented hulls on the market today, call 1-800-662-3844 for more information, and a free Skeeter brochure.

Skeeter Boats/Carmichael-Lynch

when presenting an interesting message, the use of humor has no additional impact.[8] When time is not an issue, humor can be used to produce **residual effects;** that is, the positive affect generated by the humor can place the persuadee in a favorable frame of mind for the receipt of the persuasive message. Advertisers using this principle place ads during comedy programs, hoping for residual good humor.

Though humorous persuasive strategies are effective for some persuasive ends, the effect of humor on message comprehension is equivocal. Some researchers argue that if you present a humorous message to an audience that is initially opposed to your viewpoint, you may distract the audience from thinking of arguments against your position.[9] On the other hand, if you want to teach an audience new beliefs or attitudes, or if your message is difficult to comprehend, the use of humor can be detrimental to persuasion.

In addition to selecting a type of appeal to motivate an audience, the persuader must also construct an argument, or a progression of ideas, that will elicit agreement from the receiver. In general terms, research has found that messages are perceived to be more persuasive if the message is logical, interesting, emotional, predictable, factual, not particularly concise, and not ambiguous.[10] This seems quite obvious when one considers the opposite of the message described above: illogical, boring, non-emotional, unpredictable, lacking evidence, lengthy, and vague! Nevertheless, it is not always easy to construct an effective argument or progression of ideas. At this point we will turn to the rules of reasoning for message construction guidelines.

TYPES OF REASONING

Reasoning concerns the presentation of evidence in a manner that is compelling. Consider the attorney who has all the facts to defend his or her client. It is still the manner in which the attorney ties these facts together for the jury, the manner in which the attorney lays a pattern that connects Fact A with Facts B and C, that will determine whether or not the defendant goes free. This is reasoning—a pattern of progressing from point to point to a logical conclusion. Reasoning builds the bridges that connect **claims** and **evidence.** Every claim must have evidence, support, or proof to have persuasive power. We will discuss four different types or patterns of reasoning: 1) cause-effect; 2) induction and deduction; 3) parallel case; and 4) reasoning from sign.

To elaborate each type of reasoning, we shall examine arguments used by famous trial lawyer Clarence Darrow to defend Leopold and Loeb in Chicago in 1924.[11] The legend of Leopold and Loeb was the basis for Alfred Hitchcock's psychological thriller, *Rope.* At nineteen Leopold was a graduate of the University of Chicago, and at eighteen Loeb was a graduate of the University of Michigan. Both were from very wealthy and well-known families. Leopold and Loeb beat a fourteen-year-old neighbor to death with a baseball bat—for the sport of it; they believed themselves too smart to be caught. To add spice to the trial, it was alleged that Leopold and Loeb were lovers. Darrow's argument was to persuade the judge to give Leopold and Loeb life in prison rather than death by hanging. Clarence Darrow's reasoning made this trial famous. It was this trial that established temporary insanity as a legal defense.

Cause-Effect Reasoning

In cause-effect reasoning it is asserted that an occurrence is likely to lead to a specific consequence in the future (e.g., Poor lighting on campus will lead to violent assaults). Effect-cause reasoning, the inverse, suggests that a consequence that has already occurred was caused by a particular occurrence or series of occurrences: "A careless camper caused the forest fire," or "Congressional spending caused our current economic recession," or "Increased crime rates are a result of economic recessions."

Cause-effect reasoning predicts the future, and effect-cause reasoning explains the past. In the first example Darrow employs cause-effect reasoning to predict the future, and in the second example he uses effect-cause reasoning to explain what caused the boys to commit this crime:

> "If your honor can hang a boy of eighteen, some other judge can hang him at seventeen, or sixteen, or fourteen."

> "I have spoken about the war. . . . We read of killing one hundred thousand men in a day. . . . These boys were brought up on it. The tales of death were in their homes, their playgrounds, their schools; . . . what was a life? It was nothing. It was the least sacred thing in existence and these boys were trained to this cruelty."

To evaluate cause-effect and effect-cause reasoning critically, you must question whether the connection being made between the occurrence and the consequence is logical. Is it really likely that the occurrence (cause) will produce the stated effect (consequence)? Is it likely, for example, that the death penalty for Leopold and Loeb will lead to the death penalty for younger teens in the future? In evaluating cause-effect reasoning, you should ask whether there is another cause that could produce the effect. For example, is reading about war the most logical cause of the boys' behavior, or is there some other reasonable cause?

Reasoning by Induction or Deduction

Inductive reasoning involves analyzing specific cases and drawing a general conclusion. "James Road escaped from prison and committed six murders. Darryl Knight has been convicted of murdering seven people. Can we allow murderers to kill again? The United States should implement the death penalty for all convicted first degree, multiple murderers."

When one reasons from specific to general (induction), one uses specific cases or examples as evidence and argues that the cases are representative of the whole. Do these two cases statistically represent all the multiple murderers in the United States? As a critical receiver of persuasive messages you should ask: What is the percentage of multiple murderers who are released, or escape from prison, who murder again? Before you accept this argument, you must determine if James Road and Darryl Knight are representative of most multiple murderers.

The opposite, deductive reasoning, involves applying a general principle to a specific case. For example, "No industrialized nation in the world employs capital punishment, with the exception of the United States. The United States should similarly revoke the death penalty."

When one reasons from general to specific, one progresses from a generalization that is believed to be true and applies the generalization to a specific case. Most stereotypes are born of general to specific generalizations. Conclusions (generalizations) are made about an ethnic or religious group and applied indiscriminately to specific members of that group. As a critical receiver of persuasion, you should first challenge the generalization made: Is the United States the only industrialized nation that enforces the death penalty? Is this generalization relevant to the formation of judicial policy within the United States? Before you accept this argument, you must determine if the generalization is valid and if the application of the generalization to the specific case (the U.S.) is valid.

Darrow's argument, presented below, is an example of inductive, specific-to-general, reasoning: he argues that these boys (specific) are just like all other unfortunate misled youth (general), and that mercy in this case (specific) will have great impact on human understanding and mercy (general).

> "If I can succeed, my greatest reward and my greatest hope will be that I have done something for the tens of thousands of other boys, for the countless unfortunates who must tread the same road in blind childhood that these poor boys have trod,—that I have done something to help human understanding, to temper justice with mercy, to overcome hate with love."

The next example is deductive, general-to-specific, reasoning: Darrow argues that killings throughout history were barbaric (general), and that makes the hanging of these boys barbaric (specific), and that religious doctrine condemns barbarism (general), and that religious doctrine would condemn the killing of these boys (specific).

> "For God's sake are we crazy? In the face of history, or line of philosophy, against the teaching of every religionist and seer and prophet the world has ever given us, we are still doing what our barbaric ancestors did when they came out of the caves and the woods. . . ."

Reasoning by Parallel Case

Reasoning by parallel case involves finding a situation that is similar to the current situation you are discussing. If your idea or proposal worked in a previous situation, and if the previous case is similar to the current case, then your idea or proposal should work in the current situation as well. All legal precedents are argued based on parallel case. A lawyer argues that the current case is similar in all important aspects to a previous case, and that the judge should therefore rule consistently with the previous case. In the following example Darrow argues that trying an animal is absurd. Darrow then establishes a parallel between the free will of animals and that of Leopold and Loeb. Darrow concludes that all would agree that trying an animal is absurd; therefore, trying Leopold and Loeb is absurd. (One could also contend that Darrow's argument is a bit absurd.)

> "There was a time in England . . . when judges used to convene court and call juries to try a horse, a dog, a pig, for crime . . . a story of a judge and jury and lawyers trying and convicting an old sow for lying down on her ten pigs and killing them. Do you mean to tell me that Dickie Loeb had any more to do with his making than any other product of heredity that is born on this earth?"

Receivers should critically review parallel case arguments. Are the cases being compared really similar? Are there more differences than similarities between the two cases? Do the cases differ on some critical matter that has implications for the conclusion the persuader is trying to draw? Is it reasonable for Clarence Darrow to compare trying a sow with trying Leopold and Loeb?

Reasoning from Example or Sign

People most frequently reason from example. This involves simply presenting an example to illustrate your point. Darrow argues that crimes of violence increase following times of war and supports this point by stating:

> "It will take fifty years to wipe it out of the human heart, if ever. I know this, that after the Civil War in 1865, crimes of this sort increased marvelously. . . ."

When evaluating an argument that relies upon examples, the receiver should question whether or not the examples are representative. Are the examples unusual cases? Is the speaker distorting the prevalence and importance of them?

Arguing from sign involves the use of a series of indicators from which you draw a conclusion. Trial lawyers often argue from signs: the tire tracks at the murder site that match the accused's car are a sign that the accused was present at the murder site; the gun and bullets found in the accused's car that match the bullet wounds in the victim are a sign that the accused's gun was used in the murder. We also argue from sign when making economic predictions. Economists cite signs or economic indicators in their predictions of a recession. In this case, Darrow argues that the wealth of the boys is a sign that they did not commit the crime for money:

> "These two boys, neither one of whom needed a cent, scions of wealthy people, killed this little inoffensive boy to get ten thousand dollars? . . . The

boys had been reared in luxury, they had never been denied anything; no want or desire left unsatisfied; no debts; no need of money; nothing.''

When evaluating an argument that relies upon signs, the receiver must question whether or not the signs are clearly related to the conclusion. Are the signs valid—could they be false? Are the signs merely coincidental? Could the signs predict a different outcome? Did Leopold and Loeb really have all the money they wanted? Even if Leopold and Loeb were rich, could they still desire more money?

As you can see, reasoning connects claims and evidence. Different patterns of reasoning may be used to lead receivers from evidence to claims or from claims to evidence. It is important to note (as the examples illustrate) that the use of one or more of the four types of reasoning we have discussed does not guarantee success in persuasion; nor should the receiver rely on the persuader's reasoning as an indication of truth. The quality of the reasoning may vary. In fact, the reasoning may be inherently wrong or illogical.

FALLACIOUS REASONING

A fallacy is an argument that exploits the rules of logic. The argument is not sound; this means that the conclusions may not follow from the premises, or that the evidence does not support the claim. It is unfortunate, but true, that persuaders often use fallacious reasoning. When a persuader intentionally employs fallacies to beguile an audience, this is called **sophism**. As a producer and receiver of persuasive messages you will want to be able to recognize fallacious arguments and challenge the communicators who use them. There are many types of fallacies, but we will discuss the four most common fallacies: 1) **the fallacy of generalization;** 2) **the fallacy of false cause;** 3) **begging the question;** and 4) **ignoring the issue.**

Fallacy of Generalization

As discussed earlier, one can reason inductively or deductively; that is, you may use a specific case and draw a general conclusion, or you may apply a generalization to draw a conclusion about a specific case. A fallacy of specific-to-general (**inductive reasoning**) may occur when the specific example is not representative of the whole. For example, it would be fallacious to argue that because my friends were laid off their jobs, unemployment is on the rise. My friends' jobs (specific cases) may not be representative of layoffs across the country. This type of fallacy is very common: following publicity about an airplane disaster, people argue that airline travel is unsafe. Statistically we know that air travel is quite safe; hundreds of flights reach their destination each day, and crashes are a relatively rare occurrence. Therefore, concluding that air travel is unsafe based on an example of a single airline disaster is fallacious.

A fallacy of general-to-specific (**deductive reasoning**) occurs when the generalization cannot be applied to the specific case. We know that prejudices are fallacies. Even if you believe that Germans are good mathematicians, it is fallacious to assume that Claus, a German exchange student, is likely to excel in mathematics.

Fallacy of False Cause

A fallacy of false cause occurs when the relationship between a cause and an effect are not valid. In essence, the conclusion does not logically follow from the premise. We will discuss two specific types of false cause: "affirming the consequence," and "after this, therefore because of this."

Affirming the Consequence

In an if-then statement or a cause-effect statement one asserts a consequence, "This will happen." Often, people assert consequences that are unlikely to happen. For example, Darrow argues that "if these two boys are sentenced to death, and are hanged, on that day there will be a pall settle over the people of this land that will be dark and deep. . . ." Darrow is affirming the consequence, and this consequence is not necessarily a logical or likely result of an execution.

There is always the risk of committing the fallacy of affirming the consequence when presenting a cause-effect or if-then argument. Therefore, we must be wary of the conclusions persuaders draw. Do the arguments and examples really suggest that the consequence will occur? Or does the persuader present the consequence so vividly that receivers are forgetting to evaluate the premises upon which the consequence is based?

After This, Therefore Because of This

This false cause fallacy results from an assumption that because two events follow each other in time, the first event causes the second event. If I argue that it snowed last night, and my car wouldn't start this morning, therefore the bad weather caused my car problems, I may be guilty of a fallacy. It is conceivable that my car problems are the result of mechanical defects quite independent of the weather conditions. Darrow's arguments that the war preceded the murder case, therefore the war was somehow responsible for the crime is also a fallacy.

False cause fallacies reflect illogical or invalid reasoning from premises to conclusions. Affirming the consequence and after-this-therefore-because-of-this are two types of false cause fallacies. The name "false cause" can help you remember these examples and help you to identify additional types of false cause fallacies.

Begging the Question

There are at least two ways in which one can commit the fallacy of "begging the question": by basing an argument on an erroneous assumption and by using circular reasoning. Begging-the-question is commonly used to describe an argument that cannot be falsified or counter-argued as a result of its circularity or faulty assumptions.

Erroneous Assumption

If I argue that "you can be as beautiful as Tammy Faye Bakker if you use Mary Kay make-up," I am begging the question. My whole argument is based on the assumption that Tammy Faye is beautiful! I have not stated that assumption as a premise to my conclusion; I have implied that the assumption is true without stating it. If I reasoned that: a) Tammy Faye Bakker is beautiful; b) Tammy Faye uses Mary Kay make-up; therefore c) Mary Kay make-up makes a person beautiful; and d) if you use Mary Kay make-up, you can be beautiful, too, I have presented each premise of my conclusion for your scrutiny. When persuaders base their conclusions on assumptions, we say that the persuader is "begging the question."

Let's look at another example. If I argue that "American college students can achieve educational excellence comparable to European students if the college curriculum is extended to five years," I am begging the question. The issue (increasing the quality of college graduates) is based on the assumption that American college students are not as smart as their European counterparts. The manner in which I have structured the argument precludes the discussion of whether or not American students are ill-prepared. Relying on an implicit assumption constitutes fallacious reasoning. Even if the assumption were true, I provided no evidence or support for the assumption upon which I based my conclusion.

Circular Arguments

A circular argument cannot be put to a test or disproven. A circular argument is similar to the dilemma, which came first? the chicken, or the egg? There is no way to disprove either answer. The book *Catch 22* is based on circular arguments: The Army tells the flyer that the only way he can get out of flying bombing missions is to ask to stop flying because he is crazy.[12] He says he's crazy. The Army asks, "Do you want to fly more missions?" He says, "No." The Army says, "Then you're not crazy!"

An example of how circular reasoning is used in persuasion is this: "To prevent an attack on the U.S. we must have more bombs than other countries. When we build more bombs, the other countries build more bombs, thereby increasing the risk of an attack."

Darrow uses a circular argument by reversing the prosecution's argument that the murder was particularly cruel because the victim was a boy: "Well, my clients are boys, too, and if it would make more serious the offense to kill a boy, it should make less serious the offense of the boys who did the killing."

Ignoring the Issue

The inclusion of arguments or evidence irrelevant to the primary issue can constitute a fallacy of ignoring the issue. Specifically, we will discuss two examples of ignoring the issue: appeals to pity and personal attacks.

Pity

Politicians often employ variations of this fallacy in campaign publicity. Appeals to ethnic background or modest roots are not relevant to a person's performance in office. Darrow also plays on pity in his defense of Leopold and Loeb by calling one of the murderers "Babe" and by describing the trauma the murderers' mothers were experiencing:

> "Babe took to philosophy. I call him Babe, not because I want to affect your Honor, but because everyone else does. He is the youngest of the family and I suppose that is why he got his nickname. We will call him a man. Mr. Crowe thinks it easier to hang a man than a boy, and so I will call him a man if I can think of it."

> "(their mothers) nourish them and care for them, and risk their lives, that they may live, who watch them with tenderness and fondness and longing. . . . Here is the faithful uncle and brother who have watched here day by day, while Dickie's father and mother are too ill to stand this terrific strain, and shall be waiting for a message which means more to them than it can mean to you or me."

Personal Attacks

Ignoring the issue, especially in the form of personal attacks, seems to be a frequent rhetorical device of politicians. A personal attack is a fallacy when it distracts from the primary issue, focusing attention on the alleged merits of a person, rather than the merits of the person's arguments. Darrow uses this device quite well, guilding surface compliments with caustic blows:

> ". . . my friend Mr. Savage—did you pick him for his name or his ability or his learning?— . . . I marveled when I heard Mr. Savage speak. He is young and enthusiastic. But has he ever read anything? Has he ever thought?"

Though Mr. Darrow used many fallacies in his defense of Leopold and Loeb, his fallacies did serve to persuade the judge to give Leopold and Loeb life sentences in prison rather than the death penalty. Since fallacious reasoning often goes undetected, it is often persuasive. And, because it is persuasive, you are likely to encounter fallacious reasoning on a daily basis.

As a critical receiver of persuasive messages one must constantly question and evaluate the step-by-step development of a persuasive argument. Once the type of reasoning is recognized, the validity of the reasoning should be questioned.

Thus far in this chapter, we have discussed various types of appeals that a persuader may use to motivate receivers, and various types of reasoning patterns that a persuader may use to lead receivers to accept a particular conclusion. The progression of arguments in a message is related to the organization of the message. In the following section we will explore how the organization of a message can influence persuasion.

MESSAGE ORGANIZATION

Research has shown that the sequential development of a message affects its persuasiveness. In the 1950s a group of scholars now referred to as the Yale School conducted the first systematic research experiments on persuasive messages.[13] These scholars conducted many studies of message organization effects, such as whether the strongest argument should go first (primacy effect) or whether the strongest argument should come last (recency effect). The frustration with this research is that there are unlimited conditions that may change the effectiveness of primacy or recency (when you're facing West, speaking to a group of Aborigines, etc., etc. primacy is definitely best). For this reason we will not attempt a comprehensive discussion of message organization research, but rather we will focus on two of the more interesting and useful findings on message organization: one versus two-sided arguments, and the Door-In-The-Face (DITF) versus the Foot-In-The-Door (FITD) strategy.

One- versus Two-Sided Arguments

A one-sided argument presents only one point of view—the view the persuader hopes the receiver will adopt. A two-sided argument presents the persuader's preferred position and the position of the opposition. One- and two-sided arguments are effective in different situations.

The use of a two-sided argument can enhance the persuader's credibility.[14] People perceive a two-sided argument to be more honest and trustworthy. Honesty is not always the reason a persuader chooses a two-sided argument, however. The persuader often presents strong evidence for his or her own position and presents an uncharacteristically weak version of the opposition's position. Politicians, for example, may present their own economic promises and simply dismiss their opponents' economic plans as "tax and spend."

There are certain situations in which two-sided arguments are more effective than one-sided arguments. Two-sided arguments can prepare the audience to resist future persuasion by the opposition.[15] Having presented a relatively weak version of the opposition's position, the persuader can then proceed to teach the receivers arguments against the opposition. Presidential hopeful Ross Perot uses this tactic when he claims that the Republicans and Democrats don't know how to run a business, aren't talking about the deficit, and aren't winning the economic battle with the Germans and the Japanese. When confronted with the opposition's messages in the future, the audience has preconstructed counterarguments to resist persuasion.

Two-sided arguments are also most effective when the audience is: 1) **intelligent;** 2) aware that there are **two contradictory sides to an issue;** and 3) **not already in agreement** with your position. Conversely, persuaders should use a one-sided argument when: 1) the audience is **already in favor** of your position—why confuse the issue with two-sided arguments? 2) the audience is **easily confused** on the issue; 3) the audience is **not aware of the opposition;** and 4) when **attitude change,** rather than resistance, is the persuader's primary goal.

As illustrated in Box 6.2, a one-sided message produces a greater degree of attitude change than a two-sided message. A one-sided message is a stronger, more direct way to present a new idea, whereas a two-sided message may dilute the impact of a new idea by discussing both sides of an issue. Two-sided arguments are more effective than one-sided arguments, however, in preparing the receivers to argue against the opposition. Consider the case of a politician who is behind in the polls. Under what condition should he or she use a one-sided or a two-sided argument? Why?

Sequential Message Organization

The Foot-in-the Door (FITD) and Door-in-the-Face (DITF) techniques involve sequencing requests. Using a sequential request strategy can increase the likelihood of persuasion by approximately 20 percent.[16] That is, if you had a 30 percent chance of successfully persuading a person, using a sequential strategy could increase your chances to 50 percent.

The Foot-in-the-Door strategy involves two steps: 1) presenting a small request that the receiver is likely to accept, and 2) making a second, larger request, after ascertaining the receiver's agreement to the first request. The second, larger request reflects the persuader's original goal.

BOX 6.2

The effects of one- and two-sided messages on attitude change and resistance to the opposition.

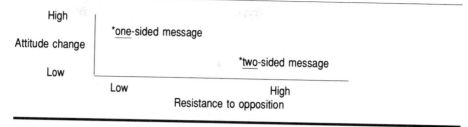

Getting the receiver to agree to a small request increases the likelihood that the receiver will agree to the larger request.

Many marketers use FITD techniques. Consider the door-to-door salesman who asks you to sign up for a free encyclopedia. After you agree to the first request, you are more likely to agree to the second request—that is, buying a complete set of encyclopedias. Interpersonally, you might use FITD to get a date. According to the FITD theory you should first get the person to agree to a small request, such as working on a class project together, and then follow up with the larger request of going out on a date.

It is generally believed that the FITD phenomenon can be explained by self-perception theory. Though some scholars have argued that self-perception theory does not adequately explain FITD processes, self-perception is clearly the best explanation we have at this point in time.[17] **Self-perception theory** suggests that we look to our behaviors to infer our attitudes and beliefs. For example, if you go to a smorgasboard and pig out, and then reflect, "My, I must have been very hungry; look how much I ate," you are acting consistently with self-perception theory; your belief was derived from your behavior.

Applying self-perception theory to FITD strategies, we would predict that people agree to the first request, reflect upon their behavior, and conclude that they are the type of person who believes in, and values, such requests. When the second request is presented, people perceive the requested behavior as consistent with their beliefs and values. The person is therefore more likely to grant the larger request. For example, according to self-perception theory, if you agree to a small request, such as signing a petition to save the whales, you may reflect upon your behavior and conclude that you are the type of person who is concerned about environmental and wildlife issues. When presented with the larger request, to go door-to-door and obtain signatures, you may be more likely to grant this request in light of your self-knowledge that you a person who is concerned about wildlife issues.

There are many conditions that influence the success of a FITD strategy. Although marketers and interpersonal persuaders often use FITD techniques for self-gain, research suggests that FITD is most effective for **pro-social causes,** when the persuader's self-interest is not apparent. In other words, you are more likely to activate FITD effects when the issue of persuasion is environmental conservation, educational benefits, or feeding the poor, rather than selling a product.

Research has also shown that giving the receiver an **incentive** for the first request essentially neutralizes any FITD benefits. Have you ever received a card offering you a gift (usually a TV, VCR, microwave, or personal computer) for visiting a time-sharing resort? These marketers are attempting to use FITD strategies but are committing grievous errors, according to FITD research. The marketers want prospective buyers to agree to a visit (first request) and then agree to buy into a time-share resort (large request). According to FITD research, providing an incentive for agreeing to the first request wipes out the effects of self-perception. If you receive an incentive for the first request, your analysis of your behavior will be that you agreed to the first request to get your prize, not because you are the type of person who is interested in time-share resorts.

Another condition influencing the effectiveness of FITD strategies is that the first and second requests must be based upon the **same self-knowledge.** The requests must concern a **similar issue or topic.** If the first request helps formulate self-knowledge (e.g., you see yourself as an environmentalist), the second request must rely upon this same self-knowledge (e.g. collect signatures to save the Great Lakes) to be effective. Likewise, if you want to get a date, don't make your first request borrowing the person's class notes and your second request going out on a date. The first request could lead to self-perceptions that the person helps out other classmates in need, rather than the perception you hope to generate, that the person likes to spend time with you.

A final consideration in structuring your FITD strategy is deciding **how large to make your first request** and the appropriate discrepancy between your small and large requests. Obviously, the larger the first request you get your receiver to agree to, the larger your second request can be. However, if your first request asks too much, and it is rejected, you stand no chance of achieving your persuasive goal. Similarly, if the discrepancy between your first and second request is too large, your second request is likely to be rejected. For example, if your persuasive goal is to get your dream date to go to Reno with you for the weekend, and your first request is to go out for coffee, the discrepancy between your first and second request is too large. However, if your first request is a date, and your larger request is a weekend in Reno, you stand a greater chance of achieving your goal.

The DITF strategy is just the opposite of the FITD strategy. The DITF strategy involves making a large request that you know will be rejected and following the large request with a smaller request that you hope to achieve. DITF strategy is usually explained by **reciprocal concessions theory.** When the receiver rejects your first request, and you counter with a smaller request, the receiver perceives that you are making a concession. Since you are making a concession, the receiver feels guilty and believes that, to be fair, he or she should also make a concession. Salespeople directly emphasize reciprocal concessions when using the DITF strategy: "O.K. I'm not going to make any money off this, and my boss is going to kill me, but I really want you to have this car. I'll make a special deal just for you. How about $7,500?"

An alternative explanation for DITF is **perceptual contrast.**[18] This explanation suggests that the second request is perceived to be smaller than the first request, and possibly perceived to be even smaller than it really is. This perception increases the likelihood that the person will comply with the request. If it is indeed perceptual contrast instead of reciprocal concessions that underlies the DITF strategy, persuaders should focus on the size of the concession: "I'll take a huge cut. You can drive this car home today for just $7,500. Don't ask me to go any lower—I might as well give the car away!"

It seems apparent that either or both reciprocal concessions and perceptual contrast may be operating to produce DITF effects. Salespeople often emphasize both concession and perceptual contrast in their appeals: "I'll meet you halfway—we'll split the difference between your offer and my sale price! How about $7,500?"

The DITF strategy is often used in negotiating contracts. The union makes a large demand that they know will be rejected. When this demand is followed by a counteroffer, the management perceives that the union is making a concession, and management also makes a concession. Similarly, time-sharing resorts start by asking $20,000 or more for a two-week timeshare and eventually offer you a special concession ("just for you!") of five or six thousand dollars.

There are several conditions necessary for DITF requests to work. First, there can be only a **brief delay** between the first and second requests. In addition, the **same person** must make both requests. If the time lapse is too long, or a new person is introduced, the receiver perceives the situation as a new bargain, rather than a continuation of the previous bargaining situation.

If both DITF and FITD strategies work to increase the likelihood of persuasion by 20 percent, which strategy should you use? If baseline compliance is less than 25 percent, you should use a FITD strategy. In other words, if your chances of persuading people are not good, then you should first "get your foot in the door." If baseline compliance is greater than 25 percent, you should use a DITF strategy. A baseline compliance of over 25 percent suggests that your receivers have some motivation to comply, and, in this situation, DITF is likely to ensure greater compliance. If people are initially against you, a DITF strategy is likely to result in rejection of both requests.

The organization of a message is an important determinant in whether or not your message will be favorably received. Depending on the situation, one might choose a one-sided message to bring about direct attitude change, or a two-sided message to enhance credibility and increase resistance to persuasion by the opposition. Also depending on the situation, one might choose a FITD strategy to lure receivers into agreeing to a second, larger request, or one might choose a DITF strategy to get receivers to perceive that you are making a concession and to get them to agree to a larger request than they otherwise might.

SUMMARY

The construction of a message is an important factor in determining its efficacy. As noted in this chapter there are many decisions to be made regarding the construction of a persuasive message. The construction of a message involves selecting message appeals, proofs, and manners of presentation. It involves supporting the argument through various types of reasoning, and then checking the validity of the reasoning. It involves organizing the message, and teaching the receiver of the message to resist persuasion by the opposition. The construction of persuasive messages is also important to the critical receiver. As targets of persuasion we must learn to recognize persuasive appeals, fallacious reasoning, and the influence of message organization on our ability to resist persuasive influences.

It is important to realize that the construction of an eloquent argument does not guarantee persuasion. The message receiver may or may not perceive the intended meaning of the message, and even if the receiver shares the intended meaning, the receiver may decide not to think, feel, or do what the message suggests. In the next chapter we discuss how to select a message for a particular type of receiver and, conversely, how to recognize when a persuader is constructing a message that targets our weaknesses.

Study Guide

logos, pathos, and ethos
sanctions, needs, and rationales
directness, positivism, and control
conditions governing use of fear appeals
conditions governing use of humor appeals
four types of reasoning
four types of fallacies
    sophism
    two types of generalization fallacy
    two types of false cause fallacy

two types of begging-the-question fallacy
two types of ignoring-the-issue fallacy
one- versus two-sided arguments
FITD and DITF organizational sequences
    conditions governing the use of FITD and DITF
    self-perception theory
    reciprocal concessions theory and perceptual contrast

Discussion Questions

1. Study the model in Box 6.1 that integrates Aristotle's classification of strategies by logos, pathos and ethos, with Schenck-Hamlin's classification of strategies by sanctions, needs, and rationales.
    a. Generate additional examples of persuasive strategies for each cell in the table.
    b. Now add a third dimension to the table—Schenck-Hamlin's three modes of presentation (direct-indirect, positive-negative, and persuader control-receiver control). Produce messages for each of the nine cells that demonstrate direct and indirect, positive and negative, and persuader control and receiver control modes of presentation.
2. Think of an advertisement that uses fear appeals. What level of fear is used in the message? Is the fear appeal persuasive or overwhelming?
3. Have you ever worked as a salesperson? How could you have used DITF or FITD strategies in your job? Which would be most effective? Why?

References

1. Roberts, W. R. 1954. *Aristotle* (A translation of Aristotle's Rhetoric). New York: Modern Library.
2. Sanders, A. L. 1979. The wrath of "Maximum Bob." *Time Magazine* (Nov. 6).
3. Schenck-Hamlin, W. J., R. L. Wiseman, and G. N. Georgacarakos. 1982. A model of properties of compliance-gaining strategies. *Communication Quarterly*, 30, 92–100.
   Wiseman, R. L., and W. J. Schenck-Hamlin. 1981. A multi-dimensional scaling validation of an inductively-derived set of compliance-gaining strategies. *Communication Monographs*, 48, 251–270.
4. McGuire, W. 1973. Persuasion, resistance, and attitude change. In *Handbook of Communication*. I. Pool, et al., eds. 216–232. Skokie, IL: Rand McNally.
   McGuire, W. 1968. Personality and susceptibility to social influence. In *Handbook of personality theory and research*. E. F. Borgatta and W. W. Lambert, eds. 1130–1187. Chicago: Rand McNally.
   Leventhal, H., R. Singer, and S. Jones. 1965. Effects of fear and specificity of recommendation upon attitudes and behavior. *Journal of Personality and Social Psychology*, 2, 20–29.
   Leventhal, H., and P. Niles. 1965. Persistence to influence for varying durations of exposure to threat stimuli. *Psychological Reports*, 16, 223–233.

Brinberg, D., and L. A. Morris. 1987. Advertising prescription drugs to consumers. In *Advances in marketing and public policy, Vol. I.* P. N. Bloom, ed. 1–40. Greenwich, CT: JAI Press.

5. Boster, F. J., and P. Mongeau. 1984. Fear-arousing persuasive messages. In *Communication yearbook 8.* R. N. Bostrom and B. H. Westley, eds., 330–375. Beverly Hills, CA: Sage Publications.

6. Smith, M. J. 1982. Persuasion and human action. New York: Wadsworth.

7. Ogilvy, D. 1985. Ogilvy on advertising. New York: Vintage Books.

8. Sternhal B., and C. S. Craig. 1973. Humor in advertising. *Journal of Marketing,* 37, 12–18.

   Gruner, C. 1967. Effect of humor on speaker ethos and audience information gain. *Journal of Communication,* 17, 228–233.

   Gruner, C. 1970. The effect of humor on dull and interesting informative speeches. *Central States Speech Journal,* 21, 160–166.

9. Osterhouse, R., and T. Brock. 1970. Distraction increases yielding to propaganda by inhibiting counterarguing. *Journal of Personality and Social Psychology,* 15, 344–358.

   McGhee, P. E., and J. H. Goldstein. 1983. *Handbook of humor research, Vol. 1.* New York: Springer-Verlag New York.

10. Hazelton, V., W. R. Cupach, and J. Liska. 1986. Message style: An investigation of the perceived characteristics of persuasive messages. *Journal of Social Behavior and Personality,* 1, 565–574.

11. Bishin, W. R., and C. D. Stone. 1972. *Law, language, and ethics: An introduction to law and legal method* (pp. 670–696). Mineola, NY: Foundation Press, Inc.

12. Heller, J. 1961. *Catch 22.* Pinebrook, NJ: Dell.

13. Hovland, C. I., I. L. Janis, and H. H. Kelley. 1953. *Communication and persuasion.* New Haven: Yale University Press.

   Hovland, C. I., et al. 1957. *The order of presentation in persuasion.* New Haven: Yale University Press.

   Hovland, C. I., et al. 1958. *Personality and persuasibility.* New Haven: Yale University Press.

14. Jones, R. A., and J. W. Brehm. 1970. Persuasiveness of one- and two-sided communications as a function of awareness: There are two sides. *Journal of Experimental Social Psychology,* 6, 47–56.

   Kamins, M. A., and L. J. Marks. 1987. Advertising puffery: The impact of using two-sided claims on product attitude and purchase intention. *Journal of Advertising,* 16, 6–15.

   Lumsdaine, A. A., and I. L. Janis. 1953. Resistance to counterpropaganda produced by one-sided and two-sided propaganda presentations. *Public Opinion Quarterly,* 17, 311–318.

15. Hovland, C. I., A. A. Lumsdaine, and F. D. Sheffield. 1949. The effects of presenting one side versus both sides in changing opinions on a controversial subject. In *Experiments on Mass Communication,* 201–227. Princeton, NJ: Princeton University Press.

16. Freedman, J. L., and S. C. Fraser. 1966. Compliance without pressure: The foot in the door technique. *Journal of Personality and Social Psychology,* 4, 195–202.

Cialdini, R. B., et al. 1975. Reciprocal concessions procedure for inducing compliance: The door-in-the-face technique. *Journal of Personality and Social Psychology*, 31, 206–215.

Dillard, J. P., J. E. Hunter, and M. Burgoon. 1984.

Cantrill, J. G., and D. R. Seibold. 1986. The perceptual contrast explanation of sequential request strategy effectiveness. *Human Communication Research*, 13, 253–267.

17. O'Keefe, D. 1990. *Persuasion: Theory and research*, 172–173. Beverly Hills, CA: Sage.

18. Dillard, J. P., J. E. Hunter, and M. Burgoon. 1984. Sequential-request persuasive strategies: Meta-analysis of foot-in-the-door and door-in-the-face. *Human Communication Research*, 10, 461–488.

7

Presentation of Self and Impression Formation of Others

A businessman is aggressive; a businesswoman is pushy.

A businessman is good on details; she is picky.

He loses his temper because he's so involved in his job; she's bitchy.

When he's depressed (or hungover), everyone tiptoes past his office. She's moody so it must be her time of the month.

He follows through; she doesn't know when to quit.

He's confident; she's conceited.

He stands firm; she's impossible to deal with.

He's firm; she's hard.

His judgments are her prejudices.

He is a man of the world; she's been around.

He drinks because of excessive job pressure; she's a lush.

He isn't afraid to say what he thinks; she's mouthy.

He exercises authority; she's power mad.

He's close-mouthed; she's secretive.

He's a stern taskmaster; she's hard to work for.

(Taken from Tubba, S. L. 1978. A systems approach to small group interaction. Addison-Wesley Publishers)

Although we would like to believe that we can manage our self-presentation to make a desirable impression on others, this is not entirely true. Yes, the impression we make on others is partly based on our personality, appearance, and demeanor. These things are, to some extent, under our self-control. Yet the impression we make is ultimately dependent upon the perceptions of others.

In this amusing, yet alarming, comparison of businessmen and businesswomen, the writer contends that the same behaviors are perceived positively when performed by a man, and negatively when attributed to a woman. Thus, there are two facets of source impressions: how the source manages his or her self-presentation; and how others perceive and evaluate the presentation. The discussion of the impact of self-presentation and impression formation on persuasion is presented in four sections that identify: 1) the persuader's characteristics; 2) the attributions we use to form impressions about others; and 3) the self-presentation strategies we use to manage impressions.

CHARACTERISTICS OF THE PERSUADER

Scholars, since the time of Aristotle, have attempted to define the characteristics that make a speaker effective and persuasive. The biggest obstacle to integrating the research on persuader characteristics is the tendency for each researcher to give the characteristics a new name—resulting in significant overlap in the discussion of characteristics. Most of the research in this area can be integrated, however, under the following four headings: 1) credibility, 2) charisma, 3) attractiveness, and 4) power. Although these characteristics are sometimes called by different names the underlying concepts remain the same. **Credibility** is often discussed in terms of trustworthiness, expertise, and composure. **Charisma** includes discussions of personality, enthusiasm, and dynamism, as opposed to **attractiveness,** which focuses on perceptions of similarity, sociability, and identification. **Power,** which is most clearly defined as the perception that a source can distribute real or imagined rewards and punishments, also influences evaluations of a persuader.[1]

Credibility

Two dimensions of persuader credibility were identified by Aristotle: **expertise** and **trustworthiness.** According to Aristotle, a speaker is evaluated according to his or her knowledge on a topic—the extent to which the speaker is believable (expertise) and the extent to which the audience feels the speaker has its best interest at heart (trustworthiness).

Numerous studies have attempted to compare the relative importance of these two dimensions of credibility.[2] The **self-interest** of the persuader is one factor that influences the relative importance of trust and expertise. If the persuader has a great deal to gain by your acquiescence (e.g., a commission on a sale), finding a trustworthy person is imperative. If the persuader has little to gain, trust is not an issue, and expertise may take on increased importance. If you are on a sinking ship and a sly, but

FIGURE 7.1   The effects of the use of evidence on credibility assessments.

nevertheless expert, shiphand offers to help you escape in one direction, and a trustworthy, moral landlubber offers to take you in the opposite direction, you will probably entrust your fate to the expert, no matter how unscrupulous the person may be.

Credibility and the Use of Evidence

The use of evidence by the speaker is a factor that influences perceptions of credibility.[3] One would expect that the use of evidence in a persuasive message would always yield increased results. In a complicated interaction of variables, researchers have found that the use of evidence by a highly credible persuader (e.g., Robert Redford) has negligible impact. In contrast, the use of evidence by a low credibility persuader (e.g., Jane Dull) can enhance attitude change (Figure 7.1). It seems that the highly credible person is so persuasive that the use of evidence produces little additional impact.[4]

For evidence to influence perceptions of persuader credibility, and ultimately attitude change, research has shown that the evidence must be new or unfamiliar to the receivers. It seems obvious that old arguments are unlikely to produce any additional cognitive or behavioral change, and that more powerful evidence is likely to lead to greater attitude change.[5]

Another factor influencing the effectiveness of evidence is the delivery of the message.[6] Evidence does not enhance credibility when the persuader stumbles over words or bores the receivers. Thus, we can conclude that the use of evidence increases perceptions of credibility under the following conditions: 1) the persuader has low to moderate credibility; 2) the evidence is unfamiliar to the receivers; and 3) the message delivery is of high quality.

Credibility and the Acceptance of Messages

The highly credible persuader has greater freedom in the selection of message strategies. A source who is highly credible may use: 1) more intense fear appeals; 2) more intense language; and 3) more opinionated language.

In chapter 6 we discuss the use of **fear appeals,** and how a moderate level of fear is usually most effective. High levels of fear can scare receivers and cause them to be overwhelmed. Receivers who are overwhelmed do not change their attitudes; they go into denial—refusing to believe in the fearful stimulus. A high credibility persuader is perceived as believable and trustworthy. For this reason a highly credible persuader can pull off an intense fear appeal that might backfire on a person characterized by low to moderate credibility.

Intense language includes the use of metaphors, adjectives, and modifiers—it is highly descriptive and often emotionally charged. Former President Reagan's reference to the Soviet Union as the "evil empire" is an example of intense language. Research has found that intense language may backfire for a persuader unless the persuader is highly credible, and the receivers are favorable to the advocated position.[7]

Opinionated language cuts down people who do not believe in the advocated position or people who adhere to the counter position. Studies have found that the highly credible persuader can use more opinionated language, whereas the low credibility persuader may alienate receivers with the use of opinionated language.[8] If a highly believable and trustworthy persuader uses opinionated language, receivers perceive that the person feels very strongly about this issue. Since the person is highly credible, receivers believe and trust the person's judgement and are more likely to change their attitudes. The low credibility source is more effective when he or she uses non-opinionated language; with the use of opinionated language, the receivers begin to question the low credibility person's trustworthiness.[9] Note that the use of opinionated language typically works best when the audience is neutral regarding the issue; even a high credibility person may alienate receivers with the use of opinionated language on a topic that the receivers perceive negatively.[10]

Credibility affects the construction of a message in several ways: low credibility speakers must use evidence, and high credibility speakers can use more intense, opinionated, and fearful messages. Credibility alone, however, does not predict the effectiveness of a persuader. Scholars of this century have wondered how world leaders have risen above contenders who appeared more knowledgeable and trustworthy. Obviously these leaders attracted followers with personal characteristics other than, or in addition to, and sometimes even in place of, expertise and trustworthiness. History has taught us that the dynamism or charisma of the persuader has tremendous influence on the persuasiveness of the source.

Charisma

Charisma is often equated with personality and dynamism but is perhaps best described as a diffuse, magical, mesmerizing quality that draws people to attend to, enjoy, and genuinely like a speaker. The best example of

the charismatic speaker is former President Ronald Reagan. His very demeanor is attracting. His smile, twinkling eyes, and chuckle exude kindness, wit, and charm. Even when people portray Reagan as less-than-competent (Figure 7.2), he comes off as eminently likeable. That's charisma!

Charisma is difficult to define and difficult or impossible for a persuader to learn. Charisma is a natural ability to charm and impress people. It is perhaps a combination of modesty, wit, and rapport. The charismatic person has the ability to build a relational bond with many different types of people. The dynamic speaker makes each receiver feel special; the dynamic source can deliver messages that appeal to the special interests of each individual. The attention of a charismatic person makes us feel worthy and special—as a result of feeling good about ourselves, we intensely like the charismatic person. This liking, and sometimes blind following, makes us more likely to do what a charismatic person asks.

Attractiveness

A concept related to charisma is source attractiveness. For persuasion researchers, attractiveness encompasses both physical appearance and psychological identification. We refer to **psychological identification** as the attraction to a person based on shared values or characteristics we wish to emulate. In this regard, attractiveness is different from charisma. A person may be attractive but not charismatic. Moreover, a person may have charisma, but you may find his or her values to be very dissimilar and unattractive.

Physical Attractiveness

Research on physical attractiveness and persuasiveness suggests that attractive people are more persuasive. But why is this so? Are we so fickle that we place more credence on physical characteristics than on the merit of the argument? Research suggests that **physical attractiveness** is not just skin deep—physically attractive people develop different personalities.[11]

Attractive people are socialized differently from less attractive people. Attractive people are given increased attention and positive feedback from an early age. People are drawn to attractiveness—we find attractive people rewarding to be around. Therefore, attractive people have more diverse social experiences and more feedback with which to hone their self-presentations. As a result, these people exhibit more developed communication skills, higher grades and achievements, self-esteem, optimism, and confidence.[12] Thus, it is not only the beauty, but also the social skills of attractive people that enhance their persuasiveness.

Psychological Attractiveness (Similarity)

In addition to pleasing physical characteristics, we also consider a source's **psychological attractiveness.** An important component of psychological attractiveness is similarity. Think of your close friends. It is very likely that you perceive these people to have values, interests, and personalities similar to your own.

Within some relationships, similarity between persuader and receiver increases attraction and, consequently, persuasion. We also know that within other types of relationships, similarity between persuader and receiver can be detrimental.[13] We will discuss three factors that affect the benefits of persuader-receiver similarity: 1) short- versus long-term persuasion effects; 2) role expectations; and 3) fear or anxiety.

For **short-term persuasion,** establishing persuader-receiver similarity is less important. Even an unattractive, unlikable, and dissimilar person can, at times, elicit support on a one-time, short-term basis. If, however, the person must continually persuade the receiver, in numerous situations over time, a lack of identification between persuader and receiver can be detrimental. Consider the boss who flaunts a self-presentation of elitism over the lowly employees. This dissimilarity may work for a while, partly out of respect, fear, and awe. But over time, the dissimilarity and lack of empathy with the employees can backfire. Although the boss' power remains the same, antagonized employees may subvert the boss' persuasive goals.

Certain leadership roles are maintained by perceptions of dissimilarity. If a persuader shuns **role expectations** to create a feeling of similarity with the receiver, the persuader may destroy his or her credibility. Consider political candidates who have presented themselves as "just like you," only to have you realize that you don't want someone "just like you" running the government! It is little wonder that politicians have changed their tactics to state implicitly, "I'm not exactly like you, but I understand you."

Fear is also a powerful situational influence that determines the effectiveness of persuader-receiver similarity. When the receiver is afraid or anxious, it is better to maintain distance between the persuader and receiver. In times of fear and confusion dissimilarity allows people to place faith in leaders. Consider a visit to your doctor when you have a serious illness. You don't really desire the doctor to be similar to you; you desire the doctor to be more powerful and more knowledgeable in managing your illness. Likewise, in times of national crisis when you are scared, you don't want national leaders to be like you—scared; you want government officials to be powerful experts who are in control of the situation. For this reason queens, kings, physicians, ministers, and generals traditionally differentiate themselves, make themselves dissimilar, from the people they lead. This dissimilarity is accentuated through the use of symbols: crowns and velvet robes, white coats and stethoscopes, and hats and ribbons.

Attractiveness is an elusive quality. It is conceptualized as having both physical and personality characteristics, and it simultaneously embraces respect for differences and similarities. The impact of attractiveness on persuasion depends upon the receiver's perceptions of the persuader as attractive. One characteristic that can enhance the attractiveness of a persuader is power—we like people who have the ability to reward us. Power can also override attractiveness in the evaluation of a persuader. A powerful persuader who controls punishments may not be attractive but may still be persuasive.

Power

By definition, power is almost synonymous with persuasion. As defined in chapter 1, persuasion is the use of communication to change another's behavior, thoughts, or attitudes. Power is, similarly, the ability to change another's behavior or affect.[14] Our perceptions of a persuader's power are influenced by: 1) the interactional nature of power; 2) the power strategies the persuader employs; and 3) the verbal and nonverbal communication of power.

The Interactional Nature of Power
Power, like persuasion, is interactionally defined. Contrary to popular belief, a person cannot have power over you unless you allow the person to exercise this control. The interactional definition of power has several

Many advertisements incorporate famous people to associate their product, service, or organization with credibility and trustworthiness.

CHARLTON HESTON: Actor, Father, Gun Collector, Outdoorsman, Life Member of the National Rifle Association.

"I've always spoken out on issues I feel strongly about. Voting, civil rights, defense, the environment. Also, the Bill of Rights.

"Why am I comfortable as a member of the NRA? Because I'm comfortable with the Bill of Rights. It says the right of the people to keep and bear arms shall not be infringed. That means, in this country, we get to choose. Americans exercise their right to own firearms for several reasons. For sport, for hunting, for collecting, for protection. They are all good reasons.

"I support the freedoms our Constitution guarantees. But democracy is fragile. It's threatened all the time from many quarters. Eternal vigilance is the price of liberty. The NRA helps maintain that vigil." **I'm the NRA.**

NATIONAL RIFLE ASSOCIATION OF AMERICA
This is to certify that the person whose name appears below is a
LIFE MEMBER

The NRA's lobbying organization, the Institute for Legislative Action, is the nation's largest and most influential protector of the constitutional right to keep and bear arms. At every level of government and through grassroots efforts, the Institute guards against infringement upon the freedoms of law-abiding gun owners. If you would like to join the NRA or want more information about our programs and benefits, write J. Warren Cassidy, Executive Vice President, Box 37484, Dept. HE-27, Washington, D.C. 20013.

Paid for by the members of the National Rifle Association of America. © 1987.

National Rifle Association of America.

implications: 1) power does not reside in a person, but in the relationship; and 2) power is situational.

Power is negotiated within a relationship. People are not inherently powerful—we give people power. Your parents, for example, probably had power over you when you were growing up. The amount of power your parents exercised—the degree to which they were able to change your behavior—was dependent upon how much you let your parents influence you. There is very little parents can do to alter the behavior of a teen who is participating in extralegal activities if the teen doesn't want to change. Parents of an Ohio teen, unable to deal with the teenage rebellion of their seventeen-year-old daughter, resorted to tying her up, drugging her, stringing their $450,000 house with barbed wire, and effectively keeping their daughter a prisoner in her own home for more than a year. The parents obviously found themselves powerless to change their daughter's behavior. (Their daughter's friend exerted power by calling the police.)

A persuasive source may exert different levels of power on different individuals, depending on the individuals' willingness to acquiesce to authority. A student resident assistant in a dormitory may have considerable power over particular students living in the hall who don't want to get into trouble, but may have little power over an incalcitrant minority who care little about fines for violations or the wrath of the RA.

Power is also situational. You may grant a person power in a particular situation, but not in others. You may grant your RA power over your behavior in the residence hall but not over your behavior off-campus or in the classroom. When you grant a person power in a particular relationship or situation, there are usually rules that accompany the use of power. That is, certain types of power strategies are considered acceptable within the boundaries of particular relationships or situations.

Power Strategies

Researchers posit four different categories of power strategies: 1) previewing expectations and consequences; 2) appealing to relational loyalties; 3) appealing to values; and 4) invoking obligations.[15] Regardless of the type of strategy a persuader employs, the receiver has the power to decide if the persuader has a right to use this strategy, and whether or not the consequences of noncompliance are greater than the imposition of giving in to the source.

The first type of power, the preview of **expectations and consequences,** necessitates that the persuader have the ability and the perseverance to reward or punish the receiver. Your boss has this type of power if your boss has the authority to increase your wages or fire you.

A persuader may invoke **relational loyalty** if he or she is an expert or has some other basis to engender reverential respect. Perhaps an older sibling has this type of power over you; you will do anything for this sibling because you revere the person so.

In appealing to **values,** the persuader must make the receiver believe in the content of the message. A religious leader might have this type of power over you if the religious leader can make you believe that a particular behavior is consistent with your moral values.

If the persuader has a legitimate position of power that the receiver recognizes, he or she has the power of **obligation.** Your parents may hold obligation power over you if you believe they have the right to control your behavior.

The type of power a persuader claims is important. A particular type of power may have different effects across situations and people. You may not, for example, accept *expectation and consequence power* from a peer. You may deny that a peer has the right or ability to reward or punish you. In more equalitarian relationships we typically invoke *value* or *relational loyalty power.* The use of an inappropriate power strategy may backfire on the persuader; the receiver may perceive the persuader as untrustworthy or unattractive.

Verbal and Nonverbal Perceptions of Power

Obviously, the persuader who has power but cannot effectively communicate that power is ineffectual. If power is dependent upon the receivers' perception and acceptance of this power, the behaviors that enhance or hinder perceptions of power are important to our study of persuasion. Both verbal and nonverbal characteristics of our behavior influence perceptions of power.

Numerous experiments have been conducted to test the characteristics of speech patterns associated with perceptions of power. All other things remaining the same, speakers who talk more frequently, initiate more topics of conversation, and interrupt other speakers are perceived as powerful.[16] In contrast, asking questions, rising intonation at the end of a statement, and gesturing are associated with low power. Sources perceived as having little power are also more likely to use: hedges (e.g., "I guess," "I'm not sure you'll agree, but. . . ,"); hesitations (e.g., "well," and "uhhhh,"); and politeness forms (e.g., "please," and "thank-you") in their speech.[17]

The power and powerless speech forms noted above are remarkably similar to gender-related speech characteristics.[18] These patterns do affect perceptions of persuasive sources. Several studies have found that males are perceived as more credible (i.e., having greater expertise and trustworthiness) and powerful than females.[19]

Although this perception may be changing as social roles for men and women change, many of these patterns persist. Males are more likely than females to initiate topics that are pursued. In contrast, when females initiate topics with a male, males often do not discuss the topic for any length of time. Males interrupt females three times more often than females interrupt males. Females give more support, such as eye contact, attention, head nods, and verbal agreement when males speak, but males give little support when females speak. Moreover, females ask more questions than do males, and even when females make an assertion they often deliver it with rising intonation, which communicates uncertainty. Read statement (a) as an assertion. Then read statement (b) with a rising inflection.

a) "We have dance lessons tonight."

b) "We have dance lessons tonight?"

Women also use tag questions more frequently than do men. Consider the following statements:

a) "It's a nice day out today."

b) "It's a nice day out today, isn't it?"

The first constitutes an assertion, and the second asks for opinion validation. In sum, women should avoid these speech patterns in order to enhance perceptions of power and credibility in persuasive situations.

Nonverbal communication also influences power perceptions. As you might imagine, straight posture, arms away from the body, chin held high, open legs, and a backward lean are all nonverbals associated with perceptions of power.[20] In contrast, visualize a person with slumped posture, arms hugging body, lowered chin, closed legs, and a forward lean toward other interactants. This is not the picture of a powerful person.

Eye contact is often key to power assessments.[21] Studies on eye contact reveal that powerful speakers have more prolonged eye contact than powerless speakers. But when listening, powerful people will use less eye contact than their powerless counterparts. Try to visualize the eye contact of your family disciplinarian when you were in trouble. A powerful disciplinarian would employ long, relentless eye contact as he/she delivers the lecture and metes out the punishment. But when you speak to give your side of the story, the powerful disciplinarian is likely to communicate that you are lower than plant life by not acknowledging your eye contact.

Clearly, power does not reside with the persuader, but in the interaction between the persuader's presentation and the receivers' perceptions. The relationship and situation, the appropriateness of the power strategy employed, and the verbal and nonverbal characteristics of the speaker influence power and consequent persuasiveness.

The Impact of Source Characteristics on Persuasiveness

Imagine that you have been selected to participate in a research study. When you arrive, a professor in a white coat greets you and introduces you to your partner for this experiment. The professor explains that this is an experiment on learning, and that you will play the role of teacher, while your partner plays the role of student. You say good-bye to your partner as he enters one of the lab rooms, and you proceed with the professor to a chair in front of a control panel. The professor explains that the student is learning new words, and that every time he gives a wrong answer, a red light will flash on your control panel. Each time the student gives a wrong answer you are to give him an electric shock. On your control board you have a shock lever that ranges from "mild shock" to "danger—extreme shock." You are instructed to increase the voltage of the shock each time the student gives a wrong answer.

The student did fairly well in the beginning, but he has been missing the last set of words. As the student gives yet another wrong answer, you give him a moderate level of electric shock. You can hear the student kicking the walls of the room in which he has been contained. After a while, the student stops giving answers. The experimenter tells you that no answer is a wrong answer and to continue the shocks. Do you continue with this experiment? Do you continue to give increasingly powerful shocks up to the danger limit?

In Milgram's classic experiment, 26 out of 40 subjects continued to give shocks two stops beyond the "danger—extreme shock" level—even after the student stopped kicking the walls and all sounds and responses from the student's room ceased.[22] This experiment in obedience documents a frightening propensity for people to obey orders.

Subjects claimed that their obedience was at least partly a result of the characteristics of the research institution (the positive and credible reputation of Yale University) and the characteristics of the experimenter (the credibility and power of the "doctor" in a white lab coat). Despite kicking heard from the victim and the word "danger" on their control panel, the subjects believed that the researcher knew what he was doing. In this experiment, perceptions of credibility, attractiveness, and power led to persuasion.

In a more recent example of the same phenomena, researchers found that adolescents hold favorable attitudes toward smokeless tobacco because sports figures endorse it. As the adolescents reported increased liking for these sports figures, their beliefs about the risks of smokeless tobacco decreased.[23]

These studies show that a highly favorable persuader not only influences favorable attitudes toward him or herself, but also generates favorable attitudes for the persuasive topic as well. Persuader characteristics are a powerful impetus in the persuasion process.

The impact of persuader characteristics on persuasion does vary across situations, however. Under some conditions we rely on our evaluations of the persuader more than on our evaluations of the message content. Under other conditions the effects of the persuader are minimized. Two conditions can help us predict how important persuader characteristics will be in a persuasive encounter: 1) receivers' involvement in the issue; and 2) the time span over which persuasive effects are expected to endure.

Persuasive Impact and Receiver Involvement

Researchers have found that when involvement is high, receivers pay more attention to the message content than to the message source, and vice-versa.[24] You have probably noticed the effects of involvement on people's evaluation of political campaigns. If the person you observe has only superficial interest in the political campaign, he or she is likely to evaluate the candidates on likability, honesty, character, lifestyle, family life, experience, and other source characteristics. If the person you observe has a personal interest in politics, the policies and issues that the candidates propose will be most important to the voting decision. Under conditions of high involvement the merit of the message is primary, and the person with the most cogent arguments will persuade the receivers.

Persuasive Impact Over Time

In addition to the effects of involvement, the impact of source characteristics on persuasion also varies over time. Hovland was the first to document what is known as the **sleeper effect.** [25] Hovland found that, as expected, a high credibility source persuades people more than a low credibility source. Hovland defined credibility rather broadly to include expertise, trustworthiness, and attractiveness. Follow-up research found, however, that the persuasion effects began to decay several weeks after presentation of the message.

Specifically, those subjects who heard a highly credible source (e.g., Robert Redford speaking on environmental issues) and experienced high levels of initial attitude change reported only moderate levels of attitude change several weeks later. Most surprisingly, those subjects who heard a low credibility source (e.g., Jane Dull, college sophomore) and experienced little initial attitude change reported moderate attitude change several weeks later (Figure 7.3).

Hovland concluded that over time, receivers dissociate the message and the source. As time passes, people forget the characteristics of the source and remember the merits of the message. This is called the **sleeper effect.** Hovland's conclusion is valid, however, only if source characteristics have no impact on the comprehension and retention of a message.

Another study found that if receivers are reminded, several weeks later, of the qualifications of the source (Robert Redford versus Jane Dull), the initial attitude effects are reinstated.[26] When subjects are reminded of the highly credible source, positive attitude change occurs,

FIGURE 7.3

The Sleeper Effect. High credibility sources elicit greater attitude change than low credibility sources. But, after a time delay, the attitude change resulting from credibility effects appears to wear off. Initial attitudes may be reinstated, however, if the receiver is reminded of the source's credibility.

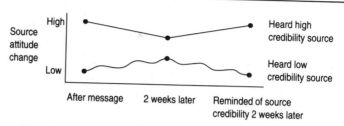

and when subjects are reminded of a low credibility source, attitude change decreases to the level recorded shortly following message reception. The sleeper effect is reversed.

Recently, researchers have had difficulty replicating the sleeper effect. In a comprehensive analysis of this research one group of scholars demonstrated that specific conditions are necessary to produce the sleeper effect: 1) receivers must comprehend and remember the salient arguments in a message; and 2) receivers must recognize the source as trustworthy.[27] The receiver must be able to remember the arguments, and the receiver must not doubt the source's arguments or intentions, if the receiver is to rely upon the merits of the arguments after the effects of source characteristics have worn off.

It also follows that if a high credibility source needs only short-term persuasive effects (e.g., getting an immediate monetary donation), the use of arguments and evidence is not very important—the impact of source characteristics can carry the persuader.[28] Conversely, if the persuader wants long-term effects (e.g., employee loyalty to the company), the high credibility persuader should use good evidence and arguments to ensure that persuasive effects will endure after the effects of source characteristics dissipate (i.e., the sleeper effect sets in).

In general then, we can conclude that source characteristics influence not only attention to the source, but the acceptance of the message as well. The relative weight of source characteristics and message arguments in determining persuasive outcome is dependent upon the receiver's involvement in the issue and the amount of time that has passed since message delivery. It is important to remember that the effects of source characteristics are short-lived. It is the merit of the message that persists to influence and maintain future attitude change.

Thus far we have looked at only one side of the persuasion equation. Though we have examined source characteristics in detail, we haven't addressed how the receiver perceives, integrates, and evaluates the source's behavior. Attribution theory explains how receivers use behavioral observations to draw conclusions about the source's credibility, attractiveness, charisma, and power.

HOW WE FORM IMPRESSIONS

In a communication encounter our minds are continually processing and evaluating information, not only about what the person is saying, but about what type of person the speaker is, what the speaker's intentions are, and even what the speaker thinks of us. Thoughts upon which we base our impressions of persuaders are called **attributions.**

We shall first discuss attribution theories that try to ascertain what evaluations are made in the mind to form an impression of another person. Based with this knowledge of attribution theory, we will move on to common errors in attribution. People, with some degree of consistency, make similar errors when making attributions about themselves and others. These errors have implications for the perception of source characteristics.

How We Judge Others' Behavior

We form impressions of others based on observations of their behavior. In evaluating this behavior we must ask to what extent the behavior we observe is a reflection of the person's personality or to what extent it is a circumstance of the situation. Attribution theorists have studied how we decide whether to attribute an observed behavior to **internal** (personality) or **external** (situational) causes.

In this section we will discuss how attributions are made on the basis of 1) responsibility, 2) noncommon effects, 3) covariation, and 4) nonrational bases. These four explanations for how people make attributions are not mutually exclusive—in other words, it is not necessary to choose one theory as correct and abandon the others. It is quite possible that we use all three methods in making attributions, depending upon situational circumstances.

Attributions Based on Responsibility

The first attribution theory we shall discuss proposes four different levels of **responsibility**: associational, causal, justifiable, and intentional.[29] According to this theory, we observe behavior, and base the decision to attribute the behavior to the person or to the situation upon the degree to which the person was responsible for the outcome, and the severity of the outcome.

People are most likely to make an external (situational) attribution, absolving another person from responsibility, when the event and person are only associationally related. If someone smashes your family car while it is parked at school, you didn't cause the accident, but the fact that you had the car parked on the street with lots of other cars around facilitated the accident. You are only **associationally responsible,** and it is likely that your parents will make a situational, or external attribution.

Causal responsibility attributes joint responsibility to the person and situation. You are causally responsible if you fall asleep at the wheel on your way home and consequently wreck the car. You caused the accident to happen, but you didn't intend for the accident to happen. Your parents will likely hold you partly responsible for the demise of the family car, but may be sympathetic to the situation that caused the accident.

If you, on the other hand, see a child blithely darting in front of your car, and you swerve into the telephone pole to avoid striking the child, you are **justifiably responsible.** You are clearly responsible for the accident, but you were justified in your actions. Your parents will probably make an external (situational) attribution (e.g., they won't make you pay for the damages).

In contrast, if you are **intentionally responsible** for the damage, you'd better get a good summer job! If you are angry at your parents, and you drive recklessly, knowing that this behavior would make them very angry, you are intentionally responsible. This is the greatest level of responsibility, and observers will likely make confident judgments about your character (e.g., irresponsible, immature, and ill-tempered) when they attribute intentional responsibility to your actions.

The legal system also makes attributions based on responsibility. If you plot someone's death, attributions of intentional responsibility will be made, and you will face charges for first degree murder. If, on the other hand, you shoot someone in self-defense, this action may be considered justifiable, and you will be charged with second degree murder. If you accidentally cause someone's death, as in a vehicle collision, you may be charged with reckless homicide and receive a third degree murder charge. And finally, if you are associated with someone's death but did not cause it (e.g., you forget to wrap the loose wire on the refrigerator, and Uncle Bob electrocutes himself while getting a snack), you will not be charged with murder, and the cause of death will be attributed to external causes.

There are also clear applications of this model to our evaluations of persuaders. In 1981, on the day of President Reagan's inauguration, the hostages held in Iran were released. Reagan had only associational responsibility for their release, as he wasn't even president yet when their release was effected. Yet, political handlers tried to convince the public to make causal or intentional attributions so that Reagan could take credit for this political coup. In this manner persuaders may be attributed blame or glory, and these impressions may influence whether a persuasive message is accepted.

Attributions Based on Noncommon Effects

This theory proposes that we evaluate an observed behavior by comparing the behavior to the alternative behaviors that could have been performed.[30] We then calculate the differences between the chosen and unchosen behaviors to discover the motivation behind the chosen behavior. The motivation is the noncommon effect among the alternatives. Noncommon effects are simply the benefits of the chosen behavior that are not common to the unchosen alternatives.

For example, your friends might be able to make attributions about your personality and values based on your choice of colleges. Your friends could evaluate all the benefits of your chosen college and all the benefits of your alternatives. Your chosen college may be close to home, have a large student population, have a good band, and have a prestigious communication department. Your alternatives may also have large student populations, good bands, and prestigious communication departments. In this scenario the only noncommon effect among your college choices is that your chosen college is close to home. Based on this information, attributions could be made about the value you place on your family and your home-town-honey relationship.

Once again, the attributions that others make based on an analysis of non-common effects will influence their impressions of you. The impression others make, will in turn, influence your ability to persuade these people.

Attributions Based on Covariation

Attributions can also be made on the basis of covariation.[31] Literally, covariation means that two entities vary in the same direction at the same time. For example, dog fleas and mosquitos covary—they both increase in numbers during rainy weather. According to covariation theory, when we observe a person's behavior, we ask three questions: Is the behavior unique to the situation? Is the behavior a unique response to a particular person involved? Do others commonly exhibit the behavior? Based on whether the observed behavior covaries with the situation, another person, or is perceived to be unique, we will make either an internal attribution regarding a person's personality or an external attribution regarding the situation. For example, if you observe your roommate at a restaurant with a person other than the significant other, the attribution you make may be based on a covariation analysis. Is the behavior unique to the situation—do you seldom see your roommate out with other people? If so, an external attribution—blaming the situation, rather than your roommate—may be in order. Is the behavior a unique response to the person involved—have you seen your roommate with this person before? If

BOX 7.1	*Attributions Made According to the Covariation Method*		
Question	**No**		**Yes**
Does this person perform this behavior in lots of situations?	situational attribution		personal attribution
Does this person perform this behavior as a response to lots of other people?	attribute to relationship with other person		personal attribution
Do most other people behave this way?	personal attribution		situational attribution

yes, perhaps this is a relative or close friend, a fact that warrants an external attribution. Do others commonly exhibit the behavior? Do other people in your social group go out casually with people other than their significant others? If yes, this appears to be an innocent situation, warranting an external attribution. Box 7.1 displays a table explaining how internal and external attributions are made on the basis of covariance.

Non-rational Attribution Processes

You may be wondering, do people really go through the laborious process of asking themselves covariance questions when making an attribution? Researchers report that people are more likely to use the covariation questions when confronted with a complex and involving situation. In boring, simple, or low motivation situations, people are likely to employ non-rational attribution processes. These non-rational processes result in judgments based on: 1) prior attributions, and 2) salient features of the situation.[32] People's **reliance on prior attributions** results in accepting congruent information at face value and being exceptionally critical of non-congruent information. We resist changing our prior attributions. For example, if you dislike Sally, and Sally gets arrested for selling dope, you don't question her guilt. However, when Sally gets a citizenship award, you are highly critical of the award selection criteria.

The **focus on salient features** means that we base our attributions on the most vivid behavior observed, rather than assessing the consistency or distinctiveness of this behavior. For example, if you observe a person crying, you may make the attribution that the person is immature. This reliance on a salient feature of the person's behavior, without garnering more information regarding the situational factors impinging upon this display, may lead to inaccurate attributions.

In persuasive conversations, we continually evaluate the persuader and make inferences about the person's personality, disposition, character, charisma, likability, friendliness, communication skills, expertise, good will, and so on. In interpersonal, mass mediated and public contexts, persuasive effects are dependent upon the attributions made by the receiver. Our attributions about political candidates, for example, determine whether or not we are likely to be persuaded by the candidate.

A candidate may be attributed blame or praise based on his or her level of **responsibility** for particular outcomes or behavioral displays. If a candidate loses his or her temper in a debate, for example, we can make an assumption that the candidate is intentionally responsible for this behavior and has little temper control, or we can assume that the candidate is causally responsible because the temper outburst was provoked.

We could also judge the candidate according to choices he or she made, and we might analyze these choices according to **noncommon effects.** The noncommon effects between going to 'Nam and staying home might be: military service versus educational opportunities; independence from family versus support for a family crisis; or personal challenge versus adherence to moral beliefs. If the candidate chose to defer the Vietnam War draft, we might conclude that the candidate is a coward, or that the candidate preferred to make other kinds of contributions to his country.

If voters have some knowledge of the candidate, they might evaluate his or her behavior on the basis of **covariation** with the situation, other people, or social expectations. If a candidate is associated with marital infidelity, we can assess whether or not this infidelity occurs across situations, with many different people, and whether or not the public commonly accepts it. If we conclude that the behavior occurs across situations, with many different partners, and that society does not accept it, we are likely to make an internal attribution and question the candidate's character.

Finally, if voters have little motivation to make evaluations, **nonrational** attributions focusing on salient features such as physical appearance or prior conceptions and prejudices may supersede more accurate attribution processes. In this case, we may dismiss the candidate's scandalous behavior because he or she looks so trustworthy, or because he or she is a war hero.

Even though attributions based on responsibility, noncommon effects and covariation require cognitive evaluations, we often make attributional errors. It is important, as a message receiver, to recognize attribution errors. Inaccurate attributions can lead the receiver to discredit a source prematurely. The critical receiver must also be alert to persuaders who use attribution errors to lead the receiver to form an unwarranted favorable impression.

Common Judgement Errors

People, with some consistency, make inferences that are fallacious. We are particularly prone to attributional errors of judgement in situations in which we are defensive—when our egos are threatened. You will also notice that these ready-made judgements most often occur under conditions of low involvement, when people make evaluations quickly and perfunctorily, with little cognitive deliberation. Upon reading this section, you may even agree that other people commit these grievous errors with some regularity, but that you are the exception. Our blindness to our own attributional errors is one of the most intriguing aspects of this area of research. There are four attributional errors that we shall discuss in turn: self versus other differences, the responsibility attribution error, the halo effect, and the "just world hypothesis."

Self versus Other Differences

We often judge others differently than we judge ourselves—even when we confront similar circumstances.[33] We are more likely to make internal attributions for others (i.e., hold the person responsible) and external attributions for ourselves (i.e., recognize situational influences).

You have probably heard a friend who has done poorly on an exam complain that "the professor put stuff on that test that we never discussed in the class!" While your friend is making external attributions for his or her failure by blaming the professor, you may be making internal attributions: "You did badly because you didn't study!" But if you were the one to do badly on the exam, you also would probably make an external attribution.

This attribution error is the basis for many social prejudices. We tend to overlook, for example, that a poor person may have lost his or her job and home, and that situational conditions, such as the lack of proper clothing and luxury of personal hygiene, make it impossible to obtain a job, even if one were available.

Responsibility Attributions

We also make errors in the degree to which we hold a person responsible for bad outcomes. The same behavior is likely to be attributed greater responsibility if the consequences are more severe.[34] Logically, the same behavior should generate similar levels of blame, regardless of the consequences. Our legal system is even guilty of perpetuating this attributional error. Attempted murderers get much lighter sentences than successful murderers. Should we give the attempted murderers a break just because they aren't very good at their chosen profession? The behavior and the potential consequences are the same, yet the attribution of responsibility varies.

Our evaluation of a persuader's arguments and strategies may be biased by whether we believe in the persuader's cause. An established church that sponsors a weekend retreat to teach children religious doctrine is evaluated positively, but a religious cult that sponsors a weekend retreat may be accused of taking advantage of people's isolation from their family and peers.

The Halo Effect

We discussed earlier how nonrational attributions are often made on the basis of prior attributions and in blatant disregard for new evidence to the contrary. The **halo effect** is the result of prior attributions.[35] The halo effect can be either positive or negative. If we form a highly favorable impression of a person, all subsequent actions by this person are bathed in a positive, redeeming light. Conversely, if we form a negative impression, this person can seemingly do nothing right. Famous rock stars, athletes, evangelists, and politicians are surrounded by halo illumination. Despite reports of murder, drug convictions, sex crimes, fraud, and extortion, we are hesitant to remove the halo. Persuaders who have the advantage of a halo effect may be particularly effective because receivers will be less likely to critically analyze the persuader's intentions and messages. As more and more of the halos of our cultural heroes slip and slide, however, we are becoming more savvy in our evaluations.

Just World Hypothesis

One of the most counter-intuitive attributional errors is the just world hypothesis. This error occurs when tragedy strikes an acquaintance and we attribute the misfortune to the victim, rather than the circumstances.[36] Consider the things you hear people say after an acquaintance has been diagnosed with cancer, has been in a car accident, or has gone bankrupt. "It's no wonder she has cancer—she's smoked like a chimney for years!" "If he hadn't been out to that party till the wee hours of the morning, he wouldn't have fallen asleep at the wheel." "She spent all the money recklessly—I guess she got what she deserved." The classic example of this phenomena is when we blame rape victims for their trauma—"she was promiscuous," or "she shouldn't have been walking alone," or "she shouldn't jog through that park!"

It is hard to imagine the frequency with which we spew vengeance and justifications rather than sympathy for our fellow humans. One of the reasons we employ the just world hypothesis is to take the randomness out of misfortune—if we can attribute tragedies to the victim, then we can be secure in the knowledge that they won't happen to us.

The just world hypothesis also affects the impressions we form of persuaders and the impressions persuaders may wish us to form of others. If we make just world attributions about the misfortunes of persuaders, we are unjustifiably blaming the persuader for something beyond his or her control. Persuaders can also attempt to lead us to a just world attribution about an opponent or a particular social group, thereby biasing our impressions of others.

Persuasion and Attributional Errors

So what does all this mean for the source of a persuasive message? As a source you should realize that your audience is likely to make internal attributions for your behavior, they are likely to ignore situational circumstances that may have dictated your behavior, they will hold you accountable for your failures and misfortunes, and if you have the good fortune to have a positive reputation, this may diffuse any negative interpretations of your future actions.

As a receiver of persuasive messages, attribution errors can result in misperceptions. A receiver may prematurely discredit a source, or receivers may be led to form an unsubstantiated positive impression of a persuader. To accurately compare the merits of competing persuasive messages, the receiver must be careful of prematurely discrediting a persuader or creating an invalid positive impression.

Up to this point, we have discussed how a source presents a self-image and a receiver forms an impression. This is a simplification of the impression formation process. Persuasion is reciprocal and mutual. As the original receiver is forming an impression of the source, the source is forming an impression of the receiver. Each person manages his or her self-presentation in communication encounters. Each person is, in fact, attempting to persuade other participants to form a favorable impression.

IMPRESSION MANAGEMENT

Your "self" is comprised of many roles: you are a student, a daughter or son, perhaps an employee, a friend, a significant other, a student leader, a musician, an artist, a volunteer, a fraternity or a sorority member, etc. Because you have numerous roles, you enact different "selves" in different situations.[37] You probably present yourself differently when with your parents than with your friends. You **manage your impressions** so that particular people will make desirable attributions. To facilitate these favorable impressions, you wear numerous **masks.** With the help of a mask, you can convince the audience that you are someone you aren't, or that you really are the someone you wish to be.

It becomes increasingly difficult to maintain our social masks under certain conditions:[38]

1) When other people respond ambiguously, and we cannot tell whether our mask is effective or not, we are plagued with uncertainty.

2) There are also times when we try to wear several masks simultaneously. Think about times when you are with your parents and your friends. Which mask do you wear? If the masks are very different from each other, you will feel quite uncomfortable. Sometimes your friends will make fun of your 'in front of the parents mask' because it is so different from your 'party mask.'

3) It is also more difficult to manage impressions in long-lasting relationships. It is relatively easy to maintain your chosen mask for an evening but increasingly difficult to role play for long periods of time. In long-lasting relationships there is a greater risk that the persons you wish to impress will catch you without your mask.

4) The most obvious obstacle to managing impressions through the adoption of a particular mask is when a person doesn't have the behavioral and communication skills to enact the role.

Enacting different roles in different situations and with different people can be difficult. Occasionally a mask we have chosen to wear slips in the middle of a performance. There are two self-presentation strategies that can help people maintain and even rescue the masks they have selected to wear: face work and aggressive and defensive tactics.

Face Work Theory

When our mask slips in a social situation, we *lose face*. That is, others notice that our behavior or statements are inconsistent with the mask we are wearing (e.g., you make an offensive, vulgar joke at a formal dinner). Fortunately, our learned communication patterns provide us with a ritualized communication pattern to manage such situations.[39]

Researchers who have studied *face work* have devised various terms to help explain the communication patterns by which face is threatened and saved. A **face-threatening act (FTA)** occurs when you exhibit a behavior that is inconsistent with your mask, or when someone challenges your mask in public. A **challenge** occurs when someone insults you—suggesting that you aren't the great mind, the great musician, or the great athlete you have presented yourself to be.

When a FTA occurs, you and the people around you can choose to engage in **cooperative face work.** This means that everyone pretends that the FTA didn't happen. So when you fall down the steps of the library and your books and papers fly in different directions, your fellow students are engaging in cooperative face work when they walk by you, avoid eye contact, hide their mirth, and pretend that it wasn't at all unusual to find your body sprawled on the steps. Similarly, if you make an inappropriate remark in conversation, your friends may quickly steer the conversation to a new topic, in an attempt to *save your face.* Cooperative face work is born from our own discomfort of seeing another person lose face. If you get uncomfortable watching old "I Love Lucy" re-runs, you have experienced this. It is embarrassing and uncomfortable just to watch Lucy lose face.

A more complex face-threatening situation occurs when someone challenges your face by direct or indirect insult. If the insult is indirect and your composure breaks (e.g., you get visibly angry, or you yell at the insulter in public), you lose even more face. Observers see that you are unable to maintain your composure and your social mask. There are two ways in which you can regain your face, however. If you maintain your composure and, jokingly, make a witty indirect insult in return—a repartee—you have regained your face—and likely threatened the face of the one who insulted you. The most effective way of regaining face is for your friends to engage in cooperative face work by challenging the insulter for you. If your friends make the challenge, you can avoid losing more face. If your friends are successful in their challenge, you can even regain the face lost during the insult.

Face work is a ritualized pattern of communicative behaviors that we use to protect the face of ourselves and others. A knowledge of cooperative face work helps communicators to reinstate lost face. In contrast, ineffective responses to face threatening acts result in additional loss of face. To manage our self-presentation as both persuaders and receivers in communication encounters, we must know the rules of cooperative face work. Moreover, as receivers we judge spokespersons, leaders, and mass media personalities on their ability to maintain face. We watch presidential debates, for example, to observe candidates' responses to face-threatening acts. The winner of the debate is usually the candidate who most successfully manages his or her face.

Assertive and Defensive Self-Presentation Tactics

An alternative way to explain self-presentation tactics is to classify impression management techniques as assertive or defensive.[40] Depending upon a person's personality, he or she may choose to use assertive or defensive tactics for impression management. **Assertive tactics** include ingratiation (e.g., flattery and obsequience) and self-promotion. **Defensive tactics** include accounts (e.g., excuses, apologies, and justifications for behaviors), disclaimers (qualifying statements to downplay thoughts, opinions, or abilities), and hedges (beating around the bush). See Box 7.2 for additional examples of assertive and defensive strategies.

Both assertive and defensive tactics are employed to manage a favorable impression; more extroverted, affiliation-oriented, dramatic, and confident people adopt assertive tactics, while more reticent, anxious, introverted, and submissive people adopt defensive tactics. For example, when John has an overdue paper to turn in, he can manage his loss of face through assertive or defensive tactics. If he chooses the assertive

| BOX 7.2 | *Assertive and Defensive Self-Presentation Strategies* |

Assertive	**Defensive**
flattery	accusations
self-promotion	helplessness
status/power	subservience
direct messages	hedges
assertions	disclaimers
positive claims	apologies/excuses

route, John will tell the professor what a great teacher she is, how hard he is working in the class, and how much he learned from writing the paper. If John were to choose defensive tactics, he might cough and wheeze a lot, discuss his concern for his mother's brain surgery, and comment on his mourning of his great-grandmother's death. Assertive tactics communicate credibility, esteem, and status, while defensive tactics communicate dependence and helplessness.

To recapitulate, as social beings we continually monitor our presentation, our surroundings, and other participants. Based on verbal and nonverbal feedback from other communicators, we may modify our self-presentation to make it more amenable to the people we are with. Through this process we develop multiple masks and learned scripts for behavior, which we can invoke to make a desired impression.

SUMMARY

The evaluation of the persuader can influence the evaluation of the persuader's message. Sources are most often evaluated according to credibility, charisma, attractiveness, and power. When short-term persuasive effects are desired, and when involvement is low, the evaluation of the source on these characteristics may have more impact on persuasive outcome than the merits of the message. The impressions we form of others have a great deal of impact on persuasive effects.

We form impressions of other people by making internal or external attributions. The attributions we make may be based upon responsibility, non-common effects, covariation, or non-rational processes. Or they may be based on attribution errors. It is important for the receiver to form an accurate impression of a source to evaluate more critically the source and the persuasive message. It is also important to remember that the impression formation process is bi-directional. Sources and receivers are involved in mutual influence, and both seek to create desired impressions.

Self-presentation skills help us to create the impressions we desire. We have many social masks that allow us to present different impressions to different people in different situations. We accomplish the presentation of our social mask through face work and assertive and defensive self-presentation strategies. Impression formation of others and self-presentation are both communication skills that have tremendous influence on the persuasion process.

Study Guide

source characteristics
    credibility: expertise, trustworthiness, and self-interest
        use of evidence, fear, intensity, and opinionated language
    charisma
    attractiveness
        physical and psychological
        short-term persuasion
        role expectations
        fear
    power
        interactional nature
        four power strategies
        verbal and nonverbal cues
impact of source characteristics versus message content
    involvement
    sleeper effect
attributions and impression formation
    internal and external attributions
four theories of attributions
    attributions based on responsibility: four types
    attributions based on noncommon effects
    attributions based on covariation
    nonrational attributions
        based on prior attributions and salient features
four attribution errors
impression management
    social masks
    face work theory: FTA, challenges, cooperative face work
    assertive and defensive tactics

Discussion Questions

1. Can you generate examples of persuasive messages you have dismissed because of the source's poor self-presentation? What aspects of the source's self-presentation did you reject? Consider the source's credibility, charisma, attractiveness, and power.

2. Harvey wants to be elected occupational safety manager of his union shop. The workers are particularly worried about health consequences of exposure to chemicals produced by the company. Should Harvey stress his similarity or dissimilarity with his fellow workers?

3. Several of the former Soviet republics are experiencing ethnic fighting, food shortages, economic hardships, and difficulties attracting foreign investors.

What attributions might you make regarding the conditions of the people living in these republics. Formulate attributions based on: 1) responsibility; 2) covariation; 3) non-common effects; and 4) non-rational attributions. Do you reach similar or different conclusions based on the attribution principle you apply? Why or why not?

4. A fellow employee continues to make cracks about your work performance. The employee never misses an opportunity to make jokes in front of other employees about how inept or helpless you are. According to face work theory, what is the best way to resolve this situation without losing 'face?'

References

1. Berlo, D. K., J. B. Lemert, and R. J. Mertz. 1969. Dimensions for evaluating the acceptability of message sources. *Public Opinion Quarterly*, 33, 563–576.
2. O'Keefe, D. J. 1990. *Persuasion: Theory and research*, 132–140. Beverly Hills, CA: Sage.
3. McCroskey, J. C. 1969. A summary of experimental research on the effects of evidence in persuasive communication. *Quarterly Journal of Speech*, 55, 169–176.
4. Norman, R. 1976. When what is said is important: A comparison of expert and attractive sources. *Journal of Experimental Social Psychology*, 12, 83–91.
5. Hample, D. 1981. *Models of arguments using multiple bits of evidence*. Paper presented at the annual meeting of the International Communication Association, Minneapolis, MN.
6. McCroskey, *op. cit.*
7. Bradac, J. J., J. W. Bowers, and J. A. Courtright. 1979. Three language variables in communication research: Intensity, immediacy, and diversity. *Human Communication Research*, 5, 257–269.
8. Miller, G. R., and J. Lobe. 1967. Opinionated language, open- and closed-mindedness and responses to persuasive communications. *Journal of Communication*, 17, 333–341.
9. Miller, G. R., and J. Baseheart. 1969. Source trustworthiness, opinionated statements, and response to persuasive communication. *Speech Monographs*, 36, 1–7.
   Infante, D. A. 1975. Effects of opinionated language on communicator image and in conferring resistance to persuasion. *Western Journal of Speech Communication*, 39, 112–119.
10. Mehrley, R. S., and J. C. McCroskey. 1970. Opinionated statements and attitude intensity as predictors of attitude change and source credibility. *Speech Monographs*, 37, 47–52.
11. Berscheid, E., and E. Walster. 1974. Physical attractiveness. In *Advances in experimental social psychology*. L. Berkowitz, ed. New York: Academic Press.
12. Chaiken, S. 1979. Communicator physical attractiveness and persuasion. *Journal of Personality and Social Psychology*, 37, 1387–1397.
    Goldman, W., and P. Lewis. 1977. Beautiful is good: Evidence that the physically attractive are more socially skilled. *Journal of Experimental Social Psychology*, 13, 125–130.

13. O'Keefe, D. J. 1990. *Persuasion: Theory and research*, p. 150. Beverly Hills, CA: Sage.
14. Berger, C. R. 1985. Social power in interpersonal communication. In *Handbook of interpersonal communication*. M. L. Knapp and G. R. Miller, eds. Beverly Hills, CA: Sage.
15. Wheeless, L. R., R. Barraclough, and R. Stewart. 1983. Compliance-gaining and power in persuasion. In *Communication yearbook 7*. R. N. Bostrom, ed. pp. 105–145. Beverly Hills, CA: Sage.
16. Scherer, K. R. 1979. Voice and speech correlates of perceived social influence in simulated juries. In *Language and social psychology*. H. Giles and R. St. Clair, eds. pp. 88–120. Oxford: Basil Blackwell.
    Stein, T. R., and T. Hellar. 1979. An empirical analysis of the correlations between leadership status and participation rates reported in the literature. *Journal of Personality and Social Psychology*, 37, 1993–2002.
17. Erickson, B., E. A. Lind, B. C. Johnson, and W. M. O'Barr. 1978. Speech style and impression formation in a court setting: The effects of "powerful" and "powerless" speech. *Journal of Experimental Social Psychology*, 14, 266–279.
18. Lakoff, R. 1975. *Language and the woman's place*. New York: Harper & Row. Kramerae, C. 1981. *Women and men speaking*. Rowley, MA: Newbury House.
19. Carmichael, C., and G. Cronkhite. 1965. Frustration and language intensity. *Speech Monographs*, 32, 107–111.
    Miller, G. R., and J. Baseheart. 1969. *op. cit.*
20. Ariers, E. J., C. Gold, and R. H. Weigal. 1983. Dispositional and situational influences on dominance behavior in small groups. *Journal of Personality and Social Psychology*, 44, 779–786.
21. Exline, R. V. 1972. Visual interaction: The glances of power and preference. In *Nebraska symposium on motivation: 1971*. J. K. Cole, ed. pp. 163–206. Lincoln: University of Nebraska Press.
    Ellyson, S. L. 1980. Visual dominance behaviors in female dyads: Situational and personality factors. *Social Psychology Quarterly*, 43, 328–336.
22. Milgram, S. 1974. *Obedience to authority: An experimental view*. New York: Harper & Row.
23. McDermott, S. T., et al. 1989. Adolescents' responses to sports figure product endorsements. *Southern Communication Journal*, 54, 350–363.
24. Chaiken, S. 1980. Heuristic versus systematic information processing and the use of source versus message cues in persuasion. *Journal of Personality and Social Psychology*, 39, 752–766.
    Petty, R. E., and J. T. Cacioppo. 1979. Issue involvement can increase or decrease persuasion by enhancing message-relevant information. *Journal of Personality and Social Psychology*, 37, 1915–1926.
25. Hovland, C. I., and W. Weiss. 1951. The influence of source credibility on communication effectiveness. *Public Opinion Quarterly*, 15, 635–650.
26. Kelman, H. C., and C. I. Hovland. 1953. Reinstatement of the communicator in delayed measurement of attitude change. *Journal of Abnormal and Social Psychology*, 48, 327–335.
27. Pratkanis, A. R., et al. 1988. In search of reliable persuasion effects, III: The sleeper effect is dead; long live the sleeper effect. *Journal of Personality and Social Psychology*, 54, 203–218.

28. McCroskey, J. C. 1972. A summary of experimental research on the effects of evidence in persuasive communication. In *The process of social influence*. T. D. Beisecker and D. W. Parson, eds. 318–328. Englewood Cliffs, NJ: Prentice-Hall.

29. Heider, F. 1944. Social perception and phenomenal causality. *Psychological Review*, 51, 358–374.
Heider, F. 1958. *The psychology of interpersonal relations.* New York: Wiley.

30. Jones, E. E., and K. E. Davis. 1965. From acts to dispositions: The attribution process in person perception. In *Advances in experimental social psychology*. L. Berkowitz, ed. New York: Academic Press.

31. Kelley, H. H. 1967. Attribution theory in social psychology. In *Nebraska symposium on motivation*. D. Levine, ed. Lincoln: University of Nebraska Press.
Kelley, H. H. 1972. Attribution in social interaction. In *Attribution: Perceiving the causes of behavior*. E. E. Jones, et al., eds. Morristown, NJ: General Learning Press.

32. Sillars, A. L. 1982. Attribution and communication: Are people "naive scientists" or just naive? In *Social cognition and communication*. M. E. Roloff & C. R. Berger, eds. Beverly Hills, CA: Sage.
Ross, L. 1977. The intuitive psychologist and his shortcomings: Distortions in the attribution process. In *Advances in experimental social psychology*. L. Berkowitz, ed. New York: Academic Press.

33. Jones, E. E., and R. E. Nisbett. 1972. The actor and the observer: Divergent perceptions of the causes of behavior. In *Attribution: Perceiving the causes of behavior*. E. E. Jones, et al., eds. Morristown, NJ: General Learning Press.
Ross, L., D. Greene, and P. House. 1977. The false consensus effect: An egocentric bias in social perception and attribution processes. *Journal of Experimental Social Psychology*, 13, 279–301.

34. Shaver, K. G. 1970. Defensive attribution: Effects of severity and relevance on the responsibility assigned for an accident. *Journal of Personality and Social Psychology*, 14, 101–113.

35. Nisbett, R. E., and L. Ross. 1980. *Human inference: Strategies and shortcomings of social judgement.* Englewood Cliffs, NJ: Prentice-Hall.
Kahneman, D., and A. Tversky. 1973. On the psychology of prediction. *Psychological Review*, 80, 237–251.
Kahneman, D., and A. Tversky. 1982. The simulation heuristic. In *Judgement under uncertainty: Heuristics and biases*. D. Kahneman, P. Slovic, and A. Tversky, eds. New York: Cambridge University Press.

36. Lerner, M. 1970. The desire for justice and reactions to victims. In *Altruism and helping behaviors*. J. McCauley and L. Berkowitz, eds. New York: Academic Press.

37. Mead, G. H. 1934. *Mind, self, and society.* Chicago: University of Chicago Press.

38. Arkin, R. M. 1981. Self presentation styles. In *Impression management theory and social psychological research*. J. T. Tedeschi, ed. pp. 311–333. New York: Academic Press.

39. Goffman, E. 1959. *The presentation of self in everyday life.* New York: Doubleday.

40. Tedeschi, J. T. 1990. Self-presentation and social influence: An interactionist perspective. In *The psychology of tactical communication*. M. J. Cody and M. L. McLaughlin, eds. Clevedon, England: Multilingual Malters, Ltd.

8

The Receiver and The Message

The headline reads, "Brain Booster Breakthrough!" In twenty-eight minutes it will zap stress, boost your brainpower, and unleash awesome creative and intuitive powers. Even more amazing is how it turns fat people thin and office clerks into mental millionaires. Another ad promises that subliminal messages will help you lose weight, stop smoking, relieve stress and anxiety, improve your memory, and be self-confident. Yet another encourages, "Develop the Einstein Within You." Marketers of subliminal programs claim we're using only 5 percent of our brains and that the other 95 percent is stagnant cerebral mush—but as Paul Chance queries, how can anyone possibly know how much of our brain is functioning[1] (aside from their booming sales)? By what fluke of evolution did 95 percent of our brains shut down? How can ten to twenty minutes of subconscious messages, electronic stimulators, and other assorted gadgets develop what twelve to sixteen years of formal education could not? But the real question is, who buys these things? These companies must be making profits, as their advertising inundates popular magazines and cable television stations! Are we, the consumer public, so gullible? Do we, as message receivers, become passive victims to persuasive messages?

The gullibility of humans has been chronicled throughout history. In mythology, the Greeks persuaded their enemies, the Trojans, to accept the gift of a large, hollow, wooden horse. Upon acceptance of the gift, the Greek soldiers hidden inside the horse emerged, sacked the city, and won the Trojan war. In the early 1600s when tulipmania struck the economically-minded Dutch, people reportedly spent the 1989 equivalent of $5,000 for a single tulip bulb. In the sixteenth and seventeenth century, at the height of witch mania, any unusual occurrence was attributed to witchcraft and many women were tortured and executed. As recently as 1950, Americans succumbed to Communist-hysteria. In this climate, Joseph McCarthy accused numerous movie stars, government workers, and other public officials of being communist or anti-American. Although McCarthy had little evidence to support these accusations, he succeeded in ruining the reputations and careers of many. History can certainly be interpreted to support the view of persuasive influence driving the powerless message receiver to stupidity.

There are two opposing views regarding the role of the message receiver in the persuasion process: the individual perspective and the socio-cultural perspective. Those who study persuasion in interpersonal contexts most often hold the individual view, and those who study mass mediated persuasion most often hold the socio-cultural view. Though neither view would suggest that all message receivers are suggestible, the two perspectives differ in the degree of control assigned to the message receiver in resisting persuasive influence.

THE INDIVIDUAL IS KING: THE INDIVIDUAL PERSPECTIVE AND RECEIVER RESISTANCE

The individual perspective has its origins in psychology and studies of individual information processing. According to this perspective, the outcome of a persuasive message cannot be predicted. No matter how masterful the persuader, the receiver has the opportunity to ignore, reject, modify, or misinterpret the persuader's message. The receiver is a person who thinks, feels, evaluates, judges, acts, and reacts. From the individual perspective, the receiver is a thoughtful, deliberate being who has some control over his or her susceptibility to persuasion.

But what, you might ask, about claims that pornography persuades people to rape, television violence persuades people to kill, advertising persuades people to suppress women, heavy metal music persuades people to worship the devil, and sexual references in movies persuade teens to get pregnant? The individual perspective suggests that these effects are limited.

There are at least three reasons that receivers are not powerless pawns of persuaders. First, a message cannot persuade a person to do something that is inconsistent with an important moral code. Receivers must be **predisposed to perform an act** for a message to motivate them to action. The receiver's conscience moderates the effects of persuasion. Second, a persuasive message is delivered in an environment in which the target receives **multiple influences** from multiple sources. The influence of a pornographic magazine, for example, may be tempered by the influences of a religious mother, a feminist wife, and a conservative boss. Third, it takes considerable **motivation** on the part of the receiver to translate a persuasive message into behavioral action. Even when we feel

Targeting is the process of adapting a message to fit the needs, values and attitudes of the message receiver.

Dilbert reprinted by permission of UFS, Inc.

strongly about an issue (e.g., environmental concerns), we often are too lazy to act upon that issue (e.g., recycle our garbage). The individual perspective suggests that the vast majority of people who read pornographic literature, watch violent television, or attend to sexist advertising do not have external motivations and conditions driving them to rape, murder, and discrimination.

Nevertheless, there are people who can be negatively influenced by persuasive messages. These individuals, according to the individual perspective, must have particular characteristics that make them unusually susceptible to a particular type of persuasive appeal, and must have limited exposure to alternative messages. Moreover, the individuals must be motivated to act out socially deviant behaviors. Finally, the actions proposed in the message can not be inconsistent with the individuals' pre-existing moral codes.

THE INDIVIDUAL AS PAWN: THE SOCIO-CULTURAL PERSPECTIVE AND RECEIVER SUSCEPTIBILITY

The socio-cultural perspective has its origins in sociology and cultural studies. We are, according to this perspective, products of our culture. The cultural values and beliefs that we learn influence our behavior and responses. The cultural perspective is used to explain how a message can have similar effects on a large group of people. The message receiver is perceived to be relatively powerless, and the receiver's responses to a persuasive message are constrained by cultural learning and cultural expectations.

In analyzing the "get smart quick" advertisement discussed earlier, the culturalist would try to identify what cultural beliefs and conditions create a need and desire for these products. The culturalist might explain this message by analyzing our cultural need for instant gratification. Compared to our ancestors who spent most of their day hunting or preparing food, we hardly have to slow down as food is thrown in our car window at the fast food drive-through, and five minutes is all that is necessary to nuke a frozen substance in the home microwave. The flick of a switch meets our entertainment needs, and computer data banks and fax machines provide instant access to information. So why should a person spend sixty hours in a class, and another sixty hours studying to take a single college course when this ad promises to charge up the brain in just ten to twenty minutes? The culturalist might argue that the instant satisfaction of our needs and desires makes this ad appealing to people in our time-conscious society.

Cultural factors clearly influence the reception of persuasive messages. Cultural conditions establish a climate in which a particular type of response to a persuasive message is clearly indicated and readily accepted. According to the cultural perspective, messages portraying pornography, violence, sexism, or Satanic ideas can create a cultural climate in which these messages become acceptable.[2] As a result, these messages could have powerful influences on particular social groups.

CULTURE VERSUS INDIVIDUAL: WHICH PERSPECTIVE IS RIGHT?

Just when we're ready to accept the portrayal of humans as blind-driven cattle stampeding to buy Cabbage Patch Dolls or Teenage Mutant Ninja Turtles, we find that many media influences on behavior are negligible. How can these two contrasting views of the power of the message receiver be resolved?

To some extent, both perspectives are correct. Receivers of persuasive messages can be influenced en masse, consistent with the cultural perspective, and, receivers, as individuals, can be critical processors of persuasive information, consistent with the individual perspective. The degree to which individual or socio-cultural forces dictate a persuasive outcome can only be determined on a case-by-case basis.

The application of one of these two perspectives is dependent upon the interaction of individual characteristics and the situation. When individual skills and motivations are evident, we are likely to see individualized responses to persuasion, and when the situational constraints are salient, we are likely to see numerous people elicit similar responses. If people with similar characteristics are exposed to a message in a similar situation, the socio-cultural perspective could be used to explain how a large group of people were motivated to respond to persuasion in a consistent manner. If, on the other hand, we notice that a particular type of message has a powerful effect on a particular sub-group—and a different effect, or no effect at all, on another group—we might compare the individual traits of people in these groups to determine what combination of variables produced the persuasive outcome.

In any persuasive encounter, the persuasive effect is the result of a combination of individual characteristics and free-will operating within socio-cultural constraints. In this chapter, we will address three questions regarding receivers' susceptibility to persuasion: 1) How do your individual characteristics influence your susceptibility to persuasion? 2) How do situational factors influence your persuasibility? and 3) How can you resist persuasive influence?

INDIVIDUAL CHARACTERISTICS RELATED TO PERSUASABILITY

How do demographic, personality, and cognitive traits influence your susceptibility to persuasion? The questions facing the persuasion researcher are these: Is there a direct relationship between individual traits and persuasibility such that people with particular traits are highly susceptible to all forms of persuasion? Or are people with particular traits susceptible only to specific types of message appeals? Persuasion scholars have researched numerous individual characteristics, such as demographics, personality, and cognitive traits, to answer these questions.

Demographic Traits and Persuasibility

You want to go to Florida for spring break, and you need to sell your 1976 Dodge Dart 'Swinger' with 137,000 miles, sans muffler, to finance your trip. What type of person would you try to find (assuming you have no conscience) to buy your car? On a multiple choice test a few students invariably pick "a stupid, old woman" as the answer to this question. Many people believe that women are more susceptible to persuasion than men, that the very old and the very young are particularly gullible, and that people of low intelligence are supposedly easy marks for a good con. Let's consider the research evidence for each of these demographic traits.

Gender

Numerous studies have reported that women are more susceptible to persuasion than men,[3] and this effect has been attributed to male dominance.[4] This dominance, whether biological or cultural in origin, supposedly makes men more inflexible to belief and attitude change.

Recent research reports no significant differences between men and women regarding persuasibility.[5] It seems that women have become less malleable in their attitudes and beliefs as they have become more assertive in their societal roles, or that the topics used to assess persuasive change may have biased the gender differences reported in earlier studies. Clearly, men and women differ in their relative expertise in different topic areas, and expertise may hinder persuasibility. That is, *some* women may be more susceptible to persuasion when the topic area has traditionally been an area of male expertise. *Some* men may be more susceptible to persuasion when the topic area has traditionally been an area of female expertise. These differences should be minimized as sex roles continue to become less exclusive.

The most compelling research on gender and persuasibility has reported differences in the types of messages used to persuade men and women. Women often demonstrate more empathy than men, and, consequently, appeals to sympathy are more likely to influence them.[6] Women, the traditional compromisers, are also more susceptible to appeals to reciprocity—that is, women are more likely to be persuaded to perform some behavior as a favor or as a payment for a favor.[7]

Age

It is generally believed that the young and old segments of our society are most susceptible to persuasion. Age, however, is a misleading and arbitrary variable. Susceptibility to persuasion is related to reasoning abilities, and reasoning abilities are related to age.

The elderly who have no deficit in cognitive function should be no more susceptible to persuasion than any other group in society. In fact, the elderly often exhibit increased inflexibility to change. You have probably had experience presenting new knowledge to an aged relative who refuses to change his or her beliefs, attitudes, or behavior despite evidence to the contrary.

Children's susceptibility to persuasion is related to their ability to analyze a message critically. There appears to be a significant change in the ability to comprehend the content of a plot, story, or argument around the age of nine.[8] Children are increasingly able to discriminate between peripheral and central information, to make inferences connecting the theme of an argument, and to recognize the motivations of other people.[9]

Reasoning skills are not the only variables that affect children's susceptibility to influence. Although young children, especially under the age of five, have limited critical thinking skills, they also have limited attention spans.[10] Young children's sporadic attention is detrimental to persuasion and may, to some extent, protect them from influence. Adolescents, on the other hand, should demonstrate more advanced cognitive functions, yet they are more susceptible to conformity appeals than are younger children. Conformity pressures seem to override reasoning skills, making adolescents susceptible to peer pressure.[11]

Clearly, different age groups are susceptible to different types of messages. To persuade a young child we must garner the child's attention by using exaggerated or peculiar voices, sound effects, and large, colorful images. To persuade a child in grade school we must present simple arguments and associations, and to persuade an adolescent we must appeal to peer pressures and conformity needs.

Intelligence

Contrary to the popular belief that people of *low* intelligence are gullible, researchers suggest that people of moderate intelligence *should be* most susceptible to persuasion. To be persuaded a receiver must: 1) **attend** to the message; 2) **comprehend** the persuasive intent; and 3) **anticipate** the outcome of the belief, attitude, or behavioral change that the message advocates. These three factors are thought to facilitate persuasion. A fourth factor, **critical evaluation** of a message, is thought to inhibit persuasion. All four of these factors (attention, comprehension, anticipation, and evaluation) are related to intelligence. Consequently, the person of moderate intelligence should have sufficient curiosity to attend, comprehend, and anticipate, but only moderate abilities to evaluate a persuasive message critically. In contrast, the more intelligent person may be highly critical of the message, and the less intelligent person may have only limited abilities to attend, comprehend, and anticipate the outcome of the message.[12]

Different types of messages may also persuade people of varying IQ levels. It follows that highly critical and intelligent receivers are more likely to be influenced by logical arguments and the use of evidence.[13] Whether or not the argument is particularly compelling, it is more likely to influence the highly intelligent receiver if it follows a logical format (e.g., if A, then B, or A causes B). Note that the intelligent receiver may be persuaded upon hearing a message that follows a logical pattern, and the receiver may or may not bother to critically evaluate logical appeals for fallacious reasoning.

Dramatic or emotional appeals may influence less intelligent receivers who may have limited attention, comprehension, and anticipation skills.[14] Emotional appeals are attention-grabbing. They are more likely to be remembered, and they dramatically portray anticipated outcomes. Consider the emotional appeal in Figure 8.1. How does the ad grab the reader's attention and dramatically portray anticipated outcomes? Most importantly, what inferences is the less critical receiver likely to make?

It is important to remember that people of both high and low intelligence are aroused by emotional appeals. The emotional appeal, however, may have a unique impact on the less intelligent receiver. The dramatic nature of the appeal may activate the less intelligent person's attention, comprehension, and anticipation—all processes necessary for message influence. Though persons of low intelligence may be more susceptible to invalid inferences in both logical or emotional appeals, the less intelligent person may be more likely to accept vivid impressions, assumptions, and literal interpretations of the emotional message appeal.

This advertisement illustrates an emotional appeal. Note the assumption that the quick headline reader will make. Also note what assumptions the reader must accept for the persuasive goal to be realized.

FIGURE 8.1

IF YOU KNEW HOW MANY DOLPHINS DIED TO MAKE THIS TUNA SANDWICH, YOU'D LOSE YOUR LUNCH.

Tuna fishermen have killed 6,500,000 dolphins over the last thirty years.

They didn't kill these dolphins for food. Or for use in any product. They killed them out of pure, blind greed.

Then they tossed their bodies back into the sea.

It's just these dolphins' bad luck that schools of tuna often swim below dolphin herds. And in the 50's, fishermen began using "purse seine" nets to catch tuna more efficiently.

After a long chase, huge nets are set around dolphin herds to catch the tuna beneath. The nets are then drawn closed.

Exhausted and entangled in the nets, many dolphins suffocate. Others are crushed to death.

The Marine Mammal Protection Act of 1972 has helped. But not enough. Over 100,000 dolphins are still being murdered by tuna fishermen every single year.

Please donate your time or money to Greenpeace so we can continue our efforts to save the dolphins.

And if you must eat tuna, buy only albacore or chunk white tuna which isn't caught "on dolphins."

Better yet, don't buy any tuna at all. It will only leave a bad taste in your mouth.

GREENPEACE

Greenpeace

In conclusion, researchers have found no demographic characteristic that makes a person more susceptible to all types of persuasive messages across different situations. Research findings do suggest, however, that receivers of a particular gender, age, or IQ level may be more susceptible to particular types of messages. People generally believe that women, children, the elderly, and the less intelligent are easy marks for persuasion. We found that this expectation is not true.

Personality Characteristics and Persuasibility

Researchers have long assumed that personality is related to gullibility. This research has led to a great number of inconsistent findings; some studies report significant relationships between personality and persuasibility while others do not. We can make sense of this research by applying the message rule we discussed in the previous section: no message receiver is susceptible to persuasion all of the time, but a person with a given personality may be more susceptible to a particular *type* of message appeal. We will discuss four personality characteristics that are frequently associated with persuasion: self-esteem, dogmatism, authoritarianism, and self-monitoring.

Self-Esteem

Low self-esteem often affects the way a person looks, talks, and acts. Persons with low self-esteem are more likely to display slumped posture, poor eye-contact, and a lack of confidence in their stance and gait. Their speech is often very soft or very boisterous, non-assertive, and marked by a great number of pessimistic, self-deprecating, and cynical statements. People with low self-esteem ask more questions and make fewer assertions than others. People with low self-esteem often preface their opinions and ideas by stating, "This may sound really stupid, but . . .;" "I really don't know what's going on, . . .;" and "You don't have to listen to me, but I think. . . ." People with low self-esteem may lack confidence in decision making, continually doubt their competence, and be perpetually anxious.

Early research on self-esteem and persuasibility reported that people with low self-esteem were more susceptible to persuasion, and people with high self-esteem were more resistant to persuasion.[15] Imagine putting low self-esteem people in one room and high self-esteem people in another, and giving the two groups the same persuasive message: "Why don't you each give me $2 so I can quit this lousy job as a communication research assistant." Would more people with low self-esteem give you money? Probably not. Just because a person has low self-esteem doesn't mean that he or she is gullible!

More recent research suggests that people of moderate self-esteem are most susceptible to persuasion. The rationale provided for this finding is that people of low self-esteem are too worried and anxious about their behavior to process a persuasive message fully, and people of high self-esteem are confident in their ability to comprehend the message but are less likely to yield to the will of another.[16] Let's analyze this hypothesis. Imagine a college party. People at the party are lying on their backs, kicking their legs in the air, dancing the "Alligator." Who is on the sidelines watching? Most likely, those persons with low self-esteem. Why didn't the persons with low self-esteem conform and join the alligator dance? People with low self-esteem often think negatively of themselves. They are afraid they won't fit in. For the person with low self-esteem, it is safer to resist conformity and stand alone than to try to conform and fail. Conversely, persons of high self-esteem love themselves and believe others love them, too. The people with high self-esteem may dance the "Shuffle" while everyone else is doing the alligator in order to stand out and lead the crowd. Thus, the people most susceptible to conformity pressures are those with moderate levels of self-esteem.[17]

It follows that people who are not secure in their self-esteem may be vulnerable to particular types of persuasive appeals. There is conventional evidence that insecure people are susceptible to persuasive appeals that communicate acceptance and social belonging. Members of religious cults are taught to recognize the posture, communication, and behavior of the low self-esteem person. Why do cults target people of low self-esteem, and why are cults so effective in recruiting people of low self-esteem? The Moonies, the Krishnas, and others are effective because they match the message to the target. These cults use a technique called "love bombing." From the time a cult member approaches a target through the time he/she persuades the target to attend a weekend retreat, he/she bombards the target of low self-esteem with messages of caring, love, respect, and belonging. Lonely persons, lacking confidence and positive self-evaluations, are likely to be persuaded by messages giving them attention, new confidence, and new respect for themselves. People of high self-esteem are already satisfying their belonging needs and are less susceptible to these appeals. Note, for example, how the ad in Figure 8.2 presents a message that appeals to the low self-esteem person who needs love, respect, acceptance and belonging.

Fear appeals are also differentially effective on people of high and low self-esteem.[18] A high level fear appeal is more effective with people of high self-esteem. For a person of low self-esteem who already lacks confidence, a high level fear appeal can be overwhelming. An integral part of our psychological well-being is a sense of control over our environment. People of low self-esteem feel powerless to alleviate the source of fear and must reject the fear appeal to maintain their mental health.

Dogmatism
The personality trait of dogmatism is easy to remember by applying the old adage, "You can't teach an old dog new tricks." A *dog*matic person is one who resists change, is reluctant to accept new information, and relies on tradition, routine, and order to make sense of a changing world. An intolerance for inconsistent beliefs and a tendency toward pessimism characterize dogmatic personalities. Rokeach's book, *The Open and Closed Mind*,[19] first introduced research on the dogmatic personality. As one might suspect, it is more difficult to persuade a dogmatic person than an open-minded person.

FIGURE 8.2

This historical advertisement demonstrates an appeal to low self-esteem. The body copy of the ad plays upon the insecurity of the hostess who does not have a socially acceptable toilet seat.

Brunswick-Balke-Collender Company.

Consider the two ads in Figure 8.3. Which one of these ads is more likely to appeal to the dogmatic personality? This campaign is trying to persuade people to change their behavior radically. People with dogmatic personalities do not like change. One ad presents a very logical, information-based appeal (Figure 8.3a), and the other ad appeals to traditional values (Figure 8.3b). The second ad also implies that unless we change, our world as we know it will change. The dogmatic person is more likely to change their behavior based on traditional values and appeals that advocate keeping things (such as our world) the same.

Many public information campaigns have faced resistance by dogmatic personalities, and once again, it is the type of message appeal that determines the success or failure of these campaigns. In Appalachia, a current literacy campaign is meeting resistance; if one's parents don't read, and one's neighbors don't read, why is reading necessary or even desirable? In the midwest, government conservation services are trying to

FIGURE 8.3

These ads request a significant behavioral change. Which of the two ads is most likely to persuade the person with a dogmatic personality?

Environmental Defense Fund and the Advertising Council

persuade farmers to plant tree lines on valuable crop land, and to use minimum tillage techniques to prevent topsoil erosion. Many older farmers oppose "college boys" telling them how to farm the land their families have farmed for three and four generations.

Authoritarianism

The authoritarian personality is motivated by power. Think of people you know who prosper in environments in which behavior is rigidly controlled, power relationships are clearly defined, and opportunities exist for exercising control over other people. Authoritarians seek positions that give them formal power over others. They revel in pomp and circumstance and formal rules of conduct. Because their behavior is governed by rigid rules and moral codes, the authoritarian person rationalizes his or her behavior by claiming it was "the right thing to do!" Good examples of authoritarian personalities in the media are: Sgt. Friday on the old *Dragnet* series or in the more recent Dan Ackroyd movie; Lieutenant Howard Hunter, commander of the swat team on *Hill Street Blues*; and Major Frank Burns on *MASH*. (Interestingly enough, authoritarian personalities are not too popular these days; it is difficult to generate examples of contemporary authoritarian media personalities.)

Lt. Col. Oliver North, the zealous marine who was involved in the 1988 Iran arms-for-hostages deal and the diversion of government funds to the Nicaraguan Contras, presented an authoritarian personality during his indictment and trial. In their advertisement for monetary aid to fund his legal defense, Ollie and his wife Betsy appealed to similar-minded authoritarian personalities. One such ad promises that ". . . every penny given through the Trust goes to assisting Ollie in his pursuit of justice and for the protection of his family. A generous gift to the North Defense Trust is a strong statement for freedom, and a bold stand for what is right."

Authoritarians are susceptible to appeals to authority or appeals to duty, such as presenting the Surgeon General as an authority on the hazards of smoking.[20] An authoritarian appeal may not be effective, however, with people whose lives are not guided by authority figures. Consider the classic "Uncle Sam Wants You" poster. Old Uncle Sam is not particularly effective in recruiting today's youth for the armed services. For an authority appeal to work, the receiver must perceive the cited authority to be a respected and legitimate source of power.

Several studies reveal that the authoritarian places more weight on the status or power of the persuader than on the validity of the arguments presented. That is, the authoritarian does not critically analyze evidence, and may not even seek evidence to support a position advocated by a person with authority. These findings have frightening implications, as, for example, when authoritarian jurors seek less evidence for a conviction and tend to support harsher sentences.[21]

Self-Monitoring

Before you read any further, answer the Self Monitoring Questionnaire in Box 8.1.[22] To get your self-monitoring score, check your answers according to the scoring table below the questions. For each of your answers that match the scoring table, give yourself one point. If you scored high on the scale (from 16 to 25), you are probably a high self-monitor. If you scored from 0 to 8, you are probably a low self-monitor. If you scored between 9 and 16, you are moderate on the trait of self-monitoring.

A **High Self-Monitor (HSM)** is a person who looks to others for social cues. If you look at the items on the questionnaire that reflect a HSM, you will notice that the HSM has a tendency to base his or her evaluations

BOX 8.1   *Self-Monitoring Questionnaire*

The statements below concern your personal reaction to a number of different situations. No two statements are exactly alike, so consider each statement carefully before answering. If a statement is TRUE or MOSTLY TRUE as applied to you, circle the "T" following the question. If a statement is FALSE or NOT USUALLY TRUE as applied to you, circle the "F" following the question. It is important that you answer as frankly and as honestly as you can. There are 25 statements for you to respond to. It is important that you answer every question in this portion of the questionnaire as being either true or false.

1. I find it hard to imitate the behavior of other people. T or F
2. My behavior is usually an expression of my inner feelings, attitudes, and beliefs. T or F
3. At parties and social gatherings, I do not attempt to do or say things that others will like. T or F
4. I can argue only for ideas that I already believe. T or F
5. I can make impromptu speeches even on topics about which I have almost no information. T or F
6. I guess I put on a show to impress or entertain people. T or F
7. When I am uncertain how to act in a social situation, I look to the behavior of others for cues. T or F
8. I would probably make a good actor. T or F
9. I rarely need the advice of my friends to choose movies, books, or music. T or F
10. I sometimes appear to others to be experiencing deeper emotions than I actually am. T or F
11. I laugh more when I watch a comedy with others than when alone. T or F
12. In a group of people, I am rarely the center of attention. T or F
13. In different situations and with different people, I often act like a very different person. T or F
14. I am not particularly good at making other people like me. T or F
15. Even if I am not enjoying myself, I often pretend to be having a good time. T or F
16. I'm not always the person I appear to be. T or F
17. I would not change my opinions (or the way I do things) in order to please someone else or win favor. T or F
18. I have considered becoming an entertainer. T or F
19. In order to get along and be liked, I tend to be what people expect me to be rather than anything else. T or F
20. I have never been good at games such as charades or improvisational acting. T or F
21. I have trouble changing my behavior to suit different people and different situations. T or F
22. At a party I let others keep the jokes and stories going. T or F
23. I feel a bit awkward in company and do not show up quite as well as I should. T or F
24. I can look anyone in the eye and tell a lie with a straight face (if for a right end). T or F
25. I may deceive people by being friendly when I really dislike them. T or F

1. F 2. F 3. F 4. F 5. T 6. T 7. T 8. T 9. F 10. T 11. T 12. F 13. T 14. F 15. T 16. T 17. F 18. T 19. T 20. F 21. F 22. F 23. F 24. T 25. T

of books, music, fashion, and movies on what other people think. The HSM is very concerned with appearances and may act very differently depending on whom he or she is with. The HSM also shows inconsistency between his or her cognitions (beliefs and attitudes) and behavior. The HSM may believe that smoking is immoral, but the HSM may smoke when with a group of friends who are smoking. Or the HSM may express dislike for a particular individual, but yet may be observed socializing, laughing, and interacting gregariously with this same person. For this reason, the HSM is sometimes accused of being superficial and insincere.

In contrast, the **Low Self Monitor (LSM)** is individualistic and an independent thinker. The LSM really doesn't care what other people think and consequently feels little pressure to conform with others. The LSM acts according to his or her beliefs and principles and honestly expresses his or her feelings. If you were to walk into the residence hall lounge and observe a person sitting alone, watching TV, and laughing out loud, it is quite likely that this person is a LSM. Though the HSM risks being superficial and insincere, the LSM risks being perceived as a bit of a geek.

One of my relatives is a low self-monitor. He does not look to others for fashion cues. When he goes to the beach, he wears a green bikini bathing suit with a congo-print skirt that covers the front and back. In his ears he places lamb's wool in lieu of earplugs, on his head he wears a bright orange bathing cap, and around his neck he places slightly mildewed noseclips held on with a shoe string. If the sun is shining, he covers his nose with vaseline instead of expensive sunscreens. As he walks toward the water in his diving flippers and large green frog-man goggles, small children scream and run! And, as a low self-monitor, this person does not mind in the least that I have used him as an example in this text!

Like other personality traits, self-monitoring is related to persuasibility if we match the right message to the right receiver.[23] For a HSM we would want to use a conformity appeal. Messages that emphasize status or prestige, or that "everyone else is doing it," or that a particular behavior or product is socially appropriate, appeal to the HSM. Appeals that stress individualism and living by one's principles are more likely to persuade the LSM.

Consider the anti-smoking campaign. If you were charged with writing a persuasive message to LSM smokers, what would you say? How would you appeal to HSM smokers? Anti-smoking campaigns target both personalities. The knowledge brochures and advertisements that give statistics related to cancer, heart disease, and emphysema will be most effective with low self-monitors. The advertisements that present smoking as socially repulsive (e.g., "Kissing a smoker is like licking an ashtray") or socially deviant ("Everyone else quit smoking, why don't you?") are most effective with high self-monitors.

| BOX 8.2 | *Examples of Construct Systems for Different Knowledge Domains* |

	Knowledge domain	
	College courses	**Music**
Constructs:	major versus non-major	instrumental versus vocal
	difficult versus easy	dance versus listening
	required versus elective	electronic versus symphonic
	interesting versus boring	fast versus slow rhythm

Similar to our conclusion regarding demographic characteristics and persuasibility, the research on personality characteristics and persuasibility demonstrates the importance of matching the message to the receiver. No personality type is more susceptible to all forms of persuasion; rather, certain personality types are susceptible to specific types of message appeals.

Cognitive Traits and Persuasibility

Personality traits and cognitive traits are in many ways very similar. A personality trait is an abstract dispositional characteristic that affects a person's behavior across different situations and points in time. A cognitive trait is a mental characteristic that affects a person's interpretation of his or her world. It follows that if people's interpretations of the world differ, their responses to persuasive messages may also differ. Simply, personality reflects how people act, and cognition reflects how people think.

Evaluative Consistency

In our minds we have **construct systems** for storing knowledge about different topic areas. We have construct systems for people, politics, religion, sports, fields of study, and numerous other topic areas. Each of these construct systems includes dimensions for evaluating our environment and experiences. For example, your **people construct system** may include evaluative dimensions such as intelligent versus unintelligent, attractive versus unattractive, generous versus not generous, witty versus not witty, and aggressive versus unaggressive. You use your evaluative dimensions to judge other people. Likewise, you have construct systems for evaluating dogs, sports, classes, books, music, and other knowledge areas important to your lifestyle (Box 8.2).

People differ in the way they evaluate their world. Specifically, people differ in the extent to which they are **evaluatively consistent.**[24] People who are evaluatively consistent have little tolerance for inconsistencies in their evaluations. Other people can easily integrate positive and negative aspects in their evaluations, a practice that reflects low evaluative consistency. If a guy who is evaluatively consistent about girlfriends experiences a break-up, he is likely to evaluate the woman as a jerk with no redeeming qualities (very consistent). Billy Joel, in contrast, demonstrates low evaluative consistency, (that is, tolerance for inconsistencies) when he sings *She's Always a Woman to Me*: "She can kill with a smile. She can wound with her eyes. She can ruin your faith with her casual lies. And she only reveals what she wants you to see. She hides like a child but she's always a woman to me."[25] We can conclude that Billy Joel's construct system for girlfriends is not evaluatively consistent, and that he integrates inconsistent evaluations in a complex way. The person who is evaluatively consistent in a particular knowledge area (e.g., wines, movies, people, places, or political ideas) has a simplistic evaluation system that categorizes entities as either all good or all bad.

Though there are no specific research studies that assess the effectiveness of different types of message appeals on people with varying levels of evaluative consistency, we can generate a few hypotheses regarding persuasive susceptibility. People who are **low in evaluative consistency** regarding a particular topic have a more sophisticated knowledge network that enables them to incorporate new and perhaps even inconsistent information into their construct systems. This type of person would be able to process messages that integrate the pros and cons of each side of the issue, and that present new ideas and information. In contrast, we know that people who are **evaluatively consistent** are likely to reject inconsistent information or distort information to make it consistent with their previous knowledge.

It follows that people who are evaluatively consistent, regarding the topic area you are discussing, would be most susceptible to a message that appeals to existing beliefs, attitudes, and values. An award-winning Budweiser advertisement illustrates this type of appeal:

	Audio	Video
	[Budweiser theme music]	
Man 1:	"Spose that's them?"	2 farmers walking across large open field . . . sunrise in background
Man 2:	"Don't know who else w'be out this early."	
Anner:	For the Caldwells the early morning is the best time to get things done . . .	
	And times being what they are, not much would make them shut down—even for a few minutes.	Farmers stop. Stand in field staring in same direction . . .

	But this summer . . . the Caldwells have shut down to see something they'll most likely never see again.	Police car/flashing lights. See Olympic runner with Olympic torch running behind squad car on country road.
SFX:	[Budweiser music accompanies sound of runner's foot steps]	
SFX:	[slow clap, picking up speed]	Caldwells clapping.
Anner:	As we host the games this summer, let's hope we all learn that the measure of the Olympics is not in the winning, but discovering the best in all of us.	
SFX:	[Budweiser theme music]	

The Budweiser ad appeals to the receivers' core values: patriotism, hard work, the pioneer tradition of farming the open land, and respect for others. The message suggests that: 1) the Budweiser company holds these values; 2) you should hold these values; and 3) if you are evaluatively consistent, your respect for these values will translate to respect and positive evaluation of Budweiser products. That is, Budweiser promotes American values, American values are positive, therefore Budweiser is positive.

Need for Cognition

Another cognitive trait that determines the effectiveness of persuasive message appeals is **need for cognition.** Before reading any further, answer the questions on the need for cognition questionnaire in Box 8.3. Check your answers according to the scoring table at the bottom of the questionnaire. Give yourself one point for each answer that matches the answer given in the scoring table. You can interpret your level of need for cognition accordingly: Low (0–6), Moderate (7–12), High (13–18).

Need for cognition reflects the extent to which a person likes to think and analyze.[26] Some people like challenging problems, reflecting a **high need for cognition.** These people may, in fact, spend their leisure time working logic problems or puzzles. Other people avoid expending cognitive effort, reflecting a **low need for cognition.**

Need for cognition is a general cognitive trait, according to Petty and Cacioppo, that is not situation specific. In other words, one may not be high in need for cognition in business and low in politics. Need for cognition is a general way of thinking that we consistently use to make sense of our world. People who are low in need for cognition will consistently

BOX 8.3	*Eighteen-Item Need for Cognition Scale*

Answer each as true or false. Give yourself one point for each answer you gave that is consistent with the answers on the bottom of the page.

Item Wording

1. I would prefer complex to simple problems.
2. I like to have the responsibility of handling a situation that requires a lot of thinking.
3. Thinking is not my idea of fun.
4. I would rather do something that requires little thought than something that is sure to challenge my thinking abilities.
5. I try to anticipate and avoid situations in which I will have to think in depth about something.
6. I find satisfaction in deliberating hard and for long hours.
7. I only think as hard as I have to.
8. I prefer to think about small daily projects rather than long-term ones.
9. I like tasks that require little thought once I've heard them.
10. The idea of relying on thought to make my way to the top appeals to me.
11. I really enjoy a task that involves coming up with new solutions to problems.
12. Learning new ways to think doesn't excite me very much.
13. I prefer my life to be filled with puzzles that I must solve.
14. The notion of thinking abstractly is appealing to me.
15. I would prefer a task that is intellectual, difficult, and important over one that is somewhat important but that does not require much thought.
16. I feel relief rather than satisfaction after completing a task that requires a lot of mental thought.
17. It's enough for me that something gets a job done; I don't care how or why it works.
18. I usually end up deliberating about issues even when they do not affect me personally.

1. T 2. T 3. F 4. F 5. F 6. T 7. F 8. F 9. F 10. T 11. T 12. F 13. T 14. T 15. T 16. T 17. F 18. T

Cacioppo and Petty—The Need for Cognition

try to avoid situations requiring a lot of cognitive effort, while people who are moderate in need for cognition will expend a moderate level of cognitive effort in many different situations, but do not enjoy or seek out opportunities to expend a great deal of cognitive effort in any situation. You can probably think of examples of people who are high in need for cognition, who seek experiences that exercise their brains.

A person's need for cognition influences how a person processes a persuasive message. A person high in need for cognition is more likely to analyze the persuader's arguments critically, is more likely to deliberate over the message content, and is more likely to seek facts to support the persuader's claims. A person who is low in need for cognition may be more persuaded by simple, high-impact information, such as image content and emotional appeals. During recent elections you may have heard people say that they would vote for Bill Clinton because "He's such a Southern gentleman." Or that they would vote for George Bush because "He looks so trustworthy." Or that they would vote for Pat Buchanan because he used so many statistics in his speech. These voters may be low in need for cognition; they do not want to expend the effort to learn all the political facts relevant to a reasoned comparison of the candidates.

Cognitive traits such as evaluative consistency and need for cognition reflect how receivers process persuasive messages. The receiver is much more likely to be active in the persuasion process and to analyze a message critically if the receiver is low in evaluative consistency regarding the topic of persuasion and high in need for cognition.

In sum, susceptibility to persuasion is at least partially dependent upon the degree to which the message appeal matches the individual characteristics of the message receiver. In the next section we will explore how situational factors beyond the individual's control can affect susceptibility to persuasion.

SITUATIONAL FACTORS RELATED TO PERSUASIBILITY

Unfortunately, much more research has addressed individual characteristics than has addressed situational factors and susceptibility to persuasion. In this chapter we will focus on the effects of **crowd behavior**—how the existence of a large group of receivers affects persuasive outcomes. The same message may have different effects when it is presented to a single receiver or a small group than when it is presented to a crowd.

A general rule of thumb regarding persuasion and large groups is that you do not want to present bad news to a group. It is more beneficial to the persuader to separate people and deliver bad news individually. An angry group can rally support for each other and create a challenging, and even threatening, situation for the persuader. The presentation of bad news to individuals isolates negative reactions. The negative reactions are more likely to dissipate in isolation than when others reinforce them. A group or crowd can reinforce itself, causing an escalation in emotion and action.

In 1989, ninety-five people were trampled to death at a soccer game in England. Several years earlier, six people were trampled to death at The Who concert in the United States. More recently several hundred Muslims were trampled to death in a pedestrian tunnel leading to Mecca.

These tragedies attest to the hysterical and frenzied nature of crowds. What happens to an individual in a crowd? Think about your own behavior—why do you do things in a crowded football stadium or on a crowded dance floor that you wouldn't do in a small group?

Le Bon, who studied the revolutionary mobs in Paris in the late 1800s, believed that crowd action was intellectually inferior to individual action, but that crowds could be either morally righteous or morally corrupt.[27] The frenzy of a crowd precludes reason, but the hysteria of a crowd may be moved to heroism or terrorism as crowd members are willing to take risks beyond those taken by the individual acting alone.

Le Bon and, more recently, Lang and Lang both attribute the contagion in crowds to a sense of **anonymity** by the individual and a **defense against anxiety**.[28] The lack of inhibition experienced in a crowd is a result of at least three factors: the **distribution of responsibility** among a number of people, rather than just oneself; the distractions of a crowd, which **preclude deliberative thought**; and changes in normative behavior, whereby the **crowd behavior becomes normative** and resistance to the crowd becomes counter-normative. Moreover, the person within a crowd cannot perceive and process the entire situation or scene. Instead, the person is reliant upon information provided through a chain of onlookers, rather than upon firsthand experience. Remember the game of telephone you played as a child? Messages, and even realities, are often distorted when they are transmitted through a number of secondhand sources.

Crowd behavior is also a **defense against anxiety.** If something happens that threatens or frustrates a common goal of a crowd, a riot may ensue. Several years ago in Austin, Texas, a riot resulted when the Ku Klux Klan organized a parade down the main street leading to the state capitol building. The crowd assembled to watch the parade were not KKK members, but KKK antagonists. The crowd, angered by the slogans the KKK chanted, tried to surge threateningly toward the KKK, and the police who were forced to protect the KKK's right to assembly intervened. The crowd felt confused and threatened by the Klan—how could the Klan be active in the 1980s? The Who concert crowd was afraid of not getting tickets, the English soccer crowd was in a hyperexcited state about a sporting event, and the Muslims traveling to Mecca were stuck in a long, hot tunnel with thousands of people. In all of these examples, the crowds were experiencing a common source of anxiety or arousal. Rationally, the crowds' actions were not constructive in solving the problems responsible for this anxiety. The crowds' impulsive behaviors served only as a release for increasing tension and an opportunity to act out salient impulses without public censure.

Everyone has probably been under the influence of crowd behavior at some time. Think about the disembodied feeling you have as you stomp your feet and yell at spectator sporting events, dance in a frenzy at parties, chant or sing at political rallies, and clap, sway, and scream at concerts. Taking only a single example, the football game, consider how easy it is to transfer the energy created by cheering, to flooding the field and tearing down the goalpost. Situational factors (e.g., situational anxiety, inhibition, tension release, and anonymity) can make a person susceptible to influence.

A crowd's potential for hysterical frenzy and influence can have tragic results. Hitler, for example, induced a crowd mentality at political rallies. Spectators were drawn into action at the rallies by the use of loud music, singing, and the chanting of slogans. These activities facilitated individual anonymity and a release of tension. As is the case with Hitler, the crowd mentality not only leads to immediate action, but it can also lead to long-term attitude and belief change. People often rationalize their behavior by changing their attitudes. That is, the impulsive crowd behavior may lead to corresponding beliefs and attitudes. The Germans at Hitler's political rallies may have reasoned, "I sang those patriotic songs, waved my arms and chanted those Nazi slogans, so I must really believe in the Nazi party!"

Individual traits and situational factors influence susceptibility to persuasion. The recognition of crowd contagion factors, and knowledge of message appeals and receiver traits, are the receiver's best defense against persuasive influence.

RESISTANCE TO PERSUASION

The resistance research reflects two divergent perspectives: 1) how to teach *receivers* to recognize and analyze persuasive appeals; and 2) how to teach *persuaders* to overcome receivers' resistance. There is usually a resurgence in studies on resistance techniques during times of powerful persuasive effects. When people become afraid of persuasive influences, efforts are made to teach resistance. During periods when persuasion is believed to be relatively ineffectual, the focus of resistance research changes to teaching persuaders how to overcome resistance and more effectively influence receivers.

Teaching Resistance

The first research to address resistance to persuasive influence was conducted by the Institute of Propaganda Analysis in the 1930's. This research was inspired by Americans' fears regarding the effective use of propaganda by the Germans prior to WWII. These researchers devised a list of seven propaganda techniques that could easily be taught to school children. They believed that if we are able to recognize propaganda techniques, we should be able to resist persuasion. The seven techniques are given simple descriptive names to appeal to school children: testimonials, plain-folks appeal, bandwagon effect, glittering generalities, cardstacking, transfer, and name calling:[29]

1.   **Testimonials** involve endorsements by a celebrity. Testimonials are effective because the credibility and liking we have for the celebrity are associated in our minds with the product, cause, or organization being promoted. Mitch Wiggenhorn, vice president of marketing for Uni-Vite (maker of the Micro Diet, and producer of 30–minute infomercials), claims that celebrity infomercials increase viewership by 25 percent. Celebrity salaries of $150,000 to $300,000, plus a 2.5 to 10 percent cut of future product sales, suggest that celebrity endorsements translate into increased sales for the companies.

2.   **Plain-folks appeals** influence us by presenting the persuader as being just like you and me. Politicians use plain-folks appeals when the candidate is shown eating BBQ at the small town Fourth of July picnic, and advertisers use plain-folks appeals when Mary Jane from Cowville, Middle-America, describes the remedy for her headaches.

3.   The **bandwagon effect** is what you use on your parents when you argue that everyone else is going to a party and that therefore you must go also. Advertisers use the bandwagon effect when they hype a sale by emphasizing that everyone is going to be there, that you're missing out if you're not there, and that there is some urgency in taking advantage of the offer.

4.   **Glittering generalities** use language that is both vague and impressive. Think about the expressions promoters have made so well-known, yet so meaningless: new and improved," "best offer ever," "lowest prices," "post-nasal drip," "guaranteed," "luxurious," etc.

5.   **Card stacking** is the presentation of a biased and one-sided message in which opposing viewpoints are either denigrated or not even acknowledged. Any time you hear a political message or advertisement that you feel is not quite fair, or is downright mean, you have probably witnessed card-stacking.

6.   **Transfer** involves either building or destroying credibility by association. When George Bush called Democratic contender Michael Dukakis a card-carrying member of the ACLU, Bush used negative transfer. When Gerald Ford's campaign promoters showed his start in Big-10 football at the University of Michigan, they were using positive transfer. Often the basis of transfer (ACLU or football) is irrelevant to the personal characteristics that should be under scrutiny (e.g., the candidates' political experience and positions).

7.   The final technique, **name calling,** is one we learn as children. The labeling of a person or group of persons in a negative, emotionally charged manner, perpetuates negative stereotypes and distracts from the real issues that should be analyzed in evaluating persuasive goals.

A more recent approach to teaching resistance to persuasion is Rank's intensification/downplay model.[30] Rank classified persuasion strategies so that receivers could recognize the intentions of the persuader. Rank contends that persuasive messages either **intensify** (exaggerate) or **downplay** (hide) certain attributes of the persuasive promise. More specifically, persuaders intensify the positive attributes of their position and the negative attributes of the opposition. Similarly, persuaders downplay the negative attributes of their position and the positive attributes of the opposition.

Rank contends that there are three ways in which characteristics of a product, person, or doctrine can be intensified: by **repetition** of particular ideas, by **association** to positive or negative ideas, and by exaggerating claims through **composition** of the appeal, such as graphics, type size, voice tone, voice pitch, or speech rate.

Receivers should critically evaluate any attempts to intensify. The Mothers Against Drunk Drivers ad in Figure 8.4 uses association and composition to intensify the fear and horror of a traffic accident. The ad associates drinking and driving with the massacre of a family of four. The headline implies the presence of young, innocent children. By vividly portraying a tennis shoe among the broken glass and car rubble. The composition of the ad intensifies the reader's reaction.

There are also three ways in which characteristics of a product, person, or doctrine can be downplayed: 1) by **omitting** negative information about the promoted idea or positive information about the competition; 2) by **diverting attention** away from the negative aspects of the promoted idea or the positive aspects of the competition; and 3) by **creating confusion** through difficult or ambiguous language or fast-moving or misleading visuals so that negative aspects of the promoted idea and positive aspects of the competition are not realized. The ad in Figure 8.5 addresses the issue of responsible drinking, yet downplays the negative aspects of drinking alcohol by promoting an alcoholic product. The use of humor diverts the negative associations of irresponsible drinking. Moreover, specific details of the effects of irresponsible drinking are omitted, and general confusion is created by the association of appealing product features with the implication that drinking the product can be dangerous.

According to Rank, resistance to persuasion can be learned. The first step to resistance is analyzing a persuasive message to determine if the persuader is using downplay or intensification. You, the receiver, can then nullify the exaggerations or omissions by using a simple rule. Intensify the ideas that are being downplayed. Then, downplay the ideas that the persuader is attempting to intensify. In this manner you dissipate the persuader's deception and exaggeration, thereby arriving at a more objective view of the product, person, or doctrine being promoted.

FIGURE 8.4

This ad sponsored by Mothers Against Drunk Drivers employs intensification by association and composition.

MADD, MN Clarity Coverdale Rueff Advertising, (Minneapolis)

FIGURE 8.5   This advertisement promoting the responsible use of alcohol employs both intensification and downplay.

Good beer is properly aged.
You should be too.

Buying beer is no minor thing. *Miller*

Teaching Persuaders to Overcome Receiver Resistance

During times when the power of persuasion is believed to be minimal, the focus of resistance research changes accordingly. Rather than teaching people how to resist the influences of persuaders, resistance research focuses on how persuaders can increase their effectiveness. It is important for receivers to recognize the six techniques that a producer of a persuasive message can use to prompt receivers to resist the opposition: 1) inoculation; 2) anchoring; 3) commitment; 4) forewarning; 5) rote learning; and 6) distraction.

McGuire proposes that the receiver of a message can be inoculated against influence by others.[31] The **inoculation effect** works much like an inoculation against a virus. A small dose of the virus or opposition's arguments is given, and the receiver is taught to produce antibodies or counterarguments against the virus or opposition. When the receiver later encounters the virus or opposition, the antibodies or counter-arguments are ready to diffuse any effect. Thus, the persuader can use a two-sided argument to increase resistance to the opposition. A two-sided argument includes the persuader's position and the opposition's position. Usually, a persuader presents an argument for the opposition that the receiver can easily and perfunctorily refute. Thus the receiver perceives the opposition to be weak.

Another way to help receivers resist persuasion by the opposition is to employ the principle of **anchoring** in the construction of a message. According to McGuire, the persuader ties the proposed belief or attitude to a belief or attitude that the receiver already holds. The persuader anchors the new belief or attitude to an established belief or attitude. As a result it is more difficult for the receiver to forsake the new belief or attitude because the established belief or attitude would also be jeopardized. For example, A.T.&T. anchors attitudes about long-distance calling to attitudes toward family relationships and the celebration of life rituals. Thus, we get an assortment of ads showing family members calling each other to celebrate birthdays, Wonderbaby's first words, and Superkid's musical talent. A.T.&T. hopes that by anchoring attitudes toward long-distance calling to attitudes about family togetherness, we won't be able to change our attitudes toward long-distance without jeopardizing family togetherness.

The third technique of instilling resistance is **commitment**. McGuire posits that if one is committed to preserving an attitude, changing that attitude will be more difficult. Therefore, if a persuader can increase a person's commitment to an attitude, the chances of the person's being influenced by the opposition decreases. There are several ways in which a persuader can instill commitment. If receivers are encouraged to ruminate upon a belief or attitude, they will likely become more rigid in their position. If receivers are encouraged to voice the belief or attitude publicly, their commitment to the belief or attitude is enhanced. Or if receivers are encouraged to act on a belief or attitude, this behavior will increase their commitment to the cognition. McGuire's theory of commitment is based upon the assumption that people strive toward consistency among their beliefs, attitudes, and behaviors.

McGuire is clearly a seminal scholar in the study of promoting resistance to opposing ideas. Building upon McGuire's work, another group of scholars addressed the effects of **forewarning** the receiver of arguments the opposition may use in influence attempts.[32] Researchers have found that the most effective method of inducing resistance to the opposition is to motivate receivers to **generate their *own* counterarguments.** People are more apt to adhere to arguments they have generated themselves, rather than arguments they have been taught. This is a method of self-persuasion. Rather than perceiving oneself as the victim of persuasive influence, the receiver believes that he or she has reached a conclusion alone. It should be noted that the effectiveness of forewarning obviously depends upon the motivation and ability of the receivers to generate their own counterarguments.

When either motivation or ability is absent, the persuader may teach receivers canned responses to the opposition. **Rote learning** of refutational arguments can be quite effective if the persuader can continually reinforce the learning.[33] For example, many religious organizations use rote learning of refutational arguments to help youth resist influence by outsiders. This is effective to the extent that the rote learning is reinforced on a continual basis, and to the extent that the learner does not have an inquisitive mind that analyzes and challenges this automatic memorization and recitation of arguments.

A final means of resistance that persuaders occasionally employ is **distraction.** If a persuader has only weak arguments and fears that the receivers will recognize the inadequacy of the arguments, the persuader can use distraction to prevent the receivers from thinking the arguments through.[34] This is obviously unethical; the free will of the receivers is jeopardized. It is important, however, to be aware of such tactics in order to resist influence by unethical persuaders. Hitler used this technique during Nazi propaganda rallies. During these rallies loud music blared from speakers, and the crowds were led in continual chantings of Nazi slogans. The noise intensity of the crowd behavior distracted people and reduced the critical analysis and evaluation of the Nazi doctrine.

SUMMARY

A variety of factors influence a receiver's reception of a persuasive message. Individual characteristics, personality, cognitive traits and situational factors are all interrelated in the persuasion process. We have discussed how matching receiver characteristics with the appropriate message appeal enhances the effectiveness of

| BOX 8.4 | *Type of Message Appeal for Various Receiver Characteristics* |

Receiver	Message appeal
female gender	sympathy and reciprocity
young age	vivid images, color, sound
high intelligence	logical appeals
low self-esteem	liking and acceptance
dogmatism	tradition and values
authoritarianism	morals, obedience and duty
high self-monitor	conformity and social acceptance
low self-monitor	individualism and practicality
evaluative consistency	association with existing beliefs and values
low evaluative consistency	new information, multiple perspectives
low need for cognition	imagery and emotional appeals
high need for cognition	facts, evidence, two sides

a message (Box 8.4). In addition, we have surmised, as a result of a lack of research in this area, that it is likely that receiver characteristics and message appeals also interact with situational factors and resistance skills in determining persuasive effect.

In this chapter we have touched only the surface of the interactional role of the message receiver in the persuasion process. To truly understand the interactional role of the message receiver, persuasion researchers should assess the combined interactive effect of the characteristics of the receiver, source, message, and situation to produce a particular persuasive outcome. This would be a master theory of persuasion. Until such time that the interaction of all the components of the persuasion process are known, we can increase the likelihood of successful persuasion and successful resistance by recognizing how receiver characteristics are matched with appropriate message appeals. Moreover, we can acknowledge that persuasive outcomes are dependent upon a complex interaction between receivers, sources, messages, and situations. In conclusion, given the complexity of the persuasion process, the passive and reactionary message receiver, who is susceptible to all types of persuasive messages across situations, appears to be mythical.

Study Guide

individual perspective on persuasion effects
    three conditions for influence
socio-cultural perspective
individual characteristics influencing persuasion
    demographics: gender, age, IQ
    personality:
    self-esteem
    dogmatism
    authoritarianism
    self-monitoring

cognitive characteristics:
    evaluative consistency
    (construct systems)
    need for cognition
situational characteristics influencing persuasion
    crowd behavior: six explanatory factors
research on resistance to persuasion
    teaching resistance to persuasion
        seven techniques
    Rank's model of intensification and downplay
        three strategies used to intensify
        three strategies used to downplay
    methods for resisting the opposition
        inoculation
        anchoring
        commitment
        forewarning
        rote learning
        distraction

Discussion Questions

1. Think about people you know who have the following characteristics. Develop a personality and behavioral profile that describes a person with each of the following characteristics.
   a. high need for cognition
   b. authoritarian personality
   c. dogmatic personality

2. You want to persuade each of the people you described in question one to join your favorite social organization. Construct the actual messages you would use to persuade each of these three people.

3. Think of a time when you were a member of a crowd and experienced the crowd mentality. Identify each of the key factors leading to the crowd behavior you experienced: 1) anonymity factors; 2) disinhibition factors; 3) anxiety or frustration; 4) tension release; and 5) consequent belief or attitude change to justify the crowd behavior.

4. Think of something you have tried to persuade a parent to do. Using this example, show how both the socio-cultural and individual perspectives help explain this situation. For example, what cultural dictated affected your parents. What cultural influences dictated your choice of persuasion strategies? What situational factors constrained your parent's behavior or your behavior? How did individual free will influence the persuasion process? What individual factors (e.g., demographics, personality, and cognitive traits) affected the persuasion process?

5. Consider your scores on self-monitoring and need for cognition. Think of a situation in which someone has tried to persuade you. How did your self-monitoring and need for cognition levels affect this persuasion? According to

these characteristics why was the person successful or unsuccessful? In general, how should a person attempt to persuade you, given your scores on these characteristics?

6. Consider McGuire's persuasion techniques for overcoming receiver resistance. Can you generate examples of situations in which persuaders tried to use these techniques to persuade you (i.e., inoculation, anchoring, commitment, forewarning, rote learning, and distraction)? How would you teach people to resist persuaders' use of these techniques?

References

1. Chance, Paul. 1989. We're only human. *Psychology Today*, November.
2. Gerbner, G., and L. P. Gross. 1976. Living with television: The violence profile. *Journal of Communication*, 26, 173–199.
   Adoni, H., and S. Mane. 1984. Media and the social construction of reality: Toward an integrated of theory and research. *Communication Research*, 11, 323–340.
   Comstock, G., S. Chaffee, N. Katzman, M. McCombs, and D. Roberts. 1978. *Television and human behavior*. New York: Columbia University Press.
   U.S. Department of Health and Human Services. 1982. *Television and behavior: Ten years of scientific findings and implications for the eighties*. Washington, D.C.: Government Documents.
3. Eagly, A. H. 1978. Sex differences in influenceability. *Psychological Bulletin*, 85, 86–116.
4. Montgomery, C. L., and M. Burgoon. 1980. An experimental study of the interactive effects of sex and androgeny on attitude change. *Communication Monographs*, 44, 130–135.
5. Cronkite, G. 1975. Cited in Reardon, K. 1981. *Persuasion: Theory and context* (p. 122). Beverly Hills: Sage.
6. McMillian, J. R., A. K. Clifton, C. McGrath, and W. S. Gale. 1977. Women's language: Uncertainty or interpersonal sensitivity and emotionality? *Sex Roles*, 3, 545–559.
   Eagly, A. H. 1983. Gender and social influence: A social psychological analysis. *American Psychologist*, 38, 871–981.
7. *Ibid.*
   Santee, R. T., and S. E. Jackson. 1982. Identify implications of conformity: Sex differences in normative and attributional judgement. *Social Psychology Quarterly*, 45, 121–125.
8. Calvert, S., and B. Watkins. 1979. *Recall of television content as a function of content type and level of production feature use*. Paper presented at the meeting of the Society for Research in Child Development. San Francisco.
9. Desmond, R. J. 1978. Cognitive development and television comprehension. *Communication Research*, 5, 202–220.
   Collins, A. W. 1979. Children's comprehension of television content. In *Children Communicating: Sage Annual Reviews of Communication Research*, Vol. 7. E. Wartella, ed. Beverly Hills, CA: Sage.
10. Anderson, D. R., and S. R. Levin 1976. Young children's attention to Sesame Street. *Child Development*, 47, 806–811.

11. Matteson, D. 1975. *Adolescence today: Sex roles and the search for identity.* Homewood, IL: Dorsey.
    Marcia, J. 1966. Development and validation of ego identity status. *Journal of Personality and Social Psychology,* 3, 551–558.
12. McGuire, W. J. 1985. Attitudes and attitude change. In *Handbook of social psychology, Vol. 2.* G. Lindzey and E. Aronson, eds. New York: Random House.
13. Eagly, A. H., and R. Warren. 1976. Intelligence, comprehension and opinion change. *Journal of Personality,* 44, 226–242.
14. In relation to intelligence and susceptibility to emotional appeals: People of both high and low intelligence are aroused by emotional appeals. As a result of limited reasoning skills, persons of low intelligence may be more susceptible to invalid inferences, whether those fallacies are found in an emotional or in a logical appeal. The dramatic nature of emotional appeals should, however, facilitate the processes of attention, comprehension, and anticipation in low intelligence people.
15. Janis, I. L. 1954. Personality correlates of susceptibility to persuasion. *Journal of Personality,* 22, 504–518.
16. McGuire, W. J. 1968. Personality and susceptibility to social influence, 1130–1187. In *Handbook of personality theory and research.* E.F Borgatta and W.W. Lambert, eds. Chicago: Rand McNally.
17. Nisbett, R. E., and A. Gordon. 1967. Self-esteem and susceptibility to social influence. *Journal of Personality and Social Psychology,* 5, 268–279.
18. Leventhal, H. 1970. Findings and theory in the study of fear communication. In *Advances in Experimental Social Psychology, Vol. 5.* L. Berkowitz, ed. New York: Academic.
19. Rokeach, M. 1962. *The open and closed mind.* New York: Basic Books.
20. Adorno, T., et al. 1950. *The authoritarian personality.* New York: Harper and Row.
21. Paul, I. H. 1956. Impressions of personality, authoritarianism, and the fait accompli effect. *Journal of Abnormal and Social Psychology,* 53, 338–344.
    Bray, R., and A. Noble. 1978. Authoritarianism and decisions of mock juries: Evidence of jury bias and polarization. *Journal of Personality and Social Psychology,* 36, 1124–1430.
22. Snyder, M. 1979. Self-monitoring processes. In *Advances in experimental and social psychology.* L. Berkowitz, ed. pp. 85–128. New York: Academic Press.
23. Snyder, M., and K. G. DeBono. 1985. Appeals to image and claims about quality: Understanding the psychology of advertising. *Journal of Personality and Social Psychology,* 49, 586–597.
24. O'Keefe, B. J., and J. G. Delia. 1982. Impression formation and message production. In *Social cognition and communication.* M. Roloff and C. Berger, eds. Beverly Hills, CA: Sage.
    O'Keefe, D., and J. G. Delia. 1981. Construct differentiation and the relationship of attitudes and behavioral intentions. *Communication Monographs,* 48, 146–157.
25. Joel, Billie. *She's always a woman.* Copyright held by Joelsongs, 1978.
26. Cacioppo, J. T., and R. E. Petty. 1982. The need for cognition. *Journal of Personality and Social Psychology,* 42, 116–131.
27. Le Bon, G. 1924. Cited in Park, R. E., and E. W. Burgess, *Introduction to the science of sociology,* p. 892. Chicago: University of Chicago Press.

28. Lang, K., and G. E. Lang. 1961. *Collective dynamics. New York: Thomas Y. Crowell Company.*

29. Lee, A. McC., and E. B. Lee. 1939. *The fine art of propaganda.* New York: Harcourt, Brace.

30. Rank, H. 1976. Teaching about public persuasion. In *Teaching about doublespeak.* D. Dieterich, ed. National Council of Teachers of English.

31. McGuire, W. J. 1964. Inducing resistance to persuasion: Some contemporary approaches. In *Advances in experimental and social psychology.* L. Berkowitz, ed. New York: Academic Press.

32. Petty, R. E., and J. T. Cacioppo. 1977. Forewarning, cognitive responding, and resistance to persuasion. *Journal of Personality and Social Psychology,* 35, 645–655.

   Watts, W. A., and L. E. Holt. 1979. Persistence of opinion change induced under conditions of forewarning and distraction. *Journal of Personality and Social Psychology,* 37, 775–789.

33. McGuire, *op cit.*

34. Petty, and Cacioppo, *op cit.*

   Watts, *op cit.*

III

The Process of Persuasion

9

Constructing a Receiver Profile

In 1929, one of the premier advertising and public relations executives of this century, Edward Bernays, organized a group of women marchers to appear in the annual New York Easter Parade. Each women smoked a Lucky Strike cigarette under a banner proclaiming the cigarettes as "torches of liberty." Up until this time, the idea of women smoking cigarettes was loathsome . . . , and the idea of women smoking in public streets was scandalous. This blatant act of social defiance paved the way for tobacco advertising directly targeted toward women.[1]

Increasing numbers of women took up smoking in the 1920s, but their smoking was usually done in secret—behind barns, in wash houses, and inside taxi cabs during lunch breaks. Smoking was a male activity. Men would retire from social interaction with ladies to go to the smoking car on a train, the library or billiard room in a house, or a smoking club.

When women adopted the smoking habit, this signified a social change much greater than a taste for tobacco. Women's smoking constituted rebellion against authority and social norms, a test of independence and equality, and an intrusion into the male domain.

Now consider Bernays' situation prior to the 1929 Easter Parade. Women represented an untapped market for tobacco products. Bernays had to identify the characteristics of women smokers—those women willing to risk social ridicule. He had to appeal to these women's needs and values, and he had to avoid alienating male smokers, many of whom were adamantly opposed to women's smoking. The controversial act of marching women through the streets of New York with cigarettes in their mouths brought women's smoking behavior into the open. Watching women march through the streets in open defiance of social norms added an aura of excitement to the act of smoking. Bernays' final touch—"the torches of liberty"—made smoking a symbol of equality, independence, progress, and change for women.

214

Bernay targeted women smokers who were primarily young, independent, and rebellious, and promoters of social change and equality.

Early advertisers of tobacco products for women not only had to appeal to women's needs, values, and beliefs, but also had to address males' resistance to women's smoking. In his study of early 1920s tobacco advertising, Schudson notes that in early advertisements women watched men smoke but were not shown smoking themselves. Schudson describes a 1926 ad in the New Yorker depicting a man and a woman in evening dress leaving the theater. The man states, "Somehow or other Shakespeare's heroines seem more feminine in modern garb and smoking cigarettes. . . ." Another 1926 ad shows a romantic couple with the man smoking and the woman looking on, with the caption, "Blow some my way." Schudson reports that in 1928 Lucky Strike was one of the first tobacco companies to target women directly. Lucky Strike used the slogan, "Reach for a Lucky instead of a sweet."[2] Though smoking may have been associated with liberty and weight loss for women (as in the current Virginia Slims advertising campaign), advertisers also attempted to persuade men that women's smoking was associated with heightened romance and sophistication.

As this example shows, the acceptance of a persuasive message is largely the result of effective targeting—selecting a clearly defined social group as the message receiver and constructing a message to appeal to this group. In chapter 2 we discussed Burke's definition of persuasion as the manipulation of symbols to establish identification between sender and receiver. Identification and shared meaning can occur only if the persuader understands the characteristics of the receiver. A key to becoming a critical receiver of persuasive messages is to recognize how the persuader has characterized you and how the persuader is using this characterization to "identify" with you. For example, the film *Silence of the Lambs* depicts a young female FBI agent (Jodi Foster) who is sent to death row to interview a psychotic murderer (Anthony Hopkins). The purpose of the interviews is to try to gain some understanding of the mind of the psychotic killer. As the FBI agent is preparing for her study, her boss warns her not to disclose any personal information about herself. Throughout the movie the audience, noting this forewarning, becomes increasingly tense as the killer tries to analyze the FBI agent's personality and psychological fears. The more personal information the killer gains about the FBI agent, the more control he has over her. The audience knows that he will use this persuasive psychological control to his advantage to escape. Identification among communicators provides opportunities for persuasion and perhaps even exploitation.

Throughout this chapter we will adopt the marketing term "target" to refer to the intended receiver/s of a persuasive message. The use of the term "target" reminds us that the most effective persuasion has an intended receiver for whom the message has been specifically constructed. You are the target of many different persuasive campaigns.

Does Bo Really Know?

A superb athlete, a hero to millions, Bo Jackson has tackled his way into the American psyche. Alas, some of his off-the-field promotional activities, namely this ad for Club Bo, leave a little to be desired. This whimsical fan club promo has appeared in *Sport Illustrated For Kids*, *Disney Magazine* and *Marvel Comics* and, at closer inspection, raises the question: "How much, if anything, does Bo really know?"

By Nathaniel Roeg

One day I was real sad and completely different! At school they voted me Most Cool and Most Likely to Marry Miss Mississippi

my dad said, "Hey, here's $17 bucks. Spend it all in one place."

So I joined Club Bo and pretty soon all this stuff showed up in the mail, like a Bo Jackson T-shirt, a gnarly newsletter, a membership certificate, and a poster of Bo to go on my mirror!

After I joined Club Bo things were

Today I'm the Ambassador to Hawaii! I fly my own helicopter!! Yesterday I bought Italy!! And a football team! Thank you Bo!

ARE YOU KIDDING? YES I WANT TO JOIN CLUB BO!

$17 may seem like a trifling sum when the stakes are a child's happiness, but it's a lot more than most stars demand of their adoring fans. In fact, the only one to charge more than Bo is the "Material Girl" herself. Membership to Madonna's fan club costs a suitably outrageous $29 (U.S.). By comparison, U2 charges nothing to join up with them, nor does Lenny Kravitz. For a mere $10, you can join R.E.M.'s fan club (along with a photo and newsletter, they send you one of their singles). For $12.50, you can sign up with Janet Jackson, Dwight Yoakum or Patty Labelle. And like U2, many athletes and bands will send you their picture and newsletter for little more than the price of the stamp.

Whatever happened to "C'mon son, let's go play a little catch"? In 1991, 50.2% of kids serving time in long-term institutions (prison, that is) came from fatherless households. Let's hope that such does not prove to be this child's lot. Fortunately, Big Brothers of America accepts applications from boys 7 to 12 who come from a male-absent home. Surely, a father who considers his child by giving him money will qualify as absent.

There are a few things this gnarly newsletter isn't likely to mention. For example, your $17 is actually going to Nike Corporation, because that's who really owns Club Bo. It should come as no surprise then, that the so-called *Club Bo Newsletter/Product Guide* offers up a panoply of "Bo-dacious Bo-ware"; everything from the Bo Mug ($7.95) and Bo Hat ($16) to the Bo Baseball Shirt ($50) and Bo Team Jacket ($166). Coming issues, no doubt, will offer the Bo Crutch and Bo Replacement Hip.

Likewise, the Air Jordan Flight Club—one of Nike's other "fan clubs"—features an impressive array of "Air-ware" with a smattering of truly incisive biographical information. For example, take the heart-stopping description of Michael Jordan's performance in Game 4 of the NBA Championship: "...So Michael laces up a new pair of Air Jordan's[*] and pours in 28 points in a 97-82 win..." The color of the winning Nike, in a display of astonishing restraint, was never mentioned.

Ahh...fantasies. What would life be without them? But then, you have what it takes to distinguish between fanciful sales pitches and real life. Does an 8 year-old? After all, that is who this ad targets—8 to 14 year-olds kids—because they're the ones who read *Sports Illustrated For Kids*, *Disney Magazine* and *Marvel Comics*.

Sadly, not all kids (or adults, for that matter) value themselves above material possessions. Suicide is the third leading cause of death among American teenagers. That is not to suggest that legions of kids are out there killing themselves for Club Bo sweatshirts, helicopters or Ambassadorships to Hawaii. For the most part, they're killing other people, and being killed themselves. Kids committed 16% of all crimes in the U.S. in 1991, and were victims of over 5.8 million crimes of violence or theft that same year. Having or "acquiring" (stealing, that is) has become one of America's national pastimes, right alongside football, baseball and being cool.

Miss Mississippi for 1991 is Mary Allison Hurdle. Mary Allison is 25 years old, is studying for her Masters of Accountancy at the University of Mississippi, and plans for a career as a chartered accountant. In her free time, she enjoys reading, storytelling and coupon clipping. She has a younger brother Eric, as well as a pet bulldog. Her favorite color is red. There is a great deal more to know about Mary Allison, should you be remotely interested in actually marrying "Miss Mississippi". It is doubtful, however, that Nike has given much thought to the person at the end of the "beauty queen" title, or to the banalities which make up real life. But then, coupon clipping doesn't sell memberships. At least they didn't mention her measurements.

This is Nike's address. What's more, Bo knows that this is Nike's address and, for that matter, a Nike ad. So why doesn't he want you to know? Probably because you wouldn't be too excited about sending your $17 to a $3 billion corporation. And after all, Bo does want you to feel special—so special, in fact, that he neglects to mention that this same address is also home to Club Andre (Agassi) and Air Jordan Flight Club (Michael Jordan's fan club). But then, what harm can there be in a few omissions? Especially when at stake is the bottom line. And with a combined membership of well over 100,000, there can be little doubt that Club Bo, Air and Andre are big business for Nike.

Juvenile crime statistics provided courtesy of the U.S. Justice Office of Juvenile Crime. Suicide statistics courtesy of The U.S. National Center for Health Statistics. Miss Mississippi bio courtesy of The Miss Mississippi Contest, Vicksburg Mississippi.

| BOX 9.1 | *Four Levels of Perspective-Taking* |

Level	Example message
1 Low	"Will you go to the TKE dance with me?"
2	"I need a date for the TKE dance Saturday night. Will you go with me?"
3	"I know I may not be your idea of a dream date, but I'd like you to go to the TKE dance with me. It's only for one night."
4 High	"The TKE's are having a dance Saturday night, and Madonna and her band are providing the music. There will be limitless champagne, and everyone who attends gets a copy of Madonna's latest CD. Would you like to go?"

WHY ANALYZE THE TARGET OF A PERSUASIVE MESSAGE?

There are two primary reasons for analyzing target characteristics: **effective communication** and **effective persuasion.** Studying the target of a persuasive message facilitates the development of shared meaning, which in turn increases the likelihood that the target will modify existing cognitions (attitudes and beliefs). Communicators must identify characteristics of each other that are likely to influence message reception.

Effective Communication and Perspective-Taking

If the persuader can see the world through the target's eyes, he/she greatly increases the chances of establishing shared meaning and understanding. The persuader can better perceive how the target's world view differs from his or her own. With this understanding, the persuader can more easily recognize his or her persuasive goal—what attitude, belief, or behavior needs to be changed—and can more easily identify a plan to accomplish this goal.

Moreover, if the target perceives similarities with the persuader, the target will be more amenable to building a relationship. People who have an appreciation for each other are more likely to work to establish shared meaning and understanding, and are more likely to select ethical persuasion techniques.

The ability to modify a message to the specific needs of the target is called **perspective-taking.** Knowledge of the characteristics of the target allows the persuader to personalize and adapt the message to the target. There are four levels of perspective-taking in persuasive messages (Box 9.1).[3] At the lowest level there is no recognition of the target's needs and perceptions, and the persuader assumes that the target is aware of his or her needs. At the second level the persuader makes his or her needs explicit and may elaborate upon personal advantages. No mention is made of the target's needs. At the third level of perspective-taking, the persuader recognizes the target's position and includes counterarguments to change the target's mind. At the fourth and highest level of perspective-taking, the target takes precedence, and an elaboration of the advantages for the target characterizes the message.

Generally, messages that take the perspective of the target are most effective. There are, however, a couple of exceptions to this rule.[4] It is conceivable that a powerful person who could control the rewards and punishments of the target would not have to produce a perspective-taking message. The target might accept a direct persuasive demand and might even perceive a perspective-taking message as weak! Moreover, it is conceivable that a person could choose to use a lower-level message strategy on purpose. Clark and Delia give the example of a teenager who selects a message elaborating *personal* advantages when persuading her parents. The teen's self-centered message may be more persuasive than a message that takes the parents' perspective. The teen may opt for the self-centered message, knowing full well that her parents' weakness is indulging their children.[5]

To summarize, we have discussed three ways in which seeing the situation through the eyes of the target facilitates communication: 1) understanding and shared meaning between target and persuader allow the persuader to discover the specific cognitive change necessary for persuasion; 2) the target may be able to identify with the persuader and will consequently be more open to communication; and 3) the persuader will be able to take the perspective of the target and may be able to produce a perspective-taking message focusing on the needs and wants of the target rather than self-needs. Let us now turn to the ways in which an understanding of the target facilitates persuasion or cognitive change.

Effective Persuasion and Understanding Cognitions

If a persuader knows the cognitions of the target—the perceptions, beliefs, and attitudes the target has on a particular topic—the persuader can use this knowledge for persuasion. It is also helpful to understand how cognitions in the mind are structured in order to understand how they may be changed. We can never know for certain what goes on in another person's mind, but a theoretical understanding of how the mind works can bolster our speculations.

Associational Memory

Psychological research has shown that attitudes and beliefs, and information in the mind in general, are organized in associational networks. When one bit of information is activated in memory, neural bridges send out reverberating stimulation to activate related bits of information.[6] The neurological pathways in the mind help us to understand and visualize how related information is brought to consciousness simultaneously.

FIGURE 9.1   Heider's Cognitive Consistency Triangle.

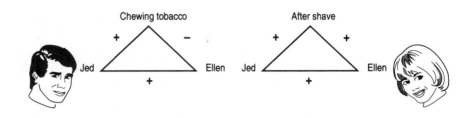

Example of Heider's Cognitive Consistency Triangle

When someone says the word "home" to you, associational pathways activate a number of memories and concepts (e.g., HOME family-house-siblings-mom-grandma-boyfriend, BOYFRIEND-highschool-dances-band-competitions, COMPETITIONS-state-city, etc.). Each concept that is brought to consciousness may activate other concepts, but the first concepts that are activated have the strongest link to the stimulus "home."

Persuasion is a process of drawing associations or bridges between existing cognitions and new attitudes and beliefs. I might persuade you to volunteer for Big Brothers-Big Sisters by associating the needs of these children with the memories activated by the stimulus "home." My persuasive attempt is likely to backfire, however, if I don't know that you activate very negative associations when confronted with the stimulus "home." Speculating about the associations that exist between a target's cognitions and the associations that need to be made to promote persuasion can help the persuader understand how the target views the topic and how the target might view the message.

Cognitive Consistency

The association among cognitions is most stable when bits of information are consistent. Fritz Heider's **balance theory** indicates that when bits of information are inconsistent, there is a state of disequilibrium in the mind and a tension or uneasiness that calls for a return to cognitive consistency.[7] Consider the simplified example in Figure 9.1. Jed loves chewing tobacco. Jed is also wildly infatuated with Sue Ellen. But Sue Ellen despises "chew." Jed is faced with cognitive inconsistency. To resolve this situation, Jed will either change his chewing habits, give up his infatuation with Sue Ellen, or persuade Sue Ellen to like "chew."

The degree to which a person can tolerate cognitive inconsistency is dependent upon the strength of the activation of related cognitions. If two bits of inconsistent information are not associated by a strong neural pathway, the inconsistent beliefs or attitudes may linger for a long time before being simultaneously brought to consciousness. If, for example, Jed has a stong neural pathway between his self-identify and Sue Ellen, and between his self-identity and his chewing habit, but a weak association between Sue Ellen and chewing tobacco, the inconsistency between his two loves may co-exist for a long time.

Clearly, the extent to which a persuader understands the association between a target's cognitions and existing or potential inconsistencies among these cognitions, the greater is the persuader's chance of changing cognitions. Recognizing that many women think "chewing" is disgusting, and that most heterosexual men who chew like to attract women, a persuader could call this cognitive inconsistency to the attention of the target to get the target to change his chewing habit.

The need for consistency in the cognitive system also allows the persuader to anchor a new idea to a pre-existing cognition. If we know that Jed wants to attract Sue Ellen, we can suggest a new after-shave that "drives women wild." We have anchored a new idea, buying Sexy You After-Shave with Jed's already established beliefs and attitudes toward attracting women.

In sum, there are at least two ways the persuader can facilitate cognitive change. The persuader can take advantage of a **cognitive inconsistency,** a state of disequilibrium system that leaves the cognitive system teetering on the brink of change, and promote a belief change that tips the cognitive system back to a state of consistency. Or the persuader can **anchor a new idea** with an already established idea in the cognitive system. Thus, the new idea is absorbed into the cognitive system because of its consistency with pre-existing cognitions. Persuasion is nearly impossible when an inconsistent idea is introduced in isolation. Without an anchor or basis for association within the cognitive system, the new idea is likely to be dismissed.

Analyzing the target of a message facilitates effective communication as well as effective persuasion. Taking the perspective of another person helps interactants reach mutual goals and understanding. Moreover, an understanding of the cognitive associations influencing a person's viewpoint informs perspective-taking. Knowledge of cognitive associations can help the persuader identify persuasive strategies and patterns of reasoning that correspond with the target's cognitions. Ideally, perspective-taking and cognitive understanding should produce more ethical persuasive strategies that lead to valid reasoning, realization of mutual benefits, and the development of shared meaning.

CONSTRUCTING A TARGET PROFILE

Joe McGinnis wrote a book entitled *The Selling of the President,* 1968 to reveal the way in which political handlers construct target profiles of prospective voters.[8] The target profile revealed voters' image of the ideal president. The political managers use this knowledge to create a candidate who fits the voters' ideal image. Richard Wirthlin, Reagan's media manager, says, "I can change the [voters'] perceptions without Reagan ever having to change the policy."[9]

The selling of the president becomes more blatant each election year. Upon meeting his political media managers, Ronald Reagan reportedly said, "I hear you sell soap. I suppose you want to see what the 'bar' looks like." From week to week George Bush's image consultants would analyze which candidate had the corner on "sympathy," "care and concern," and "support for the elderly." They would create special advertisements and messages to draw support for the candidate on key perceptions.

Target profiles allow the persuader to get inside the target's head and to imagine himself or herself in the target's position. Information about the target gives the persuader power to manipulate perceptions, and it makes it difficult for the target to distinguish claims that have been contrived for his or her benefit from claims that represent reality. For this reason, critical receivers must learn how persuaders use targeting information. Receivers must actively work to differentiate reality from the representation of reality that persuaders create.

We will explore three questions used to construct target profiles: 1) What are the demographic characteristics of the target? 2) What are the psychographic characteristics of the target? and 3) Who are the target's social referents or role models?

Demographics

Demographics are observable, factual descriptive features used to segment a large group of people. Demographics include age, income, social-economic status or class, education level, geographic residence, sex, religion, ethnic background, and so on.

Knowledge of the demographic characteristics of a person lets you modify your persuasive message according to the background of the target. Consider beer advertising, for example. Different brands of beer differ little in taste and quality. Therefore, advertisers create different images to appeal to different demographic groups. Miller Beer, for example, is targeted toward young, college-educated students or yuppies. The advertising depicts young, well-dressed, working professionals or students. In contrast, Budweiser is targeted toward the working class man, and the advertising depicts factory workers and skilled laborers rewarding themselves after a long day's work. The target of these advertisements

FIGURE 9.2 a & b

These two advertisements demonstrate how the same product can be targeted towards two diverse social groups.

a)

b)

will think, "Gee, that person is just like me—or just like I want to be. People like me drink beer X." (Figure 9.2a and b).

Psychographics

Psychographics are internal, mental characteristics and cognitions. Psychographics are not observable, but must be inferred or generalized based on the observation of behavior or lifestyle. Communication cannot change a target's demographic characteristics, but the change of a psychographic characteristic is frequently the explicit purpose of persuasion. Throughout this textbook the word **"cognition"** will be used as a generalized term that includes mental perceptions, evaluations, and thoughts. Psychographics is also a general term for cognitive characteristics. There are five different types of psychographics or cognitive characteristics that are used to construct a target profile: **beliefs, attitudes, values, needs, and ego-defense mechanisms.**

Beliefs

A **belief is an assertion we perceive to be true.** This means that *beliefs are not necessarily facts*—we may believe things that are not objectively true. There are several characteristics of beliefs that differentiate beliefs from other cognitions.

1. *Beliefs can vary in strength because beliefs are based on probabilities.* Visualize a straight line with "Buying Rainforest Crunch will help preserve the rainforests" anchoring one end, and "Buying Rainforest Crunch does not make a significant difference in the preservation of rainforests," anchoring the opposite end. What I believe to be true may fall at any point on that line, from certainty that Rainforest Crunch is the answer (point a) to a belief that it is slightly more likely that Rainforest Crunch is a marketing ploy (point b). Obviously, beliefs that fall toward the center of the line are held with less certainty and are therefore most amenable to change (Box 9.2).

2. *Beliefs are interrelated in belief systems.* We can imagine that beliefs are organized categorically in the brain, such that all beliefs about one's family are placed in the same file, and all beliefs about bombs are placed in another file. The key to the interrelatedness of beliefs is a drive for consistency within our belief system. The belief that your family is loving and caring, and the belief that your family physically and verbally abused your brother, are not consistent. Inconsistent beliefs make us uncomfortable. When inconsistency exists, one or both beliefs are vulnerable to change. The interrelated nature of belief systems is important to remember. Beliefs do not change in isolation; a

Buying	a	b	Buying
Rainforest Crunch · · · · · X · · · · · · · · · · X · · · · · · · · · Rainforest Crunch			
helps to preserve			does not significantly
the rainforest.			impact rainforest preservation.

change in a single belief may cause changes in any number of associated beliefs to maintain consistency within the system.

3. *Milton Rokeach contends that our belief systems are comprised of five different types of beliefs.*[10] According to Rokeach, our belief system is like an onion skin. We have layers of beliefs, ranging from the most superficial beliefs to the core principles upon which we guide our lives. The most superficial beliefs are represented by the exterior skin of the onion, and it is only by peeling layer after layer of beliefs that a person's core beliefs are revealed.

There are two important implications of the onion metaphor. First, this means that we have some beliefs—comprising the exterior skin of the onion—that are easily changed. But we have other beliefs, buried beneath layers of onion skin, at the core of the onion, that are resistant to change and influence. Second, this metaphor suggests that consistency among beliefs grows from the core of the onion. That is, the core beliefs are consistent with the inner layers of the onion skin, and subsequent beliefs are built upon the beliefs of the established inner layers. This means that a change in a superficial belief on the exterior of the onion does not necessarily impact upon inner beliefs. But the change of an inner belief requires a reorganization of the beliefs comprising each consecutive outer layer.

Figure 9.3 labels the five different levels of beliefs comprising Rokeach's "onion." **Inconsequential beliefs** are simple likes and dislikes—statements of personal taste, such as: "I think mini-skirts are smashing," and "My favorite food is anchovies." **Derived beliefs** are beliefs you hold based upon the recommendation of some authority, such as a religious leader, a politician, a researcher, the news media, a relative, or a friend. **Authority beliefs** are more specific beliefs regarding whom in your life you can or cannot trust, such as: Dad is always right, my friends are loyal to me, and the president knows what is best. **Primitive-without-consensus beliefs** are doctrines that guide your life, but you realize that other people may not share these doctrines. The core of your belief system is comprised of **primitive-with-consensus beliefs.** These beliefs are indisputable: "I am a student," and "Air is comprised of oxygen and nitrogen."

FIGURE 9.3

According to Rokeach, our beliefs are inter-connected like the layers of an onion. The outer belief layers are easiest to change, and any change of an inner layer may produce a readjustment of the outer layers to maintain consistency among beliefs.

Model of Rokeach's Belief System

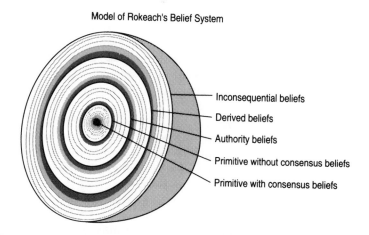

- Inconsequential beliefs
- Derived beliefs
- Authority beliefs
- Primitive without consensus beliefs
- Primitive with consensus beliefs

Knowledge of the target's beliefs, the certainty with which the target holds the beliefs, and the associations among beliefs is invaluable information for a persuader. The persuader must have some understanding of the target's belief system in order to: 1) take the target's perspective; 2) change inconsistent beliefs; or 3) construct messages that associate new ideas with existing beliefs.

Attitudes

In the past, scholars argued that there were three components of an attitude: 1) an evaluative component (e.g., good versus bad judgement); 2) a belief component (e.g., true versus false judgement); and 3) a behavioral component. In recent years scholars have decided that beliefs and behavioral intentions are separate cognitions, and that an attitude is simply a favorable or unfavorable evaluation of some object or behavior.[11] Although we have attitudes—positive or negative reactions—to every conceivable topic from fashion to people, there are several things that all attitudes have in common:

1. *Attitudes are learned responses.* We learn attitudes from observing other people's responses, from our personal experience, and from hypothetical experiences we create in our minds.

2. Because attitudes are learned responses, they are also *relatively enduring*. As we discussed earlier, humans seek some degree of cognitive consistency. Therefore, attitudes that are stable and unchanging

provide a foundation upon which consistent beliefs and behaviors can be built. If attitudes were not relatively enduring cognitive constructs, you could never be certain how you felt about an object or issue (i.e., you would never be sure whether you liked or disliked brussel sprouts), you could never learn from your past experience with an object or issue (i.e., you would have to try brussel sprouts each time you encountered them), and you would never have a stable basis to guide your beliefs and behavior (i.e., you might waste a lot of brussel sprouts ordering them at restaurants and buying them at the store, only to spit them out when you attempted to eat them).

3. As you can see from the previous example, *attitudes are mental constructs that are intricately related to beliefs and behavioral intentions.* A favorable or unfavorable attitude can lead to the development of a consistent set of beliefs. For example, the attitude that war is bad may lead to the belief that war is an unnecessary conflict resolution strategy. Conversely, a belief (e.g., war is an animalistic spinal cord fight response that doesn't involve the higher brain functions of which humans are capable) may lead to an unfavorable attitude. Both beliefs and attitudes may be used as guides for behavior (e.g., registering as a conscientious objector and refusing to participate in combat).

Attitudes are generalized and rather simplistic evaluative reactions (e.g., good or bad, positive or negative, favorable or unfavorable), while beliefs may be more elaborate claims of cause and effect. Just as a persuader must have some understanding of a target's beliefs, the persuader must also understand the target's attitudes.

Values

Values are generalized evaluations of right or wrong that we learn from our culture, and that we use to judge the behavior of ourselves and others. Values are transmitted in the communication of parents, teachers, government officials, religious leaders, and the courts. We dutifully learn these values, and we, in turn, demand that these values are upheld by the very social institutions that taught us the values. Thus, value transmission within a culture is cyclical, self-perpetuating, and consequently very static and unchanging over time.

Steele and Redding conducted a study of American values in 1962.[12] They found that American values had not significantly changed from a study conducted in 1940, or from the cultural values of the American frontier. In fact, you may be amazed that the values Steele and Redding report (see Table 9.1) are as applicable to the United States today as they were in 1962.

There are only three values that I would append to Steele and Redding's original list: the contemporary value of protecting the environment;

TABLE 9.1   Steele and Redding's List of American Values

Puritan and pioneer morality:	value of hard work, honesty, self-discipline, and cooperation
Individuality:	personal integrity, the value of the life of even one person, personal rights
Achievement and success:	personal success, money, self-made achievement, social status
Change and progress:	new and improved, future and present always better than past, change for better
Ethical equality:	all equal before God, all vote, etc.
Equality of opportunity:	all are offered free and equal education and the opportunity to achieve economic success
Effort and optimism:	no problem too big
Efficiency, practicality and pragmatism:	getting things done
Rejection of authority:	power of individual; freedom and rights over duties and obligations
Science and secular rationality:	reason, control, prediction
Sociality:	networking
Material comfort:	happiness can be bought
Quantification:	bigger, faster, more, longer, quantity over quality
External comformity:	popularity, social status
Humor:	leveling influence
Generosity and considerateness:	welfare, benevolence
Patriotism:	loyalty to values of America over nationalism

the value placed on athletic prowess and competition; and the priority of consumerism in our society. Whereas in the past, teachers, parents, and religious leaders were primarily responsible for transmitting cultural values to the young, children now learn values from television, also. One of the few recurring and socially redeeming themes of cartoons is environmental protection. The bad people in cartoons seem to commit environmental crimes as often as any other crime. In addition, the folk heroes of our youth are often athletes or musicians. Whereas we admire musicians, youth try to emulate athletes. Youth revere amateur athletes, but not amateur musicians. Americans value personal physical fitness. Meanwhile, consumerism has become our cultural entertainment. Youth "hang-out" in the malls. We watch hour-long advertisements as television entertainment. Consumer product companies, such as McDonald's, sponsor programs in the elementary schools—Ronald McDonald visits schools to tell elementary school children to read. Of course Ronald is also telling children to buy hamburgers.

Because values are relatively unchanging over time, and because members of a culture share them, values are common premises used by persuaders to argue for acceptance of their messages. By appealing to commonly held values, the persuader attempts to associate the persuasive goals with what the receiver already holds to be "good, right, and true."

Presidential candidates often campaign on "family values" and promises to cherish and preserve the "American family." Anchoring themselves to family values provides a common primitive-with-consensus belief. Yet family values have little to do with presidential policy—foreign affairs, nuclear weapons, star wars, environmental cleanup, inflation, recession, taxes, and the deficit.

As a persuader, and as a critical receiver of persuasive messages, it is important to be wary of value appeals. Although cultural values are widely shared within a given culture, individuals construe cultural values differently. As receivers of persuasive messages, we tend to forget about individual interpretations and applications of values, and, as a result, we aren't critical of value appeals.

Needs and Motivations

Human needs are what drives us to action and what motivates our behavior. Working to satisfy needs gives us pleasure. In a world where all human needs were already met, we would be lost and depressed, characterized by aimless, lethargic behavior. Human needs motivate achievement and progress.

Abraham Maslow proposes a system of human needs that are divided into seven levels: physiological, safety, belonging, esteem, self-actualization, knowledge and understanding, and aesthetic needs.[13] According to Maslow's model, needs are satisfied in sequence from the most basic level needs (physiological) to the most complex human needs (self-actualization, knowledge, and aesthetic needs). Maslow's model is often presented in five levels, rather than seven, but this omits the distinction between deficiency and growth needs. The first four needs Maslow calls **deficiency needs**—needs which, if unmet, may cause illness and/or feelings of loss and unsatisfaction. The last three needs he calls **growth needs**—needs which propel people toward their fullest potential, self-understanding, and a spiritual unity between self and the world (Box 9.3).

According to Maslow, only after basic needs for shelter, nourishment, safety, social belonging and self-worth are satisfied will a person be able to focus beyond the self to the relationship between self and others. Maslow recognizes that these needs are not strictly hierarchical. People often work on several needs simultaneously. In general, however, Maslow maintains that the satisfaction of lower level needs is a prerequisite to the ability to focus on higher level needs.

BOX 9.3 *Maslow's Hierarchy of Needs*

Growth Needs
        aesthetic needs
        knowledge and understanding needs
        self-actualization needs

Deficiency Needs
        esteem needs
        belonging needs
        security needs ·
        physiological needs

Physiological Needs. The lowest level of Maslow's hierarchy includes basic physical survival needs such as food, water, shelter, and procreation. Babies, prisoners, the homeless, and bed-ridden invalids or elderly individuals are the societal groups most likely to be at this basic need level. If survival needs are not met, all of a person's mental and physical energy is focused on acquiring food, water, and shelter. All other needs are abandoned.

Safety and Security Needs. Only after physiological needs are met is a person likely to focus on safety needs. When a person or animal is in need of food, water, or shelter, the animal will take risks to satisfy these needs. Similarly, if disease, physical abuse, crime, or war jeopardize safety, the human spends energy taking safety precautions rather than fulfilling higher needs, such as creating great books or artistic masterpieces.

In addition to physical safety, humans need stability and emotional security. Humans try to predict the future in order to gain control over their environment. The popularity of psychics and fortune tellers, our addiction to weather forecasts, calendars, scheduling, and daily routines all attest to our need for security.

Advertising campaigns appealing to safety and security needs range from home security systems to buying the right tires for your car. Product guarantees also appeal to prediction through security against unknown breakdowns. Perhaps the most famous advertisement addressing security needs is the Medical Alert advertisement with the frightened wail of an elderly woman crying into her Med-Alert speaker, "Help!! I've fallen . . . and I can't get up!"

Belonging Needs. The third level of needs on Maslow's hierarchy consists of needs for acceptance, love, and social support. Many adolescents, chronically lonely people, singles who want to be married, marrieds who want to be single, people who have recently moved to a new city, and people from dysfunctional families are stuck at this level. In addition, people who are in some way disenfranchised from society as a result of racial, religious, occupational, or socio-economic characteristics often have unsatisfied belonging needs.

Advertisers take advantage of people's need for belonging by promising that drinking a particular brand of soda or using a particular brand of shampoo will bring us friends, lovers, and even admiration from passing strangers. Advertisers also appeal to our need for roots with ads that take us back to our childhood or the house of our grandparents, or ads that depict an ethnic tradition. Even real estate advertisers promise us roots in a rapidly changing world by offering to be "our friends" at a time when we may be leaving our friends and family to move to an unknown city.

Esteem Needs. The fourth level of Maslow's hierarchy is the need for esteem. After we are secure in our sense of belonging (level three), we are more likely to progress to gratifying our ego and assuring ourselves that we are truly wonderful and unique individuals. Ego and belonging needs may be reversed in order or may be addressed simultaneously. Advertisers focus on the gratification of esteem needs by showing people celebrating success and achievement and showing people whom others revere. Money, status, power, and respect are all rewards sought at the fourth level of Maslow's hierarchy.

Self-Actualization Needs. At the fifth level of Maslow's need hierarchy we switch from deficiency needs to growth needs. As a person progresses from deficiency needs to growth needs, extrinsic rewards, such as money and status (which are so important at level four), are replaced by intrinsic rewards. Now, the person is motivated to excel for the sheer joy of the task or activity. An intrinsic reward is an ecstasy, joy, or intense satisfaction that comes from within the person.

Maslow describes the person working towards self-actualization as one who is secure and happy with his or her sense of "self," one who dares to be different, one who takes responsibility in life's endeavors, and one who presents the "self" honestly and does not stoop to protect self-identity through lies and deception. The person who is working toward growth embraces both suffering and joy in life and does not blunt experience by repressing events into the subconscious. The self-actualized individual perceives the symbolic and spiritual essence in nature and in all beings; the self-actualized individual can perceive the meaning and significance, if not the good, in all things.

Maslow also discusses the tendency of the self-actualized individual to seek peak experiences characterized by self-absorbing intensity. The struggles, disappointments, and self-exhilaration of Stacey Allison when she overcame the contraints of nature and the limitations of human strength to be the first woman to reach the peak of Mt. Everest describes such a "peak" experience! Her comments attest to her

The Infiniti advertising campaign appeals to self-actualization needs by associating the car with literature, peak experiences, and unity between human and machine.

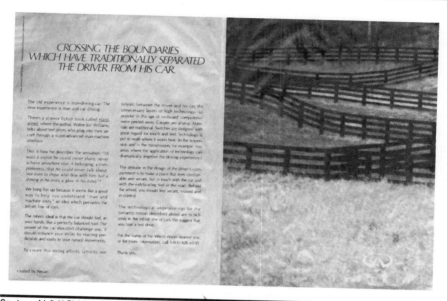

Courtesy of Infiniti Division of Nissan Motor Corporation in U.S.A. and Photographer: Greta Carlstrom

focus on self-actualization needs over self-esteem needs: "I didn't care about being first, second, or third. I came to climb. . . . I think failure is a much more valuable teacher than success."[14] Peak experiences for other people might be the birth of a child, the writing of a book, the creation and blossoming of a business, the development of an exceptional athletic skill, or an intellectual breakthrough.

Advertisers can offer all sorts of extrinsic rewards for product purchase, but it becomes more difficult to promise that a product will gratify intrinsic self-actualization needs. Nevertheless, advertisers try. Consider the ad campaign for Infiniti cars, complete with literary references, an integration of self, automobile, and nature, and a promise of "peak experiences" in your car.

Knowledge and Understanding Needs. The second level of growth needs focuses on self-awareness and an understanding of the self in relation to the world. The human curiosity for the unknown, the mysterious, and the spiritual attests to the presence of knowledge and understanding needs. Whether a person is atheistic or conventionally religious, the need to understand truth, meaning, and justice involves a spiritual quest. The

Buddhists' search for nirvana, or the pure state of being, is a poignant example of knowledge and understanding needs. The steps to nirvana focus on morality, meditation, and wisdom. The Buddhist seeks an ideal state-of-being that exalts the person beyond the base needs of passion, hatred, greed, power, and ego.

The knowledge and understanding level of Maslow's hierarchy is characterized by a need for a meaningful understanding of the relationship between self, others, and world. For this reason, a persuasive appeal to this level of needs cannot be forceful; it cannot boast of a "right way" or an intolerance of alternative belief systems. Some of the New Age literature that proposes societal reform and an egalitarian and peaceful world view is a persuasive appeal to knowledge and understanding needs. Appeals to knowledge and understanding needs cannot be manipulative or superficial, they must assume that the target is a reasoning, rational being, and they must incorporate elaborate systems of proof.

Aesthetic Needs.   Aesthetic needs are at the top of Maslow's pyramid, but they may well be gratified in conjunction with self-actualization and knowledge needs. Once basic deficiency needs are satisfied, humans have a need for beauty. We will seek beautiful surroundings or seek out the beauty of art, dance, and music.

Persuasion appeals that focus on the wonder and awe associated with beauty, rather than on the social or ego needs that beautiful surroundings satisfy, may be appealing to aesthetic needs. Wilderness vacations as opposed to resort vacations appeal to asthetic needs. Artists who are obsessed by creative visions rather than market demands may be actualizing asthetic needs.

An understanding of targets' needs is a powerful tool for a persuader. Obviously, the persuader must understand the need level of the target in order to produce the appropriate message. Persuaders can present a new idea, product, or service as an answer to our needs. We actively seek to gratify unsatisfied needs, and this blind motivation may make us unsuspecting receivers of persuasive messages.

Ego-Defense Mechanisms
The psychographic information a persuader may use to understand the cognitions of a target includes beliefs, attitudes, values, needs, and, finally, ego-defense mechanisms. Ego-defense mechanisms reflect insecurities. Ego-defense mechanisms are rationalizations that protect the self-image. (Maslow would, of course, condemn ego defenses for preventing self-development and growth. He would say that people who are struggling with deficiency needs employ ego defenses and that ego defenses are minimal or absent in people who are satisfying growth needs).

Persuasive messages often take advantage of ego-defense mechanisms to promote cognitive change. The threatened ego is particularly vulnerable to persuasive messages that bolster and protect the self-image. The five defense mechanisms most often used for persuasion are regression, denial, projection, displacement, and sublimation.[15]

Regression. A return to childlike behavior and fantasies is a form of regression. Persuasive messages that show us the disagreeable aspects of our lives and provide an escapist answer to these responsibilities and realities are encouraging the ego-defense mechanism of regression.

In modern times true drudgery is associated with housework. The old Mr. Clean commercials showed a helpless, exhausted, grease-smeared housewife scrubbing her kitchen floor, . . . when, lo and behold, a muscular, larger-than-life man with Yul Brenner sex appeal jumps out of a bottle, cleans the floor, moves the heavy dining table back into place, and, having solved all the problems, tells the helpless Cinderella that she need never worry again; Mr. Clean will help her.

Advertising for lotteries also appeals to regressive ego-defenses. When life gets too difficult and the budget gets too tight, one can vicariously live the fantasy of the weekly lottery winner, who is rescued from life's troubles by a fairy god-mother waving a money wand. Regression helps lottery players choose the fairy tale fantasy over the reality that their chance of winning is one in thirteen million.

Denial. The tendency to avoid ego-threatening information by resisting full understanding and comprehension is denial. Magical thinking, in which we minimize negative information and deceive ourselves into thinking that the problem will go away, is a result of denial.

Cigarette advertisements portray beautiful beaches and white-capped waves, snow-topped mountain ranges, or lush green vegetation to distract us from thoughts of black lungs, diseased tissue, and hospital beds. Credit card advertisements portray fine restaurants, designer clothes, luxury hotels, and exotic foreign cities to distract us from the reality that we must someday pay for these pleasures with real money.

Projection. We also protect our egos by seeing our own inadequacies in others. People who continually yell at others for poor work may be projecting their own incompetency fears.

Persuaders often help us find targets for our projections. Politicians seldom focus on individual responsibility but rather justify our projections that the government is responsible for our inability to budget our money. Some evangelists encourage us to project all our sins and wrongdoings on the "devil"; characterized by the classic line of comedian Flip Wilson, "The Devil made me do it!" In legal trials attorneys use projection to defend mass murderers by projecting blame for the crimes on society for allowing poverty, poor education, and child abuse to continue. As targets of persuasion, we often willingly believe persuaders who project our inadequacies onto others.

Displacement.   The classic example of displacement is the story of the woman who is yelled at by her boss, who then goes home, yells at her spouse, who yells at the teenager, who yells at the toddler, who kicks the dog. When we cannot confront the source of our feelings, we often displace our feelings onto other people or things. Advertisers are experts in displacing feelings of love or attraction. If the source of our infatuation is unattainable, we can displace these loving feelings onto pets, pet rocks, stuffed animals, clothing, and other material possessions. Hence, we get people who "love" their cars.

Sublimation.   A sub-conscious desire that is socially or morally inappropriate is sublimated by translating the urge into an acceptable behavior. In our consumer society we can sublimate our feelings of frustration and aggression toward a boss or family by asserting ourselves with fast cars and motorcyles. The negative characteristics of anxiety that cannot be displayed on the job may be appropriately exhibited in the context of exercise workouts and athletic competitions. Advertisers continue to suggest that we can sublimate feelings of aggression and violence through the sexual exploitation of women—a recent ad for MTV shows a woman scantily clad, handcuffed, bent over on her knees with her head touching the ground.

Reaction Formation.   The ego-defense mechanism of reaction formation is based in guilt. Consider the primal impulses that we've learned to control, but that still occasionally make their way into conscious thought. These primal impulses include being so jealous that you wish that something bad would happen to a person. The guilt associated with these inappropriate desires causes a person to protect the ego by exhibiting behavior opposite to the guilt-producing thought. In other words, thinking about the convenience of someone's death might make you react with extreme concern for the person's well-being. Or thinking about the sexual attractiveness of a married person might make you react with anger or dislike to the person in question. Persuaders can take advantage of reaction formation by drawing attention to your guilt and suggesting an opposite and appropriate reaction.

An ad promoting a college investment fund uses the startling headline, "Now we know why Guppies eat their young. . . ." The copy reads, "The guppy has a rather unique way of handling the problems of parenthood. And while we would never adopt this method, there are times when we can't help admiring its simplicity. Like when we're faced with the prospect of planning for a child's education." This ad plays on parents' unconscious desire to get rid of their kids because they cost too much money! The ad raises this guilt-producing thought in a humorous way. If the idea of eating one's young is even momentarily attractive, the reader will feel guilt and be willing to act on an opposite reaction—save more money and make more sacrifices by starting a college savings fund.

It is important to recognize the psychographic characteristics of a persuasive target, and it is also important to recognize the psychographic characteristics of ourselves. Only through self-awareness can we learn to stop—and critically analyze—those persuasive messages designed to play on our subconscious needs, values, attitudes, beliefs, and defense mechanisms. In addition to demographics and psychographics, the target is also defined by the other people with whom he or she interacts. These important people who influence our lives are called referents.

Analyzing the Target's Referents and Social Groups

As discussed in chapter 2, persuasion often occurs in two steps: an opinion leader is influenced by the message, and the opinion leader persuades friends, families, and co-workers. There are important people, referents, in everyone's life who serve the role of opinion leaders. These referents may be people you want to have favorable impressions of you, people you seek out for advice, or people you seek to emulate. Your referents might include your parents, siblings, co-workers, friends, or role models. In any event, these people play important roles in determining whether or not you will be persuaded.

Referents may serve as a sort of cognitive standard against which you compare your beliefs and attitudes. Consider the consistency triangle in Figure 9.1. It may be important for you to maintain beliefs, attitudes, and behaviors that are consistent with the beliefs, attitudes, and behaviors of your referents.

You are also a member of many social groups, including your family, school, club, work colleagues, religious organization, athletic team, and so on. These groups have cognitive and behavioral expectations for you, as a member of the group. Social groups often take the role of referents, and you adjust your beliefs, attitudes, and behaviors to make them acceptable to the social groups to which you belong.

In the movie *Wall Street*, a mid-level broker is influenced to participate in illegal trading. Recent arrests suggest that illegal trading on Wall Street is quite real. One has to wonder why successful young business people would take these risks. One explanation for their behavior is increased susceptibility to persuasion as a result of group identification.

There are three simple rules regarding persuasibility and group identification.[16] *First, if a person is highly integrated within a group, that person is susceptible to influence by that group.* We typically perform behaviors that important people in our lives reward. For the mid-level

Wall Street investors, the routes to promotion, status, and riches were controlled by high-level Wall Street investors who persuaded them to handle illegal deals.

As long as a person remains highly integrated within a peer group, that person is resistant to change from people on the outside. The Wall Street investor who is an executive in the firm and making a lot of money is not going to be persuaded by the government to change investment banking practices.

A person is susceptible to counter-persuasion when the importance of a reference group, or the motivation to conform with a particular group, decreases. The Wall Street investor is most likely to be persuaded to be a government witness when he or she becomes cynical of the banking industry, feels used by the system, and feels betrayed by clients or colleagues.

Asch's classic study demonstrates the power of group identification for persuasion.[17] Asch instructed a group of confederates before the experiment began. Asch then brought in a naive subject. All subjects were shown a picture of three straight vertical lines and a picture of one straight vertical line. The subjects were asked to judge which of the three vertical lines matched the length of the single vertical line. This is a simple perceptual task. The confederates had been instructed to give the same wrong answer. After a few trials, the naive subject began to conform with the group. That is, the group influenced the naive subject to believe that his or her visual perception was wrong! In Asch's studies, 30 percent of the subjects conformed to the group consensus even when the group's answers were wrong.

There is reason to believe that group consensus is a powerful persuasive motivator for Americans. A comparison study of American and Japanese advertising predicted that Japanese advertising would include more group consensus appeals and that American advertising would include more appeals to individualism. This hypothesis is consistent with traditional Japanese values of group loyalty and conformity. Surprisingly, the hypothesis was not supported; American advertising employed more group and consensus appeals than did Japanese advertising.[18] Bill Moyers in his PBS series *Consuming Images* argues that Americans establish their self-identity through the products they buy. We, in essence, buy our images, and our individualism is restricted to a finite set of images portrayed in advertising. In contrast, the Japanese may define themselves by their work and their achievements, not by the products they buy. From this perspective, it follows that Americans would be susceptible to concensus rather than individual appeals.

Group identification also affects resistance to persuasion. In chapter 1 we discussed how members of a group could help each other resist mind control. According to Schein's study of American prisoners of war, group identification was the most important factor distinguishing those who resisted influence from those who succumbed to their Chinese captors.[19]

The POW's who just "got along" and were least affected by the mind control attempts related well to their fellow prisoners, perceived themselves as members of an identifiable group, and used group interaction to help them maintain their individual identity.

SUMMARY

The creation of a target profile requires the persuader to study the target's: 1) demographic characteristics, 2) psychographic beliefs, needs, attitudes, values, and ego-defenses, and 3) referents and social groups. This knowledge of the target's mind helps the persuader to anchor new beliefs to pre-existing beliefs and to effectuate cognitive change by taking advantage of existing inconsistencies among belief or attitudes. In general, demographic, psychographic, and referent analysis can provide a target profile that characterizes a segment of the population. This allows mass persuaders to generate a message that appeals to a large group of people who have characteristics in common.

From our discussion in this chapter it is also clear that self-awareness of our psychographic characteristics and the influence of referents and social groups on our cognitions and behavior are very important. Recognition of our own psychographic maps and our susceptibility to group influence can help us identify persuasive appeals that seek to manipulate our beliefs and attitudes.

Study Guide

perspective-taking
associational memory
cognitive consistency: balance theory, anchoring
target profile
demographics
psychographics: cognitions
    beliefs and their characteristics
    five types of beliefs: primitive-with-consensus, primitive-without-consensus, authority, derived, and inconsequential
    attitudes and their characteristics
    values
    needs: deficiency and growth needs
        physiological, security, belonging, esteem, self-actualization, knowledge, and aesthetic needs
    ego-defense mechanisms: repression, denial, projection, displacement, and sublimation
referents and social groups
    three ways social groups influence persuasibility
    group identification
    Asch's experiment
    consensus

Discussion Questions

1. How do people differ in their acceptance of cognitive inconsistency? What factors do you think influence whether a person will withstand cognitive inconsistencies and resist changing inconsistent cognitions?

2. Think of advertisements that appeal to each of the seven levels of Maslow's hierarchy of needs.

3. What is the difference between an attitude and a belief? Give an example of your attitude on a particular topic and your beliefs about the same topic. In what ways are attitudes and beliefs similar, and in what ways are they different?

4. How do values differ in different cultures? Try to list the values of different cultures with which you are familiar. Compare and contrast these values with the American values listed by Steele and Redding.

References

1. Schudson, M. 1984. *Advertising, the uneasy persuasion*, pp. 185–204. New York: Basic Books, Inc.
2. Schudson, M. 1984. p. 192.
3. Clark, R. A., and J. G. Delia. 1976. The development of functional persuasive skills in childhood and early adolescence. *Child Development*, 47, 1008–1014. For more recent developments of this research, see: O'Keefe, B. J., and G. J. Shepherd. 1987. The pursuit of multiple objectives in face-to-face persuasive interactions: Effects of construct differentiation on message organization. *Communication Monographs*, 54, 396–419.
4. Shepherd, G. J., and B. J. O'Keefe. 1984. The relationship between the developmental level of persuasive strategies and their effectiveness. *Central States Speech Journal*, 35, 137–152.
5. Clark, R. A., and J. G. Delia. 1976. *op cit.*
6. McClelland, J. L., and D. E. Rumelhart. 1987. *Parallel distributed processing.* Cambridge, MA: MIT Press.
7. Heider, F. 1958. *The psychology of interpersonal relations.* New York: Wiley.
8. McGinnis, J. 1968. *The selling of the president.* New York: Trident.
9. Moyers, B. The public mind. Video series produced by *Public Broadcasting System.*
10. Rokeach, M. 1968. *Beliefs, attitudes and values.* San Francisco: Jossey-Bass.
11. Cacioppo, J. T., R. E. Petty, and T. R. Geen. 1989. Attitude structure and function: From the tripartite to the homeostasis model of attitudes. In *Attitude structure and function.* A. R. Pratkanis, S. J. Breckler, and A. G. Breenwald, eds., pp. 275–309. Hillsdale, NJ: Erlbaum.
12. Steele, E., and W. C. Redding. 1962. The American value system. *Western Speech*, 26, 83–91.
13. Maslow, A. H. 1968. *Toward a psychology of being.* New York: D. Van Nostrand Company.
14. Lebow, D. 1991. *Surmountable odds.* Ambassador, January 1991.
15. Talbott, J. A., R. E. Hales, and S. C. Yudofsky. 1988. *Textbook of psychiatry,* pp. 135–138. Washington, D.C.: American Psychiatric Press.

16. Siegel, A. E., and S. Siegel. 1957. Reference groups, membership groups and attitude change. *Journal of Abnormal and Social Psychology, 55,* 360–364.
17. Asch, S. 1956. Studies of independence and conformity: A minority of one against a unanimous majority. *Psychological Monographs, 416,* 70.
18. Mueller, B. 1987. Reflections of culture: An analysis of Japanese and American advertising appeals. *Journal of Advertising Research, 27,* 51–59.
19. Schein, E. H. 1956. The Chinese indoctrination program for prisoners of war: A study of attempted ''brainwashing.'' *Psychiatry: Journal for the Study of Interpersonal Processes, 19,* 149–172.

10

Understanding and Measuring Cognition

Warning
by Jenny Joseph

When I am an old woman I shall wear purple
With a red hat which doesn't go, and doesn't suit me.
And I shall spend my pension on brandy and summer gloves
And satin sandals, and say we've no money for butter.
I shall sit down on the pavement when I'm tired
And gobble up samples in shops and press alarm bells
And run my stick along the public railings
And make up for the sobriety of my youth.
I shall go out in my slippers in the rain
And pick the flowers out of other people's gardens
And learn to spit.

You can wear terrible shirts and grow more fat
And eat three pounds of sausages at a go
Or only bread and pickle for a week
And hoard pens and pencils and beermats and things in boxes.

But now we must have clothes that keep us dry
And pay our rent and not swear in the street
And set a good example for the children.
We must have friends to dinner and read the papers.

But maybe I ought to practice a little now?
So people who know me are not too shocked and surprised
When suddenly I am old, and start to wear purple.

One of the follies of human nature is to play roles that are contrary to personal beliefs. To all those who observe her, the author of this poem is living her life according to social conventions; yet she is secretly thinking about spitting, stealing flowers, wearing purple and red, and drinking brandy.

How can we hope to change cognitions and behavior if we can't determine what a person truly thinks? We certainly can't infer other people's beliefs by observing their behavior! And we certainly can't peer into the mind of another human being. Successful persuasion requires some knowledge of how an individual receiver sees the world through his or her personalized map of attitudes and beliefs. Obviously, we must know what a receiver's cognitions are before we can hope to change them. Moreover, as receivers ourselves, we must understand how cognitions are related to behavior, and under what conditions we are likely to act on our beliefs and attitudes.

In this chapter we will explore the relationship between cognitions and behavior. Under what conditions do cognitions guide behavior, and under what conditions are people likely to act at variance with their beliefs? We will also explore various methods for peering into the "black box" of the human mind and actually identifying and measuring attitudes and beliefs.

THE RELATIONSHIP BETWEEN COGNITION AND BEHAVIOR

Thus far, we have assumed that the purpose of persuasion is to alter cognitions (attitudes and beliefs). We have also assumed that a change in cognition leads to a change in behavior. That is, if I change your attitude about sororities, I assume that your behavior toward sorority women will also change.

Given this assumption, persuasion researchers were rather shocked when, in 1969, a psychologist named Wicker demonstrated that attitudes did not accurately predict behavior.[1] Wicker reviewed the existing literature on attitude experiments and found that as a whole, the correlation between attitudes and behavior ranged from 0 to .30. A perfect correlation or relationship between two variables would be represented by 1.00. As you can see, a correlation of .30 is rather low.

Rather than concluding that attitudes are unrelated to behavior in the real world, researchers concluded that attitudes and behaviors are unrelated in psychology experiments. Two major criticisms of psychology experiments are: 1) they often use self-reports as indicators of attitudes; and 2) the attitude being measured is not always relevant to the behavior being observed.

In attitude experiments subjects are usually asked to report their attitudes. There are several potential problems with this approach. It is possible that these self-reports are biased and don't represent the subjects' real attitudes at all; subjects may innocently distort their attitudes or may overtly misrepresent their attitudes to make a favorable impression. It is also possible that subjects can't recall or articulate their attitudes. Most interestingly, the very act of responding to the experimentor's questions is a behavior—therefore we are really measuring or observing a behavior, not an attitude.

The second problem with attitude experiments is that the "correspondence" between the attitude assessed and the behavior observed is often low. The **correspondence principle** suggests that attitudes and behaviors must be assessed at the same level of specificity.[2] That is, the assessment of a specific attitude (e.g., your attitude toward protesting abortion in the center of your campus) must be compared with a similarly specific behavior (e.g., whether or not you grab a protest sign and join a group of students protesting abortion laws in the center of your campus). If I tested your global attitude toward abortion—whether or not you support Roe v. Wade—this global attitude may not predict the specific behavior of whether or not you would join a campus protest. The correspondence principle states that the attitude and behavior being compared must be similar in terms of T-A-C-T: *target* of the attitude (abortion), *action* (protest), *context* (center of campus), and *time.* [3]

One way to ensure correspondence between attitudes and behavior is to assess the subject's attitude toward the behavior in question.[4] Rather than asking your attitude toward abortion, I might ask you your attitude toward *protesting* for or against abortion. This assumes, however, that a separate attitude exists for each and every behavior. This contention is not widely accepted in the communication field, and it has been argued that this weakens the attitude concept by equating it with behavior.[5]

Persuasion theorists realize that the relationship between cognition and behavior is much more complex than originally thought. Even with improvements in attitude experiments, the relationship between cognition and behavior remains elusive. Consider your own experiences and observations. Have you ever known someone who is adamantly opposed to smoking pot or drinking alcohol, yet you observe the person demonstrating this very behavior at a party? Exceptions to attitude-behavior consistency have motivated researchers to search for mediating factors—that is, variables that predict under what conditions attitudes and behaviors will be consistent.

Factors Mediating the Cognition-Behavior Relationship

There are three general categories of factors that determine whether cognitions will predict, or be consistent with, behavior: relevancy, consistency, and availability. The condition of **relevancy** requires that the attitude is perceived to be a relevant guide for the behavior in question.[6]

The fact that New Wave advocates publicly display their unique fashions suggests that they perceive consistency between their self-identity, cognitions, and behavior.

A person is also likely to use cognitions to guide behavior if the relevant cognitions are **consistent,** and if the cognitions are consistent with the self-identity the person wishes to present to others. The final factor influencing the cognition-behavior relationship is **availability** of the cognition—that is, the ease with which the attitude or belief can be activated in memory.

Relevancy

The concept of relevancy between attitudes and behavior is as cumbersome as it is obvious. There are numerous factors that may affect individual's perceptions of cognition-behavior relevancy, including personality traits, situational conditions, and decision making ability. Most of the research has focused on three representative factors: self-monitoring characteristics; direct experience; and opportunity for analysis.

Self-monitoring reflects the degree to which a person monitors his or her own behavior—that is, the degree to which a person changes his or her behavior as a result of social cues and the behavior of others. High self-monitors readily change their behavior depending upon situational factors, the people they are with, and the behavior of others. In contrast, the behavior of low self-monitors is an expression of their beliefs and attitudes. Thus, people who are low self-monitors are likely to perceive that *cognitions are relevant* guides for behavior.[7] In contrast, the high self-monitor believes that *other people,* not his or her own cognitions, are relevant cues for behavior. For example, whereas Trish-the-low-self-monitor may believe that environmental protection is the most important political issue and may vote her conscience on this issue, the high self-monitor who holds the same belief about environmental legislation may not vote for the environmental candidate. For Lori-the-high-self-monitor, the voting behavior of other people in her life is a more relevant guide for behavior than her own beliefs. When choosing a course of behavior, the low self-monitor will analyze cognitions, and the high self-monitor will analyze the behavior of other people.

A second relevancy factor is **direct experience.** An attitude that is based on direct experience with the attitude object is a more relevant guide for behavior than an attitude based on indirect knowledge.[8] Consider your attitude toward spinach. If you have tasted spinach before, you will either eat spinach or avoid spinach, consistent with your taste experience. I, on the other hand, have never tried spinach, but hold a negative attitude because I know others don't like spinach. Lacking direct experience, I may try a taste of spinach despite my negative attitude—thereby demonstrating attitude-behavior inconsistency. I am, in fact, more likely to try a taste of spinach than a person who has had direct experience with the slimy green stuff and has developed a negative attitude based on taste memories.

The opportunity to **analyze an attitude** before performing a behavior is also associated with relevancy. Experiments have shown that if people analyze an attitude prior to behavior, they often find that the attitude is not relevant to the situation.[9] If people are forced to act quickly and not given the opportunity to analyze their attitudes, they are likely to respond automatically—and their attitudes will be consistent with their cognitions. Our reactions to other people exemplify this process. If you have a negative attitude toward Chicagoans and you are introduced to a person from Chicago, your automatic response will be negative. But if you are given the opportunity to reflect on your attitude, you may find that your negative attitude toward Chicagoans is not relevant to your behavior toward this person. For instance, your attitude toward Chicagoans may be based on impressions of Chicago drivers and this attitude is irrelevant to your evaluation of this new acquaintance.

Consistency

Cognitions are more likely to guide behavior when cognitions are internally consistent, and when the behavior is consistent with one's self-identity. We know that cognitions are complex cognitive constructs that include both emotional evaluations and beliefs. Research has shown that if the affective (emotional) and reasoning components of a cognition are consistent, it is likely that the attitude will be used as a basis for behavior.[10]

Perhaps you have a set of beliefs that lead you to form a favorable stance on capital punishment. Yet the idea of frying people in an electric chair is abhorrent to your sensibilities. In this case, the affective and reasoning components of your attitude are inconsistent. This inconsistency makes predicting your behavior difficult. If a situation generates affective responses (e.g., "Ick—smoking skin!"), we would expect you to respond negatively to capital punishment. If the behavior generates reasoning responses (e.g., "Capital punishment would deter murderers"), we would expect you to respond positively.

This is called **reason analysis.**[11] Considering the example outlined above, if I wanted you to vote in favor of capital punishment, I would present a logical, belief-based appeal. If I wanted you to vote against capital punishment, I would present an emotional, affect-based appeal. If the reasons behind an attitude are inconsistent, whichever reason is focused on in a persuasive message may determine consequent behaviors.

Notice that our discussion of reason analysis further defines the conditions under which thoughtful analysis of an attitude will result in consistent behavior. Thoughtful analysis may decrease cognitive-behavior consistency if the attitude is affectively driven, and thoughtful analysis may maintain consistency if the attitude is cognitively driven.

Cognitions can also vary in the extent to which they are **evaluatively consistent**. An evaluatively consistent set of cognitions would be all-positive or all-negative. If you were to describe your best friend, your cognitions would be evaluatively consistent if the descriptors were all positive (e.g., nice, friendly, fun, intelligent), and evaluatively inconsistent if some descriptors were positive and some negative (e.g., nice, materialistic, friendly, has a temper). Evaluative consistency among cognitions leads to cognition-behavior consistency.[12] It is important to remember, however, that inconsistency among cognitions (low evaluative consistency) reflects a more complex and sophisticated view of the world. Low evaluative consistency means that you can perceive both strengths and weaknesses of your best friend, your college or university, your family, and so on, making prediction of your behavior on the basis of your cognitions difficult.

In addition to internal consistency among cognitions, the consistency between **cognitions, behavior, and self-identity** also plays a role in predicting cognition-behavior consistency. For some people (e.g., the low self-monitor) behaving in a manner consistent with internal principles and beliefs is very important. To act otherwise would violate one's self-identity. The importance of self-identity can be heightened in some situations to make all people, regardless of self-monitoring level, more concerned about consistency. That is, when a person is made to feel self-conscious, and when a person is made aware of his or her self-identity, consistency between cognition and behavior increases.[13] Experiments have tried to manipulate self-awareness by placing subjects in front of mirrors where they became observers of their own behavior. In these situations, attitudes and behavior were very consistent.

Availability

The degree to which a cognition is easily activated in memory influences the likelihood of cognition-behavior consistency. If a behavior stimulates the activation of a particular attitude, the strength of the association between the attitude and the behavior may determine if the attitude is used as a guide for behavior.

Research has shown that attitudes based on a wealth of **information,** attitudes held with great **confidence,** and **involvement** in the attitude topic all increase the availability of relevant cognitions.[14] If an attitude is based upon a wealth of information, this attitude is likely to be well-integrated into the cognitive system, resulting in more associations that may activate the attitude into conscious awareness. It follows that involvement in the attitude topic and confidence in the attitude also reflect a highly integrated cognitive system. The uncertainty surrounding attitudes for which we have little confidence or little issue involvement makes it difficult to activate these attitudes in memory and to generate these attitudes as guides for behavior. Therefore, the amount of information, the confidence with which an attitude is held, and involvement in the attitude topic all increase attitude availability.

In addition, studies have shown that people with **high need for cognition** are more likely to act consistently with their attitudes.[15] This is probably a result of attitude availability. A high need for cognition reflects a desire to think, analyze, and work through problems and complex tasks. This cognitive effort is likely to generate a large number of attitudes and beliefs. Consequently, cognitions are available for behavioral decisions. The person who is low in need for cognition is less likely to engage in deliberative evaluation of beliefs and attitudes prior to selecting a behavioral response; the person low in need for cognition is more likely to make quick, summary decisions.

A final factor related to availability is **situational competency.** Think about a situation for which you have little knowledge (i.e., low situational competence). Research has shown that in this situation your behavior is likely to be very consistent with your attitudes and beliefs.[16] In fact, your behavior may be rigid and inflexible. If you have little information to guide your behavior, you are likely to rely on your attitudes and beliefs. In a situation for which you have a great deal of knowledge (i.e., high situational competence), you have many behavioral options, many of which may not be consistent with your attitudes and beliefs.

Situational competence may also explain prejudicial attitudes. People with little contact or experience with other cultures often hold bigoted and chauvinistic attitudes. Based on a low situational competency we would predict that chauvinistic people would be very inflexible in their attitudes, and that they would behave in a manner consistent with these attitudes. Conversely, people with high situational competency in multicultural situations are more likely to invoke a wide range of behaviors that may or may not reflect their underlying attitudes.

We can conclude from this discussion that consistency between attitudes and behaviors is difficult to predict. As we have discussed, there are numerous mediating factors that may change the availability, relevancy, and consistency of cognitions, and there are probably many more that have not yet been researched. Persuaders and receivers alike must ensure that the cognitions a message activates corresponds with the desired behavior. Critical receivers must be alert to persuasive strategies that try to increase the availability of relevant cognitions (e.g., by using repetition), or that try to increase the receiver's perceptions of relevance and consistency (e.g., by making associations).

The persuader's task is not easy—and this difficulty once again supports the notion that the receiver is not defenseless against persuasion. The receiver who recognizes the role of cognitive availability, relevancy, and consistency has an arsenal of defenses with which to critique a persuader who is trying to appeal to an attitude or belief as the basis for action.

MEASUREMENT OF COGNITION

To cure an infection, a physician may run a white blood count to get a baseline measurement of the level of infection. Once this baseline measurement is obtained, the physician can repeat the test periodically to determine if the level of infection is decreasing. To treat this illness, the physician may also run a series of tests to identify the bacteria causing the infection. The doctor must identify the infectious agent to find the correct medication to kill that particular form of bacteria.

The measurement of cognition for purposes of persuasion is analogous to a physician treating an infection. A baseline measure of cognition and a post-persuasion measure of cognition are necessary to determine if cognitive change has occurred. Moreover, like the physician searching for the correct drug to treat a particular infection, the persuader must identify the cognitions of the receiver in order to select the correct message.

Why, you may ask, is it so important for you, the student of persuasion, to know how attitudes and beliefs are assessed? The measurement of attitudes and beliefs is pervasive in our society. Information gleaned from polls and opinion surveys is used to construct messages to persuade us to vote for particular politicians and causes, to persuade us to donate money to charities, to persuade us to buy new products, and to persuade us to change our behavior or opinion regarding any number of issues. Decision making groups love to have opinion data to help them predict public reactions to their decisions. You, as an ethical persuader, must understand people's opinions in order to best satisfy their needs and goals. Moreover, as a critical message receiver, you must understand that information from attitude and belief surveys is used to persuade you.

There are three approaches to measurement: scaling, ranking, and physiological assessments. **Scaling techniques** are paper and pencil tests that reflect a person's self-reported attitudes and beliefs. With a scaling procedure, the subject can indicate the degree to which the cognition is strong or weak, and/or the degree to which the cognition is positive or negative. **Ranking techniques** are similar to scaling techniques in that both are self-reports of cognitions, and both can be administered with a simple paper and pencil test. Unlike scaling procedures, ranking tests require simple yes and no responses—"I agree with this belief; I don't agree with that belief." One cannot respond, "I agree with that belief a little, and I agree with the other belief a lot." In contrast to both scaling and ranking procedures, **physiological assessments** do not rely on self-reports. The polygraph (i.e., lie-detector) test and other physiological assessments are based on the premise that subjects can't control, change, or hide physiological responses.

Scaling Techniques

Scaling techniques are by far the most commonly used technique for assessing cognitions. Even allowing for the bias of self-reports, scales are to date the most accurate cognitive measurement. Scaling techniques allow the respondent to register varying degrees of positive or negative affect (good versus bad), and/or varying degrees of confidence in the belief (strongly agree versus strongly disagree). The two most common scaling techniques are Likert scales and bipolar scales.

Likert Scales
Likert scales assess a person's response to a belief statement. It is assumed that the degree to which a person agrees or disagrees to a series of belief statements pertinent to a particular topic reflects a person's attitude toward that topic.

The belief statements used in Likert scales are generated by asking a group of subjects to write down all their beliefs about a particular topic. If the attitude topic we wish to measure is a person's attitude toward eating meat, subjects' belief lists might include: eating meat is healthy; meat is a source of protein; killing animals for meat is unethical; eating muscle tissue and blood is gross. The group of subjects who generate the list of topic-relevant beliefs must be similar to the group of people whose attitudes you ultimately wish to test. It is also important that the researcher ask a large number of subjects to generate beliefs regarding a particular topic, rather than having the researcher generate a set of his or her own beliefs.

The researcher selects the best belief statements, from all the statements generated by the subjects, and pairs them with five-point agree-disagree scales. These statements and scales comprise the final instrument that will be used to assess people's attitudes on this particular topic. There are four rules that determine which beliefs the researcher will select:

1. *Belief statements should be statements of value (good versus bad) rather than statements of fact.* For example, the statement "Americans eat meat" doesn't reveal whether the writer thinks this is a good or bad idea. If the subject writes, "Americans eat too much red meat," this statement incorporates a value judgement, and is therefore a "belief", not a "fact."

2. *Those beliefs that are listed most frequently should be considered for selection on the final measurement scale.* Beliefs that are listed most frequently are most likely to be used by the subjects you later survey. A belief that only one or two subjects voiced in the pre-test may be an unusual belief that is not widely held (e.g., "eating meat fulfills the soul"). Note that in assessing frequency, the subject of the belief is important, not whether the belief is evaluated positively or negatively. For example, "eating meat is immoral" and "there is nothing morally wrong with eating meat" reflect different evaluations of the same belief.

3. In selecting beliefs for the final instrument it *is also important to find beliefs for which there is a variance of response.* This means that all people won't respond to the belief item in exactly the same way. For example, the belief statement: "Killing is bad" is likely to invoke a universal "strongly agree" response, whereas the belief statement: "Killing animals for food is bad" is likely to result in more variable responses.

4. The final consideration is to ensure that about *half the beliefs on the instrument are positive and about half are negative.*[17] This avoids mindless or consistent responses in which a subject checks all ones or all fives on the survey scales. For example, a mix of positive and negative belief statements is likely to generate more thoughtful and less biased responses: 1) Raising cattle for meat consumption creates environmental problems; and 2) Eating meat is a good source of protein.

Once the final list of belief statements has been drawn, a five-point scale anchored by strongly agree and strongly disagree is placed after each belief statement (Box 10.1). The five points on the scale represent: 1) strongly agree; 2) somewhat agree; 3) neutral or don't know; 4) somewhat disagree; and 5) strongly disagree.

BOX 10.1   *Five–point Likert Scales*

---

1. Eating beef is healthy.
   | strongly agree | | X | | | | strongly disagree |
   | | 5 | 4 | 3 | 2 | 1 | |

2. Americans should eat less beef.
   | strongly agree | | | | X | | strongly disagree |
   | | 1 | 2 | 3 | 4 | 5 | |

3. American beef is laden with cancer-producing hormones.
   | strongly agree | | | | X | | strongly disagree |
   | | 1 | 2 | 3 | 4 | 5 | |

4. There is nothing wrong with raising cattle for food.
   | strongly agree | | X | | | | strongly disagree |
   | | 5 | 4 | 3 | 2 | 1 | |

Total Score = 16 (sum of answers to questions 1–4)
Average Score = 16/4 = 4 (slightly positive attitude toward eating beef)

*Notice how numbers on scales are reversed on some questions. This reverse numbering is usually done after the questionnaire is completed. When both positively and negatively phrased beliefs are used, the answers must be coded consistently so that the high numbers reflect a positive attitude regarding the topic, and the low numbers reflect a negative attitude.

The Likert scales can now be administered to a group of subjects to determine their attitude. The Likert scale technique is often called the Method of Summated Ratings. The scores on each belief scale are summed, and this number is used to infer a person's attitude. This allows a researcher to determine the subjects' average attitude score and to determine which subjects maintain attitudes that are greater than or less than the average score.

Bi-polar Scales

Bi-polar scales assess how an attitudinal topic is evaluated according to particular adjectives. Bi-polar scales are anchored by adjectives that have been determined to be opposites (good-bad, strong-weak, or fast-slow).[18] The scales may be five- or seven-point scales, which allow subjects to indicate the degree to which a topic is good or bad (strong/weak, fast/slow). Box 10.2 compares the use of Likert scales and bi-polar scales in assessing attitudes toward New Wave activists. Notice that Likert scales focus on very specific beliefs, while bi-polar scales assess a general affective reaction.

James McCroskey and Virginia Richmond propose a set of six bi-polar scales to determine attitudes toward ethical issues, such as capital punishment, abortion, and drinking ages (Box 10.3a).[19] They propose an alternative set of bi-polar scales to determine attitudes toward belief

BOX 10.2   *Comparison of Likert and Bi-polar Scales*

Likert scales assessing attitude toward New Wavers:

1. New Wave people are cool.

    strongly agree ____5____ __X__4__ ____3____ ____2____ ____1____ strongly disagree

2. I do not admire the goals of the New Wave followers.

    strongly agree ____1____ ____2____ ____3____ __X__4__ ____5____ strongly disagree

3. The clothing New Wave people wear makes an important political statement.

    strongly agree __X__5__ ____4____ ____3____ ____2____ ____1____ strongly disagree

4. The New Wave people's lifestyle is attractive to me.

    strongly agree ____5____ __X__4__ ____3____ ____2____ ____1____ strongly disagree

Total Score = 17 (sum of answers to questions 1–4)
Average Score = 17/4 = 4.2 (slightly positive attitude)

Bi-polar scales
New Wavers are:

Good	____	____	__X__	____	____	____	____	Bad
Beautiful	____	____	__X__	____	____	____	____	Ugly
Kind	__X__	____	____	____	____	____	____	Mean
Moral	____	____	____	__X__	____	____	____	Immoral
	7	6	5	4	3	2	1	

Total score = 21; Average score = 21/4 = 5.2 (slightly positive)

statements, such as, "The President is a good leader" (Box 10.3b). The cognition being studied is likely to determine what bi-polar adjectives are relevant to the topic.

Once appropriate bi-polar adjectives have been chosen, the measurement instrument may be administered to a group of subjects. The subjects' scores on the attitude test can be summed or averaged.

The construction of Likert and bi-polar attitude measurement instruments does take the principles of relevancy, availability, and consistency into consideration. The generation of belief statements and adjectives by a large group of people, with characteristics similar to the people whose attitudes will be assessed, attempts to ensure that the belief statements and adjectives comprising the scales are both relevant to the attitude topic and salient—or readily available—in the subjects' minds. In addition, one need only compare a subject's responses to the different scales comprising the attitude measurement instrument to analyze consistencies and inconsistencies in cognitive evaluations.

BOX 10.3a	*Bi-polar scales for measuring ethical issues*

	1	2	3	4	5	6	7	
Good	1	2	3	4	5	6	7	Bad
Wrong	1	2	3	4	5	6	7	Right
Harmful	1	2	3	4	5	6	7	Beneficial
Fair	1	2	3	4	5	6	7	Unfair
Wise	1	2	3	4	5	6	7	Foolish
Negative	1	2	3	4	5	6	7	Positive

BOX 10.3b	*Bi-polar scales used for measuring beliefs*

	1	2	3	4	5	6	7	
True	1	2	3	4	5	6	7	False
Yes	1	2	3	4	5	6	7	No
Right	1	2	3	4	5	6	7	Wrong
Correct	1	2	3	4	5	6	7	Incorrect
Agree	1	2	3	4	5	6	7	Disagree

Although these procedures attempt to ensure relevance and availability, all scales have inherent limitations in this area. It is conceivable that the beliefs or adjectives used to comprise the scales may not be relevant to a particular subject. Some beliefs or adjectives to which a subject responds on the attitude measurement instrument may be beliefs or adjectives that the subject would be unlikely to generate on his or her own—reflecting low availability. Moreover, the relevancy and availability of the *attitude* being measured as a guide for *behavior* is not addressed by Likert or bi-polar scales.

Ranking Tests

Ranking tests ask subjects to respond to a list of behaviors relevant to an attitude and to check off all the behaviors with which they agree. Box 10.4 presents a ranking test for assessing people's attitudes regarding recycling. Note that this check-list response does not allow for degrees of agreement (e.g., somewhat agree or very strongly agree). The statements are often ordered according to the most tolerant position on recycling legislation (e.g., recycling should be mandatory) to the least tolerant position on an issue (e.g., recycling is good).[20] It is assumed that a person checking off the first behavioral statement (representing the most tolerant position) would also agree with all the subsequent behavioral statements. Thus, the ranking test is interpreted as a pattern of responses (check marks) over a number of behaviors that vary in tolerance. A person who

| BOX 10.4 | *Belief statements placed on rank-order checklist* |

Directions: Please check all of the following statements that reflect your beliefs on the issue of recycling.

_____ Recycling should be mandatory for all people and regulated by federal law.
_____ The legislature should ban particular types of waste in landfills.
_____ The city should provide curbside recycling services and storage bins.
_____ People should be financially reimbursed for transporting recyclables to a recycling center.
_____ Recycling is good for the environment.

checked all the statements in Box 10.4 would be given a more positive attitude score than a person who agreed with only two statements.

The advantage of ranking procedures is that the focus is on attitudes toward specific behaviors, thereby promising greater attitude-behavior prediction. That is, an attitude toward a behavior should be both relevant and available to guide the ensuing behavior. Note that Likert and bi-polar scales typically assess attitudes toward a topic, not a behavior. Ranking procedures do not assess consistency among cognitions. The order of the items on the ranking instrument assumes consistency where consistency may not exist. It is very difficult to produce a set of statements that can be easily and accurately ordered according to attitude tolerance on an issue. For example, different subjects may perceive different rank orderings of the statements. Or subjects may perceive that the difference in acceptance between statement number 1 and 2 (mandatory recycling and landfill regulations) is greater than the difference between statement number 2 and 3 (landfill regulations and curbside recycling). Ideally, the perceived difference between all the belief statements should be about equal, and subjects should accept all the behaviors reflecting lower tolerance if they accept any behavior reflecting greater tolerance.

The primary disadvantage of ranking procedures is that the instrument does not reflect variance in beliefs. That is, a subject can not indicate the degree to which a behavior is good or bad or likely or unlikely.

Physiological Assessments of Attitude

Researchers have long sought the ultimate objective measurement of cognition—a physiological (physical) test that would indicate attitudes and or beliefs without the subject's ability to bias the response. Physiological tests have used measurements of heart rate, pupil size, EEG (brain activity), EMG (muscle activity), and even perspiration.[21] Most of these attempts have not produced a reliable measure of attitude. Heart rate, pupil size, EEG activity, EMG activity, and perspiration may all increase with arousal, but it is impossible to tell (through a physiological

Shoe by Jeff MacNelly.

test) whether this arousal is positive or negative. Your pupils, for example, may increase in size when you gaze into the eyes of a lover, and they may also increase in size when you watch a scary movie. In both cases you are aroused, but in the former the arousal is positive, and in the latter it is negative.

The most promising development in physiological attitude-assessment is the measurement of the movement of facial muscles. Researchers have found that particular facial muscles are stimulated under conditions of positive arousal, and different facial muscles are stimulated under conditions of negative arousal.[22] The stimulation of facial muscles is not apparent to the naked eye, thereby requiring elaborate equipment to measure muscle activity. For this reason this test is limited to studies conducted in research laboratories and is not as easy to administer as the simple paper and pencil ranking and attitude scales.

The relevance, availability, and consistency principles are difficult to assess in relation to physiological measures. It is conceivable that people differ in the extent to which they rely on physiological sensations in formulating attitudes and behavioral responses; that is, there may be individual differences in the degree to which physiological responses are relevant and available as behavioral guides. Moreover, physiological assessments reflect global attitudinal reactions to a topic or object and do not lend themselves to assessing consistency among specific cognitions. On the other hand, it could be argued that physiological responses are the most natural (i.e., available) and unbiased (i.e., relevant) representations of attitudes we can ever hope to measure.

The measurement of cognition prior to and following persuasion is optimal, but not always practical. Obviously, you do not hook your friends or parents up to electrodes or even ask them to fill out a short questionnaire for you before you make a request. When measurement data is not available, you must use intuition to assess a person's attitudes and beliefs. You can increase the accuracy of your intuition by considering the three conditions for correspondence between cognitions and behavior: relevancy, consistency, and availability. Ask yourself what cognitions the person will perceive as relevant to the situation. Ask yourself whether or not these cognitions are consistent with other attitudes and beliefs the person holds. If inconsistency exists, you must analyze which cognitions are likely to be activated. Also consider whether or not these cognitions are consistent with the impression the person will want to make on other people. If inconsistency exists, you can guess that the person will not use cognitions as guides for behavior. Finally, you can use attention tactics, repetition, and associations to increase the likelihood that particular cognitions will be activated in the person's mind.

THEORY OF REASONED ACTION

Martin Fishbein and Icek Ajzen have proposed a comprehensive and mathematical cognitive change theory.[23] The theory of reasoned action integrates the material we have discussed in this chapter. The theory: 1) addresses the relationship between cognition and behavior; 2) includes both beliefs and attitudes as the basis for cognition; and 3) provides a model for measuring cognition and predicting behavior. The practicality of cognitive measurement should also be apparent, as Fishbein and Ajzen's model provides guidelines for both measuring and *changing* cognitions. To fully understand Fishbein and Ajzen's model, we must examine how attitudes, beliefs, and behavior are defined and measured. Though this may at first appear to be unnecessarily laborious, this newly-gained understanding will help you appreciate how you, as well as others, formulate evaluations, and how these evaluations guide behavior.

According to Fishbein and Ajzen, the key to predicting behavior is to discover a person's behavioral intention—what the person intends to do. Fishbein and Ajzen focus on **behavioral intentions** because many spur-of-the-moment situational factors can influence actual behavior. For example, you may intend to study persuasion tonight, but the noise your roommate makes, or a special invitation to go to a movie, or a headache you develop shortly after dinner may influence your behavior.

Behavioral Intentions

According to the Theory of Reasoned Action, there are two things we must know to understand a person's behavioral intentions: the person's attitude and the degree to which other people influence this person's actions. Therefore, behavioral intentions (BI) are the sum of a person's attitude score (A) and social normative (SN) influence score:

$$BI = (A) + (SN)$$

BOX 10.5   *College students' beliefs regarding smoking pot*

1. Smoking pot causes memory loss.
2. Smoking pot is relaxing.
3. Smoking pot is immoral.
4. Smoking pot is a good social activity.
5. Smoking pot makes one think creatively.

Attitudes

Attitudes, according to Fishbein and Ajzen, are comprised of beliefs. Recall that a belief is a statement that may vary in probability—that is, the degree to which a person considers the belief to be true. The first step in Fishbein and Ajzen's model is to construct a set of beliefs about the attitude topic. The belief statements should be generated by a group of people who are similar to the group of subjects you ultimately wish to study. Box 10.5 represents a set of beliefs generated by college students about smoking pot.

Now that we have a set of beliefs about smoking pot, we can determine a college student's attitude toward smoking pot. The subjects in our study would evaluate each of the beliefs on two scales: 1) an evaluation scale, which asks whether the outcome or consequence inherent to this belief is good or bad; and 2) a strength scale, which asks the subject how likely is it that this belief is true. Seven-point scales are used for this purpose:

Smoking pot is harmful to one's health.

very good	___	___	___	___	___	___	___	very bad
	3	2	1	0	−1	−2	−3	
very likely	___	___	___	___	___	___	___	very
	3	2	1	0	−1	−2	−3	unlikely

To assess your attitude toward smoking pot, you should rate each belief listed in Box 10.6 on the evaluation scale and on the importance scale. Write in your scores in the columns provided. For example, the first belief, "smoking pot causes memory loss," would probably be evaluated as a bad thing (−3 or −2). The second scale assesses the degree to which you believe this to be true, or the strength of this belief. If you think that it is "very unlikely" that "smoking pot causes memory loss," you would record a −3 on the strength scale.

To compute your attitude score, you can multiply the number in the e column by the number in the b column and record your answer in the third column of Box 10.6. If you add all the numbers in the third column, this is the sum of the evaluation of each belief (e) multiplied by the

---

| BOX 10.6 | *Compute your attitude toward smoking pot by completing the following scales* |

e (belief evaluation: Is the consequence of this belief good or bad?)

b (belief strength: How likely is it that this belief is true?)

bad   –3 –2 –1 0 1 2 3   good

very likely 3 2 1 0 –1 –2 –3 very unlikely

Belief	e score		b score		e × b
memory loss	____	×	____	=	____
relaxing	____	×	____	=	____
immoral	____	×	____	=	____
social	____	×	____	=	____
creative thinking	____	×	____	=	____

Sum of third column is attitude score:

---

strength of each belief (b). This is your attitude score ($A = \Sigma b_i\, e_i$; $i = 1$). You will notice that the product of a negative belief evaluation (e.g., "smoking pot causes memory loss" is a bad consequence (–3)) multiplied by a negative belief strength (e.g., it is not very likely that this is true (–3)) is a positive number (+9). If you think about it, this makes sense—if a negative effect is unlikely, this has a positive influence on your attitude.

Having fun yet? To make this score meaningful, you can divide your attitude score by the number of belief statements you used to compute this score—which in our example is five. This will give you an average attitude score. (Note that the highest possible score you could receive for any one belief statement is +3 multiplied by +3, which equals nine; the lowest possible score you could receive for any one belief statement is –3 multiplied by +3, which equals negative nine. This means that an average attitude score will range between –9 and +9. Positive nine represents a very favorable attitude, and negative nine represents a very unfavorable attitude.

Social Normative Influences

You should now have an attitude score representing your attitude toward smoking pot. To predict your behavior, we also have to compute social normative influences on your pot smoking behavior. The social normative influence on your behavior is the degree to which you modify your behavior for other people. According to the Theory of Reasoned Action, your social normative influence is equal to the sum of significant others' attitudes (b_i) toward your smoking pot, multiplied by your motivation to comply (m_i) with each of these people ($i = 1$):

$$SN = \sum_{i=1} b_i\, m_i$$

BOX 10.7   *Computation of Social Normative Influence*

Referents' attitude toward my smoking pot (b_i)

Motivation to comply (m_i)

should smoke 3 2 1 0 −1 −2 −3 should not smoke

Low 1 2 3 4 5 6 7 High

Referent's Name	Referent's Attitude (b_i)		m_i		$b_i \times m_i$
1. _____	_____	×	_____	=	_____
2. _____	_____	×	_____	=	_____
3. _____	_____	×	_____	=	_____
4. _____	_____	×	_____	=	_____
5. _____	_____	×	_____	=	_____

Sum of last column is social normative score:

To compute your social normative influence, write down people who influence your decision to smoke pot in Box 10.7. For each of these people, evaluate the person's attitude toward your behavior on a scale ranging from −3: "This person thinks that I should not smoke pot;" to +3: "This person thinks that I should smoke pot." Next, evaluate how likely you are to do what this person wants you to do (motivation to comply). The motivation to comply scale ranges from 1: low motivation to comply with this person; to 7: very high motivation to comply with this person. Complete the table in Box 10.7 to compute your social normative score: 1) Multiply the referent's attitude (column b_i) by your motivation to comply with this person (column m_i) and place this number in the column labeled $b_i \times m_i$; 2) add the numbers in the $b_i \times m_i$ column; 3) to determine your average score, divide the $\Sigma b_i \times m_i$ column total by the number of people you listed. (Note that the highest possible score you could have for any one referent would be three (b_i scale) multiplied by seven (m_i scale), which equals 21. Therefore, your social normative score should range between +21 and −21, with positive numbers indicating that other people are influencing you to smoke pot and negative numbers indicating that other people are influencing you NOT to smoke pot).

Back to Behavioral Intentions

All right! We're almost through. The final step is to add your attitude score and your social normative influence score to determine your behavioral intention. This score can range from positive 30 to negative 30, because the average attitude score ranges from +9 to −9, and the average social normative score ranges from +21 to −21. Numbers approaching

| BOX 10.8 | *Summary of Theory of Reasoned Action* |

Attitude = the sum of (belief strength × belief evaluation)
Social Normative Influence = the sum of (referent's attitude × motivation to comply with referent)
Behavioral Intention = (Attitude) + (Social Normative Influence)

positive 30 represent a positive intention to smoke pot, and numbers approaching negative 30 represent a negative intention to smoke pot. For your entertainment pleasure, Box 10.8 summarizes the formulas for each step in Fishbein and Ajzen's model.

As you can see, this model attempts to assess beliefs that are relevant to a particular behavior. Generating beliefs from a large subject pool and selecting the most frequently stated beliefs address the availability of the belief statements. Each subject's rating of the strength and evaluation of a series of belief statements, in addition to the evaluation of social normative influences, provides data reflecting consistency among beliefs, and the consistency between internal (cognitive) and external (social normative) influences.

Summary of Theory of Reasoned Action

Specific ways in which persuaders can use Fishbein and Ajzen's model to change cognitions and behavior will be discussed in detail in the next chapter. The primary purpose of our detailed discussion of this model at this point is to demonstrate how cognitions and behavioral intentions can be measured, and to illustrate how cognitions and behavior are interrelated.

A strength of the Theory of Reasoned Action is that it has been used successfully in numerous public information campaigns concerning weight loss, women's occupational choices, family planning behavior, consumer behavior, and voting behavior.[24] The assessment of attitudes and social normative influences predicted behavioral intentions, and behavioral intentions were moderately predictive of actual behavior. Most importantly, attempts to change attitude or social normative components in these campaigns did lead to changes in intended behavior. For example, this model was applied to persuade alcoholics to join a rehabilitation program. Whereas previous campaigns had focused on the negative aspects of drinking, the Theory of Reasoned Action model indicated that the alcoholics' beliefs about the behavior in question—joining the alcohol treatment program—should be targeted for change. In an experiment in which some alcoholics received the traditional message focusing on changing beliefs about drinking, and another group of alcoholics received a message focusing on changing beliefs about committing to the treatment program, the merits of the Theory of Reasoned Action model were evident. Up to 30 percent of the alcoholics who were initially opposed to the treatment program but received the message that focused on behavior-relevant beliefs were persuaded to sign up for treatment, compared to only 5 percent of those who received the traditional health-oriented message.[25]

Additional research has shown that this model works best when a subject has personal control over the performance of a behavior. When the behavior is outside the subject's personal control and dependent upon external factors such as time, money, or skills, behavioral intentions may not be a good indicator of actual behavior.[26]

Interestingly enough, the best predictor of behavioral intentions is neither attitudes nor social normative influences. Research has shown that prior behavior is the best predictor of behavioral intentions. Studies have also found that of the two (attitudes or social normative influences), attitudes are usually the best predictor of behavior.[27]

The most critical problem with this theory is the assumption that attitudes and social normative influences have equal weight in predicting behavior.[28] Based on our discussions of self-monitoring, you would expect high self-monitors to place more weight on social normative influences than on attitudes. Conversely, you would expect low self-monitors to place more weight on attitudes than on social normative influences. The most critical problem with the theory of reasoned action is that researchers have found it very difficult to separate the effects of attitudes and social normative influences. The two concepts blur together. What part of your attitude is your own—what part is not influenced by other people?

SUMMARY

Getting inside a person's mind to discover attitudes and beliefs and the relationships among attitudes and beliefs is a difficult task. Subjects may lie. Subjects may make their beliefs and attitudes more socially desirable than they really are. Subjects may even bias their reports to try to please the experimenter. Moreover, knowledge of subjects' cognitions does not necessarily allow us to predict behavior. The correspondence between cognitions and behavior is dependent upon numerous variables that influence the perceived relevancy of the cognition, the consistency among cognitions, and retrieval of the cognition from memory (availability).

Although cognitive measurement is an imperfect science, we must use what tools we have. To persuade, one needs knowledge of the target's cognitions. To assess whether or not persuasion has occurred, one needs knowledge of cognitive change. To resist persuasion, one needs knowledge of the cognitions of the persuader. Like Sherlock Holmes, we need a combination of scientific method and intuitive speculation to deduce what thoughts and beliefs reside in the mental "black box."

Study Guide

two problems with attitude measurement
correspondence principle: T-A-C-T
relevancy of cognitions
    self-monitoring
    direct experience
    analysis of cognitions
consistency of cognitions
    affective and reasoning components
    reason analysis
    evaluative consistency
    self-identity
availability of cognitions
    amount of information
    confidence
    involvement
    need for cognition
    situational competency
measurement of cognition
    scaling techniques
        Likert scales
        bi-polar scales
    ranking techniques
    physiological techniques
        heart rate
        pupil dilation
        EMG
        EEG
        perspiration
        facial stimulation
theory of reasoned action
    behavioral intentions
    attitudes
    belief evaluation
    belief strength
    social normative influences
    referents' attitudes
    motivation to comply

Discussion Questions

1. Think of a situation in which your behavior was inconsistent with your attitudes and beliefs. Using the concepts of relevancy, consistency, and availability, provide a rationale for this inconsistency.

2. Write down all the words you can think of that describe yourself. Analyze this list. Are your cognitions evaluatively consistent? Do you behave consistently with these descriptors, or are there differences between your true self-identity and your actions?

3. Think of a situation for which you have low situational competency. Think of a situation for which you have high situational competency. Are there differences in the correspondence between your cognitions and behavior in these two situations?

4. How are behavioral intentions different from behavior? Is this a useful concept?

References

1. Wicker, A. W. 1969. Attitudes versus actions: The relationship of verbal and overt behavioral responses to attitude objects. *Journal of Social Issues*, 25, 41–78.

2. Ajzen, I., and M. Fishbein. 1977. Attitude-behavior relations: A theoretical analysis and review of empirical research. *Psychological Bulletin*, 84, 888–918.

3. Ajzen, I. 1987. Attitudes, traits, and actions: Dispositional prediction of behavior in personality and social psychology. In *Advances in experimental psychology*, vol. 20, L. Berkowitz, ed. pp. 1–63. New York: Academic Press.

4. Ajzen, I. 1982. On behaving in accordance with one's attitudes. In *Consistency in social behavior: The Ontario symposium*, vol. 2, M. P. Zanna, E. T. Higgins, and C. P. Herman, eds. pp. 3–15. Hillsdale, NJ: Erlbaum.

5. O'Keefe, D. J. 1980. The relationship of attitudes and behavior: A constructivist analysis. In *Message-attitude-behavior relationship*. D. P. Cushman, and R. D. McPhee, eds. pp. 117–148. New York: Academic Press.

6. Snyder, M. 1982. When believing means doing: Creating links between attitudes and behavior. In *Consistency in social behavior: The Ontario symposium*, vol. 2. M. P. Zanna, E. T. Higgins, and C. P. Herman, eds. pp. 105–130. Hillsdale, NJ: Erlbaum.
   Snyder, M., and D. Kendzierski. 1982. Acting on one's attitudes: Procedures for linking attitude and behavior. *Journal of Experimental Social Psychology*, 18, 165–183.

7. *Ibid.*

8. Fazio, R. H., and M. P. Zanna. 1978. On the predictive validity of attitudes: The roles of direct experience and confidence. *Journal of Personality*, 46, 228–243.
   Fazio, R. H., and M. P. Zanna. 1981. In *Advances in experimental social psychology*, vol. 14. L. Berkowitz, ed. pp. 161–202. New York: Academic.

9. Tesser, A. 1978. Self-generated attitude change. In *Advances in experimental social psychology*, vol. 11. L. Berkowitz, ed. pp. 289–338. New York: Academic.
   Wilson, T. D., D. S. Dunn, J. A. Bybee, D. B. Hyman, and J. A. Rotondo. 1984. Effects of analyzing reasons on attitude-behavior consistency. *Journal of Personality and Social Psychology*, 47, 5–16.

10. Millar, M. G., and A. Tesser. 1989. The effects of affective-cognitive consistency and thought on attitude behavior relations. *Journal of Experimental Social Psychology*, 25, 189–202.
    O'Keefe, D. J., and J. G. Delia. 1981. Construct differentiation and the relationship of attitudes and behavioral intentions. *Communication Monographs*, 48, 146–157.

11. Wilson, T. D., and D. S. Dunn. 1986. Effects of introspection on attitude-behavior consistency: Analyzing reasons versus focusing on feelings. *Journal of Experimental Social Psychology*, 22, 249–263.
    Wilson, T. D., D. S. Dunn, D. Kraft, and D. J. Lisle. 1989. Introspection, attitude change, and attitude-behavior consistency: The disruptive effects of explaining why we feel the way we do. *Advances in Experimental Social Psychology*, 22, 287–343.

12. Schlegel, R. P., and D. DiTecco. 1982. Attitudinal structures and the attitude-behavior relation. In *Consistency in social behavior: The Ontario symposium*, vol. 2. M. P. Zanna, E. T. Higgins, and C. P. Herman, eds. pp. 17–49. Hillsdale, NJ: Erlbaum.

13. Scheier, M. F., A. H. Buss, and D. M. Buss. 1978. Self-consciousness, self-report of aggressiveness, and aggression. *Journal of Research in Personality*, 12, 133–140.
    Ajzen, I. 1987. *op cit.*

14. Davidson, A. R., S. Yantis, M. Norwood, and D. E. Montano. 1985. Amount of information about the attitude object and attitude-behavior consistency. *Journal of Personality and Social Psychology*, 49, 1184–1198.
    Sivacek, J., and W. D. Crano. 1982. Vested interest as a moderator of attitude-behavior consistency. *Journal of Personality and Social Psychology*, 43, 210–221.
    Fazio, R. H., and M. P. Zanna. 1978. *op cit.*
    Ajzen, I. 1987. *op cit.*

15. Cacioppo, J. T., R. E. Petty, C. F. Kao, and R. Rodriguez. 1986. Central and peripheral routes to persuasion: An individual difference perspective. *Journal of Personality and Social Psychology*, 51, 1032–1043.

16. Mischel, W. 1984. Convergences and challenges in the search for consistency. *American Psychologist*, 39, 351–364.

17. Likert, R. 1932. A technique for the measurement of attitudes. *Archives of Psychology*, 140, 1–55. Quoted in Emmert, P. 1989, Attitude measurement. In *Measurement of Communication Behavior*. P. Emmert, and L. Barker, eds. pp. 134–153. New York: Longman.

18. Osgood, C. E., G. J. Suci, and P. H. Tannenbaum. 1957. *The measurement of meaning*. Urbana, IL: University of Illinois Press.
    Babbie, E. R. 1986. *The practice of social research*. 4th ed. Belmont, CA: Wadsworth.

19. McCroskey, J. C., and V. P. Richmond. 1989. Bipolar scales. In *Measurement of Communication Behavior*. P. Emmert, and L. Barker, eds. pp. 154–167. New York: Longman.

20. Guttman, L. L. 1944. A basis for scaling qualitative data. *American Sociological Review*, 9, 139–150.

21. Cacioppo, J. T., and R. E. Petty, eds. 1983. *Social psychophysiology: A source book*. New York: Guilford.
    Riccillo, S. C. 1989. Physiological measurement. In *Measurement of Communication Behavior*. P. Emmert and L. Barker, eds. pp. 267–295. New York: Longman.

22. Cacioppo, J. T., and R. E. Petty. 1979. Attitudes and cognitive response: An electophysiological approach. *Journal of Personality and Social Psychology*, 37, 2181–2199.
    Petty, R. E., and J. T. Cacioppo. 1981. *Attitudes and persuasion: Classic and contemporary approaches*. Dubuque, IA: Wm. C. Brown.

23. Fishbein, M., and I. Ajzen. 1975. *Belief, attitude, intention and behavior: An introduction to theory and research.* Reading, MA: Addison-Wesley.
24. Ajzen, I., and M. Fishbein. 1980. *Understanding attitudes and predicting social behavior.* Englewood Cliffs, NJ: Prentice-Hall.
25. *Ibid.*, 218–242.
26. Ajzen, I., and T. Madden. 1986. Prediction of goal-directed behavior. Attitudes, intentions, and perceived behavioral control. *Journal of Experimental and Social Psychology*, 22, 453–474.
    O'Keefe, D. 1990. *Persuasion.* Beverly Hills, CA: Sage.
27. Sheppard, B. H., J. Hartwick, and P. R. Warshaw. 1988. The theory of reasoned action: A meta-analysis of past research with recommendations for modifications and future research. *Journal of Consumer Research*, 15, 325–343.
28. Miniard, P. W., and J. B. Cohen. 1979. Isolating attitudinal and normative influences in behavioral intentions models. *Journal of Marketing Research*, 16, 102–110.

11

Changing Beliefs, Attitudes, and Behavior

Persuasion, or literally cognitive change, can be as inconsequential as a change in the perceptions of a brand of soap or as integral to our survival as conflict resolution. Persuasion is a prerequisite for diplomatic relations—both internationally and interpersonally. There are numerous conflicts around the world in which the body count continues to climb decade after decade: Irish Republican Army nationalists fighting Irish Protestants and Great Britain; South African Blacks fighting apartheid; Soviet Republics fighting the Kremlin; and Chinese revolutionary students fighting the communist regime. In all of these situations, persuasion is imperative to the resolution of conflict.

If all persuasion involves cognitive change, then all persuasion must necessarily involve differences of opinion. Although this chapter is not specifically about conflict resolution, it is certainly pertinent to conflict prevention. The cognitive change theories presented in this chapter are as applicable to your daily interactions with parents and roommates as they are to international problem-solving.

A persuasion theory is an elaborate hypothesis that explains and predicts how persuasion occurs. Theories are abstract and generalized—that is, they are not specific to any particular situation. For this reason, theories of persuasion should be applicable to all persuasive contexts (e.g., mass mediated, small group or interpersonal) and functions (e.g., building relationships, getting votes, getting money). This is the beauty of a theory—one explanation is applicable to many situations. In this chapter we will discuss six theories that explain and predict how a persuader can bring about cognitive change.

THEORY OF REASONED ACTION

The theory of reasoned action not only provides a comprehensive model for measuring cognition and predicting behavioral intentions, but also provides numerous options for changing cognitions, and ultimately, behavior. This theory suggests that attitudes and social normative influences (i.e., influence from friends and referents) determine behavioral intentions (i.e., the intent to perform an action). In the previous chapter we outlined the method for calculating attitudes and social normative influences. Here we will simply summarize the four components that comprise a behavioral intention: the evaluation of beliefs, the strength of beliefs, the attitudes of significant others, and the motivation to comply with significant others.[1] This means that there are many methods a persuader can employ to try to change your behavioral intentions. The persuader can: 1) create a new belief; 2) change the evaluation of an existing belief; 3) change the strength with which you hold a belief; 4) change your perceptions of what attitude other people have; 5) change your motivation to comply with others; and 6) change your referents or important others.

Let's consider an example and the options available to a persuader. If a friend is trying to persuade you to join Amnesty International, your friend could adopt any combination of the six strategies outlined above. Your friend could create a new belief, "Amnesty International helps you learn about humanitarian conditions in other countries." Your friend could change the evaluation of an existing belief: "Amnesty International is politically liberal, but this is a good thing." He/She could change the strength of an existing belief by providing you with facts strengthening the belief that Amnesty's actions save people's lives. If you thought your fellow students had a neutral or negative attitude toward the organization, your friend could change your perceptions of this attitude by telling you about the number of students who are attending the meetings. If your parents are against liberal political organizations like Amnesty, your friend might persuade you to change your motivation to comply with your parents' wishes. And finally, your friend might convince you to add a new referent to your list, by informing you that the faculty person you most respect is the faculty advisor for the organization.

The theory of reasoned action suggests at least six methods for changing a person's behavioral intentions. Any one of these changes in beliefs, attitudes, or social normative influences could produce a change in a person's intended behavior. The theory of reasoned action suggests that behavioral intentions are one of the best predictors we have of actual behavior.

FUNCTIONAL ATTITUDE THEORY

The primary tenet of functional attitude theory is that people may hold the same or similar attitudes but hold these attitudes for very different reasons. Knowing the function an attitude serves reveals how the attitude can be changed. Although functional attitude theorists have limited their discussion to attitudes, the theory could also apply to beliefs. It is likely that beliefs, as well as attitudes, serve various functions, and the knowledge of what function a belief serves indicates how the belief can be changed. Scholars have proposed at least five different functions an attitude can serve: compliance, knowledge, ego-defense, social adjustment, and value-expression.[2] The basic tenet of functional attitude theory is this: 1) two or more people may hold the same attitude but may hold this attitude for very different reasons; and 2) different approaches must be used to change these two people's attitudes because each attitude reflects different reasoning.

Compliance Function

A person may hold an attitude for reasons of compliance if holding a particular attitude brings rewards or deters punishments. For example, Bubba may hold prejudicial attitudes toward some race or sex because this attitude is rewarded. Perhaps Bubba's family laughs at his prejudicial jokes, thereby rewarding this particular attitude. A person can also hold religious attitudes for a compliance function. Melody may hold religious attitudes for compliance reasons if she knows that her parents will invoke strict rules and curfews if she doesn't voice appropriate religious convictions.

Knowing the function an attitude serves helps us to change that attitude. To change an attitude held for compliance functions, perceived rewards must change. You might change Bubba's prejudicial attitudes by refusing to acknowledge or laugh at his offensive jokes. Once this behavior is no longer rewarding, Bubba is likely to change his attitudes and behaviors. Likewise, if Melody goes to college and finds that she no longer has to avoid parental punishment, her religious attitudes are likely to change.

Knowledge Function

An attitude is held for a knowledge function if the attitude helps a person understand and explain the world. The same examples (e.g., prejudicial and religious attitudes) will be used again to reinforce the idea that two different people may hold the same attitude, but for different reasons. For Kirk, stereotyping helps to predict and understand behavior. If Kirk believes that all women are stupid, he can use this information to

FIGURE 11.1 The National Rifle Association attempts to counter the argument that banning guns will stop crime by invalidating the knowledge function. These two women sports persons contradict perceptions that people who use guns are violent criminals.

National Rifle Association of America

interpret events and guide his behavior. Faith's religious attitudes help her to explain death, natural disasters, miracles, and nature. For Kirk and Faith these attitudes serve a knowledge function.

A persuader can change an attitude serving a knowledge function by demonstrating inconsistencies in prediction. In other words, a knowledge-based attitude is changed by showing that the attitude yields inaccurate understanding. A persuader can destroy the knowledge function by showing exceptions to the attitude's predictive power, or providing alternative explanatory frameworks for predicting and understanding the world. For example, we could change Kirk's prejudicial attitudes toward women by confronting him with several intelligent, successful women. We might change Faith's religious attitudes by presenting scientific, as opposed to religious, explanations for death, natural disasters, miracles, and nature.

The brochure for the NRA in Figure 11.1 attempts to change gun control attitudes that serve a knowledge function. Many people believe that easy access to firearms is the reason behind the high rate of violent crime in America. The attitude helps them to predict and understand the frightening crimes occurring around them. A positive attitude toward gun control, likewise, helps people to control and predict an otherwise frightening environment. The NRA attempts to change this attitude by invalidating the understanding and prediction. The NRA argues that owners of firearms are "honest, decent citizens," and that stiffer crime laws, not gun control, will deter crime.

Ego-Defensive Function

Attitudes held for ego-defensive functions protect a person's ego or self-identity. People often hold prejudicial attitudes to feel superior to others. An interesting sociological phenomenon is that the most prejudicial groups in American society are those who have recently immigrated to the United States and who have experienced societal discrimination themselves. One might think that a group who has been victim to ethnic discrimination would be less likely to discriminate against others, but the opposite appears to be true. Discriminating against others makes people feel superior.

Religious attitudes may also serve ego-defensive functions. The belief that "I'm going to heaven and everyone else is going to hell" helps some people feel superior to others.

To change ego-defensive attitudes one must remove the threat to a person's ego. To change prejudices, the person must be convinced that the target of these bigoted attitudes is not a threat to his or her esteem, status, job, or income. Messages that seek to build self-esteem and security can serve to eliminate cognitions held for ego-defensive reasons.

Social Adjustive Function

Attitudes that we hold in order to be accepted by others serve a social adjustive function. We may adopt particular attitudes as a result of peer pressure, a need for social belonging, or a desire for conformity. Clearly, both of our previous examples, prejudicial attitudes and religious attitudes, could be held for social adjustive functions.

Persuaders may change social adjustive attitudes by decreasing the appeal of the peer group, increasing rewards for non-conformity, or changing the conditions for social belonging. Skinhead neo-Nazi groups are recruiting record numbers of youth in Germany and Eastern Europe. The organizations have almost become fads within certain age and socio-economic groups. To change these attitudes, people are attempting to decrease the appeal of the skinhead organizations, reward those youth who demonstrate racial tolerance, and label the skinhead organizations as deviant, counter-normative, and otherwise unacceptable.

Value-Expressive Function

Attitudes held for a value-expressive function are the only attitudes we've discussed that are held because of the intrinsic content of the attitude. In other words, the person holds the attitude because of the value of the attitude, rather than for some other gain. Value expressive attitudes are internalized; they are central to the person's cognitive system. A value-expressive attitude is held with heart, mind, and soul. Value-expressive attitudes provide the foundation for other attitudes and beliefs. For this reason, they are very difficult, if not impossible, to change. The best strategy for changing a value-expressive attitude is to show that the attitude or belief is inconsistent with other central values. As discussed earlier, inconsistency in the cognitive system can promote instability and change.

McGuire suggests that some value-expressive attitudes may be easy to change.[3] He claims that value-expressive attitudes are seldom challenged, and that people may not have ready-made arguments to defend these attitudes. If, for example, you adopted and internalized attitudes held by your parents, you may not have developed reasons and arguments to support these attitudes. In this case, the attitudes may be particularly vulnerable to persuasion.

Situational Concerns and Functional Attitude Theory

We have discussed five functions that attitudes may serve, and we have discussed how attitudes serving different functions require different attitude change strategies. One final consideration in our discussion of functional attitude theory is the role of situations.[4] It is conceivable that different situations may make a particular function of an attitude more salient or important. For example, in a situation in which you want to impress a new acquaintance, the social adjustive function may take precedence. In a situation in which you want to impress a boss, the compliance function may take precedence. In a situation in which you feel threatened, the ego-defensive function may take over. And in a situation in which you are forced to make a quick judgement, the knowledge function may be activated.

For this reason, a persuader may try to emphasize situational factors in order to evoke a particular attitude function. Let's assume you hold a social-adjustive attitude that smoking cigarettes is good because it relieves social tension. But what if you also hold a knowledge attitude that smoking is bad because it causes heart disease, cancer, and respiratory illnesses? If I want to persuade you not to smoke, I would try to emphasize elements of the situation that would make you focus on your knowledge-based attitude that smoking is bad. After images of dying, chemotherapy, and tumors were clearly in mind, I might then try to change your social adjustive-based attitude.

It is important to assess the influence of the situation on the activation of attitude functions. Trying to change a function that is not salient in a person's mind, or that is irrelevant to the situation, is unlikely to work.

COGNITIVE DISSONANCE THEORY

Cognitive dissonance theory was inspired in the 1950s when a woman claimed that she had been contacted by aliens. The aliens purportedly told Mrs. Keech that the Earth would be destroyed, but that she and her friends could be rescued on December 21. It seems that Mrs. Keech was able to find a number of "believers" in California. On the night of the scheduled destruction, Mrs. Keach and her followers said good-bye to friends and family and waited for the aliens. (They even removed all metal from their bodies because it might burn their skin as they were beamed aboard the spacecraft!) A psychologist, Leon Festinger, decided to tag along to study the reaction when the aliens didn't show (and possibly to be on the safe side in case the aliens kept their promise). Festinger, employing questionable research ethics, infiltrated the group and pretended to be a believer. When the aliens failed to show, we might expect that the followers would realize they had been duped, and that they would hurry home to get their day jobs back. Contrary to expectations, Festinger found that the followers formed even stronger beliefs and more positive attitudes toward Mrs. Keech after the aliens failed to arrive.

When people are confronted with inconsistencies (e.g., they publicly declare their belief in aliens and must face the fact that the aliens have stood them up) the people may, according to Festinger, experience **cognitive dissonance**—a feeling of mental tension, anxiety, doubt, and regret.[5] Inconsistency between two cognitions or inconsistency between cognitions and behavior can produce cognitive dissonance.

There are at least four ways to reduce feelings of cognitive dissonance: 1) *change an inconsistent cognition;* 2) *create a new cognition to rationalize the inconsistency;* 3) *agree to change the inconsistent behavior in the future;* or 4) *rationalize that the inconsistency is beyond personal control or that it isn't important.* Thus, Mrs. Keech's followers have a belief in aliens that is inconsistent with the situation—the aliens didn't show. The Keech followers could change their belief in aliens or create a new cognition that the aliens have decided to spare the world because of the loyalty of the Keech clan. The followers chose the latter option, a choice that leads us to question how we predict what route of dissonance reduction a person will take.

A person will choose the route of dissonance reduction that is easiest. A cognition that is central to a person's belief system is resistant to change. A behavior that others have observed is resistant to change. The Keech followers who had announced the alien scheme to friends and relatives found it too embarassing to go back home defeated. Therefore,

| BOX 11.1 | *Two Routes to Cognitive Dissonance* |

Decision or choice ———→ Cognitive dissonance ———→ Post-decisional spreading of alternatives
Counterattitudinal behavior ———→ Cognitive dissonance ———→ Attitude change

changing their beliefs in Mrs. Keech and the aliens was an unacceptable route to dissonance reduction. It was much easier to create a new cognition to eliminate the inconsistency.

Let's turn our attention to the two most common situations that lead to cognitive dissonance: 1) *making a decision or choosing among alternatives,* and 2) *performing a behavior that is inconsistent with pre-existing attitudes and beliefs* (Box 11.1). In the decision making scenario note that cognitive dissonance occurs only after the decision has been made. Brad, for example, has bought a new LeAuto. Dissonance—that uncomfortable, irritating, cognitive tension—sets in. Brad experiences regret: "I knew I should have bought the Honda! That blue car was much nicer. . . . Why won't my new car go over 45 mph?" To reduce this dissonance Brad must make his cognitions consistent with his behavior. To do this he will begin to rationalize his behavior and form a more positive attitude toward his new LeAuto: "Buying the LeAuto saved me $8,000. This car will last me until I get out of college and get a real job. The car gets great gas mileage!" This rationalization process is called the **post-decisional spreading of alternatives.** When a person experiences dissonance after making a choice between two favorable alternatives, the person will reduce dissonance by rationalizing that the chosen alternative is more favorable than it really is, and that the foregone alternative is more negative than it really is: "That Honda had lots of miles on it. . . . That blue plush interior probably stains easily. . . . Lots of people drive Hondas, and it would be hard to find in a parking lot. . . ."

Cognitive dissonance also occurs when you perform a behavior that is inconsistent with your attitudes. For example, if you buy a Nissan, when you firmly believe in "buying American," cognitive dissonance will set in. One way to reduce this dissonance is to eliminate the inconsistency between your belief and your behavior. This can be accomplished by changing your attitude or belief: "American companies should improve the quality of their products to be competitive with foreign products."

Conditions Increasing Dissonance

There are three conditions that increase the level of cognitive dissonance a person is likely to experience: the ratio of positive and negative factors across the alternatives; the degree to which the behavior or decision is volitional; and the importance of the decision or behavior.

BOX 11.2	*Cognitive dissonance is influenced by the number and weight of positive and negative factors affecting a decision*

Small college or large university? The factors influencing your decision may be positive or negative, and they may be very important (10) or very unimportant (1) to your decision.

Small College Factors		Large University Factors	
small class size	(+)10	university sports teams	(+)6
tuition costs	(−)10	family tradition	(+)6
close to hometown	(+)7	limited involvement in extra- curricular activities	(−)7

Ratio of Positives to Negatives:	2 to 1		2 to 1
Weight of Positives versus Negatives	17 − 10 = 7		12 − 7 = 5

*Cognitive dissonance is greatest under these conditions: the ratio of the number of positive factors to the number of negative factors is equal, and the weight of positive factors to negative factors is about equal between the two alternatives.

Cognitive dissonance is greatest when we are forced to make a **choice among alternatives that are equally positive and equally negative.** If the number of positive and negative features of each alternative are similar, and if the weight or importance of these positive and negative features is similar, cognitive dissonance increases. You may have experienced dissonance in choosing a college. If the colleges you were considering each had advantages, and each had disadvantages, and the advantages and disadvantages for each had about equal weight, you probably experienced dissonance (Box 11.2).

Cognitive dissonance also increases when the **behavior is volitional** (i.e., **voluntary**). This means that the behavior is made by choice, and that we can't blame any extenuating circumstances, or any other people, for our behavior or choice. Let's assume that you believe that a person should correct a cashier who charges too little for an item. Yet you knowingly allow a mistake to go undetected and take your money and run. You should experience more cognitive dissonance in this situation than you would if the behavior were not volitional—for example, you didn't realize the mistake until you got home.

The **importance and consequences of a behavior** also increase dissonance. You are likely to experience more dissonance over the purchase of a stereo system than over the purchase of a compact disc. You are more likely to experience dissonance over a billing mistake that nets you $1,000 than a mistake that brings you $5.

Cognitive Dissonance Experiments

Festinger set up several classic experiments that demonstrate that people employ attitude change to reduce cognitive dissonance. The first experiment we will discuss shows how Festinger created cognitive dissonance for his subjects by asking them to perform a counter-attitudinal behavior.

In the peg-turning experiment subjects reported to the experimental lab and were presented with a peg board—a wooden board with pegs stuck in it. The subject was instructed to turn the pegs in order, one quarter of a turn. When the subject completed the one-quarter rotation for each peg on the board, the subject was instructed to go to the top of the board and turn each peg another quarter turn. The subject was left to perform this extremely boring and extremely tiresome task for an extended period of time. As the bored and slightly crazed subject prepared to leave, the experimentor informed the subject that his lab assistant was sick and that he needed someone to go into the waiting room and inform the next person that the task was a lot of fun and that they would enjoy the experiment immensely. The subject was being asked to lie. Half of the subjects were given $1, and half the subjects were given $20 to lie to a fellow college student.[6]

Now, who do you think experienced more cognitive dissonance for lying to a fellow student—the subjects who were given $1 or the subjects who were given $20? Festinger found that the subjects who were given $1 experienced greater cognitive dissonance because they could not rationalize their behavior. The subjects given $20 for lying could say they did it for the money and ease their guilt.

Several days following the experiment, the subjects were given a survey assessing their attitudes toward volunteering for psychology experiments. The subjects had no idea that the survey was related to the original peg-turning experiment. Who do you think reported more favorable attitudes toward participating in psychology experiments—the subjects who were given $1 or the subjects who were given $20? The subjects who were given $1 experienced more cognitive dissonance. As a result they changed their attitude toward participating in experiments to make it consistent with their behavior (i.e., telling another person that the experiment was fun and enjoyable). The subjects who were paid $1 reported much more favorable attitudes on the follow-up survey. The subjects who received $20 didn't experience dissonance, and they didn't change their attitudes—they reported that psychology experiments were dull and tiresome.

Just in case you're considering volunteering for a psychology experiment, I'd better tell you about the grasshopper eating study.[7] College students were brought into the laboratory and presented with a tray of delectable grasshoppers. Half the subjects were paid a small sum of money, and half the subjects were paid a moderate sum of money to eat a grasshopper and complete a taste-assessment survey. (The subjects were unaware that another group of subjects was being paid a different amount). Who do you think experienced more dissonance? And who, consequently, reported more favorable attitudes toward eating grasshoppers? The group who received a small sum of money experienced more dissonance (e.g., "WHY did I eat this gross grasshopper?"), and to reduce this dissonance, they convinced themselves that the grasshoppers were rather tasty (e.g., "Crunchy on the outside . . . chewy on the inside . . . mmmmmm"). The group receiving a small reward formed more positive attitudes toward eating grasshoppers than did the group receiving the larger reward.

Using Cognitive Dissonance in Persuasion

Cognitive dissonance theory provides many insights into the persuasion process. There are three ways in which persuaders can incorporate cognitive dissonance into the production of a persuasive message. Cognitive dissonance theory can be used to: 1) create cognitive dissonance and promote attitude change; 2) create perceived choice situations; and 3) to provide the appropriate level of incentive to induce cognitive dissonance and attitude change. It is important to recognize these dissonance producing strategies. Any time you, as a receiver, realize that you are experiencing cognitive dissonance, it is a good idea to postpone any decisions until you can analyze your cognitions rationally.

Creating Cognitive Dissonance

There are at least three ways cognitive dissonance can be increased for the receiver of a persuasive message: 1) the receiver is encouraged to perform a counter-attitudinal behavior; 2) the receiver is forced to make a choice among alternatives, and the receiver's commitment to the choice is in some way enhanced; and 3) cognitive dissonance is created for a previous behavior.

If a person is persuaded to perform a counter-attitudinal behavior, and the persuader proposes specific attitude changes as a way to reduce cognitive dissonance, enduring attitude change may follow. This is the "try-it-you'll-like-it" route to persuasion. Car dealers use this technique by getting you to test drive a car you don't really like. After you've invested the time and energy to test the car, you experience dissonance, and the car dealer is on hand to suggest cars that you might purchase to reduce this dissonance. Any time a salesperson gets you to agree to listen to a sales pitch you are not really interested in, cognitive dissonance is likely to result. Why did I waste my time and this nice salesperson's time when I'm not interested in this product? The salesperson helps you to reduce this dissonance and guilt by suggesting that you purchase the product.

FIGURE 11.2

This advertisement, produced by the Madison Advertising Federation, creates cognitive dissonance for past decisions and suggests behavior changes that will lead to dissonance reduction.

Madison Advertising Federation

A second method of creating cognitive dissonance is to induce a choice and a commitment to a particular choice. Car dealers use this technique by getting you to sign a preliminary contract agreeing to the purchase of a car. The salesperson assures you that signing the contract does not obligate you to buy the car, but holds the car for you until you make up your mind. You just need to call back within twenty-four hours to cancel the contract (or you will owe the car company $16,000). Once you perceive commitment to purchasing a particular model of car, cognitive dissonance should set in. Going ahead with the purchase is one way to reduce this dissonance.

A third route to persuasion is to create cognitive dissonance for a previously performed behavior. Consider the advertisement in Figure 11.2. The ad creates cognitive dissonance for past sexual behavior. The ad is designed to make you scared and worried. You can reduce your dissonance regarding these past exploits, according to the ad, by changing your attitudes and behavior.

A study by Cialdini and Schroeder illustrates how cognitive dissonance can be created for a recent behavior, and how the creation of this dissonance can lead to attitude change.[8] The study assessed the effectiveness of persuasion strategies used in door-to-door fundraising. Half of the students in the study added the tag, "even a penny will help," to the standard request for a donation. These students collected almost twice as many donations as those students not using the tag. Cognitive dissonance theory can explain these findings. People who were ready to refuse a donation experienced cognitive dissonance upon hearing that "even a penny would help." Moreover, these people sought to reduce their dissonance about being stingy and unhelpful by acquiescing to the persuasive request—and donating far more than just a penny!

One should note that changing an attitude is not the only route to dissonance reduction. Post-behavioral or post-decisional regret may reduce the chances that attitude change will be the selected route to dissonance reduction. If a person vehemently regrets the performance of a counter-attitudinal behavior (e.g., test-driving the car or listening to the sales pitch), or the choice he or she has made (e.g., selecting a car or house), the person may not change his or her attitude to be consistent with his or her behavior. Therefore, an attempt to produce cognitive dissonance may backfire in at least two ways.

A person who has performed a counter-attitudinal behavior may reduce dissonance by **swearing NEVER to perform that behavior again**— thereby reaffirming the previous attitude. The person experiencing guilt and dissonance for an extra-relational affair, for example, may reduce dissonance by vowing never to do it again.

A person who is committed to a choice may reduce dissonance by **backing out of the commitment.** A real estate broker told me that he often gets calls in the middle of the night from panic-stricken buyers who want to reneg on a signed offer to purchase a house. The broker now sends new buyers home with a bag of M & M's with instructions to chomp on the candy if they wake up with night terrors. I'm not sure how M & M's reduce cognitive dissonance, but a person with a mouth full of M & M's is less likely to call his or her realtor at 3:00 A.M.

Since there are many ways to reduce dissonance, the persuader must suggest a preferred method of dissonance reduction. That is, once the persuader has produced cognitive dissonance in the receiver, the persuader should suggest attitude or belief change as a way to reduce this dissonance. This change decreases the likelihood that the receiver will reaffirm the pre-existing attitude or back out of a commitment.

Creating Perceived Choice

Cognitive dissonance theory tells us that people experience more dissonance when they make a choice among alternatives and when they perceive this choice to be voluntary. Festinger and his collegues conducted an experiment in the 1950s in which they presented women with a variety of new kitchen appliances. Half the subjects were told that they could choose one appliance to take home, and half of the subjects were given an appliance at random. Follow-up surveys found that the women who were given a choice were plagued by cognitive dissonance, "I should have taken the can-opener—not the toaster!" These women also established more favorable attitudes toward their new appliances as a way to reduce this dissonance.[9]

The findings of this experiment are directly applicable to product marketing. It follows that a consumer will value a product more if the consumer chooses between various brands. Perhaps this is why Procter and Gamble, which holds the largest share of the laundry detergent market, produces a variety of detergents with different packages and different names; consumers perceive a choice. Similarly, a free product sample delivered to your mailbox is not as likely to produce brand loyalty as the selection of the product from a shelf of competing products in a store.

Perceived choice is also applicable to interpersonal persuasion. If a person perceives that he or she has not been influenced by others, but has made a personal choice to support gun control, to enroll in a college, to rent an apartment, or to date a friend, more cognitive dissonance should occur. This dissonance is necessary for attitude change. Therefore, the extent to which a persuader uses indirect influence to induce perceived choice, the greater the likelihood of attitude change. If the persuader's role is too intrusive, the receiver will attribute the behavior or decision to external, rather than internal, factors. External influences (e.g, situational factors, peer influences) are less likely than internal influences (e.g., personal principles, values, and goals) to result in cognitive dissonance and long-term attitude change.

Creating the Optimal Level of Incentives

Incentives, such as monetary rewards, reduce the likelihood that cognitive dissonance will occur. In cognitive dissonance experiments the subjects receiving a moderate amount of money for their participation rationalized their counter-attitudinal behavior—"I ate the grasshoppers because I got paid $50." The subjects receiving a small amount of money in these experiments had no way to rationalize their behavior; this increased cognitive dissonance and resulted in attitude change.

Cognitive dissonance theory would suggest that many product marketing strategies are not effective. Free samples should be less effective in promoting favorable attitudes than trial samples that have to be purchased. Similarly, price-off coupons and discounts should not be effective in promoting favorable attitudes.

A series of five experiments on product pricing supports cognitive dissonance theory explanations.[10] The experimentors introduced new products in two stores. In one store the products were sold at reduced introductory prices, and in the other store the products were introduced at the regular price. Though initial sales were highest in the store offering the discounted prices, long-term sales were highest in the store offering the regular prices. The greater investment in the regularly priced items resulted in more cognitive dissonance and, consequently, the development of greater brand loyalty. The people purchasing the low priced products could rationalize that they bought the product because of its low price, not because of its quality.

Alternative Explanations for Cognitive Dissonance

Cognitive dissonance theory has generated a great deal of research—but not all of the research supports Festinger's conclusions. Self-perception theory and impression management theory provide alternative explanations for Festinger's finding that attitude change occurs following decisions and counter-attitudinal behavior.

Darrell Bem's self-perception theory suggests that behavior precedes attitudes.[11] This is not as farfetched as it may first appear. At one time or another you may have voted in an election and later concluded, "I must be a Democrat at heart," or having just bought your second red car, stated, "I must have a thing for red cars." Self-perception theory maintains that we look to our behavior to formulate our attitudes. According to Bem, attitudes reported by Festinger following a decision or counter-attitudinal behavior are merely new attitudes developed to provide a rationalization for the decision or behavior: "I must be the kind of person who enjoys turning pegs," or "I must be the kind of person who likes to eat grasshoppers." Bem says that consistency motivates us. Following a decision or behavior, we develop cognitions that are consistent with the behavior. Bem argues that the state of cognitive dissonance simply does not exist.

A second explanation of cognitive dissonance is impression management theory.[12] This theory suggests that people report changes in attitudes following a decision or counter-attitudinal behavior in order to create a favorable impression. According to this theory, inconsistencies between cognitions and behavior threaten a person's self-identity. We may perceive a person as fickle, hypocritical, or indecisive if the person behaves inconsistently or questions personal decisions. Impression management theory suggests that the attitude change Festinger observed was not real attitude change—just the public adoption of an attitude in order to appear consistent.

A recent study provides a consensus explanation for Festinger's cognitive dissonance results.[13] These researchers found that a novel and effective route to persuasion is to call into question the consensus for a belief. That is, if people perceive that they stand alone in their beliefs, they may experience dissonance, and the beliefs may become vulnerable to change.

If we compare cognitive dissonance, self-perception, and impression management theories, we find three alternative explanations for the same phenomena. Cognitive dissonance says that after a behavior, we experience dissonance, and to reduce dissonance we may change a pre-existing attitude. Self-perception theory contends that we perform a behavior and then analyze our behavior to formulate attitudes and beliefs consistent with that behavior; no pre-existing attitude exists, and a need for consistency, not cognitive dissonance, motivates the creation of an attitude. Impression management theory argues that the observed attitude is superficial lip service to an attitude, motivated by the desire to make a favorable impression.

Studies have shown that self-perception theory is likely to work in **low involvement situations.**[14] In these situations it is less likely that a person will have a pre-existing attitude to guide behavior and more likely that the person will act impulsively. In low involvement situations we may review our behavior to formulate an attitude (e.g., review our voting behavior and infer that we are Democrats). In contrast, high involvement situations necessitate cognitive deliberation. In these situations we are likely to analyze our beliefs and attitudes prior to behavior (e.g., the politically active person knows the degree to which she or he agrees with the Democratic platform before going to the polls).

There are no studies that clearly demonstrate under what conditions impression management will take precedence over self-perception or cognitive dissonance. We can speculate, however, that situations that involve the **public viewing** of a counter-attitudinal behavior, and situations that involve socially undesirable behavior, are likely to make impression management concerns salient.

In addition to its relation to cognitive dissonance theory, self-perception theory is a viable cognitive change theory in its own right. Let's turn our attention to specific ways in which the use of self-perception theory can induce attitude or belief change.

SELF-PERCEPTION THEORY

Bem doesn't give people a lot of credit for psychological insight. He proposes that we look to our behaviors to infer what type of person we really are—what we feel and what we believe. Perhaps you look at the clothes you have bought and infer that you are conservative. Perhaps you ponder the hours you have spent with a new friend and infer that you are in love. There are two interesting and rather entertaining studies that lend support to Bem's self-perception theory.

Stuart Valens' "heartbeats and nudes" study suggests that people use external cues, rather than internal emotions and feelings, as indicators of attitudes.[15] Valens placed electrodes on the chests of a group of male college students and put earphones on their heads. He told the students that he was going to monitor their heartrates and that the students themselves could hear their own heartrates through the earphones. The college students were then shown slides of nude women. After viewing each slide, each student evaluated the attractiveness of the women in the slide. Unknown to the students, the experimenter manipulated the heartrate each heard through the earphones. The researcher found that when a subject heard a fast heartrate, he evaluated the women as more attractive, and when he heard a slow heartrate, he evaluated the women as less attractive, irrespective of the appearance of the women. The subjects were using external cues (heartrates) to infer their attitudes, just as Bem suggests that we observe and analyze our behavior (external cues) to formulate an attitudinal response. If subjects had insight into their attitudes, they should have rated the attractiveness of the women based on the features of the women, not on their perceived heartrates.

Another study supporting self-perception theory involved obese people and food. Stanley Schachter used gastric balloons to blow up the stomachs of his subjects.[16] With a gastric balloon in the stomach, the researcher could manipulate stomach contractions. The normal weight subjects reported that they did, indeed, feel full when the gastric balloon was calm, and hungry when the balloon caused contractions. For the obese subjects, however, reports of fullness and hunger did not coincide with contractions of the gastric balloon. The obese subjects were responding to external cues, such as the sight and smell of food, rather than internal cues (i.e, stomach contractions) to decide if they were hungry. When subjects with full stomachs (internal cue) were presented with unlimited bowls of crackers (external cue), obese subjects ate more. Yet when hungry subjects (internal cue) were given part of a roast beef sandwich and told that additional sandwiches were available across the room in the refrigerator (no external cue), the normal weight subjects got up and retrieved more food, but the obese subjects did not. Yet if a platter of roast beef sandwiches (external cue) were placed in front of full subjects (internal cue), we could expect the obese subjects to eat more. Why? The obese subjects are regulating their eating behavior according to external cues (the appearance of food, the availability of food) rather than by internal hunger signs. Consistent with self-perception theory, the obese people used external cues to infer an internal state.

Self-perception can be an effective persuasive strategy. Persuaders can emphasize situational factors to create conditions under which self-perception is likely to occur. Situations most likely to promote attitude change based on self-perception are characterized by: 1) low involvement; 2) compliance with a small request; and 3) external stimulation.

Under conditions of **low issue involvement,** a message that points to a previous behavior and suggests an attitude consistent with this behavior may lead to persuasion. You might, for example, persuade your friend Jim to go skiing by recalling a $350 purchase of ski equipment last winter and suggesting to Jim that he must really enjoy skiing. This self-perception may make Jim vulnerable to a persuasive message suggesting that he take the weekend off and go skiing. Self-perception research suggests that you would be less successful using this strategy for a high involvment issue, such as buying a car: "Remember when you drove my sports car last summer? You really had a blast! You should buy my car."

The foot-in-the-door technique in which **a small request is followed by a bigger request** also relies upon self-perception theory. Compliance to a request increases when a persuader can convince a person to agree to a small request before presenting the original desired request. Compliance with a small request leads to attitude change as a result of self-perception, which results in greater compliance with a second, larger request. Following acceptance of a small request, such as dog-sitting for the weekend, your roommate may perceive him or herself as the type of

According to self perception theory, we look to our behavior to formulate an attitude or belief. This advertiser emphasizes a behavior in an attempt to create new cognitions.

The party begins.

I can drive when I drink.

2 drinks later.

I can drive when I drink

After 4 drinks.

I can drive when I drunk.

After 5 drinks.

I can driv when I driv

7 drinks in all.

I can drive when I dr

The more you drink, the more coordination you lose
That's a fact, plain and simple.
  It's also a fact that 12 ounces of beer, 5 ounces of wine and
1¼ ounces of spirits all have the same alcohol content. And
consumed in excess, all can affect you. Still, people drink too
much and then go out and expect to handle a car.
  When you drink too much, you can't handle a car.
  You can't even handle a pen.

The House of Seagram

For reprints please write Advertising Dept. J W. #1
The House of Seagram
375 Park Ave.   N.Y. N.Y. 10152

Joseph E. Seagram & Sons, Inc. Reprinted with permission.

person who likes dogs. Self-perception theory predicts that compliance with your first request (to dog-sit) will increase the likelihood that your roommate will accept your larger request of adopting the dog.

External stimulation also creates situations in which self-perception is more likely to occur. Years ago many restaurants kept aromatic onions frying on the grill to stimulate perceptions of hunger. This stimulated self-perceptions: "My, that smells good; I must be hungry." Television advertising employs visual images to stimulate perceptions of arousal and interest: "This commercial always gets my attention. I must really like Levi's."

It is important to remember that persuasion as a result of self-perception does not involve in-depth analysis of persuasive arguments. For this reason, self-perception is not the best cognitive change theory to promote long-term attitude change, or persuasion regarding thought-provoking or involving issues. Attitudes and beliefs created by the deliberative thought and analysis are more likely to be enduring over time than are attitudes that are reactions to impulsive behaviors.

LEARNING THEORY

Persuasion is a process of teaching and learning. Communicators teach each other new beliefs, attitudes, or behaviors. There are three approaches to learning theory: operant conditioning, classical conditioning, and social learning.

Operant Conditioning

Operant conditioning involves the use of **rewards** or **punishments** to engender attitude, belief, or behavioral change. Perhaps you've seen rats play basketball or ducks spell. These animals have been trained to produce a particular behavior through a schedule of reinforcements. The application of operant conditioning to persuasion is quite literal. A persuader can provide rewards and punishments to promote attitude, belief, or behavioral change. You may be the target of operant conditioning right now—your parents may be using money, verbal praise, or gifts to persuade you to get good grades in college. Political candidates use operant conditioning to persuade voters by promising tax cuts, labor laws, retirement benefits, national transportation, and adherence to special interests. Advertisers incorporate rewards and punishments in their persuasive messages. The implied message that you will be worthless, disliked, ineffectual, or powerless if you do not buy the promoted product communicates punishment.

Classical Conditioning

Classical conditioning should conjure up memories of Pavlov's dog. Classical conditioning begins with an unconditioned stimulus that promotes an unconditioned response. The unconditioned stimulus and response occur naturally. For example, Pavlov's dog salivated (**unconditioned response**) whenever he saw meat (**unconditioned stimulus**). Pavlov trained his dog to elicit the same response (salivation) to a **conditioned stimulus.** Every time the dog was presented with meat, Pavlov rang a bell. Over time, the dog associated meat (unconditioned stimulus) with the ringing of a bell (conditioned stimulus), and eventually the ringing of the bell alone caused the dog to salivate (**conditioned response**) (Figure 11.3). In classical conditioning the unconditioned stimulus is paired, over time, with a new stimulus. In time, the new stimilus alone can elicit the response.

Advertising frequently uses the principles of classical conditioning. Good times with friends is a natural stimulus for a positive, happy feeling. Advertisers pair the product (conditioned stimulus) with "good times" scenarios (unconditioned stimulus) and hope that, over time, the presentation of the product alone will conjure up positive, happy feelings

FIGURE 11.3   Diagram of classical conditioning.

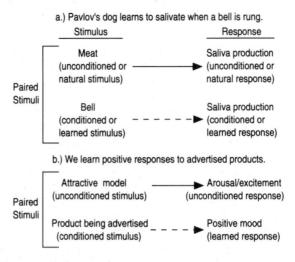

a.) Pavlov's dog learns to salivate when a bell is rung.

Stimulus   Response

Paired Stimuli

Meat
(unconditioned or
natural stimulus)   →   Saliva production
(unconditioned or
natural response)

Bell
(conditioned or
learned stimulus)   - - - - - →   Saliva production
(conditioned or
learned response)

b.) We learn positive responses to advertised products.

Paired Stimuli

Attractive model
(unconditioned stimulus)   →   Arousal/excitement
(unconditioned response)

Product being advertised
(conditioned stimulus)   - - - - →   Positive mood
(learned response)

(conditioned response). If, when you open a beer alone at home, you experience the same warm, happy feelings you learned to associate with the beer while watching commercials, you are an example of the effects of classical conditioning.

Classical conditioning also explains the popularity of sexual symbols in advertising. Sexual stimuli are unconditioned stimuli that naturally produce positive feelings of arousal (unconditioned response). When a product is associated with sex, it is the hope of the advertiser that through the association of the product with sexual symbols, the presentation of the product alone will eventually provoke positive feelings of arousal.

It is also possible, with some patience and forethought, to employ classical conditioning in interpersonal persuasion. My nephew has a particular facial expression that is cute and adorable. This expression is an unconditioned stimulus that elicits an admiring smile and warm loving feelings from his mother (unconditioned response). My nephew has learned, over the years, to pair this expression with requests for money (conditioned stimulus). It is my nephew's dream that the conditioned stimulus (asking for money) will someday elicit the conditioned response (an admiring smile, warm loving feelings, and . . . free-flowing cash).

Knowing how principles of learning are applied to persuasion, it is interesting to predict viewers' responses to particular advertisements. For example, a televised Reebok ad shows two men bungee jumping from a bridge. The two men demonstrate a beautiful swan dive as they plummet

In this advertisement, the tragic death of a teen (unconditioned stimulus) is associated with abortion parental consent laws (conditioned stimulus).

National Abortion Rights Action League

several hundred feet. As the viewer tenses for the snap of the cable and the rebound of the jumpers, the final scene shows the man wearing Reebok pumps dangling from the cable, while the man wearing a competitor's shoes evidently fell out of his shoes and plummeted to his death. Based on principles of learning, the product has been associated with the sensation of free-fall, fear, and death. One would assume that an advertiser would want a product associated with positive emotions, not negative ones. Though this ad may get viewers' attention, it may not generate positive attitudes toward the product.

Social Learning Theory

Social learning is similar to operant conditioning in that learning occurs as a result of rewards and punishments. Albert Bandura's social learning theory differs from operant conditioning in several ways.[17] First, rewards and punishments may be **real** or **imagined;** real rewards and punishments are usually concrete, such as a pay check, and imagined rewards and punishments are often abstract, such as, "people won't like me if I do this." Related to the real or imagined quality of reinforcements, social learning may occur when rewards and punishments are **immediate** or **delayed.** We may work overtime for years for the delayed reward of buying an expensive boat. Reinforcements also vary in the extent to which they are **internally** or **externally based.** External rewards are reinforcements that other people deliver; internal rewards are reinforcements that we give ourselves, such as esteem, enjoyment, and pride. The most important aspect of social learning theory is that reinforcements may be **personally experienced** or **vicariously experienced.** This means that we can learn new attitudes, beliefs, and behaviors simply by observing the rewards and punishments of others.

The most common applications of social learning theory to persuasion are role playing and identification strategies.[18] **Role playing** involves setting up a situation in which the target of persuasion is asked to role play the desired attitude, belief, or behavior. The innovative *Hang Tough* anti-drug campaign uses this strategy. Adolescents are both the targets and producers of the anti-drug messages. Teens are the writers, producers, and actors in the anti-drug raps that constitute the television ads for the campaign. Hundreds of teens worked together to produce a sixty-minute prime time television program that featured kids persuading kids to stay off drugs.

Identification with a desirable model can also promote persuasion. If a person observes a model being rewarded or punished, the observer will learn to exhibit those behaviors for which the model is rewarded. Many corporations use modeling to persuade employees to adopt particular political positions, volunteer for particular community projects, and even purchase particular products. Identification is especially effective when the observer reveres the model. Many advertisements try to persuade us to adopt modeled behaviors; famous sports figures and movie stars demonstrate products to sell us everything from deodorant to floor wax.

It is also possible, however, for people to model undesirable behavior. David Phillips has collected data over several years and presents some startling statistics. Phillips claims that homicide rates increase after nationally televised heavyweight prize fights; in these fights violent behavior is modeled and rewarded. Additional studies by Phillips show that suicide rates and single-passenger car accidents (possible suicides) increase after highly publicized suicides, and that multiple-passenger car accidents and plane crashes increase after highly publicized murder-suicides.[19]

SUMMARY

In this chapter we have reviewed five different theoretical approaches to cognitive change. Each of these approaches presents different strategies that persuaders may use to promote attitude, belief, and behavior change. Although these theoretical approaches (with the exception of the theory of reasoned action) narrowly define cognition as attitude change, these theories can be applied to belief change as well: beliefs may serve different functions for different individuals; belief change is a route to cognitive dissonance reduction; beliefs are certainly tied to self-identity and self-perception; and we may adopt particular beliefs as a result of social learning.

Based on our discussion of the relationship between cognition and behavior in chapter 10, you may have noticed that a limitation of these theories is their universal assumption that cognitive change will lead to behavioral change. Future research must integrate our understanding of the conditions that increase correspondence between attitudes and behavior, with specific theories of cognitive change.

Study Guide

persuasion theory
theory of reasoned action: six persuasion strategies
functional attitude theory: five functions
    methods for changing attitudes
    situational factors
cognitive dissonance theory
    four ways to reduce dissonance
    two situations leading to dissonance
    post-decisional spreading of alternatives
    three conditions increasing dissonance
    cognitive dissonance experiments
    three methods of persuasion
    how cognitive dissonance attempts can backfire
    alternative explanations: self-perception and impression management
self-perception theory
    attitudes inferred from behavior
    studies demonstrating self-perception
    conditions for self-perception to occur
        low issue involvement
        foot-in-the-door
        external stimulation
learning theory
    operant conditioning
    classical conditioning
    social learning

Discussion Questions

1. Think of a person whom you know very well. Using the theory of reasoned action, outline what you think this person believes about you. Estimate what you think the person's evaluation and strength ratings would be for each belief. What is this person's attitude toward you? Identify three different ways you could persuade this person to change his or her attitude about you.

2. Analyze your attitude on each of the following issues. What function does this attitude serve for you? How could a persuader use functional attitude theory to change your attitude on each of the following issues?
   a. underage drinking of alcohol
   b. religion
   c. environmental issues
   d. fashion

3. What attitudes do you hold for a compliance function? How might a persuader change these attitudes?

4. Based on your knowledge of cognitive dissonance, what advice would you give the Widget Company about each of the following marketing decisions?
   a. The purchase of Widgets is a high involvement decision. Should we mail free samples of our Widgets?
   b. The purchase of Snidgets is a low involvement decision. Should we offer price incentives?
   c. Should our distributors negotiate with the stores so that they will sell only our brand of Widgets?

References

1. Ajzen, I., and M. Fishbein. 1980. *Understanding attitudes and predicting social behavior.* Englewood Cliffs, NJ: Prentice-Hall.

2. Kelman, H. C. 1958. Compliance, identification, and internalization: Three processes of attitude change. *Journal of Conflict Resolution,* 2, 51–60.
   Katz, D. 1960. The functional approach to the study of attitudes. *Public Opinion Quarterly,* 24, 163–204.
   Smith, M. B., J. S. Bruner, and R. W. White. 1956. *Opinions and personality.* New York: Wiley.

3. McGuire, W. J., and D. Papageiorgis. 1961. The relative efficacy of various types of prior belief-defense in producing immunity against persuasion. *Journal of Abnormal and Social Psychology,* 63, 327–337.
   McGuire, W. J. 1963. Persistence of the resistance to persuasion induced by various types of prior defenses. *Journal of Abnormal and Social Psychology,* 64, 241–248.

4. Snyder, M., and K. G. DeBono. 1989. Understanding the functions of attitudes: Lessons from personality and social behavior. In *Attitude structure and function.* A. R. Pratkanis, ed. pp. 339–359. Hillsdale, NJ: Erlbaum.
   Shavitt, S. 1989. Operationalizing functional theories of attitude. In *Attitude structure and function.* A. R. Pratkanis, ed. pp. 311–337. Hillsdale, NJ: Erlbaum.

5. Festinger, L. 1957. *A theory of cognitive dissonance.* Evanston, IL: Row, Peterson.

6. Festinger, L., and J. M. Carlsmith. 1959. Cognitive consequences of forced compliance. *Journal of Abnormal and Social Psychology,* 58, 203–210.

7. Smith, E. E. 1961. The power of dissonance techniques to change attitudes. *Public Opinion Quarterly,* 25, 626–639.

   Zimbardo, P. G., M. Weisenberg, I. Firestone, and B. Levy. 1965. Communicator effectiveness in producing public conformity and private attitude change. *Journal of Personality,* 33, 233–255.

8. Cialdini, R. B., and D. Schroeder. 1976. Increasing compliance by legitimizing paltry contributions: When even a penny helps. *Journal of Personality and Social Psychology,* 34, 599–604.

9. Brehm, J. W. 1956. Post-decision changes in the desirability of alternatives. *Journal of Abnormal and Social Psychology,* 52, 384–389.

10. Doob, A. N., J. M. Carlsmith, J. L. Freedman, T. K. Landauer, and S. Tom, Jr. 1969. Effect of initial selling price on subsequent sales. *Journal of Personality and Social Psychology,* 11, 345–350.

11. Bem, D. J. 1972. Self-perception theory. In *Advances in experimental social psychology,* vol. 6. L. Berkowitz, ed. pp. 1–62. New York: Academic Press.

12. Tedeschi, J. T., B. R. Schlenker, and T. V. Bonoma. 1971. Cognitive dissonance: Private ratiocination or public spectacle? *American Psychologist,* 26, 685–695.

    Gaes, G., R. J. Kalle, and J. T. Tedeschi. 1978. Impression management in the forced compliance situation: Two studies using the bogus pipeline. *Journal of Experimental Social Psychology,* 14, 493–510.

13. Crano, W., W. Gorenflo, and S. L. Shackelford. 1988. Overjustification, assumed consensus, and attitude change: Further investigation of the incentive-arousal ambivalence hypothesis. *Journal of Personality and Social Psychology,* 55, 12–22.

14. Krugman, H. E. 1965. The impact of television advertising: Learning without involvement. *Public Opinion Quarterly,* 29, 349–356.

    Ray, M. L. 1973. Marketing communication and the hierarchy-of-effects. In *New models for communication research.* P. Clarke, ed. pp. 147–176. Beverly Hills, CA: Sage.

15. Valens, S. 1966. Cognitive effects of false heart-rate feedback. *Journal of Personality and Social Psychology,* 4, 400–408.

16. Schachter, S. 1971. Some extraordinary facts about obese humans and rats. *American Psychologist,* 26, 129–144.

17. Bandura, A. 1977. *Social learning theory.* Englewood Cliffs, NJ: Prentice-Hall.

    Bandura, A., D. Ross, & S. A. Ross. 1963. Vicarious reinforcement and imitative learning. *Journal of Abnormal and Social Psychology,* 67, 601–607.

18. Janis, I. L. 1968. Attitude change via role playing. In *Theories of cognitive dissonance: A sourcebook.* R. Abelson et al., eds Chicago: Rand McNally.

    Janis, I. L., and L. Mann. 1985. Effectiveness of emotional role-playing in modifying smoking habits and attitudes. *Journal of Experimental Research in Personality,* 1, 84–90.

19. Phillips, D. P. 1986. Natural experiments on the effects of mass media violence on fatal aggression: Strengths and weaknesses of a new approach. In *Advances in Experimental Social Psychology.* L. Berkowitz, ed. 19, 207–250. New York: Academic Press.

    Phillips, D. P. 1979. Suicide, motor vehicle fatalities, and the mass media: Evidence toward a theory of suggestion. *American Journal of Sociology,* 84, 1150–1174.

12

Interpreting Persuasive Messages

Perhaps you have heard the skits featuring Mr. Subliminal on Saturday Night Live. Mr. Subliminal manipulates people's perceptions by saying gracious things but inserting contradictory comments in a whisper. For example, a typical skit might begin:

Mr. Subliminal: "Hello Mrs. Remke (hot sex). Would you please type these letters (ask me out). And then you can go home early (work late)."

Mrs. Remke: "I'll stay late and do the letters. Say, would you like to go out to dinner with me tonight?'

Mr. Subliminal: "Sure, I'd love to. My treat (you pay)."

Information processing is the cognitive procedure by which we perceive and apply meaning to persuasive messages. Information processing includes the manner in which we **attend, comprehend, evaluate** and **integrate** messages. One area that has received a great deal of popular attention is whether or not we can process information sub-consciously. When students hear the words "information processing," one of their first questions is, "Does subliminal persuasion really work?" In this chapter we will first explore the question of conscious and sub-conscious information processing and then proceed to a discussion of the specific steps a person undergoes in the processing of a persuasive message.

Interest in **subliminal persuasion** began in 1957 when a frame of celluloid with the words "Drink Coca-Cola" was inserted in a movie reel every five seconds. This fast visual directing viewers to "Drink Coca-Cola" was not perceptible at a conscious level. Yet the experimenter claimed that concession sales of Coke tripled during the movie.

In the 1970s subliminal persuasion was quite popular. A Seattle radio station tried to increase its listening audience by inserting a sub-audial message (just below the conscious level of hearing) that said, "Television is a bore!'' A large department store inserted sub-audial messages in the department store music telling customers, "Don't steal!" In 1978 police tried to catch a serial killer by inserting sub-audial messages in the television news broadcasts of the crime, stating, "Turn yourself in! Turn yourself in!" Claims have been made over the years that satanic messages are embedded in heavy metal music, the word "sex" is inscribed in the dots on top of Ritz Crackers, and a hidden skull sends a subliminal death wish in alcohol labels.[1]

There are three types of subliminal persuasion: **embedded photos, fast visuals,** and **sub-audial messages.** An embedded photo is an image that is hidden in a picture. Remember those puzzles you did as a child in which you had to find animals or other objects hidden in a picture? These are embedded photos. A fast visual is a frame that is inserted in a video or film, and a sub-audial message is a verbal message that is embedded in other sounds. Attempts at subliminal persuasion vary in the extent to which the hidden message can be discerned at a conscious level.

Evidence for subliminal persuasion is limited. No research study has demonstrated, unequivocally, that subliminal persuasion works.[2] Let's examine the three arguments that are used to support subliminal persuasion.

Some people claim that subliminal persuasion is like hypnosis. It is true that suggestions can be given to a person in a hypnotic state, and that the person may perform this behavior even after the hypnotic state is broken. These suggestions, directed toward the sub-conscious, influence behavior; yet the subject does not usually remember being persuaded or influenced. It follows, according to proponents of subliminal persuasion, that hidden messages will be perceived by the sub-conscious and will influence the receiver without the receiver ever realizing that he or she has been persuaded.

It is also true that we often have subconscious motivations for our behavior. You may snap in anger at a person because of sub-conscious resentment. You may distance yourself from a married person because of a socially unacceptable sexual attraction. You may flirt with your brother's or sister's dates as a result of a subconscious desire to assert your superiority. In each of these examples you may not be fully aware of the motivations for your behavior. According to proponents of subliminal persuasion, these examples show that the subconscious can influence behavior.

A third argument for subliminal influence is the manner in which we make associations in our minds. We often pair a person, place, or thing with an emotional response. Sometimes we make these associations without awareness and critical analysis. You may feel sick whenever you think about eating mushrooms because at one time you got the stomach flu after eating mushrooms. Proponents of subliminal persuasion argue that associations made at a subconscious level may persist to influence conscious behavior. For example, the pairing of a picture of a nude woman with an alcoholic beverage may result in favorable responses to the product.

There are several problems with these three arguments for subliminal persuasion. First, what is sub-conscious and what is not? How do we define degrees of sub-consciousness? Can a thought influence behavior without first coming into some level of conscious awareness? Some scholars in the fields of psychology and psychiatry argue that associations between an object and an emotion must reach a level of conscious awareness to influence behavior or thought.

Subliminal persuasion becomes even more problematic when we consider that the subliminal message must be hidden to the conscious mind, yet actively perceived and processed by the brain. Which are you more likely to notice, a loud message or a sub-audial message? A clear photo, or an embedded image? A sustained visual, or a fleeting movement? There are many stimuli competing for your attention; why should your mind bother to process something so subtle? Does your mind process every matrix dot in every character on this page? Does your mind process every blade of grass when you look at a lawn? Probably not. The human animal must perceive and process whole and dominant images to be able to respond quickly to dangers in the environment. Which is more likely to save lives—a loud, intense, irritating fire alarm, or a sub-audial message in the background music stating, "Fire."

We can draw several conclusions from our discussion of subliminal persuasion. There is little research evidence supporting subliminal influences. Even if researchers were able to achieve sustained and focused attention in the research lab, subliminal messages can hardly compete with the music, film, television, and printed messages bombarding us each day. Messages with strong visual and audial images are more likely to break through the clutter and be processed by the brain. Moreover, vivid messages are more persuasive than the same message presented in a less vivid manner.[3]

Our discussion of subliminal persuasion reinforces one very important concept: knowing how receivers perceive and process persuasive messages can help persuaders predict the effectiveness of their messages. Perhaps most importantly, knowing how we perceive and process information can help us become more thoughtful consumers of persuasion.

This advertisement characterizes the response of advertising agencies to accusations of subliminal advertising.

PEOPLE HAVE BEEN TRYING TO FIND THE BREASTS IN THESE ICE CUBES SINCE 1957.

Courtesy of American Association of Advertising Agencies

FOUR INFORMATION PROCESSING FUNCTIONS

Advertisers are partial to a concept called the **persuasion continuum.** The basic tenet of the persuasion continuum is that persuasion occurs in stages, in a progressive order. Many people view persuasion as a blatant demand for a change in beliefs or actions. In reality persuasion is a much more subtle art that progresses over time. The persuader must take the receiver through a series of stages before actual belief, attitude, or behavior change is likely to occur. The four basic stages of the persuasion continuum are: **awareness, comprehension, evaluation,** and **integration.**[4] Although superficial changes in attitudes, beliefs, or behavior may occur at any stage of the process, enduring persuasive change on any important topic requires progression through all four stages.

The persuasion continuum demonstrates the parallel tasks of the receiver and sender of a persuasive message. Receivers must first perceive and attend to new information: "Multi-culturalism is the theme of the '90s." Only after attention and interest are secured can the persuader focus on increasing the receiver's knowledge of the issue: "Multi-culturalism is a widespread movement in education, business, religion, the arts, and social organizations emphasizing racial, ethnic, and cultural diversity." Following comprehension of this new information, the receiver and sender wrestle with what aspects of the information will be evaluated positively and accepted, and what aspects will be evaluated negatively and rejected: "Cultural diversity and respect are positive, but the integration and loss of cultural identity may be negative." The receiver is primarily responsible for the final task of integration. This involves storing the new attitude or belief in memory, building associations between the new cognition and existing cognitions, and establishing consistency among cognitions: "I'd better modify my beliefs regarding social interactions, work environment, entertainment choices, political issue agendas, and educational background to reflect multi-cultural concerns." New beliefs that are associated with many knowledge areas are the ones most likely to guide action.

The progression through the persuasion continuum may take a short time, or it may take years. People who sell resort time-sharing vacations speed through the continuum in a single afternoon, while public information campaigns, such as the AIDS campaign, take several years to move the public from awareness of the disease, to comprehension of its transmission, to evaluation of the at-risk populations and medical research, to actual integration of an informed belief or attitude.

The remainder of this chapter will be organized according to the four persuasion functions or stages. We will explore specific theories describing how receivers' minds work during the awareness, comprehension, evaluation, and integration stages of information processing. Though information processing is primarily concerned with the receiver of the persuasive message, it is important to remember that the actions of the persuader influence how a receiver will process information.

THE PROCESS OF AWARENESS

The theory of selective perception and theories of mindless versus mindful information processing help us understand under what conditions a person will become aware of particular information in a persuasive message.

Selective Perception

The truth is that we don't always process information to which we are exposed. Numerous studies have found that a pre-existing attitude can bias the perception of a persuasive message.[5] This is called **selective perception,** or perhaps more accurately, biased perception. This means that some parts of a message are perceived, or focused upon, and other parts are distorted or ignored.

In 1971, CBS first aired the controversial new series, *All in the Family.* This series was revolutionary in its confrontation of sensitive racial issues in the context of a situation comedy. Producer Norman Lear believed that humor could be used as a weapon against prejudice. He believed that people viewing All in the Family would see that Archie uses "convoluted logic" and that Mike is "always the one who is making sense."[6]

Viewers of *All in the Family* had different perceptions. Neil Vidmar and Milton Rokeach found that highly prejudiced viewers of *All in the Family* identified with Archie! Comparing Archie to Mike, highly prejudiced viewers reported that Archie was more likeable, Archie's arguments made more sense, and Archie usually won the arguments![7] *All in the Family* viewers were employing selective perception.

The corresponding theory of **selective exposure** suggests that people expose themselves to information that is consistent with their pre-existing beliefs. That is, we watch television shows and subscribe to magazines that support our pre-existing opinions. If you are a Republican and you watch the Republican National Convention but not the Democrat National Convention, and if you watch advertisements and coverage of Republican candidates but not Democrat candidates, and if you read Republican candidate brochures you receive in the mail but throw the Democrat brochures in the trash can, you are engaging in selective exposure. You are selectively exposing yourself to information with which you already agree.

Although this makes sense on the surface, the selective exposure hypothesis has received little research support. Numerous studies have shown that people, in some situations, do expose themselves to information contradictory to their opinions.[8] If you want to buy a red convertible Miata, you may still expose yourself to information that negatively evaluates this car, in order to make an informed decision.

Studies on selective exposure do suggest, however, that we may *bias* our perceptions of information that is counter to our pre-existing beliefs. Selective perception, for example, may lead you to distort or pay less attention to reports that criticize your favorite social cause or political candidate.

Selective perception suggests that receivers do not perceive and process all information equally. The amount of focus and attention information receives is dependent upon our pre-existing attitudes and beliefs and, as discussed in earlier chapters, our need for cognitive consistency. Selective perception is more likely to occur when people have a high need for cognitive consistency and evaluative consistency. That is, people who have little tolerance for inconsistent beliefs and attitudes are more likely to engage in selective perception and selective exposure.

Mindful versus Mindless Processing of Information

A second factor influencing the awareness stage of information processing is the degree to which the receiver employs **"mindful"** or **"mindless"** processing. Langer, Blank, and Chanowitz write that "social psychology is replete with theories that take for granted the 'fact' that people think."[9] (I guess many of us operate on this assumption—even though we observe a lot of evidence to the contrary!) Langer and her colleagues contend that people perceive a lot of information without active evaluation and analysis.[10]

When confronted with a typical or routine situation, people often rely on scripted communication. **Scripts** are pre-determined patterns of communication that are socially prescribed.[11] For example, when you sit down in a restaurant, your communication with the waiter or waitress is probably a script. The waiter says, "May I take your order?" You say, "Yes, I would like a hamburger with everything." Note that you don't typically respond by asking how the waiter is doing today, and the waiter doesn't usually initiate the conversation with a discussion of his kids. We have memorized scripts for talking with professors, doctors, friends, and family members.

Langer and her colleagues argue that scripted communication is often mindless. For example, you respond to the question, "How are you doing?" with "Fine, thank you," without even thinking about it. This occasionally gets us into trouble when someone doesn't respond according to the script and answers, "Oh, my. I've been in the hospital and I'm really quite ill," and we mindlessly respond, "Glad to hear it!"

The problem with persuasion is that persuaders can take advantage of scripted communication to achieve mindless compliance. Langer conducted a study in which people getting ready to use a copy machine were interrupted by a request to use the machine. Three different types of requests were given: 1) "Excuse me. I have five (or twenty) pages. May I use the Xerox machine?" 2) "Excuse me. I have five (or twenty) pages. May I use the Xerox machine, because I have to make copies." 3) "Excuse me. I have five (or twenty) pages. May I use the Xerox machine, because I'm in a rush." The second request gave no more explanation than the first request, but because the sentence structure included a "because" phrase, people mindlessly agreed. Specifically, few people agreed to the first request because it gave no explanation, but about the same percentage of people agreed to the second and third request because both followed the communication script that one should provide an explanation for going out of turn.[12]

Langer and her colleagues found that when a request follows an expected communication script, or when there is low-involvement or little effort on the part of the receiver, the receiver is likely to engage in mindless information processing.[13] Only when the communication issue is highly involving, requires effort on the part of the receiver, or violates the expected communication script does the receiver wake up and evaluate the merits of the message.

Have you ever driven a car in a mindless daze and wondered how you got to your destination? Cognitive psychologists have also studied mindless versus thoughtful processing of information. Studies have found that experts often perform behaviors automatically. Athletes, for example, do not consciously consider hand and foot placement but rather perform a string of behaviors and movements automatically. Similarly, musicians who have memorized a piece of music do not consciously consider hand placement or individual notes but rather perform the piece automatically from beginning to end. Experts in cognitive endeavors, such as chess, may not perform mindlessly, but they do perform holistically. Chess experts do not study the individual placement of pieces on the board; experts chunk large quantities of information together and process the information as a whole.[14] Think about times when you were learning complex behaviors; when you were conscious of every move you made when you were learning to drive, your driving was abrupt and erratic.

The advantage of automatic or holistic information processing is that experts are able to integrate large quantities of information, are able to perceive changes quickly, and are able to generate quick, efficient responses. The disadvantage of automatic or holistic processing is that the receiver may overlook details. The same advantages and disadvantages apply to mindless versus mindful processing of communication messages.

People who are skilled in communication will have many scripts and will rely on these scripts to communicate quickly, smoothly, and automatically. People who are not skilled in communication will be continually attending to details; imagine the unskilled communicator at a party, carefully choosing words, analyzing responses, and grasping for things to say.

Although the mindless processing of communication is efficient, it may place the receiver at greater risk for persuasive influence. In mindful situations, attention to detail is required, and decision making may be slow and awkward. This slower processing of information does, however, allow for careful consideration of persuasive messages.

Both selective perception and mindful versus mindless processing theories suggest that the manner in which a persuasive message is perceived determines the influence and impact of the message. Once the receiver attends to the persuasive message, the receiver may proceed to the second stage of information processing—message comprehension.

THE PROCESS OF COMPREHENSION

In the process of comprehending a message, **cognitive responses**—thoughts, reactions, associations, and emotions—are generated. We will discuss two related theories of information processing: cognitive response theory and the elaboration likelihood theory. Cognitive responses, the mental thoughts generated when a message is received, are central to both of these theories.

Cognitive Response Theory

Cognitive responses, thoughts generated by the message, may vary in evaluation and number. Cognitive responses may be either positive or negative, and the number of cognitive responses a given message generates may be small or large. Persuasion will be most effective when a receiver generates a large number of positive cognitive responses to a message. John Cacioppo and Richard Petty have found several conditions that influence whether or not the receiver is likely to generate a large number of positive cognitive responses.[15] We will explore six variables that influence receivers' generation of cognitive responses: the quality of the argument; distraction; individual or group audience; repetition; number of sources; and number of arguments. In each of these conditions, the choices the persuader makes regarding the construction of a message influences the receiver's comprehension.

The **quality of a message** is an obvious consideration. Receivers are likely to respond to a weak message with negative cognitive responses, and respond to a strong message with positive cognitive responses. Knowing this, the persuader who has a relatively weak case may attempt to discourage the thoughtful analysis of the message because the cognitive responses generated are likely to be negative. Though no persuader would purposely want to present weak arguments, there are times when the persuader realizes that the case is weak or that the opposition's arguments are stronger. Conversely, if the persuader has a strong argument, he or she would want to facilitate the receivers' generation of cognitive responses.

One of the conditions that hinders receivers' generation of cognitive responses is **distraction.** Some persuaders purposely use distraction to hinder the generation of cognitive responses to a weak message. This is, perhaps, why Hitler used distracting fireworks and loud music during many of his speeches. Persuaders who want to hinder comprehension may also distract the audience by the nature of the message. Persuaders often attack the character of the opponent or people adhering to the opposition, or attempt to distract receivers by telling emotional stories, personal stories, and anecdotes that are not representative examples of social conditions or that are not relevant to the issue. Politicians, for example, are fond of creating issues by telling vivid personalized stories: behold the dying veteran who cannot get a heart transplant as a result of lack of adequate medical care at the VA hospital. The personalized story may not be a representative example of the care provided by the Veteran's Administration Hospital, but the story may distract voters from the real issues of the campaign. Humor is yet another method of distracting the audience and getting receivers to generate positive cognitive responses about the source, in lieu of generating negative cognitive responses to a message with no substance. Receivers should therefore be leery of tactics

FIGURE 12.1

A weak argument will produce more positive cognitive responses when presented to a group than when presented to an individual. A strong argument will produce more positive cognitive responses when presented to an individual.

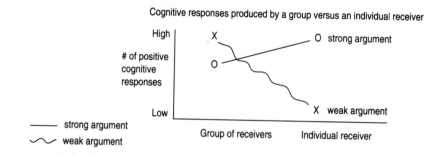

Cognitive responses produced by a group versus an individual receiver

—— strong argument

〜 weak argument

that do not facilitate the deliberate analysis and comprehension of a persuasive argument.

Cognitive response research suggests that the number of positive responses a persuasive message generates is also dependent upon whether the receiver hears the message alone, or as a member of a group. Imagine yourself on trial for murder—should you opt for a jury trial or a trial before a judge? If you have a weak argument in your defense, you should opt for a trial by jury. If you have a strong defense, you should opt for a trial by judge. A lone receiver (a judge) is more likely to generate positive cognitive responses to your strong defense and negative cognitive responses to your weak defense. In contrast, a jury or group of people will generate some positive cognitive responses and some negative cognitive responses. Figure 12.1 shows that the jury is more likely to regress toward the mean. The group is more likely to form a conclusion that averages the positive and negative nature of the cognitive responses. This leads to a more favorable reaction to a weak argument, and a less favorable reaction to a strong argument.

Advertisers seem to be ignorant of the findings that the number of **repetitions** of a message influence the number of positive cognitive responses. As shown in Figure 12.2, the number of new thoughts generated by a message increases with each repetition, up to three repetitions. After three repetitions the number of new positive thoughts levels off. Think about advertisements that you see repeatedly. You might have been interested the first time you saw the ad. The second time you might have paid more attention to get all the details. The third time you might have double-checked the accuracy of the details, but the fourth and fifth times you saw the ad you probably started to tune the ad out and generate fewer and fewer thoughts in response to the ad.

FIGURE 12.2   This graph illustrates the effect of repetition on cognitive response production.

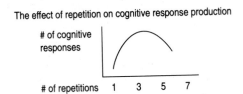

When we are listening to messages, we tend to gear up and pay more attention when we hear new information, or when we are presented with a new person to observe and evaluate. The number of **different sources** presenting an argument and the number of **different arguments** influences the production of cognitive responses. Again, three is the magic number. Cognitive responses continue to increase when three different people present three different arguments supporting the same position. More than three people and/or more than three different arguments seem to be overkill. Fatigue, boredom, or confusion results in a leveling off of cognitive responses. If you wanted to persuade people to enroll in your college or university, a brochure with three different students giving three different arguments (e.g., "I like the location near a big city," "I like the small classes," and "I like the social life") would produce an optimal number of cognitive responses.

As you can see, there are many situational and message variables that can facilitate or hinder cognitive responses. As a receiver of persuasive messages, one should be aware of tactics persuaders use to hinder comprehension. In planning a persuasive message, try to create optimal situational conditions and message characteristics to help the receiver produce a large number of cognitive responses. Thoughtful message processing is the only route to long-term persuasion. Substantive persuasive messages evaluated by thoughtful and critical receivers are ideal for effective communication and ethical persuasion. The thinking receiver can identify fallacious arguments and critically evaluate alternative positions to choose the position with the greatest merit.

Elaboration Likelihood Model

The Elaboration Likelihood Model of persuasion is also based upon cognitive responses. According to this model, there are two routes to persuasion: the **central route** and the **peripheral route.** The central route produces the greatest number of cognitive responses and requires the analysis and interpretation of information relevant to the persuasion topic. In contrast, the peripheral route may involve more mindless processing of information, snap judgements, or responses based on superficial evaluations.[16]

Alice Eagly and Shelly Chaiken have researched the type of judgements characterizing the peripheral route to persuasion. People respond to **heuristic cues,** according to Eagly and Chaiken.[17] Heuristic cues reflect the appearance of information rather than the substance and content of information. Examples of heuristic responses are:

"He is so attractive. He'd make a good president."

"He used lots of statistics—he must be very knowledgeable."

"She had many examples—her reasoning must be strong."

"She would make the best president—her speech was organized."

Heuristic cues reflect a focus on the image or credibility of the source, the length of the argument, the use of statistics or logical reasoning formats, appeals to consensus (everyone agrees), and buzz words, rather than an analysis of the substance of the persuasive appeal. The validity of arguments is never analyzed—only the surface features of the arguments are processed.

The central route to persuasion requires effort and, as the name of the model implies, elaboration of information. If you follow the central route to persuasion in Figure 12.3, you will note that there are several conditions necessary for this deliberate processing of information. First, the receiver must be motivated to expend mental effort and pay attention to the message. Second, the receiver must have the knowledge to process the message and must have a situation that facilitates the generation of cognitive responses. Third, the receiver must evaluate the positive and negative aspects of the message, and fourth, the receiver must formulate an attitude or opinion. Sound familiar? These are essentially the four stages of information processing we discussed earlier in this chapter.

If conditions are not conducive to the generation of cognitive responses and progression through the central route to persuasion, peripheral cues may be very persuasive. In an experiment designed to assess the effects of arousal on information processing, researchers found that brand image information is more persuasive when the receiver is highly aroused, and product feature information is more persuasive when the receiver is only moderately aroused.[18] In this particular experiment, exercise prior to message exposure was used to differentiate high and moderate arousal.

The central route to persuasion has three advantages over the peripheral route.[19] The central route to persuasion is necessary for enduring attitude or belief change. That is, the deliberate evaluation of information is more conducive to persuasion than the manipulation of a snap judgement or a gut response. The elaboration model suggests that tricking a receiver to make an attitude or belief change based on visual images or

FIGURE 12.3   The Elaboration Likelihood Model Persuasion.

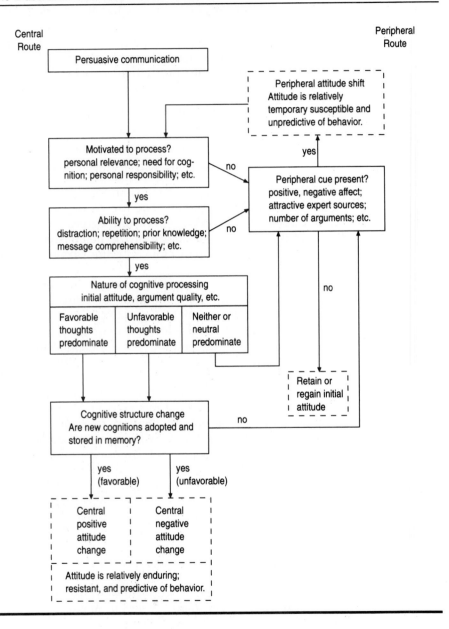

emotional reactions does not result in long-term persuasion. The attitudes and beliefs formed as a result of the central route are also more likely to predict behavior. Moreover, the central, in-depth, processing of information will enable the receiver to resist persuasion from the opposition. The in-depth evaluation of information is more likely to result in the development of counter-arguments that can be used for resistance.

The Elaboration Likelihood Model integrates much of what we have discussed regarding information processing. The mindless processing of information clearly reflects the peripheral route to persuasion. The generation of a large number of cognitive responses reflects the central processing route. Moreover, the persuader can encourage the receiver to pursue the central processing route by creating the message and situational conditions that facilitate the generation of cognitive responses (e.g., number of arguments, number of repetitions, low distraction, etc.). Perhaps most importantly, both persuader and receiver benefit from central processing of information. The persuader stands a greater change of invoking long-term persuasive change that will guide behavior and be resistant to counter-persuasion. The receiver stands a better chance of discovering faulty reasoning and resisting heuristic judgements.

THE PROCESS OF EVALUATION

One of the steps in processing a persuasive message is to sort out what parts of the message one accepts, what parts one rejects, and what parts elicit a neutral response. Though some evaluation (e.g., the generation of positive or negative cognitive responses) occurs at the comprehension stage, the process of evaluation is more in-depth. Evaluation at the comprehension stage may reflect a gut reaction or an evaluation of a specific aspect of a persuasive appeal, whereas the **process of evaluation** is geared toward the formation of an attitude. Social Judgement Theory is one of the few theories that attempts to explain message evaluation processes.

Social Judgement Theory

There are many different positions that a person could adopt for any given issue. A variety of positions on the abortion issue appear below:

a) All women have the right to a free abortion, funded by the government.

b) All women have the right to an abortion, which should be funded by insurance and Medicaid.

c) All women over the age of eighteen have the right to an abortion funded by insurance and Medicaid.

BOX 12.1	*Social Judgement Latitudes*

latitude of acceptance   latitude of non-committal   latitude of rejection

X . . . . | . . . . | X

LA   LN   LR

most preferred position   least preferred position

d) Abortion is an option only when the mother is a victim of rape or incest.

e) Abortion is an option only when the mother's life is in danger.

f) Abortion is murder.

Select your personal position on abortion. Write that position on the left end of the line presented in Box 12.1. According to Social Judgement Theory, your position on abortion is the anchor or standard you use to evaluate all other issues on abortion. According to Social Judgement Theory, you have judgement lines, like the one presented in Box 12.1, for many different issues. Each line represents a different issue, and each line is anchored by your position on that issue.

You will notice that the judgement line has three sections: a latitude of acceptance (LA), a latitude of noncommittal (LN), and a latitude of rejection (LR). Write in each of the abortion issues on the previous page on the judgement line in Box 12.1. The positions should be placed on the line, in order, such that the more favorable positions are closer to your left acceptance anchor point, and the least favorable positions are closer to the right rejection anchor point. The positions you would accept fall into your latitude of acceptance, the positions you aren't sure about fall into your latitude of non-committal, and the positions with which you disagree can be placed in your latitude of rejection.

The latitudes of acceptance, noncommittal, and rejection vary in size depending upon how many positions you placed in each latitude. Obviously, the size of your latitudes will be different for different topics. If you have a very tolerant attitude toward the issue, your LA may be very large. If you aren't very involved in an issue, your LN may be very large.

The most important factor determining latitude sizes is issue involvement. Numerous studies have shown that when involvement is high, you are likely to have a very specific position (small LA), feel strongly about all positions (small LN), and find most alternatives unacceptable (large LR).[20] For example, if you are very involved in the abortion issue, and you believe that abortion is murder, the position that abortion is murder defines your LA, and all other positions probably fall in, or close to, your LR.

FIGURE 12.4 Assimilation and contrast effects. Notice how the receiver accepts the persuader's message and perceives it to be even closer to his or her own position (X) than it really is.

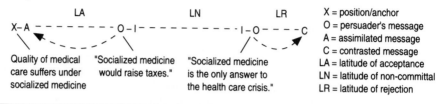

Assimilation and contrast effects

Judgment line for socialized medicine:

X = position/anchor
O = persuader's message
A = assimilated message
C = contrasted message
LA = latitude of acceptance
LN = latitude of non-committal
LR = latitude of rejection

Applying our knowledge of Social Judgement Theory to persuasion, what conditions are going to be conducive to persuasion? Who will be easier to persuade: a person with a large LA, a large LN, or a large LR? Obviously the person with the large LR is going to be the most difficult person to persuade. If you present a message that falls into a person's LA, you have not persuaded the person because he or she already agrees with you. If you present a message that falls into a person's LN and persuade the person to move this message into his or her LA, persuasion has occurred.

In the process of developing Social Judgement Theory, Caroline and Muzafer Sherif and Robert Nebergall noticed two unusual phenomena, which they called assimilation and contrast effects.[21] An **assimilation effect** is said to occur when a message falls somewhere within the latitude of acceptance. The message receiver often distorts the position advocated in a message and perceives the message to be even closer to the LA anchor point than it really is. In other words, the receiver reasons that the speaker's advocated position is acceptable and perceives that the receiver and the speaker are in perfect agreement; the receiver assimilates the position of the speaker.

Jennifer's anchor position on socialized medicine is: "The quality of medical care suffers under socialized medical systems." If a persuader says, "Socialized medicine will raise our taxes," this message falls into her latitude of acceptance but is not very close to her true position, her LA anchor point (Figure 12.4). If she assimilates this message, she distorts the persuader's position until she convinces herself that their positions on socialized medicine are the same. In reality, their positions are not the same—the persuader is concerned about taxes, and Jennifer's concerned about the quality of medical care. In the process of evaluating a message, the LA anchor point may act as a magnet to draw a message toward greater acceptance than the message warrants.

A **contrast effect** occurs when a message falls within the latitude of rejection. This may cause a boomerang effect, whereby the receiver perceives the message to be even more unacceptable and even further from the LA anchor point than it really is. Imagine a message falling into the LR. Alarms go off. Under certain conditions, the LR anchor point acts like a magnet and draws the message toward the right end of the scale. Even though the message may have fallen in the left half of the LR, the receiver responds, "That position is positively unacceptable. I see no merit in that position. That position is exactly the opposite of mine. You could not present a message that was further from the truth!"

Assimilation and contrast effects are most likely to occur under two conditions: when the receiver is ego-involved in the issue and when the message is ambiguous. Politicians frequently take advantage of assimilation and contrast effects. Knowing that you are highly ego-involved in environmental issues, a politician may say, "I believe in landfill waste reduction!" This message falls in your LA, but it falls short of your LA anchor point, "The state government should spend twenty-five million dollars to clean up landfills and lakes." You may be so excited to hear a politician present a message that communicates concern for the environment that assimilation occurs. You perceive the politician's position to be closer to your own than it really is. The politician wins. You lose.

Similarly, politicians make vague issue statements to prevent a message from falling into your LR. If the politician states, "The landfill waste problem is not my top priority." This message might fall just barely inside your LR, because you realize there are many important political issues. But if a contrast effect occurs, you would react against this message and push it toward the LR anchor, saying, "We cannot elect this politician. She is the enemy of environmentalists!" This is the reason that politicians make vague promises, "Yes, the environmental crisis is important," but do not present any specific plans for solving the problems. These vague statements will fall into an environmentalist's LA or LN, but a poor plan of action may fall into the LR.

Remember that assimilation and persuasion are not the same. Assimilation is the misperception that the position of the sender is the same as the position of the receiver. Persuasion is a change in belief. In Social Judgement Theory terms, a message must fall in the LN for persuasion to occur. If the message persuades the receiver to move the boundary of the LA to include this position, change has occurred. Study Figure 12.5. Note that the greatest amount of attitude change occurs when the receiver accepts a position that falls on the right border of the LN (point a). This is the most discrepant change a persuader can argue without falling into the LR. If the receiver accepts this position after hearing a persuasive message, the receiver will move the boundary of the LA to the right to include this position. Look at the size of the attitude change. This is the greatest amount of change the persuader can hope for. If the persuader

FIGURE 12.5   Social Judgment Theory and Attitude Change.

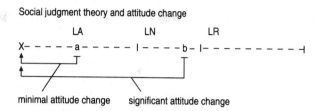

Social judgment theory and attitude change

minimal attitude change   significant attitude change

had argued a position falling within the LN at point b, the resulting attitude change would be much smaller.

The likelihood of persuading a person is obviously dependent upon
the size of the latitude of non-committal. A person with low involvement
is likely to have a large LN. This means that there are a great number of
positions a persuader could argue that might result in attitude change. If
a person is highly involved in an issue, the LN is very small. In order to
persuade the highly involved receiver, the message sender will have to
work on moving the position in the LN toward the LA, or if there are no
positions about which the receiver is neutral, the persuader may attempt
to argue a position just inside the LR and get the receiver to move the
position into the LN. Only gradually, taking one position at a time, can
the persuader hope for any significant belief change.

Social Judgement Theory explains: 1) the process of information
evaluation, 2) distortions in evaluation, and 3) how the task of the persuader changes as a result of issue involvement. The issue anchor points
help us to understand how positions or persuasive arguments are compared and contrasted. Assimilation and contrast effects demonstrate distortions in the evaluation process, which we, as message receivers,
should try to avoid. Finally, the size of the judgement latitudes visually
demonstrates the ease or difficulty of the persuasion task, under conditions of low and high issue involvement.

On the negative side, Social Judgement Theory is more theoretical
than practical. People obviously don't have latitudes drawn on their fore-
heads that we can assess prior to persuasion. We can, however, infer the
size of judgement latitudes based on knowledge of the receiver's involvement in the persuasive issue. We can also recognize our own propensity
toward assimilation and contrast and learn to resist the assimilation of
empty arguments and resist the reactionary contrast of opinions that differ from our own.

PROCESS OF INTEGRATION: SELF-PERSUASION

The process of **integration** is the procedure by which we create a new attitude, belief, or behavioral intention and associate that new cognition with our existing cognitions. Persuaders can achieve short-term changes in attitudes, beliefs, and behavior by by-passing the process of integration. Enduring changes in cognitions or behaviors, however, must be linked to existing cognitions. The process of integration may happen quickly, or slowly develop and strengthen over many years. It follows that some of your beliefs and attitudes are more integrated and associated in your cognitive system than others.

Integration is beneficial for both persuader and receiver. From the persuader's perspective, studies have shown that integration results in long-term persuasion that is resistant to change.[22] From the receiver's perspective, integration requires some reasoning and critical evaluation of arguments and suggests that the receiver develops his or her own conclusions. When an attitude or belief is integrated, it becomes part of the person. The person begins to own the attitude or belief. This is why integration is so closely tied to self-persuasion.

Self-persuasion is a difficult concept to define. How can we determine if anyone living in a community, and surrounded by messages from other people and from the mass media, changes attitudes and beliefs independently or is influenced by others? At best, self-persuasion lies in the perceptions of the beholder; we can say self-persuasion occurs when people *believe* that they have changed a belief, attitude, or behavior of their own accord. Thus, self-persuasion is one way of achieving integration.

The theories that are used to change attitudes and beliefs (chapter 11) can all be applied to processes of self-persuasion. We use the same theories to persuade ourselves as others may use to influence us. The theory of reasoned action, functional attitude theory, cognitive dissonance theory, self-perception theory, learning theory, and cognitive response theory may all involve self-persuasion processes.

The **theory of reasoned action** maintains that attitudes and the influence of other people are the basis for our behavioral decisions. If you analyze your beliefs and attitudes toward your job, and the attitudes of significant others regarding whether you should keep or change jobs, and you consequently modify your attitude toward the organization for which you work, self-persuasion has occurred.

Functional attitude theory suggests that attitudes serve various functions. If you hold a negative attitude toward "New Kids on the Block" because your little sister is a New Kid freak, and you think your sister is a dweeb, you may be holding this attitude for an identification function. If you suddenly realize your little sister shows signs of musical genius, you may change your attitude toward New Kids. Self persuasion has occurred.

One route to **cognitive dissonance** is when we perform a behavior that is inconsistent with our beliefs. Let's say you went skinny dipping at a party. As a result you feel cognitive dissonance. To reduce this dissonance you modify your attitudes and beliefs to make them consistent with your behavior—you change your beliefs and attitudes to form a more favorable and accepting view of skinny dipping and public nudity. If you performed this counter-attitudinal behavior (i.e., skinny dipping) voluntarily, you are responsible for your modified attitudes and beliefs, and self-persuasion has occurred.

The performance of a behavior may lead to the formation of a corresponding attitude, according to **self-perception theory.** Self-perception theory is most likely to be invoked when you have not spent effort analyzing a behavior, and when the behavior in question is not particularly involving or important. You may, for example, look in your closet and infer that you have a postive attitude toward yuppy clothes. Or you may reflect on the jobs you've held and decide that working with people is very important to you.

Learning theory can take many forms, including rewards and punishments and role modeling. If you decide to reward yourself for studying, losing weight or exercising, you are using learning theory for self-persuasion. Choosing a role model for athletics, academics, or your career and deciding to emmulate this model are also a form of self-persuasion.

Cognitive response theory may also be used to explain self persuasion processes. Consider a situation in which the persuader is presenting your side of an issue, but in which the persuader is presenting pitifully poor arguments in support of your position. What type of cognitive responses are you likely to generate? You will probably start thinking of arguments that the speaker should use to be more persuasive. In the process of generating these stronger arguments you are reinforcing your position.

A second way in which cognitive responses can promote self-persuasion is when audience members are forewarned that another person will try to dissuade them. This forewarning prompts audience members to generate a number of cognitive responses to support their position, thereby reinforcing the position the persuader is hoping to promote.

The attitude and belief change theories we have just discussed reflect different ways in which information may be processed. In the examples just cited we have shown how attitude change theories can be used in individual reasoning to develop new attitudes, beliefs, or behavior. In these examples we ignored the role of the message sender and other influences upon the decision maker. In the next section we will address ways in which a persuader can facilitate self-persuasion. These persuasive techniques are classified as self-persuasion because the persuader is using indirect techniques. The persuader prompts the receiver to have "insights" consistent with the persuasive goal, rather than directly telling the receiver what to believe and feel.

Insight-oriented Persuasion

Six insight-oriented persuasion techniques will be discussed. These techniques are most easy applied to one-on-one interpersonal persuasive situations, but are also used in public persuasion. The first three techniques are paradoxical. Let us begin with a definition of paradox.

Paradoxical injunctions are commands or instructions that are precisely the opposite of the desired behavior.[23] Child counselors will sometimes use paradoxical injunctions to change deviant behavior. If Ricky is missing school, the counselor may tell Ricky, "I want you to miss school three days next week. Can you do that for me? Don't tell anyone. Just skip school." If Ricky is skipping school to be deviant, being told to skip school is no longer deviant. Skipping school will no longer be fun or rewarding, and Ricky will go to school. Various forms of the paradoxical approach can be used for persuasion, as the switched role playing, teach thyself, and reductio ad absurdium techniques demonstrate.

Switched Role Playing

Let's assume your friend, Bob, is thinking about dropping out of school, and you want to persuade him otherwise. You should voice Bob's irrational beliefs as if they were your own. Argue that Bob should indeed drop out of school. Then, ask Bob what *he* would say to convince you to stay in school. Keep arguing Bob's irrational beliefs, and force Bob to come up with good arguments for getting a degree. When Bob comes up with several good arguments, give in.[24]

This technique forces Bob into a counter-attitudinal behavior. According to cognitive dissonance theory, Bob may reduce his dissonance by changing his attitude and staying in school. According to self-perception theory, Bob may reason that he really does believe in a college education—how else could he have come up with such strong arguments? According to impression management explanations, Bob may be embarrassed by the inconsistency between his original attitude and the arguments he made and decide to change his attitude to save face. Whatever the explanation, you have indirectly helped Bob to change his attitude.

In 1992 presidential candidate Ross Perot used switched role playing to intensify his followers' commitment to his campaign. Instead of staying in the race to persuade voters, Perot dropped out of the race in July, hoping that voters would persuade themselves to demand his reentry in the race. Thus, Perot placed the voters in the persuader role.

Teach Thyself

Using this method of self-persuasion, you encourage people to teach you their beliefs. In the course of teaching you their beliefs, they should recognize any inconsistencies or weak links in their arguments. To persuade Bob, you should tell him you want to understand his reasoning. Ask Bob to teach you his beliefs. Ask him to organize his thoughts and teach you each belief and each assumption behind each belief. Perhaps Bob will argue: "I'm going to quit school so I can make money. Every year I stay in school, I'm losing income. I can get a sales job at Benco Company and make $25,000 a year. Why should I pay $10,000 to go to school? I lose $35,000 every year—and over four years that's $140,000." As Bob proceeds, ask questions. Ask Bob for evidence and examples to support his arguments: "Can you get promoted at Benco without a degree? How long will you have to work to make more than $25,000?" Question Bob about inconsistencies in the arguments: "What's the average income for a person without a college degree? Do you know what the average income is for a person with a degree? Let's figure this out. How would these earnings compare over ten years, over twenty years, and over forty years?" Don't argue with Bob; just ask questions as if you're truly trying to understand his reasoning: "Is college really costing you $10,000 a year right now, or is some of that money coming from financial aid, scholarships, loans, or your parents?" If Bob's reasoning is faulty, Bob should come to this realization.[25]

Advertisers use this technique to facilitate self-persuasion regarding brand loyalty. Frito-Lay, for example, currently offers incentives (free MCI long distance calling time) if you call Frito-Lay and tell them why you like their products. By forcing you to generate arguments supporting products, the company is having you teach yourself.

Reductio ad Absurdium

For this technique you should act as if you agree with Bob. Adopt Bob's arguments. In the course of vocalizing Bob's arguments elaborate upon these arguments to the point of absurdity. Make generalizations such as: "Education is a useless waste of money;" "I'd rather work in a labor job than in an office anyway;" "If companies want to see a piece of paper to give me a promotion, I'll just quit;" "Money isn't everything—I could be very happy in a lower paying job." If you do this correctly and not too obviously, Bob should be arguing with you in no time.[26]

Probing Questions

The use of probing questions challenges a person's reasoning, but it is not a paradoxical technique because you don't "set the other person up." To persuade Bob to stay in school you could listen to his arguments and then ask probing questions to challenge his conclusions. Don't get into an argument with Bob. Make sure your questions are challenging but not insulting. Ask the questions as if you're asking for clarification or better understanding. Probing questions might be: "Did your father ever regret not getting a college degree?" "How are you going to support yourself?" "How far can you be promoted in that job without a college degree?" "What do you see yourself doing ten years from now?" "Will you get tired of always working for someone else?" "How much money do you have invested in your college education so far?" Notice that you are not telling Bob what to believe; instead, you are helping Bob to recognize any inconsistencies or oversights in his arguments.[27]

The rhetoric of religious persuaders often incorporate probing questions. Televangelists frequently pose open-ended personal questions to motivate listeners to change their lives: "What would happen if you were to die today?"

Pragmatism

Any persuasive encounter can become defensive or angry if people feel their beliefs are being challenged. You can use the pragmatism technique to avoid conflict. In this technique, you never question the validity of a person's beliefs. You do, however, challenge the utility or practicality of the beliefs. In the case of Bob's quitting school, you may communicate your support and understanding regarding Bob's beliefs about tuition costs and the value of his classes. In addition, you can challenge the practical nature of the decision: "Is it practical to go to night school when the credit hours are even more expensive?" "Is it cost effective to come back to school five or ten years from now when tuition is increasing?" Using the pragmatic approach, Bob should reach the insight that his beliefs are not practical, and he may decide to modify his beliefs or attitudes.

Political rhetoric is filled with appeals to pragmatism. Politicians try to appeal to voters by suggesting that family leave policies, for example, are very important, but just not practical: "Voters, do you really want to drive small businesses to bankruptcy by pushing this issue?" Voters often persuade themselves to abandon important issues prematurely as a result of pragmatism threats.

Self-Imagining

A final strategy used to promote self-persuasion is called self-imagining. Just as the name implies, the receiver is encouraged to imagine, and thereby vicariously experience, the desired belief, attitude, or behavior. The receiver is encouraged to visualize life after he or she takes the desired action. In an experiment by Gregory, Cialdini, and Carpenter, door-to-door salespersons asked consumers to "take a moment and imagine how cable television will provide you with broader entertainment," and to imagine how each benefit of cable programming would affect their lives. The self-imagining technique resulted in 30 percent more sales than a straight information sales pitch.[28] In the case of Bob's quitting school, self-imagining could be used to prompt Bob to visualize his life in a dead-end job, working long hours, and living away from campus and his friends.

Self-persuasion involves information integration, the final stage of information processing. Integration requires a cognitive insight, a lightbulb illumination of an idea, a flash of realization—the hand-hitting-forehead thump made famous by, "Wow! I could have had a V-8!" When this type of insight occurs, the receiver will take credit for the belief change. The receiver will validate the new belief by thinking, "I discovered that staying in school is wise," rather than, "Someone told me that staying in school is wise." A self-discovered belief or attitude is more likely to be embedded in the belief system—the new idea is more likely to be associated with existing beliefs and attitudes, such that the activation of an existing idea will activate the new idea as well.

The relationship between self-persuasion and information integration is cyclical. Self persuasion is most likely to occur when new information is integrated into the existing belief system. Moreover, the central processing of persuasive messages is most likely to occur when attitude-relevant beliefs and experiences are activated in memory.[29] That is, the activation of the belief system facilitates the integration of new information. Mindless processing, or peripheral processing of information, does not activate the belief system, and message integration is less likely to occur. Receivers who can activate beliefs in memory, base decisions more on the validity of the message than on the image. This is why ideas generated by self-persuasion are more resistant to change and are more likely to be activated in the mind at the time of a behavioral decision.

SUMMARY

Information processing theories suggest that the most effective route to persuasion is thoughtful, reasoned, and deliberative. In contrast, subliminal persuasion, mindless processing, peripheral routes to persuasion, and the adoption of beliefs without self-discovery are not likely to produce long-term beliefs that are resistant to change. Persuasion by these routes seems to promote more superficial changes that are not well integrated into the existing belief system.

There are four stages of information processing: perception, comprehension, evaluation, and integration. Though all messages must be perceived for any information processing to occur, the last three stages of information processing may or may not occur. It is quite possible that a receiver may not comprehend, evaluate, or integrate a message.

Information processing may be biased at any of the four stages. Selective perception and mindless processing result in errors in perception. The peripheral route to persuasion leads to less than adequate comprehension, and assimilation and contrast effects may cause biases in evaluation. Integration involves reasoning. And although we did not address this in depth in this chapter, it is obvious that information integration may be based on valid, or invalid, reasoning.

Study Guide

subliminal persuasion
    three types of subliminal persuasion
    three arguments supporting subliminal persuasion
    arguments against subliminal persuasion
four stages of information processing
    the persuasion continuum
perception
    selective perception
    selective exposure
    mindful versus mindless processing
    scripts
    advantages and disadvantages of mindful processing
    advantages and disadvantages of mindless processing
comprehension
    cognitive response theory
        argument strength
        distraction
        individual versus group receiver/s
        repetition
        number of arguments and sources
    elaboration likelihood model
        peripheral route
        central route
        heuristic cues
        advantages of central processing
evaluation
    social judgement theory
    latitudes of acceptance, non-committal, and rejection
    involvement and sizes of latitudes
    assimilation and contrast effects
        effects of involvement and message ambiguity
    latitudes and process of attitude change
    involvement and process of attitude change
integration
    self-persuasion
    attitude change theories and self-persuasion
    insight-oriented persuasion
        pardoxical injctions
        switched role playing
        teach thyself
        reductio ad absurdium
        probing questions
        pragmatism
        self-imagining

Discussion Questions

1. Think about how you process information about political campaigns. Is your perception of information biased by selective perception? What political scripts lead to mindless processing of information? Do you use the central or peripheral route when processing this information? Can you recall a time when you employed assimilation or contrast in processing a politician's message? To what extent do political campaigns facilitate self-persuasion?

2. Identify a current public information campaign (e.g., AIDS, anti-drug, anti-smoking, gun control, etc.). Analyze where this campaign falls on the persuasion continuum. At this point in time, is the primary focus of the campaign awareness, knowledge comprehension, evaluation, or integration? Support your claim with evidence and examples.

3. Imagine that your best friend has decided to get married. You believe that this is an impulsive decision. Divide into small groups and role play this situation for the class. Demonstrate how you could use one of the insight-oriented self-persuasion techniques to help your friend realize the folly of his/her decision. The class should try to identify what technique the role-players are employing.

References

1. Trenholm, Sarah. 1989. *Persuasion and Social Influence,* pp. 46–47. Englewood Cliffs, NJ: Prentice-Hall.
2. Dudley, S. C. 1987. Subliminal advertising: What is the controversy about? *Akron Business & Economic Review,* 18, 6–18.
   Trainer, M., and M. Simonson. 1987. Subliminal messages, persuasion, and behavior change. *Journal of Social Psychology,* 128, 563–565.
   Moore, T. E. 1988. The case against subliminal manipulation. *Psychology and Marketing,* 5, 297–316.
3. Collins, R. L., et al. 1988. The vividness effect: elusive or illusory? *Journal of Experimental Social Psychology,* 24, 1–18.
4. Hovland, C. I., I. R. Janis, and H. H. Kelley. 1953. *Communication and persuasion.* New Haven, CT: Yale University Press.
   Strong, E. K. 1925. *The psychology of selling.* New York: McGraw Hill.
   Rogers, E. M. 1962. *The diffusion of innovations.* New York: Free Press.
5. Fiske, S. T., and S. E. Taylor. 1984. *Social cognition,* pp. 188–198; 360–362. New York: Random House.
   Cooper, E., and M. Jahoda. 1947. The evasion of propaganda. *Journal of Psychology,* 23, 15–25.
   Manis, M. 1961. Interpretation of opinion statements as a function of recipient attitudes and source prestige. *Journal of Abnormal and Social Psychology,* 63, 82–86.
6. Lear, N. 1971. As I read how Laura saw Archie. . . . *New York Times,* October 10, quoted in Vidmar & Rokeach. 1974.
7. Vidmar, N., and M. Rokeach. 1974. Archie Bunker's Bigotry: A study of selective perception and exposure. *Journal of Communication,* 24, 36–47.

8. Sears, D. O., and J. L. Freedman. 1967. Selective exposure to information: A critical review. *Public Opinion Quarterly*, 31, 194–213.

9. Langer, E., A. Blank, and B. Chanowitz. 1978. The mindlessness of ostensibly thoughtful action: The role of placebic information in interpersonal interaction, *Journal of Personality and Social Psychology*, 36, 635–642.

10. Langer, E. J., and A. I. Piper. 1987. The prevention of mindlessness. *Journal of Personality and Social Psychology*, 53, 280–287.

11. Abelson, R. P. 1976. Script processing in attitude formation and decision-making. In *Cognition and social behavior*. J. S. Carroll and J. W. Payne, eds. Hillsdale, NJ: Erlbaum.

12. Langer, Blank, and Chanowitz 1978, *op cit.*

13. *Ibid.*

14. De Groot, A. D. 1965. *Thought and choice in chess*. The Hague: Mouton. Cantor, N., and W. Mischel. 1977. Traits as prototypes: Effects on recognition memory. *Journal of Personality and Social Psychology, 35*, 351–363.

15. Petty, R. E., T. M. Ostrom, and T. C. Brock. 1981. *Cognitive responses in persuasive communications: A text in attitude change*. Hillsdale, N.J.: Erlbaum.
Petty, R. E., and J. T. Cacioppo. 1984. The effects of involvement on responses to argument quantity and quality: Central and peripheral routes to persuasion. *Journal of Personality and Social Psychology*, 46, 69–81.
Petty, R. E., G. L. Wells, and T. C. Brock. 1976. Distraction can enhance or reduce yielding to propaganda: Thought disruption versus effort justification. *Journal of Personality and Social Psychology*, 34, 874–884.

16. Petty, R. E., and J. T. Cacioppo. 1986. The elaboration likelihood model of persuasion. In *Advances in Experimental Social Psychology*, vol. 19. L. Berkowitz, ed. 123–181. New York: Academic Press.

17. Eagly, A. H., and S. Chaiken. 1984. Cognitive theories of persuasion. In *Advances in Experimental Social Psychology*, vol. 17. L. Berkowitz, ed. 267–359. New York: Academic Press.

18. Sarbonmatsy, D. M., and F. P. Kardes. 1985. The effects of physiological arousal on information processing and persuasion. *Journal of Consumer Research*, 15, 379–385.

19. Petty, R. E., and J. T. Cacioppo. 1986. *Communication and persuasion*. New York: Springer-Verlag.

20. Sherif, C., M. Sherif, and R. E. Nebergall. 1965. *Attitudes and attitude change: The social judgement-involvement approach*. Philadelphia: W.B. Saunders.
Sherif, M., and C. Sherif. 1967. *Attitude, ego involvement and change*. New York: John Wiley and Sons, Inc.

21. Sherif, M., and C. I. Hovland. 1961. *Social judgement: Assimililation and contrast effects in communication and attitude change*. New Haven, CN: Yale University Press.

22. Ullman, W. R., and E. M. Bodaken. 1975. Inducing resistance to persuasive attack: A test of two strategies of communication. *Western Journal of Speech Communication*, 32, 240–248.
Petty, R. E., and J. T. Cacioppo. 1979. Effects of forewarning of persuasive intent and involvement on cognitive responses and persuasion. *Personality and Social Psychology Bulletin*, 5, 173–176.

23. Frankl, V. 1960. Paradoxical intention: A logotherapeutic technique. *American Journal of Psychotherapy*, 14, 520–535.

24. McMullin, R. E. 1986. *Handbook of cognitive therapy techniques.* New York: W.W. Norton & Co.

25. *Ibid.*

26. *Ibid.*

27. *Ibid.*

28. Gregory, W. L., R. B. Cialdini, and K. M. Carpenter. 1982. Self-relevant scenarios as mediators of likelihood estimates and compliance: Does imagining make it so? *Journal of Personality and Social Psychology, 43,* 89–99.

29. Wood, W., and C. A. Kallgren. 1988. Communicator attributes and persuasion: Recipients' access to attitude-relevant information in memory. *Personality and Social Psychology Bulletin, 14,* 1172–1182.

13

Analyzing Symbolic Meaning

Symbols are the basis for communication, yet the meaning of symbols varies, and the basis for our interpretation of symbols and our response to symbols is not always apparent. Symbols change meaning over time, contexts, and people. Moreover, as receivers of persuasive messages, we often fail to explore the conscious and sub-conscious associations that determine our positive or negative responses to particular symbols. One of the best examples of a symbol with implicit associations, which had a powerful persuasive effect on our culture, is the Cabbage Patch Doll.

In 1983, hordes of parents and grandparents battled their way through Christmas shopping lines to buy overpriced and admittedly homely, stuffed dolls. Enterprising entrepreneurs responded to the shortage of Cabbage Patch Dolls by scalping these toys for over $100 apiece through classified ads.

What can account for this crazed reaction of American consumers? J. Soloman in *The Signs of Our Times* presents a symbolic analysis of this phenomena.[1] He contends that parents, most of whom work full-time, are plagued with guilt for not spending enough time with their children. Furthermore, children must be kept occupied so that parents can attend to household chores during their off-duty hours. Guilty parents who want to occupy their child's time, but not deprive their child in any way, saw the large, homely, stuffed doll as a human surrogate, according to Soloman's analysis. The Cabbage Patch Kids were made to look pitifully ugly and fat, not artificially beautiful. The Cabbage Patch Kids were personalized; each doll came with a name and set of adoption papers. Soloman claims that the Cabbage Patch Kids filled a need in our children for human, or pseudo-human, interaction, and a need of parents to pamper and occupy time-neglected children. It was easier for parents to buy a human surrogate for their children than to spend time with their children. Moreover, parents spending over $100 for a simple stuffed doll had physical proof—for themselves, for the child, and for the public—that they were good parents who made sacrifices for their children. The meanings associated with the symbol of the homely Cabbage Patch doll make it difficult for parents to refuse buying Cornela Lenora for their child.

Soloman's analysis of the Cabbage Patch Doll phenomena is far from superficial—Soloman analyzes the deep-rooted cultural beliefs and conditions that influenced the meaning assigned to a simple doll. This type of analysis of symbols, meaning, and persuasion is called critical analysis. Rather than analyzing the definitional meaning of symbols or the obvious relationship between persuasion and action, critical analysis focuses on the underlying cultural influences that affect the interpretation of a persuasive message, within both conscious and sub-conscious awareness.

In this chapter we will explore several approaches for analyzing the meaning of symbols and messages. We will discuss how personal and impersonal persuasive contexts, and cultural ideals and values influence the construction of meaning. The process of **critical analysis** is a method for studying how cultural factors influence the meaning of persuasive messages. Though it is useful for you to understand how qualitative analyses of messages are conducted for persuasion research purposes, it is even more important that you learn to recognize the factors that influence your interpretation of the persuasive messages you encounter in your daily life.

THE DEVELOPMENT OF MEANING

How can we identify the meaning of a persuasive message if meaning resides in people, not symbols or messages? How is "meaning" created by the persuasion process? How can we determine what a symbol or message means if meaning lies within the intentions of the speaker and the interpretations of the receiver?

The construction of meaning varies depending upon whether the persuasive encounter is face-to-face (i.e., interpersonal) or mediated (i.e., channeled through television, radio, or print). Yet in either context (face-to-face or mediated), meaning emerges from the unique interaction of the communicators; meaning is constructed by the speaker's intentions, the receiver's interpretation of these intentions, and the modification of intentions and interpretations by both speakers and receivers. In this chapter we will examine several theories that help explain how meaning is constructed in persuasive interactions, and how the construction of meaning may vary according to the personal or mediated nature of the persuasive context.

| BOX 13.1 | *Coordinated Management of Meaning: Seven levels of meaning used to interpret communication* |

7. Cultural patterns

6. Lifescript of receiver

5. Contract (relationship)

4. Episode (situation)

3. Speaker's intent

2. Content of message

1. Raw sensory data

EMERGENCE OF MEANING IN DYADS AND SMALL GROUPS

In face-to-face interpersonal situations the persuader may receive immediate feedback from the receiver, and this feedback increases the likelihood that they will define symbols similarly, resulting in shared meaning between the two interactants. In face-to-face interaction, feedback allows the communicators to actively negotiate the meaning of symbols and messages. Although the emergence of meaning in small groups provides similar opportunities for feedback and negotiation, small groups provide the opportunity for increased interaction of ideas, interpretations, and meanings. Thus, the group may develop a meaning that is different from the meaning any individual member originally assigned.

Coordinated Management of Meaning

The Coordinated Management of Meaning theory provides an explanation of the negotiation of symbolic meaning in interaction.[2] As the name implies, CMM outlines how persuaders and receivers coordinate individual meanings to reach a shared understanding. CMM provides a model for the emergence of meaning in face-to-face interaction, in which both persuaders and receivers are active participants in the construction and negotiation of meanings.

According to CMM, there are seven levels of meaning for any message (Box 13.1). At the base level, **raw sensory data,** such as sounds in verbal communication or visuals in written communication, are perceived. At this base level there is no specific meaning attributed to the sounds or letters.

At the second level, the **content** of a message is interpreted at face value. What do the words mean? If you answer the door in your bathrobe and your friend responds, "Cute!" you would first interpret this statement according to the dictionary definition of "cute."

At the third level of meaning, the **intentions** of the speaker are inferred to understand the true meaning of the message. A speech act defines the intended purpose of a message. Questions, statements, requests, promises, and threats are all different types of speech acts. Resurrecting the previous bathrobe example, using the third level of meaning to interpret this statement, you might conclude that the speech act intended by your friend was humor.

The fourth level of meaning requires the analysis of the **episode** in which the statement is made. An episode is the conversational situation. In the bathrobe example, the episode is *greeting a friend who has arrived unexpectedly.* You might interpret the remark, "Cute!" very differently if the episode were *trying on clothes at a store* or *falling down while playing basketball* or *scoping out attractive persons.*

The fifth level of meaning is the **contract** between sender and receiver. The contract is the expectations one has for the type of communication that should occur based on the relationship between sender and receiver. Contracts include teacher/student, doctor/patient, salesperson/consumer, daughter/mother, wife/husband, etc. Again, the statement, "Cute!" might have different meaning coming from a salesperson, your mother, or your teacher, as opposed to your friend.

At the next level of the meaning hierarchy, messages are analyzed in terms of **lifescripts**—one's style of living, personality, world view, and social roles. One's lifescript determines how one defines contracts and conversational episodes. If your lifescript is *engaged to be married* and your friend's lifescript is *looking for action* and you go to a party together, you are likely to define contracts and episodes differently. Were a mutual friend to approach the two of you and say, "Cute!" you might define this as an innocuous compliment in a platonic relationship, but your friend might interpret this comment as a sign of interest in an intimate relationship.

The final level in the meaning hierarchy is the analysis of **cultural patterns.** Different cultures and sub-cultures have different communication rules. The meaning we attribute to messages is dependent upon the application of cultural expectations. In our culture, friendship communication operates under rather loose politeness rules. You would probably interpret your friend's response to your bathrobe in good humor and would not be shocked that your friend would make such a personal comment about your private apparel. In other cultures, even communication among friends is governed by rules of formality and politeness. In another culture, you might expect a friend to pretend not to notice your bathrobe, and a blatant reference to your nightwear would be rude.

There are numerous examples of cultural and sub-cultural communication rules. If a person does not understand the cultural communication rules being applied to a conversation, meaning is altered. My Italian friend talks a great deal and interrupts frequently. If I were to apply my own cultural expectations to my friend's communication, I would conclude that she is boorish and rude. But if I apply my knowledge of her Italian upbringing, in which everyone in her family talks loudly and at the same time, I conclude that she perceives our relationship to be a close and intimate one. When leading a group of students in Puerto Rico, I was guilty of applying my own cultural communication rules to people within that culture. I was informed that when I asked Puerto Ricans to commit to a time schedule, my message was considered quite rude and pushy.

One of the first steps toward multi-cultural understanding in the United States will be for us to learn different cultural communication rules. Many misunderstandings among people of different ethnic and racial groups result from the application of one's own cultural expectations to a message, without realizing that the meaning of the message was created with different cultural communication rules in mind.

One of the amazing faculties we possess is the ability to make judgements of all seven levels of meaning, instantaneously, in the course of a continuing conversation. Our interpretation of a single message may involve many levels. The disadvantage of this is that it is easy for people to attribute different meanings to the same conversation. Meaning may derail at any of the seven levels of interpretation. The implications for persuasion are profound—establishing shared meaning between communicators requires that the communicators apply similar interpretations to all the levels of meaning.

Rules Guiding CMM

You might be asking how it is possible to analyze all seven levels of meaning for each message in a conversation. In reality, we often focus on one level of meaning and assume that all other levels are consistent. Constituative and regulative communication rules further explain the interrelationships among the seven levels of the Coordinated Management of Meaning model and the procedure for interpreting messages. Constitutive and regulative rules are shortcuts for interpreting meaning. Only if the meaning of a message is confusing, based on the analysis of constitutive and regulative rules, are we likely to explore all seven levels of meaning.

Constitutive rules specify how the **speech act,** or the speaker's intent, influences the interpretation of all other levels of meaning. Identifying the constitutive rule of a message involves asking, "In this particular context, what does this message constitute? A question, a request, a promise, a compliment . . . ?" Your answer to this question is your perception of the sender's intentions. If you determine that the speech act of the message "Cute!" is humor, you are likely to analyze the contract consistently, as a friendship. You are less likely to infer a friendship contract if you decide the speech act is an insult. Similarly, if your lifescript includes liking to debate, and your contract with your friend includes debating issues, it is unlikely that you will label the episode of a volatile conversation about feminist theory as an argument. Constitutive rules allow us to make quick judgements in evaluating the meaning of a symbol or message, based on the assessment of: "This symbol or message *constitutes* X type of speech act when used in Y context, which means that the speaker's intention is Z."

Regulative rules provide guidelines for how we should react based on our interpretation of meaning. If you conclude that the message "Cute!" (content), was intended as humor (speech act), and spoken in greeting (episode), by a close friend (contract), who knows of your vanity (lifescript), in a culture in which greeting guests is not commonly conducted in a bathrobe, regulative rules tell you to respond by laughing or making a joke of the incident. In contrast, if the same message "Cute!" (content), was intended as an insult (speech act), yelled across a street (episode), by a loitering group of young males (contract), and you are a female feminist (lifescript), ignorant of the male gang's subculture, regulative rules may suggest the response of a mean glare or a choice gesture.

In brief, we apply constitutive and regulatory rules to tell us how to interpret a persuader's intentions, and based upon our interpretation of the persuader's intentions, what behavioral response is appropriate. To the extent that a persuader can influence what constitutive rule the receiver applies, the persuader can also influence the receiver's behavioral response (the regulatory rule). Thus, a persuader may phrase a message to constitute a concession, so the receiver will apply a regulatory rule of offering a counteroffer. Or a persuader could phrase a message to constitute flattery, to get the receiver to enact a regulatory rule of owing the persuader a favor.

Symbols, Rules and Meaning in Conversation

The use of constitutive and regulative rules also explains problems in interpersonal communication. Let's consider the following scenario: B.J. is playing baseball and hits a ball into Mr. McGreggor's garden. As a result of different analyses of the situation, B.J. and McGreggor apply very different constitutive and regulative rules and continue to talk at cross purposes, with neither party able to accomplish his persuasive goal.

B. J.:

B. J.'s perceptions	—culture (neighborhood)
	—lifescript (peer group leader)
	—contract (old man)
	—episode (retrieving a ball)
Constitutive rule	—simple task of retrieving ball
Regulative rule	—direct request
Message	—"Can have I my ball back?"

McGreggor:

Perceptions	—culture (neighborhood)
	—lifescript (respected adult)
	—contract (disciplinarian)
	—episode (garden trampled)
Constitutive rule	—message reflects lack of respect
	—message is an affront and an insult
Regulative rule	—challenge the child
Message	—"No."

B. J.:

Constitutive rule	—message reflects a threat
	—using power/dominance over me
Regulative rule	—establish my rights
Message	—"It's my ball!"

McGreggor:

Constitutive rule	—message is disrespectful
	—threat to authority
Regulative rule	—force kid into submission
Message	—"It's in my garden!"

As in all persuasive conversations, B. J. and Mr. McGreggor must reach some agreement in constitutive and regulative rules before persuasion is successful. The meanings associated with age, roles, rights, respect, authority, property, and neighborliness must be negotiated before B. J. will persuade McGreggor to return his baseball. Without agreement regarding what constitutive and regulatory rules govern a conversation, shared meaning, understanding, and persuasion are unlikely to occur.

Symbolic Convergence of Meaning

The unique role of symbols in groups is best explained by Earnest Bormann's symbolic convergence theory.[3] **Symbolic convergence** is the phenomenon by which symbols come to assume a unique meaning that is shared by members of a social group. As a result of face-to-face communication and persuasion among a group of people, the members of the group begin to construe similar meanings for particular symbols. The meanings that emerge as a result of the group process may be unique to the group itself; that is, the meanings that emerge may be different from any meaning any individual member originally applied. Meanings and ideas communicated by one member inspire new meanings and ideas for another member, who then inspires another. This process leads to the eventual convergence of meaning, whereby the group begins to share a new perception of reality.

Carib Indians, for example, believed that they acquired the prowess of their enemies by eating them. Cannibalism was a symbolic event, the meaning of which members of this tribe clearly understood.

A psychiatric condition called folie au deu, "shared delusion," is another example of symbolic convergence. A delusional person may assign particular events and people symbolic meaning—e.g., "the police are part of a conspiracy to get me committed to a hospital so that they (the police) can take over my business." Symbolic convergence occurs if a person associated with the delusional person begins, over time, to adopt the delusional person's perceptions of reality. The relative or friend begins to assign similar meanings to occurrences (e.g., "the police cruiser driving by the house is spying on us," "there was no mail delivered today because the police intercepted it," etc.).

There are numerous additional examples of symbolic convergence. Several writers have explored the symbolic convergence of Dungeons and Dragons addicts, claiming that some groups become so obsessed with the fantasy that the symbols of the game invade their daily life. Families also experience symbolic convergence—you can probably generate examples of photos, holiday decorations, heirlooms, cherished rituals, and even words or phrases that have acquired symbolic meaning that all members of your family share, but that outsiders do not know.

Symbolic convergence describes how social groups create meanings for particular symbols. A persuader cannot assume that all people assign the same meanings to symbols, and the persuader must attempt to learn the symbolic significance of symbols that a group employs. A classic case of this dilemma occurred when advertisers attempted to persuade people to wear motorcycle helmets. The campaign was successful with formally-educated, recreational bikers, but it was an abysmal failure with motorcycle gang members. Eventually, the advertisers discovered the symbolic significance of riding without a helmet in motorcycle gangs—the helmets hid the men's gorgeous faces, making it more difficult to attract women and threatening their macho, risk-taking image. The advertisers tried, with moderate success, to appeal to this symbolism by portraying helmet use as a sort of Darth Vader eroticism.

Symbolic convergence differs from the coordinated management of meaning in qualitative ways. Symbolic convergence is almost mystical—the construction of a shared meaning is inspirational. Whereas symbolic convergence is mystical, the coordinated management of meaning is methodical. In the latter case, shared meaning is negotiated, not inspired. Yet, whether meaning is constructed through symbolic convergence or coordinated negotiation, both processes depend on the immediate feedback characteristic of face-to-face interaction.

EMERGENCE OF MEANING IN MEDIATED CONTEXTS

The construction of meaning in mass mediated communication differs from the negotiation and inspiration of shared meaning in interpersonal and small group contexts. The mass media can construct social reality for a large number of people, and individuals have little opportunity to provide feedback, much less challenge, the meanings assigned by the media. Any feedback that does occur is delayed and impersonal.

Imagine the process of *coordinating meaning* when a single message can reach millions of receivers, yet the receivers cannot easily communicate with the disembodied message source. Receivers must either accept the meanings assigned by the media source, ignore the message, or organize a political action group to try to negotiate the meanings assigned to messages and symbols.

The process of symbolic convergence in mass mediated persuasion is also disturbing. Consider the power the media have in defining symbols and facilitating symbolic convergence in our society. Whereas symbolic convergence as a result of face-to-face interaction is based on inspiration, symbolic convergence as a result of mediated messages is characterized by a mindless acceptance of predetermined meanings. The construction of meaning in mass mediated persuasion is passive and one-sided; it takes a great deal of effort for the receiver to counterargue the meanings assigned by the mass media when it is difficult to interact with the message source directly.

Does symbolic convergence of meaning actually occur as a result of media messages? Do we adopt the meanings assigned by the mass media, resulting in a shared social reality? Have we all begin to think alike and to interpret symbols in a similar way? The power of the government and media to define the reality of "the masses" was accomplished by "doublespeak" in George Orwell's science fiction novel *1984.* [4]

Doublespeak

Doublespeak is the process of making symbols meaningless. If the purpose of communications is to establish shared meaning, the purpose of doublespeak is to bury meaning and to convey as little information as possible. Ambiguous message symbols, in turn, breed apathy regarding social issues. In Orwell's novel, *1984,* the government convinced the people that "war is peace." Why are we fighting a war? To keep peace. Therefore, war is peace. In this manner, the symbols "war" and "peace" both become void of meaning. As a result, the "masses" become confused and apathetic, and began to accept the meaningless communication without critical thought.

William Lutz is a college professor whose hobby is doublespeak.[5] Lutz collects media examples of doublespeak—and he doesn't have to look very far to find them. One of his favorite examples is the response of Oliver North in the Iran-Contra hearings: "The additional input is radically different from the truth . . . and I assisted in furthering that input. . . . I received a different version of the facts which was inconsistent with the truth. . . . I have no specific recollection of that conversation."[6] What was the truth, what wasn't, where did the truth and the false facts come from, and did this conversation occur or not? Lutz also cites the communication of politicians in his examples. When asked what he would do about the federal deficit, a presidential candidate replied: "I am from all these people as to what—not only what the situation is but what we do about it."[7] No, this is not a typo—this is really the candidate's verbatim answer to the question!

Lutz describes four types of doublespeak: euphemisms, jargon, bureaucrat-ese, and inflated language.[8] **Euphemisms** are phrases used to minimize the emotional impact of reality. We talk about people "passing on" instead of dying. In the military, killing is "termination with extreme prejudice." A junker car in the classifieds is referred to as a "good work car." Our government calls tax increases "revenue enhancements" and military conflicts "actions of peacekeeping forces."

Jargon is technical language usually adopted by an occupational group. Medical terms, for example, qualify as jargon, and they qualify as doublespeak if they are used to confuse the patient. If your doctor tells you your illness is "idiopathic," you'd best run. Though you may be tempted to breathe a sigh of relief that the doctor has pronounced a diagnosis, a closer look reveals that idiopathic means "of unknown origin." If you are similarly comforted by a diagnosis of "iatrogenesis," you are in even greater trouble because this means that your *doctor* has made you ill.

Bureaucrat-ese includes political statements that are nonsensical, but are produced with the intent to distract the public from the truth. The movie *The Best Little Whorehouse in Texas* parodies bureaucrat-ese in the scene of the governor dancing before the reporters, singing: "I just do the little sidestep. . . ."

The final type of doublespeak, **inflated language,** is the exaggerated use of a word or phrase to the point at which the words become meaningless. Our current health craze has rendered the label "fat free" meaningless. Comedians joke that the label really means you pay for the rest of the contents, but that the fat is free! A label of "low fat" can mean anything from 5 percent fat to 95 percent fat. One of the best examples of inflated langauge used for purposes of deception is the phraseology used in car advertisements. A brief visit with a salesperson reveals that the car advertised for $7,500 is really $12,500. Upon closer evaluation you realize the ad reads "as low as $7,500," and upon quizzing the salesperson, you find the single car on the lot selling for $7,500 does not have tires, a steering wheel, or seats. Expressions such as "zero percent financing" are similarly meaningless when you realize the inflated price of the car and the impossible conditions that a buyer must meet to qualify.

Euphemisms, jargon, bureacrat-ese, and inflated language are all forms of doublespeak that can be used in many interpersonal as well as mass media contexts. The research interest in doublespeak, however, focuses on its use in public address and by the mass media. In face-to-face, feedback-oriented situations, doublespeak is not particularly powerful—the receiver has the opportunity to challenge the persuader's use of ambiguous symbols. In public address and mass media contexts, however, the receivers' access to the speaker is restricted, and the receivers are more likely to accept doublespeak uncritically.

In a PBS television series, *The Public Mind*, Bill Moyers explores examples of doublespeak in the mass media and weaves the frightening conclusion that doublespeak thrives in our society.[9] Moyers contends that we believe what we see on television, and that we do not scrutinize visual images in the same way we've been taught to evaluate the truth or falsity of verbal claims. The result, according to Moyers, is that visual media images, which communicate skewed views of reality and very little substantive information, create our individual realities. We are products of media images—these images govern our lives, our thoughts, and our behavior.

Moyers provides numerous examples of the influence and uncritical acceptance of this visual "doublespeak."

1) Rather than create a personality, we borrow a self-identity through products we buy.

2) Rather than form educated opinions, we readily adopt the perspectives that the media voice.

3) Rather than explore the character and positions of a political candidate, we vote according to the candidate's media image.

Moyers concludes that we have supplanted reality with media illusions—meaning is lost and doublespeak reigns supreme. It is true that this is not a new argument. Walter Lippmann, in his book *Public Opinion* published in the 1920s, and even Plato in the "Allegory of the Cave," have made similar criticisms about our tendency to rely on illusion and perception over reality. The degree to which artificial representations created by media technology have become *truth* is arguably much more pervasive today than at any other point in history. Camera angles and the editing of video segments and interviews bias what we accept as "truth" and "reality". Even the positioning of stories biases their interpretation—the release of American hostages in Iran was interspersed and associated with the inauguration of President Reagan, leading people to conclude that the two events were one. Reality may well lie on the editing room floor.

Meaning is illusive—persuasive context is one of many factors that influence how symbols are presented and perceived. Symbolic meaning can be "coordinated" and "managed" in interpersonal contexts when interactants become aware of the regulative and constitutive rules being applied by others. Symbolic meaning may "converge" in groups such that, over time, members of a group may increasingly share similar meanings and significance for important symbols. The media go one step further. Rather than using symbols to *represent* reality, the media's definition of symbols has *become* reality. The mass media propagate "doublespeak"— the use of euphemisms, jargon, bureaucrat-ese, and inflated language to replace reality. The responsibility for this "mass management" of meaning lies not only with the media, but also with the people who rely on the media to define their world.

As critical receivers of persuasive messages, we must learn to analyze the meanings assigned to symbols and messages. A superficial analysis of a message can help us to identify the meaning a persuader wishes us to adopt, but this information is not sufficient to resist the sophisticated messages that confront us each day. Critical analysis of the symbols comprising a message can help us assess the validity of the meanings a persuader employs and help us identify the cultural influences that may make us susceptible to a particular symbolic meaning.

ANALYZING SYMBOLS IN PERSUASION

Any message in our society may be laden with symbolic meaning—a television program, a book, a conversation, or a work of art. The analysis of symbolism can help the recipient of a persuasive message to critically assess the validity of the symbol. To respond critically to persuasive messages we must be able to identify how the persuader is constructing the presentation of symbols. Is the persuader altering the level of abstraction, the emotional intensity, the aesthetic form, or the cognitive associations of symbols, as discussed in chapter 4? Is the persuader emphasizing particular levels of meanings (the episode, the relationship, or cultural patterns)? Is the persuader toying with the convergence of symbolic meaning or using doublespeak to confuse the audience?

There are numerous methods for analyzing messages and symbols. Each method includes different steps and different theories for interpretation. For example, a movie analyzed using psychoanalytic theory would evaluate symbols for evidence of phallic images and other Freudian concepts, while an ideological criticism of the same movie would focus on how the symbols reflect the ideals of the powerful elite, the suppression of social-economic classes, and materialism. Clearly, what the researcher is looking for, and the method of analysis, influences the conclusions drawn from a symbolic analysis. Symbols can be interpreted in many different ways.

Defining the Scope of the Critical Analysis

Although there are many different methods for analyzing the meaning of a persuasive message, there are some steps that are common to all methods of analysis.[10] Prior to the analysis of the symbolic meaning of a message, the researcher must define the scope of the analysis.

At an event honoring Macolm X, sponsored by a campus Black Student Organization, a group of students performed a skit that highlighted the social hardships facing African-Americans, followed by the repetition of the Malcolm X chant: "... kill the blue-eyed devils ... kill the blue-eyed devils." Prior to analyzing the symbolic meaning of this message, the persuasion critic must address five issues that define the scope of the analysis and the context in which the message occurred:

1. *Define the purpose of the analysis.* Persuasive symbols and messages may be analyzed for a number of reasons. A **receiver-focus** leads the critic to identify the effect of the persuasive symbols and messages on individuals or society. A critic with a **cultural-focus** may analyze a message in order to reveal the heartbeat of the culture—the values and ideology that govern the culture. A **historical-focus** leads the critic to analyze the context, speaker, and effect of a message at a given point in time, in order to identify the historical implications of the message. The **educational approach** to persuasion analysis seeks to explain how the speaker produced a message that had an impact on the receiver/s. The purpose of the educational approach is to guide theory and research on persuasion, teach persuaders how to communicate more effectively, and to teach receivers how to recognize and evaluate persuasive strategies.

   To analyze the Malcolm X quote, we must first decide what the purpose of our analysis will be. A cultural analysis of the African-American culture would yield a much different interpretation of the message than an educational approach.

2. Once the purpose of the analysis is defined, the critic must *identify the location of meaning.* The meaning of a message may change depending upon whose perspective is considered. There are nine different perspectives, or places, in which meaning can be located: 1) the meaning intended by the author; 2) the unconscious intentions of the author; 3) the interpretation of the message by the author's contemporaries; 4) the interpretation of the message receiver; 5) the interpretation of the *ideal* message receiver; 6) the society at the time

the message was created; 7) contemporary society; 8) social critics; or 9) the literal use of language in the message.[11] If we were to analyze the symbol "Nova" used to represent a make of car, we would reach different conclusions were we to focus on the creator's intentions, the dictionary definition—a star that increases in light, then fades away to its former obscurity, or the interpretation of Spanish speaking message receivers—"no va," meaning the car doesn't go.

If our purpose is to address the effects of the Malcolm X message on receivers (step one), then we have to define the receivers in which we are interested. We could choose either the receivers attending the Black Student Organization event or the receivers of Malcolm X's original message.

3. *Review the historical and social context, and the central issue/s reflected in the message.* The context in which a message is received clearly influences the meaning of a message. Historical factors may have as much of an influence on the meaning of a message as the current social conditions under which the message is received. Moreover, the central controversial issue underlying the message may not be readily apparent in the message itself. It is important to analyze the conditions or issues that motivated the message.

Both historical and contemporary social factors influence the interpretation of the Malcolm X message. We must recognize the period of social strife, discrimination against African-Americans, and anger that defined the context of Malcolm X's remarks. Yet to interpret these words as spoken in the 1990s, we must contrast the symbols with the goals of multi-culturalism and tolerance for ethnic diversity. Moreover, what dominant issue might have driven the students' decision to incorporate the "blue-eyed devil" chant into their skit?

4. *Analyze the audience.* The critic must clearly identify the receivers for which the message was intended. The demographics, the attitudes, beliefs, and values of the audience all influence the speaker's intentions and the audience's interpretations.

If our purpose is to analyze the receivers' interpretation of the Malcolm X quote in the context of the Black Student Organization skit, and bearing in mind both the contemporary and historical social issues underlying the selection of this particular Malcolm X message, we must analyze the audience attending the "Celebrate the Life of Malcolm X" event. It is conceivable that the message would have a different meaning for the different people comprising the audience (African-American students, the students' parents, and non-African-American students and professors who were interested in Malcolm X and in African-American issues).

5. *Analyze the speaker.* The ethics, credibility, charisma, eloquence, and attractiveness of the speaker all influence the reception of a message. Moreover, the speaker's adherence to expected rhetorical conventions is also worthy of note. Rhetorical conventions are the rules of behavior that govern a speaking situation. These rules differ by culture and by historical period. The rules govern a variety of factors from the length of the speech, the grammar employed, the dialect, the manner of addressing the topic, and the relevance of the topic, to the quality of the arguments.

An analysis of the rhetorical conventions the students employ in the Malcolm X skit might reveal their intentions and persuasive goals in choosing this particular message. One of the speakers responded to the shock of some non-African American audience members by explaining that the quote referred to white racists, and that the whites attending the event were not racist and therefore not included in the "blue-eyed devil" category. The credibility and intentions of the speaker certainly influence the meaning the receivers assign to this message and the Malcolm X skit.

These five steps reflect the type of background information needed before embarking on an in-depth critical analysis. Once the critic has defined the purpose, perspective, social and historical context, intended audience, and speaker characteristics that will influence the meaning assigned to the symbols comprising a message, the critic can pursue an in-depth analysis of symbolic meaning. In the Malcolm X case, for example, the critic might explore the symbols "blue-eyed" and "devil" to determine their social and historical interpretation and significance.

To provide some insight into the power of symbol analysis, we will explore the method of **semiotics**. This method is very applicable to our study of persuasion because semiotics is based on the assumption that the meaning of symbols does not reside in the message strategy, the delivery, or the stylistic devices employed—the meaning can be derived only from the interaction of the communicators. Semiotics is the study of how the communication of symbols reflects underlying cultural meanings. For example, a semiotic analysis of Appalachian women would analyze the symbols employed by these women to represent their experiences and would explore what these symbols or words mean to these particular women. Meaning, therefore, lies in the social significance of the symbols and how people perceive and use them to make sense of their worlds. Semiotic analysis assumes that people construct meanings in their minds as a result of the historical, cultural, social, and individual situation in which they encounter symbols.

Semiotic Analysis

Semiotic analysis may focus on a conversation, the use of music, the positioning of a product, a film genre, or most any other communicative event. The purpose of semiotic analysis is to study what the communication text means for its audience, and how the text reflects or influences the culture in which it is received.

For example, Eric Peterson conducted a semiotic analysis of Cindy Lauper's hit, "Girls Just Want to Have Fun."[12] He concluded that there are three distinct audiences and interpretations of this song: liberal individualists, liberal feminists, and teeny-boppers. For liberal individualists the song symbolizes fun and youth. For this audience the song is fun and provides pleasure partly because it distinguishes the young and "in" crowd from older generations. For liberal feminists rock and roll has political as well as entertainment functions. For this audience the song symbolizes rebellion from cultural norms and the definition of new ways for women to have fun, or conversely, the trivilization of women. Teeny boppers emphasize the danceability and social aspects of the music. For this audience the song symbolizes community with other girls, and a silly, carefree time of adolescence.

Just as there are many methods of message criticism, there are many different approaches to semiotic analysis. Each approach may incorporate different types of questions. As previously noted, the questions directing an analysis influence how symbols are defined and how meaning is interpreted. Malcolm Sillars presents one of many approaches to semiotic analysis. He has outlined seven factors that a semiotic critic may explore to flesh out the dominant symbolic meaning of a text.[13] Sillars provides a good checklist for the semiotic critic. It is important to note, however, that not all of the seven categories may be relevant to the analysis of every persuasive text.

Connotations

We have already discussed how connotation reflects the deeper, emotional meanings associated with a symbol (chapter 4). What associations and emotions are generated by receivers when confronted with a particular symbol? We could, for example, explore the connotative meaning responsible for the public outcry against thong bikinis on public beaches. At a literal level the thong is simply a swimsuit (which allows the wearer to get a more extensive tan!). In France and Spain bikinis are often one piece, not two, and the thong has been popular for fifteen years. Why the controversy in America? Whereas Europeans may perceive the buttocks as natural, beautiful and artistic wonders, Americans associate buttocks with uncleanliness, promiscuity, and obscenity; the exposure of buttocks is associated with immorality, the downfall of our social system, and a widespread disregard for societal decency. Although Kevin Costner

A semiotic analysis of the symbols in this 1989 East German poster reveals fears of being consumed by Western capitalism. The symbol of the hamburger presents a negative connotation of Western (especially American) glitz and epitomizes a perceived lack of substance in our "McDonald's culture." The person sandwiched between the buns is a metaphor for the voracious appetite of Western consumerism. The lack of power exhibited by the person who is about to be eaten reflects the myth that the powerful West is attempting to export our way of life and is seeking to subsume all other cultural traditions.

Eastburger by Thomas Gübig, 1989, Courtesy of Marta Sylvestrová, Moravian Gallery Brno and Dana Bartelt, NCSU Raleigh

is challenging this viewpoint with bare buttocks scenes in his recent movies, the thong remains inconsistent with our country's puritanical roots and nudity phobia.

Metaphor

The application of one concept to a second, unrelated concept, in order to provide a new perspective, is a metaphor. Describing the role of missionaries as warriors marching off to conquer new souls, or describing eating a piece of cheesecake as an erotic, tender, and sexual experience is an example of a metaphor.

The caterpillar metaphor in this ad generates images of a dangerous, uncontrollable, voracious insect that could threaten our survival.

IN AFRICA THERE IS A TYPE OF CATERPILLAR THAT CONSUMES HUNDREDS OF ACRES A DAY.

In the two minutes it takes you to read this ad, about 300 acres of African, South American, and Asian jungle will be cut down, burned, or bulldozed.

This senseless destruction increases global warming and the greenhouse effect. It destroys the cultures of those who've lived in the jungles for centuries. Perhaps worst of all, it causes at least one entire plant or animal species to become extinct every single day.

Right now, all of this is happening thousands of miles away. But there are things that you can do right here at home to stop it.

You can write to your representatives and senators urging them to support legislation protecting tropical forests. You can tell them you don't want your tax dollars spent on projects that are destroying the ancient jungles.

And you can support Greenpeace Action. We'll work to stop funding for new roads and logging operations.

We'll also let people know how they can help the rainforest natives keep their homelands.

There. Two minutes are finished. And so are about 300 acres of rainforests.

*GREENPEACE*ACTION

Greenpeace

In semiotic analysis, it is important to highlight the metaphors that instill new meanings into symbols. During his trial, Oliver North enacted a warrior metaphor to force the public and the legal system to try him as a soldier, not as a government worker. Why? Soldiers often operate outside civilian laws. It is unpatriotic to interrogate the actions and to incarcerate a soldier, but not a government worker. Moreover, the actions of soldiers are shrouded in secrecy, but the public expects access to the actions of the government. North enacted this metaphor in his costume, language, and demeaner. Although he was a civilian, he wore a military uniform to his hearing. He answered questions with the alert "Yes, sir!" or "No, sir!" customary in the military. His discussion of "duty," "love of country," and "following orders" further elaborated the war metaphor. In fact, his act was so compelling that many of us forgot that America was *not* at war.

Metonymy

In the production of any message, we can choose among similar symbols (synonyms). Metonymy is the characterization of a part, or a specific, with a more abstract symbol (e.g., replacing "I paint" with "I am an artist"), or the characterization of an abstract symbol by a more specific symbol (e.g., replacing "I am a teacher" with "I am a professor"). Does the change in symbols in the preceding examples produce a change in meaning? The symbols "artist" and "professor" convey different image than "painter" and "teacher."

Metonymy can also influence meaning by focusing on a part to the exclusion of the whole. Sillars gives the example of filling a camera lens with a densely packed group of six protesters, implying the presence of hundreds of protesters off-camera. In fact, John Fiske argues that "all news films are metonymies and all involve an arbitrary selection" of reality.

Receivers of persuasive messages should be on guard for gross generalizations, or the opposite, the myopic focus on a concrete symbol in persuasive arguments; the selection of symbols influences meaning. Consider the advertisement in Figure 13.1. The choice made by the advertiser to use the symbol "man" instead of "person", and "heart" instead of "stomach" in the headline creates a very different meaning. The implications are numerous: a wife is responsible for a man's happiness; and the way to achieve a man's love and respect is through good cooking—if she's not a good cook, he has no reason to love her.

Tokens

Tokens are objects that have cultural meanings. Sillars gives the example of mascots for athletic teams, such as Rams, Cubs, Lions, Tigers, and Bears. These symbols do not represent mere animals in our culture, but they are tokens of physical prowess and regional loyalty. Name brands and chic products are tokens of wealth and status. Money is itself a token for prestige. The donkey is the symbol of the Democratic party and the elephant the symbol of the Republicans. An office may be a token of occupational status and a class ring a token of educational achievement.

Tokens are used and abused for persuasive ends. Television evangelists use the bible, a token of Christianity, to convey morality and honesty. FTD, a symbol for the floral delivery service, is explained as a token of love, and used to communicate affection to long distance relatives and friends for whom we've forgotten to buy a gift. Cute children, tokens of nurturance and affection, are used to sell car tires. Glamorous women, tokens of sex and beauty, are used to sell everything from cosmetics to oil drilling equipment. Though the use of objects as tokens for persuasive ends may corrupt the true meaning of the token, the use of people as tokens is an ethical affront.

Metonymy is the strategic selection of abstract or concrete symbols. The choice to use "man" instead of "person", "heart" instead of "stomach", and "love" instead of "respect", influences the meaning of the message.

FIGURE 13.1

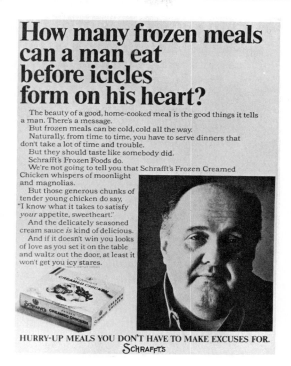

Schrafft's Frozen Foods

Values

Values, relatively enduring cultural beliefs used to evaluate our world, are discussed in chapter 6. For the semiotic researcher, the values embedded in the language of a persuasive text help explain how the message reflects the culture in which it is received, and how the message will influence the culture in which it is received. A message that is consistent with the values of a particular social group or sub-culture is likely to be readily accepted without scrutiny.

Think about what values are embedded in consumer advertising directed towards college students. You should be able to compile a list of values such as physical health, environmental awareness, sex appeal, heterosexual relationships, and consumerism that are reflected in the magazines that you read.

Myths

Myths are the stories that are told and retold within a social group and that are used as a basis for our self-identities. Myths that influence your self-identity include pioneer stories that instruct you what it means to be an "American" and family myths, often passed down through generations, that instruct you what it means to be a "Johnston" or a "Dumerauf." Similarly you have myths that define your circle of friends, myths that define your religious heritage, and myths that define your sexual and political preferences.

The myths we adopt as rationalizations for our lifestyle and personalities provide standards upon which we evaluate persuasive symbols and messages. The myth that my great-great-great Scottish Grandpa Johnston dropped a nickel down a gopher hole and consequently single-handedly created the Grand Canyon tells me that Johnstons are . . . thrifty. My husband's family myth of Great-grandpa Flynn obliviously drunk, floating down the Mississippi in a row boat with Grandma Flynn running and yelling along the shore, bespeaks to the laid-back, fun-loving nature of his clan. And, occupational myths, such as "professors are absent-minded," continue to provide useful excuses for my errant behavior.

We use myths such as these in attributing meaning to messages and in seeking guidelines for action. To understand the impact of a message we must understand the myths embedded in the message and the myths of the people who will interpret the message. The advertisement in Figure 13.2 makes fun of the myth that superior beings from outer space visit Earth. The advertisement plays on the myth that these encounters with aliens usually occur in rural areas, involve the sighting of "shiny discs," and result in some phenomenal insight on the part of the human involved. The advertisement taps our secret fantasy that extraterrestrials do exist, and that these alien beings can make us better humans. Note how the symbols of the cow and the pitchfork instill the advertisement with trustworthiness—Iowa farmers don't lie!

Ideology

The definition of ideology is a hotly contested one. For our purposes, ideology is the dominant social theory of a particular culture or subculture. Ideology is often described as dialectical—it represents opposites. For example, if your ideology focuses on social empowerment, you might view the world in terms of the white, rich, power elite versus the disenfranchised minorities. If your ideology focuses on gender issues, you might view the world in terms of males versus females, or feminists versus male chauvinists. Marxist ideology views the world in terms of the working class versus the business owners (the proletariat). Other dialetical social ideologies include conservatives versus liberals, green-lovers versus polluters, and Muslims versus non-Muslims.

The ideology one imposes on the interpretation of symbols in a persuasive message obviously influences the meaning. The case of

This advertisement makes fun of UFO myths and rural sightings of aliens. Notice how the UFO myth is trivialized by the cow, farmer, pitchfork, and shiny disc.

FIGURE 13.2

FIGURE 13.3

The people of Kazahkstan in Central Asia give the honorary dinner guest a ram's head to dissect. The guest is expected to dole out the eyes, nose, and ears, giving a piece to each person at the table. The eyes symbolize great vision, the ears symbolize great wisdom and learning, and so on. Each part of the ram's head has symbolic significance.

Milwaukee serial killer Jeffery Dahmer illustrates the existance of variant ideologies in the city. Dahmer killed and dismembered up to eighteen victims in his inner-city apartment, many of whom were homosexuals or minorities. The homosexuals view the case in terms of homophobia— specifically, hatred and violence directed toward gays. Blacks view the case in terms of racial hatred and insufficient police protection in inner city neighborhoods. Suburbians could, conceivably, view the horror of the case from a distance, with a survival-of-the-fittest-my-money-got-me-out-of-the-city ideology.

The meaning a particular group of people attribute to particular symbols may be derived from an analysis of the connotations, metaphors, metonymy, tokens, values, myths, and ideologies that the message's sender and receiver employ and negotiate (Figure 13.3). A common language does not ensure that symbols will have the same meaning for all message recipients. Symbols carry tremendous emotional, political, social, and cultural meaning.

SUMMARY

The emergence of meaning is a process which is influenced by many variables. Receivers may apply up to seven levels of meaning in the interpretation of a message. The meaning of symbols may converge within a social group—resulting in a meaning unique to the members of the group, and symbols may be used for doublespeak, in an effort to confuse, rather than to convey, meaning. The ethical persuader must understand how these factors affect meaning, in order to produce a message that clearly communicates his or her intentions.

Message receivers can learn how to critically evaluate the symbols embedded in a message by learning Sillars' seven factors. Semiotic analysis provides a method for analyzing the hidden meanings in messages. A thoughtful analysis of the values, myths, and tokens associated with the symbols in a message can help the receiver identify the true intentions of the persuader.

Study Guide

coordinated management of meaning
    seven levels of meaning
    constitutive rules
    regulatory rules
symbolic convergence
doublespeak
    four types of doublespeak
steps for critical analysis
    purposes
    locations of meaning
    analysis of historical, social, and cultural factors
    analysis of source and audience
semiotic analysis
    connotation
    metaphor
    metonymy
    token
    values
    myth
    ideology

Class Discussion Questions

1. Ask members of the class to find an example of doublespeak in the media and bring it to the next class for discussion. How pervasive are examples of doublespeak in the media? Are most examples of doublespeak found in political statements, advertising, newspaper reports, etc.? What kind of effects do you think doublespeak has on the receiver and on our society? If the purpose of doublespeak is to make people believe that information is being released, when in reality the messages are meaningless, what are the implications of this for our society and our form of government?

2. What are the ethical implications of doublespeak? Is it ethical for a persuader to hide his or her intentions? Is it ethical for a persuader to withhold information? Is it ethical for a persuader to avoid communicating information?

3. What are the ethical implications of using symbolic tokens in persuasion? Discuss examples in which people are used as tokens. Is this common?

References

1. Soloman, J. 1988. *The signs of our times.* Los Angeles: Tarcher, Inc.
2. Pearce, B. W., V. Cronen, and F. Conklin. 1979. *Communication, 4,* 195–220. Cronen, V., and B. W. Pearce. 1981. *Communication, 6,* 5–67.
3. Bormann, E. G. 1983. *Symbolic convergence: Organizational communication and culture.* Communication and organizations: An interpretive approach. L. L Putnam and M. E. Pacanowsky, eds. Beverly Hills, CA: Sage.
4. Orwell, G. 1949. 1984. New York: New American Library.
5. Lutz, W. 1989. *Doublespeak.* New York: Harper & Row.
6. Lutz, W. 1990. *Doublespeak.* Princeton, NJ: Films for the Humanities.
7. *Ibid.*
8. *Ibid.*
9. Moyers, B. 1989. *The Public Mind.* New York: Public Broadcasting Service.
10. Andrews, J. 1990. *The practice of rhetorical criticism.* New York: Longman.
11. Sillars, M. O. 1991. *Messages, meanings, and culture: Approaches to communication criticism,* p. 18. New York: Harper Collins.
12. Peterson, E. E. 1987. Media consumption and girls who want to have fun. *Critical Studies in Mass Communication, 4,* 37–50.
13. Sillars. 1991. *op cit.,* pp. 109–127.

IV

The Impact of Persuasion on Society

14

Political and Sociological Propaganda

In the early 1980s, President Ronald Reagan attempted to have a Canadian film, *The Atomic Cafe*, banned in the United States. Unable to ban the film's release, Reagan did succeed (for a short time) in requiring that a disclaimer be inserted at the beginning of the film, labeling the film as "Anti-American Propaganda."

The film *The Atomic Cafe* is a mosaic of film clips that the government produced and distributed during the Cold War, and that Canadian film producers subsequently collected.[1] Tensions between the U.S. and the Soviet Union were high during the 1950s, and the threat of nuclear war was ever-present. American citizens feared the new nuclear age, yet the U.S. government justified widespread testing and development of nuclear weapons by propagating fears of nuclear attack. Americans responded by building bomb shelters in their backyards and canning and storing food for survival.

Some of the most startling footage from *The Atomic Cafe* includes a film shown in public schools to instruct children how to protect themselves during a nuclear blast. The children are taught a jingle called "Duck and Cover!" According to the school film, if you are out riding your bike, and you see the atomic bomb go off—all you need to do is curl up next to the curb with your forearms protecting your head! If you are in school when the bomb goes off—duck under your desk! The announcer in the film yells, "Hey! It's a bomb! Duck and cover!" and the school children dutifully cover their heads.

Another segment of *The Atomic Cafe* shows U.S. military personnel persuading the natives of the Bikini Islands to abandon their homeland to aid U.S. "humanitarian efforts." The naive islanders agree to help these Americans, and they are boarded onto ships while singing "You

Are My Sunshine.'' Government film footage shows the Bikini Islanders watching as the nuclear test bomb hits their homeland, and sand, palm trees, and coconuts disintegrate into the ocean.

A U.S. Army training film included in *The Atomic Cafe* seeks to reassure soldiers about the risk of radiation. Soldiers are told that there are three effects of a nuclear bomb: falling debris, heat, and radiation. The soldiers' anxieties are obviously soothed when they are told that if they are close enough to receive lethal doses of radiation—they will be ''dead from heat and flying debris anyway!'' Following the detonation of a nuclear test bomb, the soldiers in the training film demonstrate how to run toward the explosion, as a powerful wind of radioactive sand and debris flies into their faces and mouths. Just prior to the blast a chaplain in a fox hole explains that a nuclear bomb ''is one of the most beautiful sights'' he has ever seen.

The Atomic Cafe generates many questions regarding what constitutes propaganda. Was the original government film footage that comprises *The Atomic Cafe* propaganda at the time of its release in the 1950s? Is the movie, *The Atomic Cafe*, as released in the 1980s, anti-American propaganda as President Reagan claimed? What is, and what is not, propaganda? In this chapter we will explore the characteristics of propaganda and discuss two specific types of propaganda: political propaganda and sociological propaganda.

CHARACTERISTICS OF PROPAGANDA

There are three characteristics that help us to define propaganda: concealment, absence of reasoning, and the manipulation of symbols. One or more of these three themes recur in numerous definitions of propaganda.[2] There has been a tendency to view propaganda as an either/or phenomena—either the message is propaganda, or it is not. There are many instances in which the manifestation of even one of these characteristics was considered sufficient to classify a message as propaganda. It is far more useful, however, to view propaganda on a continuum. Messages may be purely propaganda, messages may have some elements of propaganda, or messages may have no elements of propaganda—it's all a matter of degree.

Concealment

The omission of facts and details necessary to achieve an informed opinion is a form of propaganda. These messages may prevent the receiver from making an informed judgement, through the concealment of: 1) the source of a message, 2) the intentions of the message sender, 3) the methods

the source employs to persuade the receiver, or 4) the harmful consequences of the persuasive goal on people involved.[3]

In the 1970s, the communication strategies of the Unification Church
were criticized. The "Moonies" (followers of the Reverend Sun Moon),
sought contributions for their cult by selling candy and flowers. Vanloads
of Moonies were dropped off in residential neighborhoods to solicit donations, and many people would buy the candy, never questioning the
organization they supported. According to our standard of deception, the
Moonies were employing propaganda. They never mentioned the sources
of the message (the Reverend Sun Moon and the Moonie cult). The
Moonies concealed their intentions—to turn the money over to the Reverend Sun Moon—and they told people that the money would be used to
feed hungry children, support orphans, or for some other social-humani-
tarian cause. Finally, they concealed the ill-effects of this promotion—the
deplorable living conditions of the cult members, the lack of freedom
given cult members to leave the organization, the labor abuses of making
solicitors work twelve- to sixteen-hour shifts, the recruitment of teenagers
and young adults for cult membership, and the growing coffers of the
Reverend Sun Moon.

Although the Moonie promotions have some propagandistic elements, the most clear-cut cases of propaganda demonstrate all three characteristics. Note how the examples of propaganda become more
elaborated and powerful as we add each characteristic.

Absence of Reasoning

"Propaganda," according to E. D. Martin, "offers ready-made opinions
for the unthinking herd." Other writers note that propaganda generates
an emotional reaction from the receivers. Maxwell Garrett defines propaganda "as any organized effort to make people think of something . . .
otherwise than it would be thought of by a perfectly impartial person
aware of all relevant facts."[4]

Each of these definitions associates propaganda with an absence of
logical reasoning. Propaganda intends to prevent the receivers from establishing accurate and informed opinions—propaganda may actually
seek to create barriers to rational analysis and evaluation. There are at
least three ways to discourage thoughtful analysis of an issue: provide
the receiver with ready-made opinions; activate the receiver's emotions;
and bias the primary source of information while controlling alternative
sources of information.

The television news and many radio talk shows can be criticized for
presenting ready-made opinions for the adoption of uncritical listeners.
Many people avoid investigating alternative presses to find the "other
side" of an argument—thereby relying solely on Dan Rather's, Tom
Brokaw's, or Peter Jennings' world view. Similarly, radio talk shows

ostensibly encourage debate, but in reality they discourage thoughtful analysis by stating a ready-made opinion. Rather than seeking the truth through debate, the host proclaims the truth and often ridicules callers who disagree with witty put-downs.

Emotional responses to messages often flood our senses and prevent an impartial analysis of the facts. In the grips of an emotional reaction we may even forget to notice that the facts are missing. Political television advertisements have made emotional characterizations an art form. The ads feature patriotic music, slow dissolves from a waving American flag, footage of the candidate smiling and greeting his family—in slow motion—at an All-American family picnic, and end with a dazzling, sun-filled close-up of the candidate grinning and lifting a grandchild up over his head—again, in slow motion—with a slow dissolve to the waving American flag. The ads are beautiful—no one can deny it. But where are the facts; where are the issues? The ads pull on the heartstrings, and we simply forget to ask about nuclear weapons, world peace, environmental destruction, economic recession, homelessness, and hunger.

Impartiality in a message is always a question of degree. Many people argue that humans can never be impartial reporters or researchers—individual biases always influence what we decide to notice, how we perceive and interpret what we notice, and what details we include and omit in the final report. In contrast, propaganda occurs when a source intentionally biases the message. In this regard, much of advertising and legal discourse have characteristics of propaganda. Yet we don't get too concerned about advertising and legal impartiality because we know that competing advertisers and the prosecution or the defense lawyers will present alternative viewpoints.

True propaganda occurs when the source intentionally biases a message, knowing that there are no other sources of information on this issue. Communist propaganda in the former Soviet Union is a good case in point. Recent Russian visitors to our college explained how propaganda messages from the government convinced them that the Soviet Union had the highest standard of living, the best medical care, and the longest life expectancy in the world. They believed that they lived under the most socially humanitarian government in the world. With no information from the outside world, the Soviets had no reason to doubt the government's messages. Only with peristroika and increased contact with the West did the Soviets come to the realization that these messages were blatantly false. The Soviet visitors expressed resentment and anger toward the government that had tricked them into accepting a false reality for decades. Even this realization did not prepare the visitors for the discrepancy between propaganda and reality; the visitors were shocked at American's stocked refrigerators, large houses, personal cars, and closets full of clothing.

Manipulation of Symbols

We've discussed that persuasion often involves the exaggeration or downplay of symbols to induce change in attitudes and beliefs. We become concerned about the possibility of propaganda only when the symbol manipulation is significant. When symbols are used for high impact shock effect, distracting the receiver's critical evaluation, important aspects of the message may be concealed, and the receiver may not process alternative interpretations of the issue.

Both the pro-life and pro-choice movements practice the manipulation of symbols in this manner. Even the names of the movements are loaded with symbolic baggage. Who would deny being pro-life? If anti-abortion activists are pro-life, does that mean that pro-choice activists are anti-life? The pro-life movement's pictures of developing babies and fetuses and bloody tissue in garbage cans are loaded with emotional meanings and certainly achieve high impact shock effects. The pro-choice literature also resorts to the use of emotional, high-shock symbols to vividly portray the health risks associated with anti-abortion laws. These tactics can be labeled as propaganda if they discourage or distract receivers from seeking medical facts before forming an opinion on the issue.

A final example of the manipulation of symbols for the purpose of propaganda is when the fight over symbols supplants the issue itself. There are several recent examples of this. The pro-life activists' tactics, calling physicians "executioners" and women seeking abortions "babykillers" and employing violence to communicate their message, often backfire. Some people form opinions on abortion based on opposition to the symbols and tactics used, rather than on the merits of the issue.

We can find another example of the focus on symbols over substance in our personal lives. The emphasis on consumerism in our society has resulted in an interpersonal focus on possessions and name brands over character. Too often, we evaluate people on the basis of the car they drive, the house they live in, or the clothes they wear, rather than on their personal integrity and character.

Characteristics of Propaganda: Conclusions

We may evaluate messages for elements of propaganda by looking at the three characteristics we have discussed: concealment, obstacles to critical analysis, and manipulation of symbols. Based on these indicators, was President Reagan right? Is *The Atomic Cafe* anti-American propaganda? Or was the original U.S. government film footage (the basis of the film) propaganda fed to Americans to influence public opinion during the Cold War?

The pro-choice movement, like the pro-life movement, employs vivid, emotional, and even repulsive symbols to promote its cause.

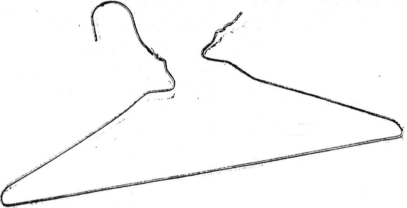

TO MANY OF OUR DAUGHTERS, THIS LOOKS LIKE A COAT HANGER.

PLEASE. SIGN THE PLEDGE TO KEEP IT THAT WAY.

"JOIN THE MARCH
FOR WOMEN'S LIVES, APRIL 9TH,
IN WASHINGTON, D.C."

Just sixteen years ago, a coat hanger was more than a coat hanger.

For countless desperate women, it looked like the only way out of a crisis pregnancy.

Infection, uncontrolled bleeding, a perforated uterus, sterility, abuse at the hands of back-alley butchers, these are just some of the horrendous risks women were forced to endure. Thousands died.

Then the Supreme Court acted to protect women's private medical decisions. Abortion was made legal and safe. And the women of America stopped dying.

It's frightening that anyone could seriously propose returning to the bloody, brutal, desperate past.

Yet the *Webster* case, which will soon be heard by the post-Reagan Supreme Court, could make it practically impossible for millions of American women to obtain a safe, legal abortion.

Already anticipating victory, an extremist, vocal minority, personally opposed to abortion, has launched a savage nationwide assault on our right to decide for ourselves.

Their view of women does not allow for personal choice. They block the doors to health clinics. Lobby to limit birth control methods. Impose obstacles to abortion unlike any other medical procedure. Try to withhold information about abortion from poor patients. And unceasingly demand that abortion be outlawed. Under all circumstances...at any cost.

They would involve lawyers and politicians in a decision now made between a woman and her doctor. They would make women and their doctors into criminals. Most shocking of all, they just might win.

Your right to choose has never been in greater danger. Sixteen years after safety was assured, a single Supreme Court decision could rip away protections now taken for granted. Please act now. Sign the pledge. Defend every woman's right to choose.

We know restrictive abortion laws kill women.

Must we learn the same lesson twice in a lifetime?

ADD YOUR NAME TO MINE. AFTER SIXTEEN YEARS OF SAFETY, TIME IS RUNNING OUT.

Kate Michelman
Executive Director, NARAL

MY STATEMENT OF PRINCIPLE AND PLEDGE.

I believe our Constitution protects every woman's right to make her own decision about abortion, according to her own personal convictions, free from the dictates and intrusion of government. Others want to take away this right. They seek to impose their beliefs on the rest of us by making abortion illegal. The women of America must never be thrown back to that degrading and dangerous time of illegal abortions when they risked their lives and health, and thousands died. I therefore pledge to oppose any attempt to interfere with the fundamental right of a woman to make her own decision about abortion.

National Abortion Rights Action League
and the NARAL Foundation
1101 14th Street, N.W. Washington, D.C. 20005

National Abortion Rights Action League

It does not appear that *The Atomic Cafe* employed concealment of source, intentions, methods, content, or effects. The source of the film appears in the credits. In the early 1980s the film was often distributed with an introduction by Helen Caldicott, President of the Physicians for Social Responsibility. The intentions of the movie are clear—to make people question the government's rhetoric regarding nuclear weapons. Viewers can readily see that the method for presenting the information involved splicing film clips from government archives. Viewers should also recognize that they are seeing clips taken out of context, clips placed in a sequence to exaggerate their absurdity, and many clips to which the film producers added musical background.

The Atomic Cafe is far from impartial, however. Emotional symbols, like test bombs being dropped on screaming pigs to assess survival rates, are used to shock the viewer. Graphic footage of Hiroshima survivors makes the viewer forget the hundreds of thousands of Allied deaths during World War II. The film presents only one side to the nuclear weapons issue—a frightening portrayal of ethnocentrism (viewing one's culture as superior to all others) and ignorance about the effects of nuclear weapons. The film does not provide evidence of ethical and safe government testing of nuclear weapons, the training and protection of military personnel in the use of nuclear weapons, and follow-up statistics supporting the implied cancer risks for military personnel and people living near test sites. Thus, *The Atomic Cafe*, as released in the 1980s, exhibits elements of concealment and the use of vivid and emotional footage that may restrict critical reasoning.

The final characteristic of propaganda—the manipulation of symbols—is also evident in *The Atomic Cafe*. Although the film footage comprising the movie was derived from actual U.S. government films and 1950s news reels, the viewer of the movie sees only selected segments of those films. Moreover, the producers of *The Atomic Cafe* integrated film footage with radio broadcasts and inserted music over the original film footage. The producers' artistic license could bias the viewers' response— the juxtaposition of horrifying film footage and light-hearted music conveys a mocking disregard for human decency that may not have been as poignant in the original films.

In conclusion, the film *The Atomic Cafe* has some elements of propaganda. *The Atomic Cafe* was released, however, at a time (the 1980s) and in an environment (a country that has recently relinquished control on volumes of classified information in the government archives) in which the viewer has access to alternative sources of information. Rather than distracting the viewer from the issue, the film tends to inspire viewers to seek more information, and to critically evaluate messages that the government and the mass media propagate.

The original film footage released by the U.S. government in the 1950s also meets the criteria of concealing information, creating obstacles to reasoning, and manipulating symbols. The film footage makes it clear that our government released information that minimized the risks of nuclear war. If the government's intent was to garner public support for nuclear weapons testing, this was concealed. If the government had no knowledge of the effects of nuclear weapons, it concealed this information and presented the public with comforting messages that they need only "Duck and Cover." If the government did have knowledge of the harmful effects of nuclear weapons, the government minimized these threats in their messages to military personnel and to the public.

Consider how these reassuring public information messages discouraged critical reasoning and questioning: 1) fallout from nuclear test sites is not a health risk; 2) soldiers running toward a nuclear bomb blast are at little risk for radiation poisoning; 3) building bomb shelters and storing food is a fun-filled family activity; and 4) looking at the bright lights from a nuclear blast may blind you, but watching the mushroom cloud following the blast is one of the most beautiful sights one can behold. In addition to concealment and absence of reasoning, the government manipulated symbols regarding the threat of communism. Communists were represented by larger-than-life cartoon figures—making it clear that we would need extraordinary military means to conquer this menace.

From our analysis, it appears that both *The Atomic Cafe* and the original government film footage upon which the movie was based incorporate elements of propaganda (i.e., concealment, absence of reasoning, and manipulation of symbols). Yet when we compare the effects of these two propaganda messages—the 1950s films and the 1980s movie—the impact is very different. The key difference is that in the 1950s, the government was the primary, if not the only, source of information regarding nuclear weapons and Cold War relations.

Before the FBI comes and whisks away my computer, let's move on to the differences between political and sociological propaganda. Since Jacque Ellul is the one who makes this distinction, I will employ his definitions.[5] **Political propaganda** is promoted by a special interest group, a political party, or a government or administration, to change public opinion on some particular political issue. In contrast, **sociological propaganda** consists of measures taken by a society to unify members, to gain support for common themes and ideals, and to spread its influence in other cultures. Sociological propaganda promotes a style of life—a world view, and is often propagated by educational, religious, or family systems and transmitted to future generations.

The purpose of political propaganda is to change attitudes and beliefs regarding a political or social cause. The headline of this 1954 German poster reads: No Atomic War.

ERNI, Hans. *Atomkrieg Nein* ("Atomic War No"). 1954. Offset lithograph, printed in black, 50 × 35". Collection, The Museum of Modern Art, New York. Gift of the designer.

POLITICAL PROPAGANDA

Garth Jowett and Virginia O'Donnell have conducted considerable research on political propaganda.[6] Political propaganda has a **specific source,** a **specific behavioral goal,** and a **specific audience.** Any organization disseminating messages for social or political gain, with the explicit purpose of changing the way you think or act, may be using political propaganda. Political parties, the National Organization for Women, Mothers Against Drunk Driving, and civil rights groups all disseminate persuasive messages with political and/or social agendas. These messages may constitute propaganda if they use concealment, absence of reasoning, and/or manipulation of symbols to exert power or unfair influence over the receiver.

Political propaganda is so pervasive in our society that we may not recognize it as propaganda. Jowett and O'Donnell propose ten steps for analyzing messages for elements of propaganda.[7] Each of these ten steps will be discussed and applied to Jowett and O'Donnell's analysis of televangelism.[8] Although the televangelism movement is a religious movement, it constitutes political propaganda. There is an identifiable source, a specific behavioral goal, and a specific audience. Moreover, many televangelists are seeking personal and political power (e.g, Pat Robinson's presidential candidacy and Jerry Falwell's Moral Majority political action group). As you may recall, televangelism reached its peak in popularity in the 1980s. Jerry Falwell, Pat Robertson, Jim and Tammy Bakker, and many other evangelists gained national recognition and collected millions

This memorial to the 28 soldiers who defended Moscow (with hand grenades) against a German armored division in WWII reflects several ideological themes. What ideology underlies this giant soldier with superhuman muscles that appears to jump out of the granite in which he is sculpted?

of dollars through their cable television ministries. Coinciding with the televangelist movement, the "Moral Majority" became a political lobby and promoted issues consistent with conservative religious doctrine, hypernationalism, and consumerism.[9]

Identify Purpose and Ideology

The first step in analyzing a message is to identify the purpose of the message and the ideology upon which the message is based. Specifically, what beliefs, attitudes, and values does the message promote? What attitude or behavior change is asked of the receiver? Ideology consists of societal assumptions, such as implicit rules of gender, race, social status, distribution of wealth in society, and philosophies of government.

The ideology of the televangelist movement is based on the literal translation of the Bible, a male-dominated society, nationalism, militarism, the work ethic, and traditional family values. This particular interpretation of the Bible contends that the government should support business and that people should take care of themselves, rather than relying on social welfare programs for food, housing, or medical care.

The ostensible purpose of the televangelists' messages is to spread the Christian gospel and to save souls for Christ. Underlying purposes include forming political action groups to support conservative candidates and organizing groups to protest "abortion, gay rights, pornography, sex education, feminism, gun control, busing, civil rights, welfare, labor unions, socialism, and communism."[10] Christian tolerance for diversity is not a priority with this group. This example emphasizes the importance of looking for multiple and implicit purposes in analyzing messages; creating a voting block appears to be as important to this movement as teaching Christian values.

Explore the Political Climate

The historical events preceding the release of the message, the priority of current events, conservative versus liberal trends, and current social and political attitudes constitute the context in which the message is received. Understanding the audience's general mood—their anxiety, frustration, or risk-taking exuberance—determines the effect of a message.

The 1980s were ripe for a religious and conservative movement. Many people felt the presidency of Jimmy Carter was ineffectual, the liberal civil rights and feminist movements of the last two decades were losing momentum, and drugs, sexual mores, and crime were threatening traditional morality. In addition, a rapidly changing society (VCR's, space travel, recording technology, and microwaves) created a nostalgia for the slower paced, more predictable years of the 1950s.

Identify the Message Source

The third step in analyzing a message is to identify the source. The apparent source may not always be the real source. The scandal alleging that Ronald Reagan's political handlers arranged for the release of American hostages to coincide with the President's inauguration demonstrates that the apparent source of the message (the Iranian terrorists) may not be the real source (U.S. political handlers). One of the key questions for identifying sources, according to Jowett and O'Donnell, is to ask: Who has the most to gain?

According to the analysis by Jowett and O'Donnell, the source of the televangelist movement includes a new group of preachers: James Robinson, Jim Bakker, Robert Schuller, and Jerry Falwell. If we ask who has the most to gain, we learn in retrospect that many of these preachers accrued tremendous personal fortunes during the 1980s. Hidden behind the preachers is another powerful source. Jowett and O'Donnell reveal the role of the National Conservative Political Action Committee (NCPAC), which helps to finance the "moral movement," and uses the money collected by the movement to launch campaigns against liberal politicians and issues.

Analyze the Structure of the Organization

The structure of the organization reveals the power, leadership, and chief objectives underlying the message under question. The hierarchical or consensus-based leadership of the organization, an analysis of the decision-making process, the long and short-term goals, the recruitment of members, and the size of the organization all influence the power of the message.

Jowett and O'Donnell explain how the very structure of the televangelist movement is cable television. Television allows the preachers to reach millions of viewers. Computer technology allows the ministries to track people who call or write the ministry so that they may be solicited for funds. Television audiences are usually anonymous—the producers know basic demographic characteristics of their audience but no more. Televangelists make television personal. Viewers call in prayer requests, and televangelists mention many by name during the broadcast. Telephone workers collect names, telephone numbers, addresses, and other pertinent information to maintain contact with audience members.

Identify the Target

Understanding the target of the message may also reveal underlying goals of the political organization. The elderly are an important target group for the televangelists. One potential benefit is that the elderly may leave money to the ministry in their wills. The televangelists gear their messages toward the needs of this target by emphasizing interest in the plight of the elderly, companionship to the lonely, and inspiration to the depressed.

Note Media Technology

The analysis of the media technology used may reveal how the propagandist manipulates information. For example, media choices that emphasize music and emotional visuals may reveal image-based emotional persuasion, while media choices that are primarily print-oriented may invoke logical or psuedo-logical information processing.

Clearly, cable television is the lifeline of the televangelist movement. In addition to the personalized call-in television format, the televangelists rely heavily on direct mail to disseminate political information, solicit funds, and to sell everything from books, cassettes, magazines, and videos to coffee mugs. Direct mail has the advantage of being very personalized—letters can be addressed to individuals, and the excitement of receiving goodies in the mail may inspire the elderly, home-bound target. The media choices of the televangelist movement lead the target to perceive that an intimate, personal relationship exists between the follower and the personable, charismatic preacher.

Examine Special Techniques

One can learn a great deal about a message by analyzing the special persuasive techniques employed. The critical receiver should question the symbols, including the slogans, language, and visuals that the propagandist employs. Moreover, how is the credibility of the source communicated, and how does the message appeal to the needs of the audience?

The primary symbols of the televangelist movement are the cross and the Bible. These Christian symbols appeal to the predispositions of the target, and anything associated with these symbols is believed to be good, moral, and just. Though the true meaning of these symbols may evolve around anti-materialism, love, giving to the needy, and peace, the messages of the movement teach the target to associate these Christian symbols with money and selling, shame and guilt, reduction of public assistance programs, and military build-ups. The power of the cross and the Bible is so strong in our society that the contradictions are never questioned.

The movement also uses language effectively. The initiated learn a new language: born-again, witness, testimony, sin, and saved. Vivid descriptions and graphic stories are incorporated in the sermons to evoke audience members' emotions. Jowett and O'Donnell note that listeners readily adopt and repeat pithy slogans: "God created Adam and Eve, not Adam and Steve," and that evaluative judgements are conveyed in vivid language: "homosexual perverts," "babykillers," and "godless communists." Audience members can ride the wave of emotional response by waving arms to the music, yelling "Amens," and releasing emotion through tears. The evangelists also use immediate and personalized language as if they were speaking to a single person—the individual "you"—not an audience of millions.

Perhaps the most effective technique the movement uses is the establishment of a charismatic leader. The televangelists look wholesome and attractive; they communicate power and confidence—with an occasional small dose of humility and human frailty thrown in. They use the speaking techniques of yelling, Bible thumping, and crying, to scare, intimidate, and finally to embrace the target.

Assess Audience Reaction

Yet another step in analyzing propaganda is to assess the effects of the message on the intended audience. Do the messages evoke belief, attitude, or behavioral changes? Do these effects have an impact on the targets' lives? Perhaps most importantly, are the effects of the message harmful to the target and the target's well-being?

In the case of the televangelist, the messages do seem to be effective. The target may experience increased loyalty to the program and its

Analyze this rape prevention poster. How are words and visuals used to produce a "shock effect"? What special techniques are used to accomplish this effect?

SOME RAPISTS USE LOADED WEAPONS. OTHERS USE LOADED VICTIMS.

Most rapists aren't strangers. They're acquaintances. Often they get their victims drunk before attacking. But be aware that any time a woman is unable to give her consent to sex—drunk or not—it's rape. A felony punishable by prison. No means no. And no answer means no, as well.

ALCOHOL ABUSE CAN LEAD TO SEXUAL ASSAULT.

© 1992 Minnesota Department of Human Services

leader, may make the program a central part of daily or weekly life, and may contribute money to the organization. It is conceivable that elderly people on fixed incomes send more money than they can afford to these organizations, thereby shorting themselves of proper food and medicine. It is also apparent that at least in some cases, the money sent—in good faith—to be used by the ministry is actually added to the personal wealth of the leader.

Seek Counter-propaganda Messages

Messages that present alternative views to one-sided propaganda are considered counter-propaganda. The communication of alternative perspectives lessens the power of propaganda. In extreme cases of propaganda, the propagandists suppress alternative viewpoints. In less extreme cases, alternative viewpoints may not be voiced as a result of apathy or lack of coordination. Situations in which many alternative views are openly communicated and disseminated effectively can be described as persuasion rather than propaganda.

Groups attempting to counter the messages of the televangelist movement are not as well organized as the movement itself. Moreover, it is difficult to counter the televangelists without appearing to argue against Christianity and religion. Several special interests groups, such as the National Organization for Women, gay and lesbian groups, and pro-choice groups have attempted to counter the televangelists, but these groups are on the fringe of the power structure in our society and are often not taken seriously.

Assess Effects

The final step in analyzing propaganda is to assess the effects of the propaganda on society. How much impact does the propaganda have? Has the movement been effective in bringing about changes within certain social groups or within the society as a whole? Has the propaganda influenced politics, economics, or legislation?

The televangelist movement probably reached its height during the 1980s. The propagandists were successful in placing particular issues, such as prayer in school, flag burning, abortion, and militarism on the national agenda. The messages were somewhat effective in squelching support for minority, gay and lesbian, and women's issues. The organizations also served to activate voters and increase the grassroots support for conservative issues. In the late 1980s the public exposure of several televangelists' fraud, homosexual encounters, extra-marital affairs, and income tax evasion deflated the momentum of the movement. It is doubtful that the movement will ever regain its previous power.

Jowett and O'Donnell's ten steps for analyzing political propaganda and corresponding analysis of the televangelist movement remind us not to accept media messages at face value. Jowett and O'Donnell's ten steps are most applicable to the analysis of political propaganda messages that are designed to change public opinion on a social or political issue. Sociological propaganda, which promotes a lifestyle or a world view, is a pervasive force in society that has many sources, and that has widespread effects on many people, not just a specified target. Thus, many of Jowett and O'Donnell's steps are not applicable to the analysis of sociological propaganda. We could, for example, analyze and identify the purpose and ideology, the political climate, and the role of the mass media in sociological propaganda. Yet it would be nearly impossible to identify the source, organizational structure, and the specific target of sociological propaganda. It is this elusive nature of sociological propaganda that makes it so difficult to detect and so potentially dangerous in its effects.

SOCIOLOGICAL PROPAGANDA

J. F. MacDonald provides a nice description of sociological propaganda. He argues that propaganda is a "social adhesive (that) . . . amalgamate(s) the individual with the modern state. . . [P]ropaganda reiterates mutually respected values, (and) skews events and phenomena to harmonize with the national viewpoint. . . ."[11] Jacque Ellul, who is largely responsible for the concept of *sociological propaganda,* describes propaganda as integrating society and teaching people a particular "way of life." In essence, a particular person or organization does not design sociological propaganda for a particular audience—it is a pervasive societal and cultural force that yields social conformity in thought and action.[12]

Sources and Causes of Sociological Propaganda

Various systems of our culture (education, religion, law, family, politics, etc.) propagate a culturally shared belief system through the communication of values and mottos. We do not evaluate or critically analyze these culturally shared beliefs because opposition to social values would be considered socially deviant. In essence, individual opinion is devalued— any opinion that deviates from the social propaganda is believed to be a minority opinion, and people, believing that they are alone in their doubt or disagreement, keep silent. The propaganda functions to suck up individual diversity and opinion and spit out conformity and public opinion. The disseminator of public opinion doesn't have to believe personally in the opinion—he or she just propagates the opinion for the 'public good' or for the 'good of the organization.' The result is an endless loop

Sociological propaganda makes us conform to societal norms. Sometimes the tension produced by the illusion of free will, paired with social controls on our behavior, is overwhelming.

KIESLER, Gunther. *Der stillgelegte Mensch* ("The Incapacitated Man"). 1981. Offset lithograph, printed in color, 46 13/16 × 33 1/16". Collection, The Museum of Modern Art, New York. Gift of Hessischer Rundfunk.

whereby social institutions profess a belief or value that the mass media reiterate, the individual adopts, and all of society appears to accept.

One of the ways this is accomplished, according to Ellul, is through the simplification of public issues. Ellul claims that the mass media simplify issues into clear-cut good or bad evaluations. The more complex an issue, the more diffuse public opinion will be. Therefore, the goal of sociological propaganda is to simplify and reach consensus. Ellul quotes Goebbels, Hitler's propaganda expert, who said:

> "By simplifying the thoughts of the masses and reducing them to primitive patterns, propaganda was able to present the complex process of political and economic life in the simplest terms. . . We have taken matters previously available only to experts and . . . hammered them into the brain of the little man."[13]

Consider the degree to which the nightly television news simplifies public issues—complex international problems are boiled down to a sixty-second sound bit. Moreover, media talk shows provide opinions on these issues that we can adopt as our own and spout knowingly to impress friends and acquaintances.

We live in a society in which rhetoric can change public opinion, without a change in the underlying situation. In the recent Gulf War we discussed our "peacekeeping forces," and it did not seem the least bit ironic that our peacekeepers were at war. At the time, we opted to call the military action "Desert Storm" rather than "War." Couched in the rhetoric of freedom and liberty for the sovereign nation of Kuwait, we downplayed our oil and business interests. In the press conferences, General Schwartzkoff told us jokes. The rhetoric of *peace, freedom, justice,* and *jokes* defined our reactions of pride, excitement, and patriotism. Consider how different Americans' reactions were to the Vietnam War. *War, death, destruction,* and *grief* characterized the rhetoric, especially in the later years of the war. The rhetoric employed in each of these cases shaped our perceptions and reactions.

Sociological propaganda is an outcome of modern society, according to Ellul. In our highly mobile, industrialized society, the individual is isolated. Our relationships with family, church, and community are not as strong as they once were, and an individual moving to a large metro area may have few close social contacts. Moreover, modern people suffer from fears of inadequacy. Technology that few of us understand provides our basic needs. No matter how much we excel in our given professions, our individual contribution to the social order is small. Sociological propaganda gives us a raison d'etre—a reason for living. The simplification of social issues, the adoption of opinions, and the lip service to common values and beliefs make us feel that we are personally knowledgeable and involved in our social order. The ever-cynical Ellul proclaims: "The propagandee, if deprived of one propaganda, will immediately adopt another; this will spare him the agony of finding himself vis-a-vis some event without a ready-made opinion, and obliged to judge it for himself."[14]

Ellul argues that the educated people in society are most at risk for sociological propaganda because they are exposed to large amounts of secondhand information, and they have a strong motivation to have an opinion on every important issue. Ellul states that:

> "Everywhere we find men who pronounce as highly personal truths what they have read in the papers only an hour before, and whose beliefs are merely the results of powerful propaganda. Everywhere we find people who have blind confidence in a political party, a general, a movie star, a country, or a cause, and who will not tolerate the slightest challenge to that god. Everywhere we meet people who, because they are filled with the consciousness of Higher Interests they must serve unto death, are no longer capable of making the simplest moral or intellectual distinctions or of engaging in the most elementary reasoning. Yet all this is acquired without effort, experience, reflection, or criticism. . . ."[15]

How Does Sociological Propaganda Affect You?

Sociological propaganda constrains our opinions and behaviors and reinforces conformity. It is characteristic of modern societies. The propaganda succeeds as a result of the simplification of issues and the public's need for instant information. But what, you might ask, constitutes sociological propaganda in our society and in our lives?

We live with the illusion of free will and individualism—but in reality our society largely controls us. Think about the degree to which sociological propaganda dictates your life. How does consumer propaganda influence your motivation for success, money, and possessions? To what extent do social messages telling you how a person of your age, sex, and background should act dictate your personal image, your demeanor, your clothing, your speech, and your mannerisms? Think about your individual identity. What part of your identity can you claim as a unique aspect of your true self, and what part of your self is defined by sociological propaganda?

Resisting Sociological Propaganda

At this point you should be asking how we can avoid being sucked up by sociological propaganda. How can we maintain individualism, identity, and diversity? If sociological propaganda is as pervasive as Ellul argues, the future of our democracy and culture are at stake. How can democracy survive without individualism, free will, and diversity of thought and opinion? The diversity of thought and opinion must be real. Differences of opinion regarding which candidate has the greatest wimpfactor, or which candidate is more patriotic, and which candidate gives the best speech with the best jokes is not real diversity.

Ellul contends that the key to diminishing the power of sociological propaganda is non-conformity.[16] We must question cultural myths and truisms. We must allow rebellious social groups that contest the reality of these myths to speak. We must rephrase propaganda myths in humanistic terms (e.g., evaluate peacekeeping forces in terms of human deaths). Most importantly, individuals must embrace diversity of opinions. We must continually shake society out of its complacency and force members to acknowledge different ideas and to respect individuals' thoughts and opinions. This is, in essence, the purpose of this book—to challenge you to question and analyze critically persuasive messages and symbols.

The media influence our self-identities by presenting images that we try to emulate. Too often advertisements try to influence us to be things that we are not.

Reprinted with permission of NIKE, Inc.

College students in Washington, D.C. protest U.S. involvement in Nicaragua.

SUMMARY

It is clear from our review that government communications, social and political information campaigns, advertising, legal communication, and broadcast news all, at times, contain elements of propaganda. The key to analyzing propaganda is to rate messages on a continuum reflecting the extent to which the message incorporates propagandistic elements.

Although we've discussed the existence of propaganda in messages produced by many different sources, we should note that the availability of alternative sources of information limits the power of propaganda. We need not be too concerned about propaganda that is delivered in a context in which alternative perspectives and viewpoints are available to the receiver.

If we agree with Ellul that sociological propaganda is becoming increasingly powerful, we are creating a society in which propagandistic messages may flourish. Sociological propaganda promotes conformity and wipes out diversity of opinion and alternative perspectives. Most would argue that Ellul presents an extreme view. Nevertheless, his arguments serve to make us aware of some frightening trends leading to the blind acceptance of information, the mindless adoption of opinions, and the creation of a social, rather than an individual, personal identity.

Study Guide

three characteristics of propaganda
    concealment
    absence of reasoning
    manipulation of symbols
political propaganda
    three characteristics of political propaganda
ten steps for analyzing political propaganda
sociological propaganda
    simplification of public issues
    rhetoric and public opinion
    modern society
    impact on intelligent people
steps for resisting sociological propaganda

Discussion Questions

1. Generate examples that support Ellul's concept of sociological propaganda. What forces in society shape our reasoning, enforce conformity, and discourage critical thinking?

2. Discuss the effects of sociological propaganda on you. Who are you? What is your individual identity? What parts of your self have been defined by sociological forces?

3. How is sociological propaganda necessary and beneficial? In what ways is sociological propaganda harmful to you as an individual and to society?

4. What can we do to resist sociological propaganda and encourage reasoning and analysis? In what ways are you a nonconformist? In what ways do you challenge and question societal systems?

References

1. *The Atomic Cafe.*
2. Schur, E. M. 1980. *The politics of deviance.* Englewood Cliffs, NJ: Prentice Hall.
   Gordon, G. N. 1971. *Persuasion: The theory and practice of manipulative communication.* New York: Hastings House.
   Trenholm, S. 1989. *Persuasion and social influence.* Englewood Cliffs, NJ: Prentice Hall.
3. Lulofs, R. S. 1991. *Persuasion: Contexts, people, and messages.* Scottsdale, AZ: Gorsuch Scarisbrick.
4. Choukas, M. 1965. *Propaganda comes of age.* Washington, D.C.: Public Affairs Office. (Choukas presents a series of definitions that were summarized in this chapter).
5. Ellul, J. 1965. *Propaganda: The Formation of men's attitudes.* New York: Alfred A. Knopf.
6. Jowett, G., and V. O'Donnell 1986. *Propaganda and persuasion.* Beverly Hills, CA: Sage Publications.
7. *Ibid.* (pp. 153–170).

8. *Ibid.* (pp. 181–186).
9. *Ibid.* (p. 180).
10. *Ibid.* (p. 181).
11. MacDonald, J. F. 1989. Propaganda and order in modern society. In *Propaganda: A pluralist perspective. Media and society series.* T. J. Smith III, ed. New York: Praeger.
12. Ellul (*op cit.*), p. 65.
13. *Ibid.* (p. 206).
14. *Ibid.* (p. 170).
15. *Ibid.* (p. 173).
16. Christians, C. 1981. Ellul on solutions: An alternative buy no prophesy. In *Jacques Ellul: Interpretive Essays.* C. Christians and J. M. Van Hook, eds. Champaign, IL: University of Illinois Press (pp. 147–173).

15

Social Movements and Public Information Campaigns

Michael McGee, a city alderman in Milwaukee, Wisconsin, has announced that his Black Panther organization will resort to terrorism if steps are not taken to improve conditions of African Americans living in the inner city.[1] To draw attention to the rampant crime, unemployment, and poverty of the inner city, McGee threatened that unless city officials responded to his demands, violence would erupt during the 1990 Great Circus Parade, which attracts several hundred thousand spectators to the city. At about the same time, McGee reported that Usinger's sausage, a local product distributed nationally, had been poisoned with cyanide, forcing the company to recall thousands of pounds of sausage. Some city residents applaud the audacity of McGee's tactics to shake up the white male city government, others fear that he is a mad man with an armed militia.

McGee is a leader of a **social movement.** The purpose of a social movement is to bring about changes in a social system. Social movements are typically anti-establishment and liberal and progressive. The rhetoric of social movements occasionally threatens violence, it escalates conflict, it is motivated by moral outrage, and it is guided by lofty intellectualism. In contrast, **public information campaigns** work within the existing social system to promote changes in behavior at the individual, as opposed to the social, level. Campaigns are well-organized and are governed by rules, procedures, and preplanned timetables for the release of information and the staging of events. If McGee were to organize a public information campaign, he might use the media to increase people's awareness of racism and implement programs in the schools to teach children how to overcome social and cultural barriers. A **professional movement** is similar to a social movement in its challenge of existing policy and similar to a public information campaign in its organized use of the mass media. If McGee were to organize a professional movement, he might use shocking television and newspaper messages to challenge the city government and its policies.

Social movements, public information campaigns, and professional movements are three types of organizations involved in mass persuasion. In this chapter we will compare the definition, organization, and tasks of these three types of persuasion organizations.

ANALYZING SOCIAL MOVEMENTS

There are two defining features of a social movement. A social movement is a **grassroots** or bottom-up collective of concerned members whose explicit purpose is to **promote** or **resist a social change issue.** [2] Examples of social movements include: Christianity, Nazism, the Equal Rights Amendment movement, the pro- and anti-abortion movements, and the 1960s peace movement.

Simons identifies three types of social movements according to the focus of social change.[3] A social movement may be classified as a **political movement** if its purpose is to change political power or political policies. A **value movement** differs in its focus by attempting to change perceptions of what is moral or right. And finally, an **ego-expressive movement** exists primarily for the gratification and needs of its members. It follows that McGee's black panther organization is a political movement, Christianity is ostensibly a value movement, and Nazism is in part an ego-expressive movement. Obviously, many movements, such as the National Organization for Women, have components of all three types of movements and defy classification. The NOW seeks political change, purports values of equality and constitutional rights, and also serves as a lobby for the advancement of individual women and women's issues.

Any or all of the following features also characterize social movements:

1) Social movements usually grow from an **overt moral conflict** (e.g., "When does life begin—at conception or at birth?")[4]

2) The rhetoric (i.e., messages) of a social movement is usually **agitational** in nature. Bowers and Ochs identify several agitational strategies, including: mass protest meetings and leafleting; nonviolent resistance, such as sit-ins or boycotts; derogatory messages or jargon; escalation of verbal attacks; and token violence.[5] The purpose of these activities is to agitate movement supporters, as well as the movement's opposition, to some sort of response or action. Social movements may use symbolic behavior (e.g., fasting), symbolic violence (e.g., bombing abortion

centers), and mass messages (e.g., articles, books, and brochures) for purposes of agitation.

3) Social movements are usually **marginal to the established power structure.** [6] This means that the organization is an *out-group* that is not legitimized or institutionalized by mainstream society. Because marginal groups are at odds with the power structure, the established policy making body resists their proposals for social change.

4) The focus of change promoted or resisted by a political or value social movement is at the **societal level,** not the individual level. That is, social movements are not as concerned with changes in individual behavior as they are with changes in societal norms, laws, and values.

IN-DEPTH ANALYSIS OF SOCIAL MOVEMENTS

When you consider the diversity of social movements (e.g., the Moral Majority, the gay activism movement, the civil rights movement, and the Moonies and Hare Krishnas), it becomes obvious that there are many ways in which social movements are similar, and there are many ways in which social movements are different. Social movements are similar in tasks and developmental stages. Social movements may differ, however, in their purpose, membership, and tactics.

Stages and Tasks of Social Movements

Social movements have to accomplish certain tasks to progress and develop into successful collectives. In this section we will expand and elaborate upon the five stages of social movements identified by Blumer.[7] Within each stage we will discuss the specific tasks the social movements must accomplish. The five stages Blumer discusses are: agitation, espirit de corps, morale development, group ideology, and tactics. It is important to note that these five stages are necessary for the organization of a collective, but that *the order in which these functions are accomplished may vary.*

Agitation

Scholars have found that situational factors, such as economic conditions and governmental policies, are not sufficient to mobilize a group of people to social action. The **interactionalist view** of social movements purports that social conditions must be accompanied by an intellectual or group of intellectuals to lead the *masses* to action.[8] This rather elitist view claims that intellectuals must construct and define the social problem for the masses, because the masses are too enmeshed in the struggle of daily living to recognize and label the source of their problems. The agitational leaders serve to label the problem, identify the enemy or opposition, and propose alternatives to the current social morass.

Gamson has determined that there are two factors that will lead the masses to agitation and mobilization: 1) perceptions of **high political efficacy,** and 2) **low trust** in the existing power structure.[9] Political efficacy means that the people perceive that they can accomplish their goals and improve their condition, and low trust suggests that the people don't believe that the existing power structure will work to meet their needs.

The process of agitation requires that the leaders appeal to the existing beliefs and values of the people and motivate these people to organize. Communication scholar Michael McGee (not to be confused with the social activist of the same name!) describes this process best.[10] According to McGee, there exists a culturally shared belief system of idealistic values and myths. In the United States cultural values and myths include: all people are free, all citizens are equal, and hard work will lead to success and riches. These cultural values are ideals and do not necessarily reflect reality. Yet most Americans would agree that we must fight to uphold these ideals. Prior to agitation, a group of people share cultural ideals that are highly valued, yet as a result of the demands of daily life, these people have not considered whether or not these values are actually realized.

According to McGee, reformists can take advantage of these cultural values and "dangle" idealistic visions before the masses. The reformists can then proceed to demonstrate the disparity between the culturally shared ideals and the realities of everyday life. As the people begin to ponder these ideals, the reformers usually elaborate upon the injustice of current conditions. As agitation begins to take hold, people respond to the idealistic visions of change and give up their individual lives to join together for the cause. Only at this point do the roots of an organized group begin to take hold.

One of the key tasks of the social movement is to translate idealistic intellectual goals into vivid symbols and pithy slogans for mass consumption. If the intellectual leaders can not construct messages that identify with the populace, the social movement is not likely to progress beyond the agitational stage.

Esprit de Corps

The developing social movement must also establish esprit de corps by motivating individuals to unite and form a collective. To maintain this collective and to prevent people from leaving the group to resume their individual lives, the leaders of the group must provide a group identity and a group consciousness.[11] At this point, outsiders begin to perceive the individuals as a group, group values are articulated, and group norms and patterns of interaction are established. These processes are necessary to validate individual members' contributions. After all,

Speaker's Corner, Hyde Park, London is traditionally a place where activists can freely voice their opinions to passersby.

individuals need security and ego support to pursue the risky venture of social change.

Slogans, logos, symbols, costumes or uniforms, special food, rituals, ceremonies, or simply a group name may create group identity. It is hard to say whether the Shriners first organized for a good cause or a good time, but they do provide a nice example of group identity: funny tassled hats, costumes, silly cars, and mysterious names for local chapters. MADD facilitates group identity by tying red ribbons to the right side of cars to remind people of drunk driving deaths. These symbols of group identity promote group consciousness—a feeling of belonging to a particular group, a common bond among members, and perceptions of grandeur as the lowly self rides an important cause at the crest of social change.

As discussed earlier, the "outgroups" in society often comprise the memberships of social movements. People who have been refused social rewards, power, or status may rebel against the oppressors or victimize themselves through self-degradation, low self-esteem, and guilt. When

Social movements often personify the opposition in a negative way. The "This is the Enemy" posters created by the U.S. and other allied countries during WWII portray the Japanese as rapists and Hitler as a satanic fireball.

a)

b)

c)

c) ANCONA, Victor and KOEHLER, Karl. *This is the Enemy.* 1942. Offset lithograph, printed in color, 34¼ × 23¾″. Collection, The Museum of Modern Art, New York. Poster fund.

rebels choose to rebel, they need a focus for their wrath. The destruction of neighborhood property by juvenile delinquents and the violence between gangs are examples of unfocused wrath—these groups would do better to focus their anger on the source of oppression—prejudice and poverty—rather than on each other. Outgroups also victimize themselves by internalizing their anger, resulting in a lack of pride and esteem. In either case—unfocused anger or internalized anger—the outgroup lacks the cohesiveness necessary for action.

Social movements serve to focus this anger by personifying the threat—identifying a person or group of persons who are responsible for the social plight. Prior to WWII, Germany faced serious economic crises. Hitler personified the threat by blaming social hardships on the Jewish people. The United States responded in kind by creating posters associating Hitler and the Japanese with evil, fire, destruction, and the violation of women. More recently, Ann Richards, keynote speaker, built espirit de corps at the 1988 Democratic convention, by personifying the social problems facing the American people. She described homelessness, unemployment, and the federal deficit. Following each descriptive story she repeated the query, "Where's George?" in an effort to discredit the vice-president and Republican candidate, George Bush.

In sum, esprit de corps is necessary to form a cohesive collective. Group identity, group consciousness, and a personified threat that provides a clear "us" versus "them" distinction may all serve to promote esprit de corps.

Morale Development

Once people have been recruited, an important task of the social movement is maintaining its membership. At various points in the progression of a social movement, members must be reassured. The leaders or voices of the movement must justify the purpose of the movement. Members want to be convinced that the just and moral purpose for which they rallied can really be accomplished.

There are researchers who study the **rhetoric of self-justification.** Ware and Linkugel, for example, propose four communication strategies for justifying one's position or actions: denial, bolstering, differentiation, and transcendence.[12]

Denial is the outright refutation of any responsibility for bad outcomes. Former President Richard Nixon used denial in an attempt to rally support when he was confronted with the Watergate break-in. Saddam Hussein attempted to deny any responsibility for the hardships experienced by his people following American bombing raids during the Gulf War.

Bolstering is used to help the target audience identify with the speaker. When Jim Bakker, the leader of the PTL (Praise the Lord) Club, got into a sex scandal, he attempted bolstering by producing messages that implied, "I'm just like you, so I can't be the villain." His bolstering attempts became ineffective, however, when the media released pictures of his multi-million dollar home with an air-conditioned dog house.

Differentiation suggests that *if* the target could understand all the intricate details of the situation, the target would understand why certain actions were necessary. The target is taught to differentiate—take apart and analyze—the situation. David Duke, the former KKK member who has run for governor of Louisiana, and even president of the United States, uses differentiation in justifying his position. He attempts to differentiate the situation by arguing that he is no longer a Ku Klux Klan member, and that his positions on welfare and civil rights are not racist. He maintains that he's going to take back America for the hard-working American—he's going to revamp the welfare system to stop free handouts. He maintains that once we have all the facts and details regarding the use of our tax dollars to support people who aren't working, that we will see that his position is justified.

Transcendence is perhaps the most common strategy that social movement leaders use to justify their actions. In using this strategy, leaders don't deny controversial actions but attribute these actions to a universal value or code of conduct. The United States used transcendence to justify involvement in WWII. Pro-war posters justified military action by associating our involvement with the preservation of Christianity.

American messages employed the persuasion strategy of transcendence to justify American involvement in WWII.

"ONE IS EITHER A GERMAN OR A CHRISTIAN . . . . . YOU CANNOT BE BOTH." —ADOLF HITLER, 1933.

Michael McGee, the Black Panther leader in Milwaukee, also uses transcendence when he justifies violence as a means to the universal value of the eradication of racism.

To maintain followers, the social movement leaders must be able to justify the actions of the movement. During periods of morale development, the rhetoric of the social movement is likely to reassert the importance and morality of the movement's purpose, reassure followers that the goals can be accomplished, and validate the *sacred mission* of the movement through the four justification strategies discussed above.

Group Ideology

Every movement needs a doctrine to guide its purpose and its actions. Often the doctrine of a social movement is developed by the intellectual leadership and is quite scholarly in form. According to Blumer, the doctrine usually includes: 1) a **statement of purpose;** 2) a **criticism of the existing power structure;** 3) **defensive arguments to be used against the** opposition; 4) **policies and tactics that guide the actions** of the movement; and 5) the **cultural myths, values, and higher ideals** upon which the movement is grounded.[13]

An example of this type of doctrine is Karl Marx's Das Kapital, written as the handbook of the communist movement. As is the case with many social movements, the very people the leaders are hoping to inspire are unlikely to read and/or understand the dense scholarly ideology written by the movement's intellectuals. In Marx's case, the laborers he hoped to inspire to revolution were largely illiterate (and even most graduate students have to struggle to get through Das Kapital!). For this reason, the movement leaders have to translate the esoteric doctrine into forms that will inspire and motivate the followers. Many movements translate ideology into pithy slogans, visual symbols, and stories that take on a folktale quality. During the American Revolution, for example, the complexities of a democratic republic form of government were translated into folktales about Paul Revere, the Boston Tea Party, and the creation of the flag by Betsy Ross.

Tactics

The tactics of a social movement are the nuts and bolts used to recruit followers, keep these followers involved, and accomplish the political objectives of the movement. These are not easy tasks. The movement leaders must secure resources (e.g., money, offices, printing services, and workers), they must organize a disparate group of activists into a disciplined unit, they must continually work at discrediting the opposition, and they must fight the power structure that is trying to disband the movement. Consider the tasks of Martin Luther King during the Civil Rights Movement. He had to solicit churches and community organizations for money and supplies, and he had to organize a highly volatile group of activists into non-violent demonstrations across a wide geographic area. Most incredible are his efforts to work both with, and against, the opposition to negotiate legislation with the President and Congress on the one hand, and fight police brutality and bail supporters out of jail on the other. King had the finesse to agitate the power structure, yet he recognized that he had to work *within* that same power structure to bring about legislative change and accomplish his objectives.

Types of Social Movements

Although all social movements are similar in their need to produce agitation, esprit de corps, morale development, ideology, and procedural tactics, social movements differ in purpose. We will discuss three types of social movements: reform movements, revolutionary movements, and expressive movements.[14] These three types of movements differ in purpose, membership, and in the tactics they use to accomplish goals.

Reform Movements

Purpose. A reform movement seeks to work within the existing power structure to change a specific policy. Therefore, the reform movement embraces the values of the existing order and appeals to cultural myths and shared morality to change a specific policy. The women's movement and the civil rights movement are good examples of reform movements. Both of these movements embraced the cultural values of freedom and equality and sought to work within the democratic system to bring about a specific change in public opinion and policy.

Membership. The membership of reform movements is usually educated and economically secure. It is interesting to note that the membership of the reform movement is often not the beneficiary of the reform. In other words, middle-class reformers often work for reforms that benefit disenfranchised groups in society. For example, when Sara Weddington (the lawyer representing Jane Roe in Roe versus Wade) organized a group to fight for poor women's abortion rights, the reformers were people who had the money and contacts to acquire an abortion if they so desired.

Perhaps the most important characteristic that distinguishes reform movements from other types of social movements is that the movement satisfies the ego-expressive needs of its members. This means that the movement empowers its members to grow, to spread their wings, and to reach their potential.

Tactics. The reform movement usually uses value, benefit, and dramatic strategies to accomplish its goals. **Value strategies** appeal to cultural myths, loyalty, morality, and social responsibility.[15] The Moral Majority movement uses value strategies. It is hard for people and groups in the existing order to refute these appeals without being labeled immoral and unresponsible. **Benefit strategies** propose that the followers of the movement and the general social order will all benefit from the proposed change.[16] Environmental groups such as the Sierra Club employ benefit strategies—we will all benefit from stronger legislation preventing pollution of our land and water. **Dramatistic strategies** create a scene, a group of characters, and a plot in order to act out the ideology of the movement.[17] Politicians seeking economic reforms often dramatize stories of homeless individuals who, for example, were bank executives and are now forced to live, with their spouse and children, out of their family car.

The strategies used by reform movements are usually non-violent. After all, the reform movement must work within the existing power structure and does not wish to alienate people in power.

Revolutionary Movements

Purpose. Social movements that seek to change the entire social order and change the cultural mores of the society are revolutionary movements. As you might expect, revolutionary movements are more threatening to the existing social order and are therefore more vulnerable to attack. The anti-slavery movement in the 1850's was considered a revolutionary movement in the Southern United States. The Black Panther movement in the United States in the 1960s, the Russian Revolution at the turn of the century, Ghandi's movement in India, and the French Revolution in the nineteenth century are all revolutionary movements. In addition to the nuts and bolts of organizing the movement, the revolutionary movement must withstand police and military opposition.

Membership. The membership of a revolutionary movement is likely to include the disenfranchised group who will benefit from the reforms. These people, according to Hoffer, are motivated to join the social movement because they are ready for a change in their living conditions and have very little to lose by abandoning their properties, jobs, and lifestyles to fight for the movement.[18] College students, the unemployed, people experiencing lifestyle changes, and people who do not have clearly defined societal roles (e.g., criminals) are particularly susceptible to recruitment by revolutionary movements. Criminals in particular may have a variety of skills that a revolutionary movement at odds with the police or military may value.

Tactics. The revolutionary movement may employ unity, countermovement, and violence strategies. The use of **unity strategies** may be important to all types of movements but are particularly important for revolutionary movements. Unlike other movements, revolutionary movements are fighting against an established social order and must present a strong, unified front.

According to Hoffer, **unity strategies** take six forms.[19] **Hatred** directed at the opposition places more distance between the followers of the movement and the people of the opposition. This decreases the likelihood that the follower will be able to abandon the movement and return to mainstream society. The second unity strategy, **uniformity,** is accomplished through the use of uniforms, musical themes, symbols, flags, chants, salutes, handshakes and slogans. The peace movement of the 1960s provides a good example of uniformity. Followers of the movement wore particularly long hairstyles, hip hugger jeans, tie-dyed tee-shirts, headbands, and peace symbols. **Propaganda** may consist of exaggerated, one-sided arguments supporting the movement's ideals, and **suspicion** makes the followers trust the movement and distrust the opposition. These two strategies help dilute the influence of any countermovement messages or arguments. A final tactic for establishing unity is the use of **charismatic leaders.** The power of attraction to a personable and dynamic leader can inspire people to be loyal to the cause and do whatever the leader asks.

Countermovement strategies incorporate messages of victimization and crisis in the rhetoric of the movement.[20] Michael McGee's threats of terrorism against whites in Milwaukee invoke a sense of urgency and

Ku Klux Klan members use white sheets, signboards, and chants to achieve uniformity as they march past 600 state troopers and national guardsmen in Austin, Texas.

crisis, forcing the city government to respond. Similarly, McGee's messages elaborate the continuing exploitation of blacks by the white power structure, motivating his followers to take action before more people fall victim to crime, unemployment, and poverty. The sense of urgency in these messages serves to inspire followers and to agitate the city government.

As a result of the out-group status of revolutionary movements, they are more likely to employ **violence.** [21] The revolutionary movement is proposing radical social change and may be defending itself against police and military action. Violence may be the only bargaining chip a societally powerless group has available.

Expressive Social Movements

Purpose. Unlike revolutionary and reform movements, the expressive movement does not seek social change. The expressive social movement is the outcome of frustration with societal conditions and an inability to change those conditions. Therefore, rather than a collective effort to change the society, expressive movements represent individual efforts to relieve personal tension. Whereas the revolutionary and reform movements focus on changing society, expressive movements focus on creating a sub-culture. Expressive movements include religious cults, such as the Moonies, the Hare Krishnas, and Jim Jones' People's Temple. In this section we will first focus on the characteristics of cult-like expressive movements. At the end of this section, however, we will address recent expressive movements that vary in membership and tactics.

Membership. The members of an expressive social movement often suffer from low self-esteem. People in transition—people without jobs, close family ties, friends, social groups, or clearly defined life plans—are susceptible to recruitment by expressive social movements. To people who face ambiguous opportunities, the expressive social movement provides security and structure.

Whereas a reform movement serves ego-expressive functions for its members, expressive movements develop ego-defensive responses. Ego-defensive responses include self-sacrifices, strict rules of conduct, restricted expression of ideas and abilities, subserviance to authority, and guilt and self degradation. Whereas the reform movement seeks to help its members grow, expressive movements are more likely to suppress the development of the individual. Hoffer discusses how the faith in the cause substitutes for a faith in the self, and how the cause is used to provide worth to lives that are perceived to be meaningless.[22]

The most successful expressive movements require extensive sacrifices from members, require members to surrender their individualism and autonomy, and require members to give up all personal decision making.[23] In addition, members are asked to break outside ties, especially ties to family. Members of the Hare Krishnas, for example, are required to give up sex, meat, jobs, television, material possessions, and alcohol. Members are required to submit to the authority of the Hare Krishna leaders and to let the leaders dictate their personal decisions. Members are asked to break communication ties with their families and let the cult become their new family.

Members of expressive social movements are often attracted to the movement for the sake of joining a movement, rather than for the specific doctrine of a particular movement.[24] In other words, the members are ripe for any movement that comes along. Expressive movements usually provide direction, rules, structure, clothing, housing, and food for its members. Many recruits are attracted by the lifestyle more than the ideology.

Tactics. Whereas revolutionary and reform movements have to communicate an ideology to people outside the movement, the communication strategies of expressive movements are primarily internal. Expressive movements use religion, symbols and rituals, and sacrifice and guilt to recruit and maintain members.

Religious strategies are used to invoke a higher calling for the purpose of the movement.[25] Religious strategies emphasize moral and spiritual development and extravagant hopes for a utopian community here on earth.

In 1973, Jim Jones, leader of the People's Temple, and 1,200 followers left the Los Angeles area to establish a utopian community in the country of Guyana. Jones' messages to his followers were based in Christian

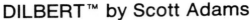

DILBERT™ by Scott Adams

Dilbert reprinted by permission of UFS, Inc.

scriptures and emphasized racial equality, solutions to poverty, and a humanitarian government. In 1977, an article in *The Sun Reporter* states that the People's Temple "follows the precepts of Jesus Christ more diligently than any other group."[26] Yet, in November of 1978 Jones and 900 followers committed mass suicide by drinking cyanide punch on the grounds of their "utopian" commune in Guyana. The image of 900 people strewn across the compound provides a stark contrast to Jones' description of life in the commune written earlier that fall:

> The warm and gentle tradewinds have come up and the flow of the
> evening is subsiding quickly into the clear starfilled night. There is such
> peace here. . . . We watered the garden today . . . we sang and laughed and
> joked the whole time . . . in the spirit of joy in our accomplishment. It
> strikes me as immensely sad that the vast majority of people submit to the
> regimentation and extreme tension of a highly technological society. . . .
> Cooperative living provides such security. It provides the structure to see
> that everyone's needs are met. It maximizes everyone's own individual
> creativity and allows time for pursuit of individual interests. . . . We enjoy
> every type of organized sport and recreational games. . . . Our lives are
> secure and rich with variety and growth and expanding knowledge."[27]

Symbolism and ritual invoke a sense of mysticism in the movement.[28] Ceremonies can provide structure and focus to the lives of the followers, and even serve to unite the followers through shared experiences. At the very least, the symbolism and rituals add excitement to the movement.

One of the rituals at Jonestown was to partake in mass suicide gestures. A former member reports:

> At least once a week, Reverend Jones would declare a "white night," or
> state of emergency. The entire population of Jonestown would be awakened
> by blaring sirens . . . fifty (people) would arm themselves with rifles (and)

move from cabin to cabin . . . we would be told that the jungle was swarming with mercenaries . . . that our situation was hopeless and that the only course of action open to us was a mass suicide for the glory of socialism . . . (we were) told to line up . . . (and we were) given a small glass of red liquid to drink. . . . When the time came when we should have dropped dead, Rev. Jones explained that the poison was not real and that we had just been through a loyalty test.[29]

Other rituals practiced by Jones included faith healing. In his church in the United States Jones employed a group of compatriates who would break into houses and steal medical records to provide Jones with personal information about people in his congregation. During the services, Jones would amaze his followers with his psychic revelations. To the doubtful he even presented chicken organs as examples of cancerous tumors removed before their very eyes. Perhaps Jones' best trick was slipping drugs into the church punch of an unsuspecting victim, and then convincing observers he could raise people from the dead by praying over the body at the time the victim was regaining consciousness.

Sacrifices and appeals to guilt are used to keep members in the movement.[30] The more personal sacrifices a person makes to the movement and the more alienated the movement's lifestyle is from societal norms, the harder it is for a follower to leave the movement and re-enter mainstream society. Much of the rhetoric of expressive movements plays on the guilt of the followers; recruits are aware of their failures, sins, and character flaws. The followers are made to feel worthless, thereby increasing their dependence on the movement.

Jones skillfully targeted his messages to different audience members. To the religious he offered a disciplined Christian lifestyle. To the ideological he offered plans for a new world, free of crime, poverty, and racism. To liberals he offered promises of socialism and an equality based government. To the poor he advocated a philosophy of plenty—a promise of land without rent, free food, free medical treatment, and freedom from bills and taxes. To the ignorant he offered deceptive faith healing and mind-reading miracles. For the lonely or lost he provided a caring "family."

At the same time Jones attracted followers with his promises, he discredited alternative sources of support. He broke up families, he spread fear and paranoia regarding the practices of the U.S. government, and he spread rumors of racial terrorism and nuclear holocaust. He further isolated the members from society by making them financially dependent upon the movement. As one ex-member states, "We had nothing on the outside to get started in. We had given up our money. We had given up our property. We had given up our jobs."[31] Financial sacrifice, and psychological guilt for abandoning the ideals of the movement kept at least 900 Jonestown followers loyal to the tragic end.

Recent expressive movements. The recent popularity of the New Age movement, Native American spirituality movements, the men's movement, men's warrior weekends, and women's goddess retreats suggest a new form of expressive movements. These movements differ from cults in that participation in the movement accompanies, but does not subsume, one's secular lifestyle. That is, a person can participate in the movement without forsaking his or her occupation and family and social life. Membership in these expressive movements is probably characterized more by spiritual fulfillment than low self-esteem. Whereas the cult movement promotes ego-defenses, these expressive movements are characterized by ego-expression (e.g., expression of ideas, uninhibited conduct, and release from guilt and self-degradation). These movements also rely on religious tactics, symbolism, and ritual, but avoid tactics incorporating sacrifices and appeals to guilt.

To summarize our discussion of social movement, we can conclude that social movements face similar tasks that are necessary for the survival of the movement. Social movements must all progress from agitation to group identification, and from the communication of an ideology to a translation of ideas into action. Social movements also share the perpetual problem of balancing internal communication to its members with external communication to people within the existing social order.

Social movements differ, however, in their social change goals, the characteristics of their members, and the communication strategies they employ. The characterization of social movements as reform, revolutionary, or expressive helps to distinguish among these different goals, followers, and communication strategies.

PUBLIC INFORMATION CAMPAIGNS AND PROFESSIONAL MOVEMENTS

There are three general categories of public information campaigns in the United States: 1) **political** campaigns focus on voting behavior or the acceptance of a particular political candidate; 2) **product** campaigns promote buying behavior; and 3) **idea** campaigns attempt to increase awareness and knowledge of a pro-social cause, for the public good.[32] As you can see, public information campaigns are designed to promote awareness, knowledge, and behavioral action. Or, in Rogers and Storey's words, the purpose of public information campaigns is to inform, persuade, and mobilize.[33]

Persuasive messages sponsored by "idea" public information campaigns seek to increase awareness for pro-social causes.

VIESTOLA, Jukka. *UNICEF*. 1969. Offset lithograph, printed in color 39½ × 27½". Collection, The Museum of Modern Art, New York. Gift of the designer.

Public information campaigns differ from social movements in several ways:

1) Public information campaigns are characterized by **clearly defined communication goals.** These campaigns have established awareness, knowledge, and behavioral goals that can be accomplished through communication. For example, the public information campaign against smoking has clearly defined goals to increase awareness that smoking is bad for one's health, increase knowledge of the specific health risks associated with smoking, and change the behavior of smokers. In contrast, social movements may have a clearly defined cause but ambiguous plans for how the cause should be promoted. For example, the civil rights movement involved large numbers of people, identified with various civil rights organizations, each communicating different messages, employing different persuasive strategies, and identifying different civil rights issues. Social movements often communicate that

change is necessary but do not communicate what steps are necessary to effectuate change.

2) It follows from the first point that public campaigns are also **more organized** than social movements.

3) Public information campaigns **focus on individual knowledge and behavior** rather than social values.

4) Public information campaigns are not necessarily organized by "out groups" or by grassroots movements. The existing power structure may promote public information campaigns in the name of *the public good*. For this reason, **agitational persuasive strategies are less likely** to characterize public information campaigns.

5) In contrast to social movements, public information campaigns are promoted through the mass media and **do not employ symbolic behaviors and symbolic violence.**

Professional Movements Defined

In recent years we have witnessed the birth of **professional movements.**[34] Professional movements advocate a social cause and promote change like social movements but strategically use the mass media like public information campaigns. Examples of professional movements include the Sierra Club, the Association for the Advancement of Retired People, and consumer advocacy groups such as Ralph Nader's organization.

According to McCarthy and Zald, professional movements have full-time leaders, they use the mass media extensively, and they are organized by professional leaders who purportedly represent a group of dis-enfranchised citizens.[35] Unlike social movements, the constituency of the professional movement may not be involved in the administration or work of the movement. Professional movements have *paper memberships* —lists of members who may support the movement through signatures and donations, but who do little real work for the advancement of the cause. Simons, et al. note that a potential problem of social movements is that they may "create grievances out of whole cloth for the sake of their own perpetuation."[36]

A common criticism of professional movements is that they spend more resources on the maintenance of the organization than on promoting the social cause. Recent reports indicate that for every dollar donated to MADD, 27 cents goes to prevent drunk driving, and the remaining 72 cents is spent to maintain the organization. Furthermore, professional movements may co-opt the needs and desires of individuals in the bureaucratic mechanisms of the large, centralized organization. For example, the Sierra Club's environmental lobbying may do little to meet your individual needs of radium-free and lead-free city water in your community.

One advantage of professional movements is that they tend to even the score between social movements and public information campaigns. Ideally, social causes may be best served by professional movements that adopt the cause of an *out group* and use highly sophisticated methods to secure money and resources. Remember that social movements are peopled by *out-groups* and must continually struggle to secure money and resources. In addition, social movements must survive the opposition's attempts to destroy and discredit them—and the opposition often carries the weight of the government and law (e.g., consider the resistance that the civil rights movement experienced in the 1960s—Governor Wallace called in the National Guard to prevent a black woman from entering the state university). The less radical tactics of the professional movements result in more acceptance of the *out-group* and less resistance from the law or government. As a result, the power structure often legitimizes and supports professional movements, giving them ready access to resources.

Analyzing Information Campaigns and Professional Movements

There are two premises necessary to fully understand the effects of media campaigns. First, persuasion occurs in stages, and second, the effects of persuasion vary across time.

Persuasion occurs on a continuum, in progressive stages, beginning with awareness, comprehension (knowledge), evaluation (liking), and integration, and ending with action. This model of persuasion, which was discussed in chapter 12, suggests that **awareness** is a prerequisite to persuasion. The campaign must first establish recognition of the slogan, logo, product, brand, or campaign cause. The drunk driving campaign would first need to establish awareness of the acronym MADD. Only after the movement establishes awareness can its members address the **knowledge and comprehension** of problems, features, or benefits. At this stage, MADD would present statistics and examples that support their cause. After they successfully impart knowledge of the product or issue, the campaign can progress to messages promoting positive attitudes, desire, image, and loyalty. The **evaluation and liking** of the MADD organization is addressed through various activities, including the sponsorship of after-prom parties and the dissemination of red ribbons during the holiday season. **Integration** is accomplished when the target internalizes MADD's messages and shares the values of the MADD organization. Once a campaign has established awareness, knowledge, liking, and integration, the target is encouraged to take appropriate **actions**. At this stage, MADD asks for monetary donations to support their organization. In any given campaign, the level of awareness among the campaign target will be highest, followed by decreasing levels of knowledge, liking, integration, and action.[37] This means that the level of action is small compared to the amount of information disseminated (Figure 15.1).

FIGURE 15.1

This exposure drop-off graph illustrates that the level of action generated by a persuasive message is small compared to the amount of information disseminated.

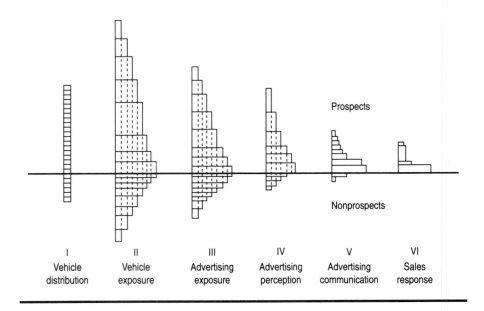

I	II	III	IV	V	VI
Vehicle distribution	Vehicle exposure	Advertising exposure	Advertising perception	Advertising communication	Sales response

A second principle of information dissemination is that the effects of persuasion vary across time. Marketing analysts have identified four adoption categories to explain the rise and fall of persuasive effects over time.[38] You can apply the adopter model to the acceptance of compact disc players. When something new is presented, people who are **innovators** enthusiastically adopt the new idea or product. These people are trendsetters. The innovators bought CDs in the early 80s. With the passage of time, a second, larger group of people, called **early adopters,** become interested in the new idea or product. It is at this time that the product or idea has reached its peak in popularity. The early adopters waited to see how this new technology would take hold, and bought their CDs in the late 80s. The **late adopters** jump on the bandwagon after the idea has withstood the test of time. The late adopters waited for the price of CD players to go down, and bought their players at the turn of the decade. And finally, **the laggers,** who are resistant to change, adopt the new idea as it wanes in popularity. The laggers will buy their CDs just as the new digital recording technology revolutionizes the industry, making compact disc players obsolete.

From these two premises we can conclude that the task of the media campaign organizer is to move the target through the sequential stages of awareness, knowledge, liking, and action, and to adapt the campaign message to the varying needs of innovators, early and late adopters, and laggers.

Steps for Creating Media Campaigns

There are seven parts of an information campaign plan:

1) situational analysis,
2) marketing research,
3) target analysis,
4) market analysis,
5) communication plan,
6) creative message strategy, and
7) media selection and scheduling.

In this decision-making approach to campaign planning, the decision made at each step becomes the foundation upon which decisions in the next stage are made. Thus, there is a logical progression to the plan, beginning with the analysis of the problems facing the organization, to the placement of a message in the media. As we progress through this plan, think about how these questions might be applied to the development of a campaign convincing grade schoolers to stay drug-free.

Situational Analysis

The first step facing the campaign planner is to analyze the current situation of the organization. Pertinent information includes a/an:

Industry analysis—what is going on in other organizations that have goals similar to yours? (E.g., the *industry* of a downtown development organization would be other downtown development organizations across the country, and the *industry* of an anti-drug use organization would be other organizations that promote similar anti-drug use messages.)

a) What economic indicators are affecting the industry?
b) What demographic changes are affecting the industry?
c) What changes in values and lifestyles are affecting the industry?
d) Are there technological changes affecting the industry?
e) Is there legislation pending that affects the industry?
f) What is the public's perception or image of the industry?

Market analysis—what is the purpose and scope of the organization?

a) How can one describe the current target of the organization's message?

b) Who are the competitors, or what groups counter the objectives of the organization?

c) Who is the opposition targeting, and what techniques and media are they using?

Client analysis—what is the image and history of the client?

a) What is the image of the organization? Has there been any bad press?

b) Were previous campaigns effective?

c) What are current problems facing the organization?

d) What are current strengths of the organization?

Problem focus

a) What is the key problem that the organization must address immediately.

b) Can this problem be addressed through a public information campaign?

Organizations can gather information for the situational analysis from a variety of sources. They can find industry trends by consulting the *Reader's Guide to Periodical Literature, The New York Times Index, American Demographics* magazine, U.S. Census data, and business periodicals. They can locate information about the organization's market by collecting publications, media coverage, and annual reports disseminated by organizations representing the opposition. The client analysis should begin with interviews with people in the organization, an analysis of any research data available to the organization, and a search for any mention of the organization in the news media.

An industry analysis for the drug-free campaign might reveal that government funding for drug education has decreased, and that new technology is making drugs cheaper and more accessible. The marketing analysis might reveal that the primary opposition to the campaign is lack of family and school involvement, negative peer pressure, and pro-drug messages in popular music. The client analysis might reveal criticism of previous campaigns for general ineffectiveness and for not using multicultural messages. This situational analysis might lead to a decision to focus on a youth-centered message that realistically incorporates the young person's social experiences and concerns.

Marketing Research

Based on the results of the situational analysis, the campaign organizer usually has a good idea what information is missing. What does one need to know about potential targets' attitudes, values, needs, beliefs, or actions? At this stage the campaign planner may decide to conduct a focus group interview of potential targets, a telephone survey, a mail survey, or a personal interview. The planner can use this information to assess the current levels of awareness, knowledge, liking, and action. This information is necessary to establish accurate goals for the campaign and to provide a standard for assessing the effectiveness of the campaign after it has run.

If the key problem facing the anti-drug campaign is identifying with the youth target, a focus group of young people could be organized to address this problem. A group discussion addressing questions of drug use, peer pressure, popular music, reactions to previous campaigns, and family and school concerns could help the campaign organizers understand the experiences of this particular age group.

Target Analysis

To analyze the target is to identify the persons to whom the campaign should be directed. There are four options for the campaign planner. The campaign organizer can decide to target: 1) people who are currently using the product or currently contributing to the campaign cause; 2) people who are using the product or participating in the campaign cause on an infrequent basis; 3) people who do not use the product or are not aware or involved in the campaign cause; and 4) people who buy the competitor's product or who constitute the opposition to the campaign cause. It is best to target current supporters when brand or cause loyalty are important. Low supporters may be targeted to increase product usage or campaign contributions. Non-supporters may be targeted to increase the market opportunities for the product or campaign, and people supporting the competitors or opposition may be targeted to sway their attitudes in favor of campaign product or cause.

To understand the target of the campaign, the planner usually constructs a target profile. This profile includes a specification of the demographic characteristics of the target (e.g., age, income, sex, social-economic class, occupation, geographic region in which the target lives, education, etc.) and psychographic characteristics of the target (e.g., beliefs, attitudes, needs, motivations, etc). The campaign planner must know a great deal about the lifestyle and personality of the target to construct messages that grab the attention of the target and inspire the target to action (as we discussed in chapter 6).

Our research might show that an anti-drug campaign is necessary during the middle school years, because drug accessibility and usage increase in junior high and high school. A target analysis of middle school students might reveal that these students are strongly influenced by peer pressure, they are very concerned about social acceptance, music is a very important aspect of their lives and of their self-identities, they value pro-social causes, and they are skeptical of messages produced by adults trying to tell them what to do.

Market Analysis

The marketing analysis addresses the sales history of the client or the past effectiveness of the cause. The success of previous campaigns is reviewed, the success of the product competition or the cause opposition is analyzed, and the goals for the current campaign are established. Marketing goals are concerned with sales or monetary contributions, the geographic coverage of the campaign, the distribution of products or information, and the relative allocation of campaign funds to marketing tasks such as advertising, public relations, and promotion.

Communication Plan

Though marketing goals are concerned with sales and revenue, information goals focus on communication tasks. In the course of the information analysis, the campaign planner reviews the levels of target awareness, knowledge, liking, and action and establishes goals for the current campaign. Typically, an information campaign focuses on one of these tasks—for example, moving the target from knowledge to action. It is unrealistic to expect the target to progress through all four stages of the persuasion continuum during one campaign.

Moreover, it is at this stage that plans are made to assess the effectiveness of the campaign following its implementation. The campaign organizer may plan telephone or mail surveys, focus groups, or personal interviews at various stages throughout the campaign, or following the campaign, to assess changes in targets' levels of awareness, knowledge, liking, and action.

Our market research has shown that middle school students are aware and knowledgeable about drug use. It appears that the advertising goal of our campaign should be liking for the anti-drug cause. We must convince these students that being drug-free is desirable, and that being drug-free is socially acceptable. We must create a positive image for choosing a drug-free lifestyle.

Creative Message Strategy

Having identified the campaign target and established information goals, the campaign planner must then generate creative strategies for matching the information goals with the needs, beliefs, and other characteristics of the target. At this stage, the campaign planner must decide what sets the product or campaign issue apart from the competition or opposition. The planner must determine what specific information to convey to the target and how to present this information most dramatically through images, words, and/or sound. The campaign planner must identify the specific mood to convey through images and sounds and what techniques to use to convey this mood. Next, the campaign planner may identify one or more attitude change theories (chapter 9) to guide the construction of messages.

The problem with previous anti-drug campaigns is that the message has not appealed to the target. Moreover, in the past, the source of the message is adults, and kids at this age believe that adults don't understand kids. A new creative strategy would be to have kids tell other kids not to do drugs. The kids could actually create their own television, radio, and print messages to persuade other kids. The graphics, music, and language—all created by kids—would attract the target's attention. This strategy would also communicate to the target that being drug-free is socially acceptable because kids (just like themselves) are voicing this message on television for everyone to see. This creative strategy incorporates social learning theory—the target learns the concepts of the campaign by watching the behavior of their peers.

Media Selection and Scheduling

The final step to campaign planning is to determine what media to use to convey the campaign messages. The planner may choose to use any combination of media, including television, radio, billboards, busboards, magazines, newspapers, direct mail, posters, handbills, brochures, or promotional items (e.g., pens, stickers, hats, or tee-shirts). The planner selects media according to several criteria: 1) which media best communicate the campaign information? 2) which media does the target use? and 3) which media reaches the greatest number of targets, with the highest impact, for each dollar expended?

A second decision facing the campaign planner is whether to use campaign money to reach a lot of different people or to reach a few people many times. Most information campaigns focus on either high reach or high frequency, not both. If awareness is low, the planner may decide to reach the greatest number of people possible. If knowledge or action are the goals of the campaign, persuasion is more likely to occur if the planner tries to reach a few people with high frequency.

Another important decision to make is the scheduling of the messages. The planner may decide to deliver a large number of messages over a short period of time for high impact—(more bang for the buck, so to speak) and/or to announce an important event. Or the campaign planner may decide to spread the budget out over the entire campaign period by keeping a low frequency message before the target at all times.

The media plan for our anti-drug campaign would probably involve television, because television is a primary source of entertainment and information for middle school-age children. Since television is expensive, and—as we noted in the situational analysis—budgets have been cut, we should concentrate our budget on one big impact and make sure that our target audience is watching. We could, for example, schedule a special half-hour program featuring the student messages and extensively promote this one big event to capture our target audience.

The anti-drug media campaign described in the preceding examples was, in fact, a real media campaign, and it was very successful. The middle school students within a city competed for the privilege of participating in the half-hour television show. The students wrote and produced anti-drug messages for their peers. The very act of writing messages and participating in the production of the message persuaded many of the students to adopt drug-free beliefs and actions. The television show was heavily promoted and attracted viewers to watch their peers, friends, and relatives on television.

The seven steps in the creation of a media campaign reflect the careful planning, decision making, and research that guide the construction and release of messages in information campaigns and professional movements. The persuasion strategies are carefully planned and executed. In contrast, recall the strategies that social movements use. The environment surrounding the social movement is constantly changing, the membership is motivated by emotions and reactions, and the movement is responding to threats from the power structure. It is unrealistic to expect the movement to stop and collect marketing research and test messages for target appeal and effectiveness. It is important to note that although information campaigns and professional movements are both media campaigns, the key factor that differentiates the progression of a media campaign from a social movement is the strategic planning and research that guide message production.

SUMMARY

In our democratic society we prize our power to bring about social change. Any social change brought about by the people, for the people, is likely to be the result of one of the three types of mass persuasion organizations discussed in this chapter: a social movement, a public information campaign, or a professional movement.

In our modern media age one could argue that the success of a social change cause is dependent upon the effective use of the mass media. For this reason a public information campaign or a professional movement would be the most efficient organization for the dissemination of information.

Yet social movements are alive and well in our society. Why? The social movement provides camaraderie among people. The members of a social movement are acting together in defiance. The members are living the drama of organizing social disobedience, protesting, shouting slogans, and being arrested for a cause. Symbolic action is exciting—it is human. In contrast, the construction of media messages is cold, mechanic, and removed from human struggle, emotion, and experience. And, perhaps most importantly, part of our American identity is associated with fighting the system. Every once in a while we have to test our freedom to fight and our power to win.

Study Guide

social movements
  defining features
  three types
  five stages
  four justification strategies
  three purposes: reform, revolution, and expression
      three strategies of reform movements
      three strategies of revolutionary movements
      three strategies of expressive movements
public information campaigns
  three types
  five characteristics
professional movements
  advantages and disadvantages
media campaigns
  persuasion continuum
  adopter categories
  seven steps of media campaign planning

Discussion Questions

1. To what degree does each of the following reflect the characteristics of a social movement?

Christianity	NAACP
Democratic Party	Queer Nation
National Rifle Association	Communist Party in the U.S.
U.S. Army	Greenpeace
labor unions	1960s War Protests

2. Discuss the ethics of professional movements. What professional movements are you familiar with? How do these movements use their money?

References

1. *Time Magazine,* 23 April 1990, 26.
   Christian Century, 30 May 30–6 June 1990, 557–8.
2. Stewart, C., C. Smith, and R. E. Denton Jr. 1984. *Persuasion and social movements.* Prospect Heights, IL: Waveland Press.
3. Turner, R. H. and L. Killian, 1972. *Collective behavior.* Englewood Cliffs, NJ: Prentice-Hall.
4. Cathcart, R. S. 1972. New approaches to the study of movements: Defining movements rhetorically. *Western Speech,* 36, 82–88.
5. Bowers, J. W. and D. J. Ochs, 1971. *The rhetoric of agitation and control.* Reading, MA: Addison-Wesley.
6. Simons, H. W. 1970. Requirements, problems, and strategies: A theory of persuasion for social movements. *Quarterly Journal of Speech,* 56, 1–11.

7. Blumer, H. 1969. Social movements. In *Studies in social movements: A social psychological perspective*. B. McLaughlin, ed. New York: The Free Press.

8. Simons, H. W., E. W. Mechling and H. N. Schreier 1984. The functions of human communication in mobilizing for action from the bottom up: The rhetoric of social movements. In *Handbook of rhetorical and communication theory*. C. C. Arnold and J. W. Bowers, eds. Boston: Allyn & Bacon.

9. Gamson, W. 1968. *Power and discontent*. Homewood, IL: Dorsey Press.

10. McGee, M. C. 1975. In search of "the people": A rhetorical alternative. *Quarterly Journal of Speech*, 61, 235–249.

11. Blumer, H. 1969. *op cit.*

12. Ware, B. L. and W. A. Linkugel 1973. They spoke in defense of themselves: On the generic criticism of apologia. *Quarterly Journal of Speech*, 59, 274–283.

13. Blumer, H. 1969. *op cit.*

14. Blumer, H. 1969. *op cit.*

15. Fireman, B. and W. Gamson 1979. Utilitarian logic in the resource mobilization perspective. In *The dynamics of social movements: Resource mobilization, tactics and social control*. J. D. McCarthy and M. N. Zald, eds. Cambridge, MA: Wintrop.

16. Turner, R. H. and L. Killian 1972. *Collective behavior*. Englewood Cliffs, NJ: Prentice-Hall.

17. Griffin, L. M. 1969. A dramatistic theory of the rhetoric of social movements. In *Critical responses to Kenneth Burke*. W. H. Rueckert, ed. Minneapolis: University of Minnesota Press.

18. Hoffer, E. 1951. *The True Believer*. New York: Harper & Row.

19. Hoffer. 1951. *op cit.*

20. Griffin. 1969. *op cit.*

21. Simons, et al. 1984. *op. cit.*

22. Hoffer. 1951. *op cit.*

23. Kantor, R. M. 1972. *Commitment and community: Communes and utopias in sociological perspective*. Cambridge, MA: Harvard Univ. Press.

24. Neal, A. 1970. Conflict and the functional equivalent of social movements. *Sociological Focus*, 3, 3–12.

25. Blumer, H. 1969. *op cit.*
    Bittner, E. 1963. Radicalism and the organization of radical movements. *American Sociological Review*, 28, 928–940.

26. *The Sun Reporter*, 21 April 1977. Thomas Fleming's Weekly Report.

27. Rose, S. 1979. *Jesus and Jim Jones*. New York: The Pilgram Press (p. 132).

28. Kantor. 1972. *op cit.*
    Stewart, C., et al. 1984. *op cit.* See: Persuasive Use of Music, and Persuasive Use of Slogans.

29. Krause, C. A. 1978. *Guyana Massacre: The Eyewitness Account*. New York.

30. Kantor. 1972. *op cit.*

31. Rose. 1979. *op cit.*

32. Larson, C. U. 1986. *Persuasion reception and responsibility*. Belmont, CA: Wadsworth.

33. Rogers, D. M. and J. D. Storey 1987. Communication campaigns. In *Handbook of communication science*. C. R. Berger and S. H. Chaffee, eds. Newbury Park, CA: Sage.

34. McCarthy, J. D. and M. N. Zald 1973. *The trends of social movements in America: Professionalism and resource mobilization.* Morristown, NJ: General Learning Press.
35. McCarthy, J. D. and M. N. Zald 1977. Resource mobilization and social movements: A partial theory. *American Journal of Sociology,* 82, 1212–1241.
36. Simons, H. W., et al. 1984. *op cit.* p. 822.
37. Lavidge, R. and G. A. Steiner 1961. A model of predictive measurement of advertising effectiveness. *Journal of Marketing,* 25.
38. Rogers, E. 1962. *Diffusion of innovations,* p. 185. New York: Free Press.

Index